D0152605

JOURNAL FOR THE STUDY OF THE OLD TESTAMENT
SUPPLEMENT SERIES
121

JSOT Press
Sheffield

KING SAUL
in the
HISTORIOGRAPHY
of
JUDAH

Diana Vikander Edelman

Journal for the Study of the Old Testament
Supplement Series 121

To my parents, June and Arthur Vikander

Published by JSOT Press
JSOT Press is an imprint of
Sheffield Academic Press Ltd
The University of Sheffield
343 Fulwood Road
Sheffield S10 3BP
England

Typeset by Sheffield Academic Press
and
Printed on acid-free paper in Great Britain
by Billing & Sons Ltd
Worcester

British Library Cataloguing in Publication Data

Edelman, Diana Vikander
King Saul in the historiography of Judah.—
(Journal for the study of the Old Testament.
Supplement series. ISSN 0309-0787; 121)
I. Title II. Series
222.4092

ISBN 1-85075-321-0

CONTENTS

ACKNOWLEDGMENTS

I want to express my gratitude to the American Council of Learned Societies from whom I received a Grant-in-Aid in 1984 to help fund research for a historical investigation of the Saulide era. The present volume is a spin-off from the historical project, which is still under way. I am very grateful to the Council for its support of my endeavors.

I want to thank my colleague and friend, Stuart Lasine, for reading large portions of the manuscript and offering responsive comments and suggestions. His careful scrutiny of most of the chapters has helped me to fine-tune some of my initial observations and to polish my final product.

I also want to thank my family, Lee, Will and Evvie, for their unflagging support and patience during the long writing and revision process. My son's question, 'Mom, will you *ever* be done with the computer?', reminded me very poignantly of the degree of commitment, dedication and sacrifice that a scholarly life requires.

Finally, I want to thank Philip Davies for accepting this volume into the supplement series and expediting its publication. The final manuscript was completed in March 1990 and Phil has moved with lightning speed after assuming responsibility for the project in February, 1991. I also owe special thanks to Andrew Kirk, the assistant editor who had to reformat my bibliography and footnotes to conform to Sheffield style and who labored many hours editing the manuscript and deciphering unfamiliar American idioms and translating them into phrases that are understandable by the international English-speaking community at large.

Abbreviations

AB	Anchor Bible
AJBA	*Australian Journal of Biblical Archaeology*
ARM	Archives royales de Mari
ASTI	*Annual of the Swedish Theological Institute*
BA	*Biblical Archaeologist*
BARev	*Biblical Archaeology Review*
BASOR	*Bulletin of the American Schools of Oriental Research*
BBB	Bonner biblische Beiträge
BETL	Bibliotheca ephemeridum theologicarum lovaniensium
BEvT	Beiträge zur evangelischen Theologie
Bib	*Biblica*
BJRL	*Bulletin of the John Rylands University Library of Manchester*
BZAW	Beihefte zur *ZAW*
CamB	Cambridge Bible
CBQ	*Catholic Biblical Quarterly*
ConBOT	Coniectanea biblica, Old Testament
EBib	Etudes bibliques
ExpTim	*Expository Times*
FRLANT	Forschungen zur Religion und Literatur des Alten und Neuen Testaments
HSM	Harvard Semitic Monographs
HUCA	*Hebrew Union College Annual*
ICC	International Critical Commentary
IEJ	*Israel Exploration Journal*
JANESCU	*Journal of the Ancient Near Eastern Society of Columbia University*
JAOS	*Journal of the American Oriental Society*
JBL	*Journal of Biblical Literature*
JNES	*Journal of Near Eastern Studies*
JSOT	*Journal for the Study of the Old Testament*
JSOTSup	*Journal for the Study of the Old Testament* Supplement Series
JTS	*Journal of Theological Studies*
KAT	Kommentar zum A.T.
KHC	Kurzer Hand-Commentar zum Alten Testament

MDAIK	*Mitteilungen des deutschen archäologischen Instituts Abteilung Kairo*
NCB	New Century Bible
OBO	Orbis Biblicus et Orientalis
OTL	Old Testament Library
OTS	*Oudtestamentische Studiën*
PEQ	*Palestine Exploration Quarterly*
RB	*Revue biblique*
RHR	*Revue de l'histoire des religions*
SBLDS	SBL Dissertation Series
SBLSBS	SBL Sources for Biblical Study
SBT	Studies in Biblical Theology
SHANE	Studies in the History of the Ancient Near East
SWBAS	Social World of Biblical Antiquity Series
TynBul	*Tyndale Bulletin*
VT	*Vetus Testamentun*
VTSup	*Vetus Testamentum*, Supplements
WMANT	Wissenschaftliche Monographien zum Alten und Neuen Testament
WTJ	*Westminster Theological Journal*
ZAW	*Zeitschrift für die alttestamentliche Wissenschaft*
ZDMG	*Zeitschrift der deutschen morganländischen Gesellschaft*
ZDPV	*Zeitschrift des deutschen Palästina-Vereins*
ZKT	*Zeitschrift für katholische Theologie*

Chapter 1

INTRODUCTION

This volume began as a chapter of another book, entitled *Saulide Israel: A Historical Investigation.* It was to be the initial step in an evaluation of the literary evidence for Saul's reign, but as it became clear that the literary study would approach 300 pages, it seemed logical to publish it as a separate work. Although it is a necessary and integral step within the historical investigation of Saul's career, a literary analysis of the narrative concerning the career of Saul ben Kish can stand on its own merits without being linked to questions of historicity.

Coming to the narrative of Saul's career as a historian, I feel it is essential to try to put myself in the shoes of a member of the intended ancient audience so that I can understand the author's allusions, structuring techniques, and idioms to the most detailed degree possible. My primary focus is on understanding how, when, and why the writer created this narrative about Saul, with the ultimate goal of deducing what parts might have been based on pre-existing sources and what portions are likely to have been the product of creative artistic invention or guesswork. I readily admit that I can never become a fully initiated member of the ancient Judahite audience, so that in reality, my reading of the text and decisions about the author's methods and intentions will represent the opinions of an American female at the end of the 20th century who has tried to immerse herself in ancient Judahite culture as it can be reconstructed from its artifactual and textual remains or posited on the basis of analogy to neighboring ancient Near Eastern cultures that in turn have been reconstructed from their artifactual and textual remains.

To a casual observer, my stated goals might well seem foolishly impossible to achieve. Nevertheless, in spite of the tremendous holes in the fabric representing my reconstruction of ancient Judahite society, the few warp and weft threads that I am able to set in place and interweave provide me with the ability to read the narrative of Saul's career in a way that is more in tune with the ancient author's world and world-view than one who does not undertake this task. My fabric may have an open weave that allows the cloak I make from it to leave me somewhat exposed, but at least I have an actual piece of cloth from which some sort of visible clothing can be made, unlike the emperor in his new clothes. In my opinion, this approach is necessary for anyone who is attempting to understand the ancient narrative writer's techniques as fully as possible; one must try to read 'like an ancient Judahite'.

Like every reader, I am faced with the problem of 'overreading' or 'underreading'—of missing some of the writer's intended signals to help guide the audience to a particular view, or of creating signals for the same purpose that were not originally intended by the writer. Since we are not in the enviable position of being able to talk to the writer in person and correct these inevitable shortcomings, we must be content to acknowledge that they will occur in spite of our best intentions. The most that readers can expect to establish about the biblical writer's 'intended meaning' can only be a wide range of possibilities derived from readers' reactions to the text. A certain consensus can be established, which can in turn produce a 'definitive meaning' for the group involved, although there is no guarantee that that meaning will correspond to the one originally intended by the writer.

All readers of the Bible are faced with the additional handicap of working with a text that has undergone centuries of 'updating' and reinterpretation. This means that, in addition to the pitfalls of 'overreading' and 'underreading', the reader is faced with the problem of knowing when 'signals' stem from the author or when they stem from subsequent hands that have created new connections of meaning by adjusting the author's world-view to their own. When working with the final form of the text, we must be aware that it is a composite product with its own coherence and network of meaning, so that to speak of it as a product of a single author is an oversimplified fiction. Nevertheless, it is an acceptable working fiction because it is based on the underlying presumption that the narrative's structural coherence and the majority of its literary devices derive from a single author whose vision has remained predominantly intact through the centuries. Working with the final form of the text, we are in fact exploring the world-view of the last 'hand' that made adjustments to it. At the same time, though, we are experiencing a narrative that was conceived and shaped several centuries earlier, even though we cannot know for certain what that narrative looked like in its pristine form. After completing a close reading of the final form of the text, those so inclined can attempt to identify what may be secondary additions or reworkings.

Different groups of readers most likely will establish different 'definitive readings' based upon their own cultural presumptions and patterns of communicating. It is my hope that in the future, readers who are interested in using the biblical texts as a potential source of evidence for historical reconstruction, or who are sympathetic to such a use of the literature, will undertake their literary analyses of various biblical narratives by announcing their intentions to try consciously to neutralize their own cultural biases and read 'like an ancient Judahite'.[1] The results can then be pooled to create an open-ended 'consensus' concerning the techniques, patterns, idioms and devices that the author of a particular biblical narrative used, which historians can then use as a starting point for their long process of weighing the potential historicity of details in a given biblical text. The resulting consensus will be open to constant revision as more warp and weft threads concerning the ancient Judahite world become available and as more readings are undertaken.

A literary analysis of any biblical narrative raises an important set of questions that need to be recognized and borne constantly in mind, even if they cannot be answered for certain. The first set concerns the interpretive context in which the analysis is to be made. Granted that one will work with a critically adjusted text of the selected narrative, is one to limit the analysis to that segment of text alone, treating it as a self-contained piece of literature with no relationship to other biblical narratives? Does a literary analysis have to be done 'canonically', taking the entire set of biblical writings, whether defined as the Tanak

1. Although the characterization 'read like an ancient Judahite' is my own, here I reiterate the call made by J. van Seters (*In Search of History: Historiography in the Ancient World and the Origins of Biblical History* [New Haven: Yale University Press, 1983], p. 52). For a more specific definition of levels of audience, see below.

or one of the Christian Bibles, as the interpretive context in which its message and the literary conventions employed within it will be established and potential intertextual allusions uncovered? Or is it permissible to take a middle ground and analyze the narrative within the framework of larger divisions that have been deduced to be present within the collection of books now called the Bible, such as the Pentateuch, the Hexateuch, the Deuteronomistic History, or the Chronistic History, recognizing that these divisions may well be modern fictions? One's final decision about the interpretive context will inevitably affect the reading of the narrative and will likely yield a different 'consensus' concerning the literary conventions used by the writer.

In the ensuing analysis of the narrative of Saul's career, I will take the following approach and interpretive context. First, I have established as the boundaries of the narrative to be investigated 1 Samuel 8–2 Samuel 1. My decision has been determined by what I perceive to be larger structuring patterns that the biblical writer has used in the material that mark these chapters of text as an intentional subunit within a larger account of Israel's relationship to its god Yahweh through time. Thus, the delineation of the narrative has resulted from my completion of the literary analysis and has not been imposed beforehand according to a set of preconceived ideas about the author of the narrative, the nature or extent of his sources, his social or chronological setting, or the nature of his goals. It is possible that these factors may ultimately have influenced my decisions in subconscious, unintentional ways, but I have tried to eliminate them from consciously predisposing me to particular narrative parameters or analytical 'tendencies'.

Secondly, I will analyze the narrative sequentially, as if I were hearing or reading it for the first time. This means that I will not use later story developments, occurrences of idioms, *Leitwörter*, or literary techniques to influence my interpretation of preceding ones. While I readily admit that my ability to recognize a given phrase's literal or idiomatic meaning ultimately derives from a comparison of all biblical and extrabiblical occurrences of that phrase, my focus will center on how a given word or idiom functions within its immediate context as part of a sequence of episodes comprising the narrative of Saul's career. I will not anticipate later occurrences of similar expressions or phenomena, since I would not know that they were coming up. Links between different episodes will be drawn and commented upon at the subsequent occurrence of a technique, convention or phrase. This approach maintains the integrity of the author's development of the plot and use of strategic intertextual comparison or allusion.

I do not deny that my familiarity with the narrative will influence my results and allow me to read or hear in a more sensitive and informed way than I would have done had I analyzed it during the course of a first reading. Nevertheless, my chosen approach will allow me to focus with more precision on some of the more subtle techniques the writer has used to lead his audience to experience a desired view or effect. Often, clues encountered along the way come into sharper focus in retrospect. My approach has the advantage of being able to highlight the clues as they appear sequentially, simultaneously highlighting the writer's chosen writing strategies. In its canonical form at least, and probably in its precanonical form as well, the narrative would have been read or heard periodically by ancient audiences (Deut. 11.18-21; 31.9-13; 2 Kings 23; Nehemiah 8), who would have experienced the same opportunities for hindsight realizations and more 'insightful' readings informed by reflection.[1]

Thirdly, I will limit the wider context in which the narrative devoted to Saul's career is to be analyzed to the body of literature traditionally designated as the 'Deuteronomistic History', the Books of Deuteronomy–2 Kings. Because of my decision to work sequentially, my field of comparative vision will be limited to materials preceding the Saulide narrative—Deuteronomy, Joshua, Judges and 1 Samuel 1–7 and in practice, the vast majority of my remarks will involve possible comparisons to and contrasts with the material in the Book of Judges and the early narratives in 1 Samuel. My attention and comments will be focused primarily upon patterns, themes, *Leitwörter* and stylistic devices used by the writer to interconnect the twenty-five chapters of text that comprise the narrative of Saul's career. Secondarily, however, links to the wider context of the preceding divisions of the 'Deuteronomistic History' will be made, as deemed

1. For the nature of the Bible as canonical literature and some of the literary strategies used within it to educate its audience, see S. Lasine, 'Fiction, Falsehood and Reality in Hebrew Scripture', *Hebrew Studies* 25 (1984), pp. 26-27, 29, 32, 34.

appropriate or useful. There are a few, rare instances in which I will be forced to comment on textual parallels outside the 'History' because of the appearance of a quotation in the Saul narrative and in that wider body of literature. I will include in the footnotes links to texts located outside Deuteronomy–1 Samuel that have been proposed by others.

I find compelling M. Noth's delineation of a coherently conceived and structured account of the vicissitudes of Israel's relationship to its god Yahweh as his covenantal people, whose author divided his account of that relationship into five consecutive eras: the Mosaic era (Deuteronomy); the era of the occupation of Cisjordan (Joshua); the era of *šōpᵉṭîm* (Judges 1–1 Samuel 12); the era of Saul, David and Solomon (the 'United Monarchy') (1 Samuel 13–1 Kings 11); and the era of the kingdoms of Israel and Judah (1 Kings 12–2 Kings 25).[1] More problematic for me are his proposed date of composition for the work during the exile and his proposal to limit the Mosaic era to the Book of Deuteronomy. Because of the apparent use of administrative lists and royal annals within the material, I favor an initial date of composition for the so-called Deuteronomistic History within the late monarchic period, when such records would have been available to the author. Notwithstanding, there are clear indications that the work was subsequently revised during or after the exile.

The chronological and literary relationships between the so-called Pentateuch and the so-called Deuteronomistic History need much further elucidation. Suffice it to say that the narrative frameworks of the Book of Deuteronomy, with their reflective summary of Israel's past history, presume the existence of the Books of Exodus, Leviticus and Numbers. Whether they also presume the patriarchal traditions as a means of getting the Israelites into Egypt is open to debate. Has the author of the so-called Deuteronomistic History picked up where a pre-existing body of tradition left off, to 'update' events that transpired between Yahweh and his people and narrate the continuing story of Israel's disobedience to the covenant down to Judah's exile in 587 BCE? Has his work preceded the existence of the presentation of

1. So M. Noth, *The Deuteronomistic History* (trans. J. Doull *et al.*; JSOTSup, 15; Sheffield: JSOT Press, 1981). The characterization of the third period as the United Monarchy is my own. The deliberate inclusion of Judah within Saul's domain in the literary history justifies this labeling.

Israel's origins and earliest trials in (Genesis), Exodus, Leviticus and Numbers, perhaps prompting the subsequent composition of the latter sequence to explain in more detail the sketches presented in the narrative sections of Deuteronomy? Have the two groups of texts been composed separately, either contemporaneously or not, and joined together by a third party at some later point?

For the purpose of this book, I have gone with the conventional definition of the boundaries of the 'Deuteronomistic History', but I am not convinced that they are accurate. I hope to be able to explore this issue in a more systematic way in the future; without the proper ammunition at the moment to explode the conventional definition, I have used it for the sake of clarity, but with hesitation.

Finally, I will not attempt to make any judgments concerning the historical reliability of the events being depicted, nor address the issue of historical inconsistencies within the narrative itself or between the narrative and other biblical texts. I will not attempt to delineate potential sources used by the author. All of these concerns must be approached from the groundwork of close literary reading, but need not be addressed within such a reading. I will pursue them in my forthcoming volume, *Saulide Israel*, in connection with my evaluation of the literary evidence for Saul's reign.

A second set of important questions involves the nature of the ancient audience: who were they, where did they live, when did they live, and what was their level of education? Can we even speak of a single 'ancient audience', or should we not distinguish at least four levels of audience, as P. Rabinowitz has proposed? These include: 1) the 'actual audience' reading a given piece of literature in any chronological or cultural setting; 2) the 'authorial audience' for whom the writer has rhetorically designed his work and with whom he has presumed a shared set of beliefs, knowledge and set of conventions; 3) the 'narrative audience' whom the authorial audience is asked to become a part of by pretending to share the world-view of the narrator, which may or may not correspond to their own world-view; and 4) the 'ideal narrative audience' who accept everything from the narrator's point of view, even if he or she is unreliable. The ideal narrative audience relates to the narrative audience roughly in the same way that the authorial audience relates to the actual audience.[1]

1. 'Truth in Fiction: A Reexamination of Audiences', *Critical Inquiry* 4 (1977),

These four levels of audience all need to be constantly borne in mind, since one's presumptions about them have major repercussions for any literary analysis whose focus is on understanding the conventions used by the biblical writer.

Decisions about the authorial audience hinge in some ways upon one's perception of the author himself. Having written anonymously, we are forced to deduce aspects of his character and life-setting from his work itself. I would presume that the author of the Saulide narrative and the larger 'Deuteronomistic History' was a member of the literate upper class and was probably attached to the Jerusalemite court. It seems logical to presume that he had formal training as a scribe, since his literary product reveals a high level of complex, artistic achievement that would have been beyond the abilities of one not schooled in literary endeavors. The larger 'History' shows a strong interest in promoting Jerusalem as the only place that Yahweh 'would choose to place his name to dwell' in the monarchic period. It also reveals a strong pro-Judahite, anti-Israelite bias in its use of David in the Books of Kings as the measuring rod for the ideally obedient king and of Jeroboam, the founder of the re-established independent state of Israel, as the epitome of the rebellious, wicked king.

As to the author's period of writing, this is a hotly debated issue, with the period immediately after the fall of Israel to the Assyrians in 721 BCE, during the reign of Hezekiah,[1] or the period of the eclipse of the Assyrian Empire in the closing years of the 7th century, during the reign of Josiah,[2] being the two most favored ascriptions among

pp. 125-30, 134-35. I am indebted to Stuart Lasine for bringing this article to my attention.

1. So, for example, H. Weippert, 'Das "deuteronomistischen" Beurteilungen der Könige von Israel und Juda und das Problem der Redaktion der Königsbücher', *Bib* 53 (1972), pp. 310-19, who points out reasons to posit a pre-Josianic date, but does not specifically propose a date; W.B. Barrick, 'On the "Removal of the High Places" in 1–2 Kings', *Bib* 55 (1974), p. 259; M. Weinfeld, 'The Emergence of the Deuteronomic Movement: The Historical Antecedents', in *Das Deuteronium: Enstehung, Gestalt, und Botschaft* (ed. N. Lohfink; BETL, 68; Leuven: Leuven University Press, 1985), pp. 76-98. A. Lemaire ('Vers l'histoire de la rédaction des livres de Rois', *ZAW* 98 [1986], pp. 224, 230, 232) posits a Hezekian edition, but believes that the first assembling of the extended history took place even earlier, under Jehoshaphat.

2. So, for example, W.F. Albright, *The Biblical Period* (Pittsburgh: Pittsburgh University Press, 1950), pp. 45-46; J. Gray, *I and II Kings* (OTL; Philadelphia:

those who favor a pre-exilic date for the initial composition. Those in favor of the earlier date have based their conclusions in large part upon variations in the standardized regnal formula in the Books of Kings. My work with the Saulide narrative has uncovered two details that point to a date at the close of the 7th century, but both could be the result of later 'updating' rather than part of the original work, so they cannot be used in isolation to argue for a particular date of composition for the larger 'History'. They must be combined with other potential indicators of date drawn from all the books included within the 'History' before an informed decision can be made concerning the probable date of initial composition and the likely period(s) of later 'updating'.

The first detail with chronological implications is the identity of Doeg, the purported slayer of the Elide priesthood, as an Edomite (1 Sam. 22.9, 18-19). Such an ethnic slur would be particularly meaningful to an audience at the end of the 7th century, when the Edomites were already beginning their incursions into southern Judah. Similarly, I suspect that the reference to the people's request for a king (constituting Yahweh's rejection in favor of a divinized human king) in 1 Sam. 8.7 is meant to be a disapproving allusion to the Egyptians' concept of Pharaoh as a living god. This reference would be meaningful to an audience living under Josiah and his successor, Jehoiakim, the latter of whom was a bona fide Egyptian vassal to Necho II and the former of whom was walking a dangerous tightrope between his waning Assyrian overlord and the newly resurgent Egyptian empire builder, Psammeticus 1.

The following observations lead me to favor a date of initial composition for the 'History' near the end of the 7th century, although I am willing to be persuaded by any evidence that might favor an 8th-century date. First, the strong anti-Egyptian sentiment that flavors the

Westminster Press, 1963), pp. 35-36; F.M. Cross, Jr, *Canaanite Myth and Hebrew Epic* (Cambridge, MA: Harvard University Press, 1973), pp. 274-89; P.K. McCarter, Jr, *I Samuel* (AB, 8; Garden City, NY: Doubleday, 1980), p. 15; R.E. Friedman, *The Exile and Biblical Narrative* (HSM, 22; Chico, CA: Scholars Press, 1981), pp. 1-26; R.D. Nelson, *The Double Redaction of the Deuteronomistic History* (JSOTSup, 18; Sheffield: JSOT Press, 1981), pp. 120-21; A.D.H. Mayes, *The Story of Israel between the Settlement and Exile: A Redactional Study of the Deuteronomistic History* (London: SCM Press, 1983), p. 136; I. Provan, *Hezekiah and the Books of Kings* (BZAW, 172; New York: de Gruyter, 1988), p. 172.

retrospective views of Israel's bondage to Egypt throughout the 'Deuteronomistic History' would have been particularly poignant and instructive to Judahites who were experiencing or had just experienced vassalship to Egypt in the last years of the 7th century and the opening years of the 6th century.[1] Secondly, as is commonly recognized, the idealization of a united twelve-tribe Israel dating from the pre-monarchic period is understandable in terms of a plan for Josiah to regain control over the territory that had once been controlled by David and Solomon in the wake of the crumbling of the Assyrian empire. Although the plan was not realized, it was one that certainly could have been formulated in light of the political atmosphere of the day, Egypt notwithstanding.

As a final example that would lead me to favor a date in the late 7th century for the author, I would suggest that the particular interest expressed in Gilgal and Bethel within the 'Deuteronomistic History' is due to the inclusion of these two former Israelite sanctuaries within the boundaries of Judah at the time of Josiah as the first and apparently only successful move northward to re-establish the golden-era borders of Judah.[2] I suspect that the Elijah–Elisha stories (at least the traditions that have been included in 2 Kings, which focus particularly upon those prophets' associations with Bethel and Gilgal) as well as perhaps the Book of Hosea and possibly also Amos, first became avail-

1. This point was made by Michael Astour in his presidential address to the Midwest SBL/AOS/ASOR Regional Meeting, 30th January, 1989, entitled 'The Birth and Growth of the Egyptian Bondage Story'.

2. This point was expressed publicly in a paper I gave on 28th October, 1988 at the 289th meeting of the Chicago Society for Biblical Research, entitled 'Boundaries and Deuteronomistic Source Materials'. In the paper I sought to delineate the northern border of Judah from Josiah until the end of the southern monarchy, using as source material the Benjaminite city list in Josh. 18.21-28, the Asherite genealogy in 1 Chron. 7.30-40, the Manassite genealogy in 1 Chron. 7.14-19, and the Ephraimite genealogy in 1 Chron. 7.20-29. I concluded that Josiah was able to move the northern border slightly into southwestern Mt Ephraim, including the former northern sanctuaries of Bethel and Gilgal within Judah's confines. In so doing, the southern court would have gained access to any northern records kept at the sanctuaries. My analysis and dating of the Asherite genealogy has now been published as 'The Asherite Genealogy in 1 Chronicles 7: 30-40', *Biblical Research* 33 (1988), pp. 13-23, while my analysis and dating of the Manassite genealogy has been published as 'The Manassite Genealogy in 1 Chronicles 7: 14-19: Form and Source', *CBQ* 53 (1991), pp. 179-201.

able to the southern court and Judahite population at large after Judah gained control over the records kept at these two former northern sanctuaries.

Returning to the questions concerning audience, I would propose that the authorial audience consisted of members of the Jerusalemite court during the middle and closing decades of the 7th century and probably also the wider Judahite citizenry at large. If we can rely upon the appeals to 'the people' to uphold the Horeb covenant, teach it diligently to their children and put it on their doorposts (Deut. 18.19-20) as expressions of the original author and not secondary expansions by a later hand, then the authorial audience would appear to include the entire Judahite citizenry. The emphasis on the responsibility of the people for continuing to uphold the terms of the Horeb covenant even after they have received kingship as their supreme office of civil authority in 1 Sam. 12.14-15, 25 and the fact that their repeated religious apostasy was to have led to the punishment of the entire nation by Yahweh throughout the Book of Judges seems to target the citizenry at large as the intended audience. The stereotyped references to the people continuing to commit religious apostasy during the monarchic period by sacrificing on the *bāmôt* (i.e. 2 Kgs 12.3; 13.4; 15.4, 35) also reinforces this impression.

It is not yet clear if the ability to read and write would have been limited to the upper classes within the second half of the 7th century, but this would seem to be the likely case. Given, for example, the simplified alphabet that had been adopted over the incredibly complex cuneiform system for writing Hebrew, a widespread and high level of literacy could have been achieved with relatively little effort expended. However, the few extrabiblical examples of Hebrew letter-writing that have been recovered through excavations that date to this general time period (including the Meṣad Hashavyahu letter, the Lachish ostraca, and the Arad ostraca) tend to indicate that literacy was restricted to administrative and upper-level military personnel and, perhaps, members of the upper classes. The uncharacteristic repetitiveness of the Meṣad Hashavyahu letter suggests that its 'author', the complaining reaper, was not used to such correspondence and probably dictated it to a scribe rather than writing it himself.[1]

1. So D. Pardee, *et al.*, *Handbook of Ancient Hebrew Letters* (SBLSBS, 15; Chico, CA: Scholars Press, 1982), p. 23. I include this letter as an example of

The Arad ostraca suggest that common soldiers were given prewritten instructions that were presented at their destination to a literate member of the local administrative personnel to be acted upon. Other letters between the Arad commander Elyashib and his brother Hananyahu, or subordinate administrators and Elyashib tend to suggest that literacy was restricted to specially trained government personnel. Finally, it is noteworthy that the use of different formulae within the Arad corpus tends to indicate that they stem from different scribal schools, suggesting again a tight and limited control over literacy at this time.[1] The Lachish letters also bear indications that they were written by different scribes, even though five are on sherds from the same vessel.[2]

Although the inscribed seals and seal impressions that have been recovered from the 7th century belonged to private individuals as well as government officials, both types of seals would have been used as 'signatures' for official correspondence or business transactions, whether or not their owners themselves could read or write.[3] They therefore cannot serve as proof for growing literacy in the late monarchic period. The few samples of abecedaries that have been found at 'Izbet Ṣarṭah, Gezer, Lachish, Qadesh Barnea and Quntillet 'Ajrud and the few samples of writing exercises from Arad, Aroer, Qadesh Barnea and Quntillet 'Ajrud provide evidence for limited interest in literacy during the course of the monarchic period.[4] While

attested correspondence written in Hebrew, but do I not believe that it testifies to Judahite control over Meṣad Hashavyahu in the late 7th century. I belong to the growing minority who suspect that the site was built and controlled by the Egyptians, into used Judahite and Greek mercenaries.

1. Pardee, *Handbook*, p. 29.

2. S. Birnbaum, 'The Lachish Ostraca', *PEQ* 71 (1939), pp. 20-28, 91-110; Pardee, *Handbook*, p. 77.

3. See, for example, R. Hestrin and M. Dayagi-Mendels, *Inscribed Seals, First Temple Period, Hebrew, Ammonite, Moabite, Phoenician, and Aramaic. From the Collections of the Israel Museum and the Israel Department of Antiquities and Museums* (Jerusalem: Israel Museum, 1979); N. Avigad, *Hebrew Bullae from the Time of Jeremiah* (Jerusalem: Israel Exploration Society, 1986).

4. For details, see A. Lemaire, *Les écoles et la formation de la Bible dans l'ancien Israël* (OBO, 39; Fribourg: Editions Universitaires, 1981), pp. 7-33. The dates of some are problematic since they were not found in stratified contexts. The only one that might be premonarchic is the one from 'Izbet Ṣarṭah. For discussion of the existence of formal education in Judah, its date, and its possible locales, see, for

it is true that papyrus was used widely as a writing surface by the late monarchic period, so that the few writing samples that have managed to survive on ostraca cannot be taken as indicative for the general level of literacy, it also is likely that literacy was restricted to government-trained personnel and the upper classes, even if it became more available to these groups as time passed.

We must ask, however, whether the 'Deuteronomistic History', though a piece of written literature, would have been intended only for a literate audience or whether it could have been composed with the goal of being read aloud periodically to a largely nonliterate audience. In light of its theological interpretation of history, it seems likely to me that it was composed to be presented at major religious festivals to the citizenry at large, to explain to the people the history of Yahweh's 'saving deeds' for his nation and the nation's infidelity and need to rely upon their god's ongoing revelations. It also presents existing requirements represented by the laws propounded in the Horeb covenant to ensure blessings of economic prosperity and national peace. The narratives are didactic in nature and do not express concerns that would have been limited to an upper-class audience only. Their goal seems to be to teach the audience to be loyal to the national god and to accept government policies propounded on his behalf by his earthly representatives, the king and the prophet. With our present knowledge, it is impossible to determine if the proposed religious function was a secondary development and if, originally, the 'History' was composed for court circles only, perhaps as a means of denigrating their northern counterparts who had fallen victim to the Assyrians, while bolstering their own self-images and positions of relative power on the eve of the eclipse of the Assyrian empire. One's decision as to the *Sitz im Leben* and purpose of the 'Deuteronomistic History' will be greatly influenced by one's decisions concerning the nature and extent of later editorial work within the body of material. In addition, one's views about the social and political situation at the

example, B. Lang, 'Schule und Unterricht im alten Israel', in *La sagesse de l'Ancien Testament* (ed. M. Gilbert; BETL, 51; Gembloux: Ducolot, 1979), pp. 186, 201; F. Golka, 'Die israelitischen Weisheitsschule oder "des Kaisers neue Kleider"', *VT* 33 (1983), pp. 257-70; J. Crenshaw, 'Education in Ancient Israel', *JBL* 104 (1985), pp. 601-15; and D.W. Jamieson-Drake, *Scribes and Schools in Monarchic Judah: A Socio-Archeological Approach* (SWBAS, 9; Sheffield: Almond Press, 1991).

end of the monarchy and during the postexilic community, the type of audience intended, and the nature and extent of underlying source materials used to create the document will impact on one's ultimate understanding of the social setting and function of the 'History'.

Finally, in connection with the issue of the ancient audience, we need to bear in mind the problems of shared literary conventions and a common world-view between the author and his intended readers or listeners. My attempt to read the narrative of Saul's career 'like an ancient Judahite' is an attempt to share the world-view and literary conventions of the authorial audience. Whether this means as a citizen of Judah in the last decades of the 7th century, the time I have tentatively targeted for the composition of the 'Deuteronomistic History', or as a member of a Judahite audience that begins in this period but includes future generations of unknown number is an important point to bear in mind. Did the author write only for an immediate audience, using literary conventions of his day and addressing issues facing his immediate generation, or did he write with future generations in mind, addressing issues he felt transcended the immediate situation of his day using literary conventions that he felt would be shared by future audiences as well as his contemporary one? Again, this question cannot be answered definitively, but has implications for how one chooses to approach the text and the kinds of literary conventions that are sought.

At the very least, we can conclude that 1) the author's work is based upon a world-view and a set of literary conventions that he believed he shared in common with his contemporary audience, and 2) the work addresses concerns of his contemporary audience that may or may not have continued to be problems for subsequent audiences. In order to convey the points he wished to communicate to his audience, the author would have relied upon the audience's ability to recognize his use of standard literary devices and structuring patterns, as well as his possible deliberate alteration of structuring patterns to convey a point. Since such patterns and devices are regularly used to create oral literature as well as written literature, the audience's literacy level should not have affected their ability to discern the use of the expected repertoire of standard devices and patterns in the 'Deuteronomistic History'.

All actual audiences, whether part of the same cultural tradition and time period as the author or not, are faced with the problem of immersing themselves in the world-view and set of accepted literary conventions in vogue during the author's lifetime if they are seeking to understand the author's 'intended meaning' in a given text. Decisions concerning the genre of a given piece of literature, which in turn have important ramifications for one's understanding of the author's intentions and message and the type of narrative audience being sought, must ultimately be based upon a knowledge of the range of genres in use at the time the author wrote, as well as their means of relating to the world-view of that time. As members of an actual audience far removed in time and culture from the ancient biblical writer, we need to become members of the authorial audience to the best of our abilities in order to function properly as members of the narrative audience and the ideal narrative audience. As an actual audience, we need to know when we can decide that a piece is intended to confirm existing reality, challenge some aspect of existing reality, or deliberately go beyond reality. To be efficient members of the two levels of narrative audience, we need to know something of the author's conventions and world-view, that is, be an informed authorial audience, so that we can judge in what ways the narrative before us imitates the writer's reality and in what ways it deliberately upends or overturns that reality.

Thus, whether or not any actual audiences share the identical set of literary conventions and the same world-view as the author of the 'Deuteronomistic History', all of them would share the same need to recover the author's *Sitz im Leben* and to become part of the hypothetical authorial audience in order to attempt to understand the original intended reading of the narrative. Of course, it is not always necessary to try to establish the 'intended meaning' of a piece of literature. A hermeneutical approach to reading literature leaves actual audiences free to determine what will be a 'definitive reading' of a given piece for their own era, without feeling compelled to determine whether or not that reading corresponds in any way to the author's intended reading. Such an approach eliminates the intermediate step of becoming part of the hypothetical authorial audience. I would only make a call for close readers to set out their goals and presumptions clearly and honestly in print so that others can easily judge whether their reading will be done from the perspective of a member of an actual modern audience or as an attempt to become a member of the ancient authorial audience.

Literature on the narratives in the Books of Samuel continues to grow annually and cannot be included *in toto* within the confines of the ensuing close reading. I will concentrate my attention upon the more recent works that have also focused on close literary readings of 1 Samuel 8–2 Samuel 1, whether or not their primary goal has been to understand how, when, and why the ancient author created the narrative of Saul's career. In addition, I will include discussions concerning philology, textual reconstruction, and ancient social customs or structure where I deem them to be crucial for understanding the narrative. However, the bibliography will by no means be exhaustive.

Chapter 2

STRUCTURING DEVICES: AN OVERVIEW

Within the 'Deuteronomistic History', 1 Samuel 8–2 Samuel 1 forms a coherent, yet not independent subunit that explores the career of Saul ben Kish, the first king of Israel. The disproportionate amount of space that these chapters occupy within the larger 'History' is an indication of the importance of Saul's reign as a critical juncture within the author's purview of Israel's development. Saul's pivotal role within the 'History' is apparent from the use of his career to bridge two of the larger periodizations, the era of the Judges and the era of the United Monarchy. The former era, marking the final stages of Israel as a premonarchic polity, officially closes with Samuel's farewell speech in 1 Samuel 12. The accession formula in 1 Sam. 13.1 formally introduces the succeeding era of the United Monarchy, which ends with Solomon's death and burial in 1 Kgs. 11.43. 1 Samuel 8–12 represents a subsection within the era of the Judges, which details the transition to monarchy with its account of Saul's elevation to kingship (1 Samuel 9–11) and which defines the meaning of kingship in relation to the pre-existing, ongoing Horeb covenant (1 Samuel 8; 12). Since it is only after the official act of coronation that kingship exists as a fact, it is logical that the account of the institution of monarchy be placed as the conclusion of the premonarchic era rather than the beginning of the monarchic era.

The account of Saul's career is not coterminous with formal temporal divisions within the 'History'. In addition, as will be seen in the ensuing discussion, it is inextricably intertwined with the account of David's unusual accession to the throne of Israel. Thus, while it justifiably can be studied as a coherent subsection within the larger 'History' in terms of 'the story of Saul's career', it cannot be studied in this way from a structural perspective within its larger setting within the 'Deuteronomistic History'. Whether it once formed an independent narrative remains to be determined.

The ensuing discussion of the literary structure of the account of Saul's career presumes the completion of a close reading of all twenty-five chapters of text. Structuring patterns and devices can only be recovered during the course of actual analysis, since they form the skeleton of the narrative. While some might feel that to be methodologically consistent one should reserve a delineation of structuring patterns and devices for the conclusion of the book after the completion of reading, this is not necessary; the presentation of findings need not replicate the investigative process to be valid. I prefer to present an overview of what I consider to have been the structuring patterns and devices that the ancient writer used to create the Saulide narrative before I launch into the more detailed analysis, as an aid to the reader. In this way, each person can decide as they work through the chapters of text whether the patterns I have distilled are indeed organic parts of the narrative or whether they seem to be outside patterns that I have tried to impose upon the narrative with only limited success.

Only one discussion of the literary structure of the majority of the Saulide complex, 1 Samuel 9–31, has been made to date. W. Lee Humphreys has proposed that the chapters follow a three-part pattern that has been employed three times over the course of the narrative. The elements of the pattern are defined as: 1) an encounter between Samuel and Saul, in which Samuel announces privately what will be worked out publicly (9.3–10.16; 15.1–16.13; 28.3-25); 2) a constructive phase of Saul's kingship (10.17–11.15; 16.14–19.10); and 3) a destructive phase tending toward disintegration (13–14; 19.11–28.2; 29–31 [steps 2 and 3 merged]).[1]

While initially attractive, on closer inspection Humphreys' scheme reveals inadequacies. His characterization of 16.14–19.10 as a 'B' element, a constructive phase of Saul's kingship, which is required by the constraints of the deduced pattern, leads him to overlook the significance of Saul's loss of Yahweh's good spirit in 16.14 and the meaning of the preceding summary of Saul's productive career in 14.47-48. After 16.14, without the guidance of a benevolent divine spirit, Saul can no longer have a constructive phase in his career, and David's arrival at court and personal success, under the guidance of

1. W.L. Humphreys, 'The Tragedy of King Saul: A Study in the Structure of 1 Samuel 9–31', *JSOT* 6 (1978), pp. 18–27

God's good spirit, only heightens Saul's loss of divine favor and military ability. For the same reason, there can be no constructive phase in chs. 29–31: Saul never regains a benevolent guiding spirit. The characterization of chs. 13–14 as a destructive phase also needs qualification. Even though Saul's disobedience leads to a warning about his divine rejection for any future disobedience, the battle of the Michmash pass ends with a Saulide victory and the summary in 14.47-48 indicates that Saul, working under Yahweh's guiding spirit, has indeed had a very successful career until that point.

The recovery of structuring principles and devices used in ancient Hebrew narrative is an area of inquiry that is only recently being investigated in depth and on a large scale, through the broad range of biblical texts. The discernment of literary patterns is a task that requires that comparisons be sought both intrabiblically and within the wider ancient Near Eastern literary tradition. The widening of horizons to include the latter body of material is particularly crucial so that single or infrequent occurrences of established ancient patterns can be duly recognized in the Bible. The following discussion will focus on what appear to be *ancient* patterns or devices that the author used to help structure his account of Saul's career and convey his understanding of that era to his contemporaneous actual, authorial and narrative audiences.

In our quest to read 'like an ancient Judahite', we must ask what kinds of patterns were used in ancient Judah in connection with kingship. How were kings made? How were their deeds proclaimed to the public? Did royal annals follow a standard pattern for recording events during a king's reign? It is likely that the author would have employed patterns that would have been familiar to his audience from their monarchic world to portray how the first king was installed and to highlight events in his life, even if these patterns would not necessarily have been in existence or common use at the onset of the monarchy. To make Saul's reign meaningful to his contemporaneous audience, who had experienced centuries of monarchic rule, he would have needed to have used familiar patterns and conceptions associated with royalty in his own day.

In my work with 1 Samuel 9–2 Samuel 1, I have uncovered four main structuring devices, three overlapping patterns and one theme that I believe the author used to facilitate his audience's ability to follow plot developments and to grasp his understanding of the significance of the introduction of monarchy under Saul for Israel's ongoing covenantal relationship to Yahweh. The patterns are: 1) the three-part coronation ceremony, 2) the regnal account pattern, and 3) a division of Saul's career into two segments, the first 'under Yahweh's benevolent spirit' and the second 'under Yahweh's malevolent spirit'. The theme is Jonathan's covenant with David. In addition, battle scenes within the larger narrative follow what seems to be a set literary pattern for that genre. However, the 'battle narrative' is not used like the other patterns and theme to interrelate segments of the larger story, but merely to structure individual battle accounts.

The four structural elements will be briefly discussed below. A chapter by chapter examination of the entire narrative of Saul's career will then follow, to illustrate how I understand the major patterns and theme to have been employed and to point out some of the smaller-scale literary devices, motifs and strategies that the ancient author has used to shape some of the individual episodes and interrelate them within the larger narrative block.

From comparative ancient Near Eastern material and intrabiblical evidence, it appears that Israel shared with its ancient neighbors a three-part kingship installation ceremony.[1] The three main elements of the rite included the designation of the candidate, his testing as a worthy candidate through his performance of a military deed, and his subsequent coronation as king upon successful completion of the testing. Within Israel's normative coronation ceremony that evolved during the course of the monarchy, the first stage would probably have included the search for the successful candidate, his anointing, and his public acclamation as candidate. The second stage may have included the bestowal of regalia and weapons, the sounding of the trumpet to represent the battle cry, and some form of mock battle. The final stage probably would have included a dynastic promise, investiture, divine 'adoption' of the king into the divine council, and public proclamation.[2]

1. T.D.N. Mettinger (*King and Messiah* [ConBOT, 8; Lund: Gleerup, 1975]) and B. Halpern (*The Constitution of the Monarchy in Israel* [HSM, 25; Chico, CA: Scholars Press, 1981], pp. 51-148) both describe two steps, but seem to be aware that the testing element is an integral part of the ritual. For the three-part division, see D. Edelman, 'Saul's Rescue of Jabesh-Gilead (1 Sam. 11: 1-11): Sorting Story from History', *ZAW* 96 (1984), pp. 198-99.

2. So suggested by Halpern, *Constitution*, pp. 125-47 and adopted by

The ancient Judahite audience should have been familiar with the three-part coronation ceremony both from royal investitures that they might have witnessed and from cultic myths about Yahweh and the national gods of surrounding lands. The pattern was applied equally to heaven and to earth, its mirror image, so that what was expected of the divine king of the heavenly council was also expected of his chosen earthly vice-regents. Echoes of Yahweh's military deed, his slaying of the watery chaos monster, are preserved, for example, in Isa. 11.15; 51.9; Hab. 3.8-9; Nah. 1.4; Job 26.12; Pss. 64.7; 74.13-14; and 89.9-10,[1] while the Psalms seem to preserve remnants of Yahweh's election as champion of gods (e.g. 29.1-2; 86.8; 89.6-8) and his coronation after his slaying of the waters (e.g. 24.7-10; 29.10; 33.14; 44.4; 47.2-8; 68.24; 74.12; 93.1-2; 95.3; 96.10; 97.1, 9; 98.6; 99.1, 4; 123.1; and 145.1).[2]

In narrating how Saul became the first Israelite king, an ancient writer almost certainly would have shaped his account to include the three steps that his audience would have equated with the process of king-making: designation, testing and coronation. In other words, he would have 'historicized' the familiar cultic rite to satisfy the cultural expectations of his audience: since Saul became king, he must have been designated in some way, he must have passed some sort of military test, and he must have been subsequently crowned. In recounting Saul's elevation to kingship, then, the writer would have sought to portray concrete events that corresponded to the three stages of the familiar king-making process.

Edelman, 'Saul's Rescue', p. 198.

1. For studies of the divine battle, see, for example, G.A. Barton, 'Tiamat', *JAOS* 15 (1893), pp. 1-27; H. Gunkel, *Schöpfung und Chaos in Urzeit und Endzeit* (Göttingen: Vandenhoeck & Ruprecht, 1895); M. Wakeman, *God's Battle with the Chaos Monster* (Leiden: Brill, 1973); J. Day, *God's Conflict with the Dragon and the Sea* (Cambridge: Cambridge University Press, 1985).

2. The classic formulation of this position was made by S. Mowinckel, *Psalmenstudien*, I (6 vols.; Kristiana: Dybwad, 1921-1924), pp. 94-185, although he built on the work of P. Volz, *Das Neujahrsfest Jahwes (Laubhüttenfest)* (Tübingen: Mohr, 1912). Other useful studies of the divine coronation ceremony and its cultic setting in ancient Israel include, for example, A.R. Johnson, *Sacral Kingship in Ancient Israel* (2nd edn; Cardiff: University of Wales, 1967); J.H. Eaton, *Kingship and the Psalms* (SBT Second Series, 32; London: SCM Press, 1976).

A 'historicized' version of the three-part coronation ceremony appears to have been used three times within the Saulide narrative: to describe Saul's rise to kingship over Israel (1 Sam. 9.1–11.15), to describe Jonathan's possible rejection as Saul's successor for his failure to pass the second testing stage (1 Samuel 13–14), and to describe David's progression to the Israelite throne as Saul's successor (1 Sam. 16.13; 17; 2 Sam. 2.4; 5.1-6). In addition to fulfilling audience expectations concerning the necessary stages a person would have taken to become king, by using what became the normative pattern for the kingship ritual to help structure the account of David's progression to the throne, the writer may have been hoping to imply that David's succession followed the normal pattern and so was legitimate. Unfortunately, we do not know how well-informed he and his audience would have been about events surrounding David's accession to the Saulide throne, so we cannot gauge whether it would have been necessary for him to counter long-standing 'golden age' traditions or not.

The second pattern in evidence in the Saulide narrative is the standard regnal account. The elements of the pattern are derivable from the accounts of the reigns of subsequent kings of Israel and Judah in the Books of Kings. An initial accession formula, which includes the name of the king, his age at accession, and the length of his reign (13.1), is followed by an account of some of the king's accomplishments (13.2–14.46), a summary of his deeds (14.47-48), and finally, a report of his death, burial, and succession (1 Samuel 31; 2 Sam. 2.8-11).[1] While a reference to the Book of Deeds of the Kings of Israel or Judah is normal in the summary of deeds in the accounts in the Book of Kings, there is no such source reference for Saul. In addition, in Saul's case, the death, burial and succession notices do not immediately follow the summary of deeds, as is standard practice in the Book of Kings. Instead, they are separated by some sixteen chapters. This slight deviation seems to have been intentional; it allows the writer to use Saul's career to depict the consequences a king would face for disobeying the central principle of the pre-existent Horeb covenant,

1. For a slightly different delineation of the basic pattern and an attempt to demonstrate how its formulaic language has been derived from underlying sources, see S. Bin-Nun, 'Formulas from Royal Records of Israel and Judah', *VT* 18 (1968), pp. 414-32.

obedience to Yahweh's revealed command.[1] At the same time, it allows him to prepare the audience for David's eventual succession to the throne of Israel in place of a legitimate Saulide.

It is not clear whether the regnal account pattern was a new schematization created by the biblical writer as an abridgment to longer annalistic entries or whether it was a pre-existing convention known both to him and his audience. It does not seem likely that royal annals would have been written for popular consumption, so if the pattern has been derived from them, it would not have been readily known to the general populace. On the other hand, inscriptions on Assyrian and neo-Babylonian victory stelae include formulaic royal titles, stereotyped phrasing, and a basic pattern for reporting that could have influenced the development of the regnal account pattern within either oral or literary circles.[2] Such monuments were erected for public display and consumption. Thus, if the regnal pattern can be linked with patterns used within the public realm, whether or not they could have been read by every passer-by, then we can presume that the elements would have been familiar to the author's audience and expected to appear as elements in any standard account of a king's reign.

The third pattern, which divides Saul's career into life 'under Yahweh's good spirit' and life 'under Yahweh's evil spirit' (1 Sam. 16.14), need not have been a common literary structural device in the narrator's own day to have been successfully employed in the account of Saul's career. Since it reflects a cultural belief system that sees the existence of good and bad spirits that can possess a person's body and dictate behaviour, the pattern would have been readily accepted by an audience who shared the same cultural belief system, regardless of its novelty or familiarity. It would have been instantly plausible.

1. Cf. D. Gunn, *The Fate of King Saul. An Interpretation of a Biblical Story* (JSOTSup, 14; Sheffield: JSOT Press, 1980), p. 125.

2. For the conventions of commemorative stelae, see, for example, M. Miller, 'The Moabite Stone as a Memorial Stela', *PEQ* 107 (1975), pp. 9-18; J. Westenholtz, 'The Heroes of Akkad', *JAOS* 103 (1983), pp. 327-36. For the problems of determining the origins of such patterns among scribal forms or traditional oral structuring patterns, see, for example, D. Gunn, 'Narrative Patterns and Oral Tradition in Judges and Samuel', *VT* 24 (1974), pp. 303-11; J. van Seters, 'Oral Patterns or Literary Conventions in Biblical Narrative', *Semeia* 5 (1976), pp. 139-54.

The third pattern shares with the regnal pattern the same two purposes. Primarily, it allows the writer to demonstrate that as Yahweh's anointed, who has received divine spirit, the king will remain in office and possess some form of guiding divine spirit throughout his lifetime. The same principle is evident in the previous period of the Judges, where the term of judgeship lasts for the rest of a chosen individual's life; once divine spirit is bestowed, it remains until death (Judg. 2.18). Nevertheless, possession of divine spirit does not guarantee success; disobedience to God will lead to the king's divine rejection and his inability to continue to serve his nation adequately as God's earthly vice-regent during the remainder of his reign. The king will lose God's benevolent guiding spirit, which will result in his failure to be able to discern the divine will and act appropriately. As a consequence, his nation will suffer. A similar structuring device seems to have been used in the account of David's career.[1]

A possible fourth pattern, 'the rise of the lowly and fall of the mighty', has been suggested by T. Preston to have been employed by the ancient writer to shape the Saulide narratives. Preston argues that the Saulide materials are part of a larger narrative complex extending from 1 Samuel 2–1 Kings 1–2, in which the lives of Samuel, Saul and David are 'intertwined in such a way that they follow the same basic pattern, foreshadowing and reflecting each other as the narrative progresses'.[2] Upon examination, however, his scheme is not applicable to Saul, nor probably to either Samuel or David. Saul is not a 'lowly man' who is raised to kingship. The seven-generation genealogy in 9.1 indicates that he is a man destined for greatness from birth,[3] and his status as the son of a *gibbôr ḥáyil*, a man of wealth or importance,[4]

1. R.A. Carlson, *David, the Chosen King* (trans. E.J. Sharpe and S. Rudman; Stockholm: Almquist & Wiksell, 1964), p. 243 n. 17.

2. T.R. Preston, 'The Heroism of King Saul: Patterns of Meaning in the Narrative of Early Kingship', *JSOT* 24 (1982), p. 28. His structural analysis is cited approvingly by R. Polzin, *Samuel and the Deuteronomist* (St Louis: Harper & Row, 1989), p. 18.

3. J. Sasson, 'A Genealogical "Convention" in Biblical Chronology?', *ZAW* 90 (1978), p. 18.

4. For the semantic range of this term, see J. van der Ploeg, 'Le sense de *gibbôr ḥâīl*', *RB* 50 (1941), pp. 120-25; W. McKane, 'The Gibbôr Ḥayil in the Israelite Community', *Glasgow University Oriental Society Transactions* 17 (1957–58), pp. 28-37.

also dispels any possible rise from lowly origins. Preston has not understood that Saul's profession of humility in 9.21 is a requisite part of the kingship pattern: the candidate for king is *always* humble. It seems best to reject his proposed pattern as a legitimate ancient structuring device in the Saulide narratives.

The theme of Jonathan's personal covenant with David also serves as an important structuring device within the Saulide narrative and beyond, into the story of David's career as Saul's successor. It is introduced after Jonathan has been passed over as Yahweh's new king-elect in favor of David, in 18.1-5. After David reportedly kills Goliath, Jonathan is said to have made a covenant with David, 'because he loved him as his own soul' (v. 3). He is then said to have given Jonathan his own robe, his armor, his bow and his girdle (v. 4). With this act, Jonathan has symbolically endowed David, the secretly anointed king-elect, with the formal instruments associated with the second 'testing stage' of the three-part coronation ceremony. In so doing, he has demonstrated his acceptance of David as Saul's divinely chosen successor, instead of himself, the heir-elect by birth, thereby signalling his understanding of the guilty verdict rendered by Yahweh in 14.42. As in the case of the third pattern, the intended audience would have shared with the author an understanding of the semantic range associated with the term *b^{e}rît* that would have made it possible for them to understand the intended symbolism and recognize the deliberate use of the term as a theme in the larger narrative, whether or not 'covenant' was a common theme in the ancient Judahite literary realm.

The covenant between Jonathan and David is skillfully used to chronicle Jonathan's immediate and willing acceptance of David's status as Saul's successor and to contrast it with Saul's refusal to accept the divine plan. In this way, the rejected Jonathan serves as a foil to his rejected father Saul. As has been pointed out by D. Jobling,[1] the covenant theme is developed progressively through scenes that alternately focus on Jonathan and David or Saul (18.1-5; 19.1-7; 20.1-21; 23.15b-18) and ones in which David and Saul interact (16.14–17.58; 18.6-30; 19.8-25; 21.2–23.15a [with other material]; 23.19 onward [with much other material]). It is important to realize that the theme

1. D. Jobling, *The Sense of Biblical Narrative*, I (2nd edn; JSOTSup, 7; Sheffield: JSOT Press, 1978), p. 15.

continues into 2 Samuel in the five sections that depict David's involvement with Jonathan's son Meribaal (2 Sam. 4.4; 9; 16.1-4; 19.24-30; 21.7).

Finally, before beginning the close reading, I will mention the writer's use of the contrasting pairs *ṭob* and *rāʻâ*, 'good' and 'evil'; *lēb* and *'ênáyim*, 'heart' and 'eyes'; and the key word *yād* as a symbol of political power as recurrent motifs that help focus the audience's attention on the precepts of royal power and its potential abuses throughout the course of the narrative. Additional terms will serve as *Leitwörter* or motifs in individual episodes or sometimes will recur in such a way as to link two or three episodes together. They will be acknowledged and discussed during the course of the close reading that will now begin.

Chapter 3

1 SAMUEL 8

The chapter introduces the subsection 1 Samuel 8–12, which recounts the author's understanding of the institution of monarchy within Israel as the final phase within the era of the Judges. Chapter 8 builds directly upon the experiences Israel has undergone within the preceding era and serves as the introduction to the final resolution to the problem Israel has experienced since Judges 1: a need for continuous, uninterrupted leadership that can maintain the community's faithfulness to the Horeb covenant and Yahweh's ongoing demands. In particular, ch. 8 introduces the elders' realization, which they were depicted to have gained especially from the harsh lesson of the long period of Philistine dominion beginning under Jephthah and ending only with Samuel's victory at Mizpah (Judg. 10.7–1 Sam. 7.12), that peace and divine favor can only be secured through uninterrupted, dynastic leadership.

In the narrative's flow of events, Samuel's purported victory in 7.3-12, leading to a long-overdue routing of the Philistines from Israelite territory[1] during the remainder of his career as well as economic and social recovery and peaceful respite, finally prompts Israel's elders to attempt to break the cyclic pattern characteristic of the era of the judges (Judg. 2.11-23) by avoiding the inevitable backsliding into idolatry after the death of a divinely raised judge. Samuel's success as

1. The length of Philistine oppression from the days of Jephthah has previously been emphasized by D. Jobling, *The Sense of Biblical Narrative*, II (JSOTSup, 39; Sheffield: JSOT Press, 1986), pp. 49-51, 53. It is implicitly set under Jephthah, but is overtly associated with Samson's unsuccessful judgeship (1 Sam. 13.5) by H.W. Hertzberg, *I & II Samuel* (trans. J.S. Bowman; OTL; Philadelphia: Westminster Press, 1964), p. 69. While 1 Sam. 7.13 has been considered problematic by many, it represents no challenge if the Philistine withdrawal is understood to refer to the rest of 'Samuel's days' as judge, in the way years were dated according to a king's reign.

a judge is portrayed to have stemmed from his close relationship with Yahweh and his ability to discern the divine will, obey it, and so lead Israel effectively, in obedience to the Horeb covenant. As many have noted, in the account of the Battle of Mizpah, it is Yahweh who is portrayed as the active military leader of Israel, not Samuel. Samuel is depicted as a passive deliverer, in contrast to earlier judges, to drive home this point. Similarly, the benefits of obedience to Yahweh—peace and prosperity—are reportedly maintained by Samuel's continued communication with Yahweh, indicated by his erection of the altar in his home town of Ramah and by his administering of justice or continued governance. Realizing that Samuel was an effective leader but that he has grown old and could die at any moment, the elders of Israel decide that the only way to ensure the continued peace and prosperity they have come to enjoy after much hardship is to maintain an unbroken chain of effective leadership, which can mediate between the people and Yahweh and hold them to obedience.[1]

In 8.1-5, the elders' request for a king is predicated on two important grounds: the realized desirability of continuity of effective leadership to secure ongoing divine blessing and the customary use of familial continuity to achieve an unbroken line of succession. Samuel's own sons do not follow his role as obedient, mediating leaders but, instead, pervert justice and are corrupt. Searching for an adequate solution to their dilemma, the elders reportedly turn to successful examples of mediation from surrounding nations and conclude that kingship, which is predicated on a dynastic principle that ensures unbroken representation, seems to be the tried and true method of mediated leadership.

The phrasing of the elders' initial request for a king seems to be deliberately ambiguous. It is addressed personally to Samuel, the existing *šōpēṭ*, with the actual request stated as a *qal* imperative, *śîmâ-lānû mélek lᵉšopṭēnû*: 'make for us a king to govern us' (v. 5). The request does not specify whether they expect Samuel, as the existing human leader, to use his personal judgment to name a worthy

1. So too, in previous discussion, Jobling, *Sense of Biblical Narrative*, II, p. 54. Compare the common suggestion that it had no basis whatsoever, in light of Samson's success as an ideal judge: Hertzberg, *I & II Samuel*, p. 70; Mettinger, *King and Messiah*, p. 80; McCarter, *I Samuel*, p. 151; R. Klein, *I Samuel* (Word Biblical Commentary, 10; Waco, TX: Word Books, 1980), pp. 70, 79.

replacement or whether they are expecting him, as their covenantal mediator, to secure for them a divinely chosen and approved candidate. The concentrated use of the root *špṭ* to designate judiciary functions in the immediately preceding verses (7.15, 17; 8.2, 3) would seem to be intended to indicate the elders' desire to maintain Samuel's achieved state of peace and covenantal harmony with God through the installation of the dynastic office of king, even though the root also has a dimension of meaning associated with military leadership, which is mentioned subsequently in 8.19.

Contrary to the common view,[1] Israel's depicted request for a king does not reflect their attempt to move to a 'secular' government away from theocratic rule. Throughout the ancient Near East, the king was the national god's earthly vice-regent, who carried out his god's commands and served as mediator between god and the larger community. Within the larger schematization of the 'Deuteronomistic History', the elders' request for a king 'like all the nations' seems to express the people's desire to move away from the disastrous cycle experienced under the noncontinuous form of mediating leadership represented by judgeship to a permanent, unbroken form of mediating representation offered by dynastic kingship, a prevalent and apparently effective form of political leadership in the surrounding world. In light of the common view of the relationship between national god and king, the elders' request would seem to presume that the appointed king would attune himself to Yahweh and would faithfully execute his commands.

In ch. 8, the author reinforces the ambiguity of the people's request for a king through the heavy use of discourse for plot development. As is widely noted, Samuel's reported focus on the first part of their request only, a king to 'judge' (root *špṭ*), ignoring the qualification 'like all the nations', leads him to misinterpret the request as a personal rejection, an attempt to oust him from office without cause (8.6). Yahweh's reply that Samuel has not listened to 'all that they have said to you' (8.7) is accurate; Samuel has failed to grasp the true meaning and import of the request. Yahweh then interprets the request for Samuel: the people have not rejected Samuel, they have

1. The most detailed argument of this position can be found in L. Eslinger, *Kingship of God in Crisis. A Close Reading of 1 Samuel 1–12* (Bible and Literature Series, 10; Sheffield: Almond Press, 1985), pp. 255-59.

rejected God himself from ruling over them. He reportedly understands the request to be a rejection of his abilities to protect and govern his covenantal people continuously without a human mediator. He associates the request for a king 'like all the nations' with other instances of Israel's deeds, which ended up by leading them to abandon their God and serve other gods (8.8).[1] His sentiments imply that royalty could become a form of idolatry, alluding to the belief known from surrounding nations, particularly Egypt, that the ruling king was a god incarnate.[2]

Yahweh is depicted to be anticipating the people's eventual downfall, not because of their installation of a king *per se*, but because of their desire to imitate surrounding nations, who inevitably become a snare for them. His statement seems designed to lead the audience to reflect over the source of affliction during the preceding period of the *šōp*^{e}*ṭîm*: the people's continual decision to do 'what was right in their own eyes' instead of doing 'what was right in Yahweh's eyes'. If a temporary human mediator was not always successful in holding them to the Horeb covenant, then there would be no guarantee that a permanent one could either. In Yahweh's eyes, the people do not seem to be facing the real issue, which is their own human weakness; their seeking to adopt the practices of other nations in the hope of finding a solution to their oppression is a stopgap measure that does not address the underlying problem of human free will and weakness.

After Samuel is made fully aware of the larger implications of the people's request for a king by Yahweh, in his role as mediator he purposely uses the ambiguity of the term *mišpāṭ* in Yahweh's command in 8.9 to his own advantage. God commands him 'to testify against the people and declare to them the "ways" of the king' as a condition of accepting their request. Construing *mišpāṭ* in the sense of 'custom, manner' rather than in the sense 'ordinance', he tries to dissuade the people from their decision by explaining the physical and

1. Following Eslinger (*Kingship in Crisis*, p. 265), I adopt S.L. Harris's proposed restoration of an *m* before the final *lk* to read *gm mlk* ('1 Samuel VIII 7–8', *VT* 31 [1981], p. 79). For a plausible interpretation of the existing text, see P. Miscall, *1 Samuel. A Literary Reading* (Bloomington, IN: Indiana University Press, 1986), pp. 48-49.

2. So previously, G. Auzou (*La danse devant l'arche* [Connaissance de la Bible, 6; Paris: Editions de l'Orant, 1968], p. 122), who cites Amos 5.26 as a possible example of a non-Yahwistic cult of a god-king connected with Sinai.

economic burdens that accompany kingship, rather than by testifying about Yahweh's understanding of their request as a potential source of further entrapment and covenant-breaking.[1] He fails to restate to them the 'ordinance of the king', the conditions under which kingship is to operate within Israel, which have already been spelled out by Yahweh, through Moses, on the plains of Moab (Deut. 17.14-20).

Samuel's speech in 8.11-18 fails to persuade the people and, ironically, confirms Yahweh's misgivings about introducing a king in Israel. It prompts the people to reiterate their desire to be 'like all the nations' (8.19) and to adopt whatever conventional administrative measures and practices, including those that have just been spelled out by Samuel in vv. 12-17, are necessary to secure the dynastic leadership of a king. It is the potential abuse of standard practices and the adoption of 'foreign' practices that Yahweh purportedly fears will eventually lead the Israelites to transgress the legal stipulations contained in Deuteronomy that are part of the ongoing covenantal regulations. In their steadfast confirmation of their desire for a king, the people add that in addition to his judiciary functions, *ûšᵉpāṭānû malkēnû*, he is to go out before them and fight their battles (v. 20).

The Israelites' addition of military leadership to the duties of a king may have been intended to appear as an afterthought, in response to Samuel's reminder in 8.11-12 that kingship includes this function as a primary task, but again it confirms Yahweh's misgivings. Their initial request focused on the need for continuous mediation, particularly in a judicial capacity, and in its restatement, the judicial aspect was again given priority in the repeated request. Notwithstanding, their unfortunate phrasing of the additional, military dimension of kingship in terms of a human figure who could 'go out before them' unintentionally points to another potential pitfall of kingship: the potential failure to acknowledge that God is the true source of victory in war. The people seem to intend only that an added bonus of dynastic mediation that would secure covenantal blessing for the nation could be military domination over other nations and the reception of wealth

1. This discrepancy has been stressed previously by, for example, K. Budde, *Die Bücher Samuel* (KHC, 8; Tübingen: Mohr, 1902), p. 55; Eslinger, *Kingship in Crisis*, pp. 270-71; A. Wénin, *Samuel et l'instauration de la monarchie (1 S 1-12)* (European University Studies Series, 23.342; New York: Peter Lang, 1988), pp. 140-41; Polzin, *Samuel*, p. 84.

through tribute. T. Mettinger is probably correct to connect 8.20 with Joshua 8; 23.2, 10,[1] although I would argue that the cross-connection is intended to allow the reader to see the ironic nature of the statement and situation and so realize the potentially grave consequences of which the people seem unaware.

Samuel, fully aware of the misleading aspect of the people's second request, nevertheless is said to repeat it in full ('all the words') to Yahweh, acting as covenant mediator. As L. Eslinger has pointed out, there may be some intimation of whispering in the phrasing *way-dabb^{e}rēm b^{e}'oznê yhwh.*[2] Yahweh appears to accept the final request and commands Samuel to install a king for the people (8.22). The use of a hiphil conjugation, *w^{e}himlaktā*, indicates that the office will remain under divine authority and, indirectly, that it has been approved by God. Samuel's sending everyone home in response to the divine command comes unexpectedly, introducing ambiguity. Has he not obeyed God because he is upset about his personal loss of leadership?[3] Is the narrative audience to understand him to be stalling because he fears Israel's inability to remain faithful to the stipulations of kingship? Or are we to conclude that Samuel is merely awaiting more specific divine initiative in the selection and announcement of a suitable candidate?[4]

1. Mettinger, *King and Messiah*, p. 81. For even broader citations, including Exod. 14.14; Deut. 20.1-14; Josh. 10.14, 42; Judg. 4.14; and 2 Sam. 5.4, see Klein, *1 Samuel*, p. 78.

2. Eslinger, *Kingship in Crisis*, p. 281.

3. So especially, R. Polzin, 'The Monarchy Begins: 1 Samuel 8–10', in *SBL Seminar Papers 1987* (ed. K.H. Richards; Chico, CA: Scholars Press, 1987), p. 122.

4. So, for example, Hertzberg, *I & II Samuel*, p. 74; P. Ackroyd, *The First Book of Samuel* (CamB, 9; Cambridge: Cambridge University Press, 1971), p. 73; McCarter, *I Samuel*, p. 162; Klein, *1 Samuel*, p. 78; Eslinger, *Kingship in Crisis*, p. 282; Miscall, *1 Samuel*, p. 51.

Chapter 4

1 SAMUEL 9

1 Sam. 9.1–11.15 is an account of Saul's elevation to kingship in Israel, apparently structured according to the three-part coronation ceremony outlined in Chapter 2. Various literary devices are clearly visible in the structuring of the material.[1] The opening genealogy employs the seven-generation pattern to depict Saul as one destined to greatness,[2] and the reference to Saul's physical stature (v. 2), a trait of many heroes, immediately reinforces Saul's future potential. Saul is sent in search of asses, the symbol of royalty in the ancient Near East.[3] The narrator's care to identify the lost animals as females would seem to be intended to emphasize the importance of producing offspring and creating/carrying on a royal line. Saul's trek through the southeastern portion of the Ephraimite hill country in search of the she-asses seems to serve as an anticipatory tour of his future kingdom and thus should function to foreshadow plot developments. It is probable that the four regions visited are identical with the territory

1. Contrast the structure proposed for ch. 9 by Polzin, *Samuel*, pp. 91-92.

2. J. Sasson, 'A Genealogical "Convention"', p. 18.

3. For the use of the ass as a royal mount during the coronation ceremony, see 2 Sam. 16.1-2; 1 Kgs 1.33-35, 38-40; Zech. 9.9. This use continues symbolically in the New Testament in Mt. 21.2-13; Mk 11.1-11; Lk. 29.28-48. The royal archives from Mari provide an excellent extrabiblical example from the MB II period. In ARM VI 76.20-25, the prefect of Mari, Baḫdi-Lim, sends word to the king, Iaḫdun-Lim, advising him not to ride a horse in the forthcoming ceremonies in Mari, but rather an ass, because 'you are king of the Haneans, but you are secondly king of the Akkadian'. For state occasions, the ass was still considered to be the royal mount *par excellence*. The MB IIA Hyksos royal tombs at Tell ed Dab'a provide a graphic illustration of this concept with their ass burials just outside the royal burial chambers. For details, see M. Bietak, 'Vorläufiger Bericht über die erste und zweite Kampagne der österreichischen Ausgrabungen auf Tell ed Dab'a im Ostdelta Ägyptens (1966, 1967)', *MDAIK* 23 (1968), pp. 90-100.

covered in Samuel's reported annual sanctuary circuit (1 Sam. 7.16-17).[1] Bearing this in mind, the plot should go on to explain how Saul took over control of Samuel's domain.

The brief scene between Kish and Saul in v. 4 highlights Saul's filial status and his obedience. Both are key themes from the previous chapter, where the elders are depicted to have asked Samuel to petition Yahweh to institute a form of hereditary government passing from father to son, in response to the disobedience and irresponsibility of Samuel's own sons and their unsuitability as candidates for such an office. In v. 4 Saul obeys his father's command instantly, without questioning motive or purpose, thereby revealing his filial loyalty, in contrast to Samuel's offspring. The narrator seems to intend Saul's response and actions to be a positive trait as a means of further developing his previously introduced destiny to royal greatness in the preceding three verses.[2]

In ch. 9 the author initiates wordplay centered on the root *ngd* that will continue through 10.16.[3] Beginning in v. 6 with Saul's weapons-bearer introducing innuendo in stating that perhaps the seer in the nearby town can 'declare' (*yaggîd*) concerning the nature of their journey, it continues in v. 18 with Saul unknowingly asking Samuel, the man who will anoint him as *nāgîd* ('king-elect'), for directions to the seer's home to learn his 'declaration' (*haggîdâ-nā' lî*). Samuel then responds to Saul's question in v. 19 by stating that in the morning he will 'declare' to him (*'aggîd lāk*) all that concerns the young man. The following morning, Samuel purportedly anoints Saul as Yahweh's *nāgîd* ('king-elect') (10.1). Finally, upon his return home, Saul's 'uncle' is said to have ordered Saul to 'declare' (*haggîdâ-nā*) what

1. D. Edelman, 'Saul's Journey through Mt Ephraim and Samuel's Ramah (1 Sam. 9: 4-5; 10: 2-5)', *ZDPV* 104 (1988), pp. 44-58, *contra* for example J. Mauchline, *1 and 2 Samuel* (NCB, 6; London: Oliphants, 1971), p. 94; Eslinger, *Kingship in Crisis*, p. 290.

2. So Eslinger, *Kingship in Crisis*, p. 289, who has not correctly understood, however, how v. 4 continues to develop the traits introduced in vv. 1-3.

3. So also previously noted by, for example, M. Buber, 'Die Erzählung von Sauls Königswahl', *VI* 6 (1956), p. 126; Auzou, *Danse devant l'arche*, p. 126; McCarter, *1 Samuel*, p. 176; S. Shaviv, '*Nābî'* and *nāgîd* in 1 Samuel IX 1-X 16', *VT* 34 (1984), pp. 108-12; Eslinger, *Kingship in Crisis*, pp. 293, 335; Miscall, *1 Samuel*, p. 62; Polzin, *Samuel*, p. 98. Wénin (*Samuel et l'instauration*, p. 351 n. 21) points out the additional use of *mṣ'* as a *Leitwort* in 9.4, 8, 11, 13.

Samuel had said to him (10.15). Saul reportedly replies by stating that Samuel 'certainly declared' (*haggēd higgîd*) that the asses had been found. The narrator explicitly intrudes to tell the audience that Saul did not tell him about (*lō' higgîd*) the matter of the kingdom (10.16). However, to the discerning audience, Saul's response would have symbolically revealed his new status.

Suspense is introduced in v. 6 in the reference to the well-known but unidentified seer. The audience is led to wonder about his identity and how it will impact on Saul's quest. Immediately, however, attention is diverted to the wordplay introduced in Saul's seemingly innocuous question in v. 7, *ûmah-nābî' lā'îš*, 'What shall we bring the man' as a gift for his prophecy since the food is gone? By construing *nābî'* as a noun rather than a first person plural imperfect verbal form, Saul, the seeker of a royal destiny, asks the question 'What is a prophet to mankind?',[1] thereby raising an issue to be explored throughout the remaining Saulide narrative and onward into the Books of Kings: the function of the prophet in the new era of kingship. Will the king replace the prophet as mediator of the divine will, or will this role continue to be played by the priest/prophet? Thus, as chs. 9–10 focus on the establishment of kingship in Israel, they will also explore the related, yet subsidiary question of the role the prophet will play within the monarchy.[2]

As pointed out by J. Blenkinsopp and popularized by R. Alter,[3] the

1. The double meaning of the question has been noted previously by, for example, Buber, 'Die Erzählung', p. 126; McCarter, *1 Samuel*, p. 176; Eslinger, *Kingship in Crisis*, p. 294; Miscall, *1 Samuel*, p. 53; M. Sternberg, *The Poetics of Biblical Narrative* (Indiana Studies in Biblical Literature; Bloomington, IN: Indiana University Press, 1986), p. 95; Polzin, *Saul*, p. 93.

2. *Contra* Polzin (*Samuel*, p. 97), who states that the ideological purpose of chs. 9–10 is to discover *who* a prophet is in Israel. The Hebrew Text reads *what*, not 'who', and the issue of the role of prophecy is not an independent concern but rather an aspect of the larger question of authority structure within the monarchic era. Sternberg (*Poetics*, pp. 94-95) argues that vv. 6-20 are designed to shatter the inflated prophetic image that he thinks would have been part of the ancient popular imagination.

3. J. Blenkinsopp, '1 and 2 Samuel', in *A New Catholic Commentary on Holy Scripture* (ed. R.C. Fuller; London: Nelson, 1969), p. 311; R. Alter, *The Art of Biblical Narrative* (New York: Basic Books, 1981), p. 61. Alter was also preceded in his 'discovery' by R. Culley, *Studies in the Structure of Hebrew Narrative* (Missoula, MT: Scholars Press, 1976), pp. 41-43.

ensuing scene (vv. 11-13) where Saul meets the eligible young women going out to draw water as he approaches the seer's town is the beginning of a possible marriage betrothal type scene. With it, the author introduces momentary suspense into the plot development as Saul, an eligible young hero on an adventure, is put in a position to seek a wife and abandon his original course. The scene is quickly ended, however, as Saul continues his primary quest. Finally, the identity of the well-known seer is revealed to be Samuel (v. 15), thereby resolving the earlier suspense generated by the question of the seer's name. At the same time, the revelation begins a new episode, thereby allowing the naming to serve as a minor climactic focal pivot in the story.[1]

Verses 12-24 form a loose subunit that is characterized by stress on alternating temporal phrases and by stress on 'eating'. The phrase *hayyôm* occurs with varying meanings twice in v. 12, once in v. 13, and once in v. 19, while the expressions, 'one day before Saul's arrival' (v. 15), 'tomorrow' (v. 16), 'about this time' (v. 16), 'the past three days' (v. 20), 'the appointed time' (v. 24), and 'that very day' (v. 24) appear in the space of the twelve verses. The cumulative effect stresses the issues of temporality and the implementation of Yahweh's will concerning the people's earlier request for a king, which was left in an unresolved state at the end of ch. 8. The time references climax in v. 24 with Samuel's presentation to Saul of the reserved thigh from the sacrificial animal that has been kept 'until the appointed time'. References to 'eating' by the people, by invited quests, and by Saul with Samuel occur five times, three concentrated in v. 13 and one

1. I agree with B. Birch (*The Rise of the Israelite Monarchy: The Growth and Development of 1 Samuel 7-15* [SBLDS, 27; Missoula, MT: Scholars Press, 1976], pp. 34-35) that the withholding of Samuel's identity is to be attributed to literary strategy and not to Samuel's editorial insertion into the narrative. The geographical circuit described in vv. 4-5 seems to presume his identity with the old seer from the story's beginning, and no one has doubted the authenticity of these verses. Others who have stressed a unified reading of the chapter, rather than using the different terms as a means of carving it up into sources, include Buber, 'Die Erzählung' pp. 124-25; A. Weiser, *Samuel: seine geschichtliche Aufgabe und religiose Bedeutung. Traditions-geschichtliche Untersuchungen zu 1. Samuel 7-17* (FRLANT, 81; Göttingen: Vandenhoeck & Ruprecht, 1962), p. 50; Eslinger, *Kingship in Crisis*, p. 299; R. Gordon, *I & II Samuel: A Commentary* (Regency Reference Library; Grand Rapids, MI: Zondervan, 1986), pp. 32, 113; Polzin, *Samuel*, pp. 89-91; V.P. Long, *The Reign and Rejection of King Saul* (SBLDS, 118; Atlanta: Scholars Press, 1989), pp. 198-99.

each in vv. 19 and 24. The progression of those involved in the eating follows the typical Hebrew pattern of moving from the general to the specific, narrowing focus to a spotlighted Saul. Since the act of eating is intimately tied up with a sacrifice and takes place within the confines of a private room in the town's main sanctuary, the depicted action again highlights the divine presence and central role in the unfolding events. The action does not center on the relationship between Saul and Samuel, but rather on that between Saul and God, with Samuel serving as Yahweh's earthly middleman. The eating references reach their climax simultaneously with the chronological references, with Saul's presentation and eating of the reserved thigh at 'the appointed time'.

The purpose that the ritual meal plays in the narrative action needs further consideration. Mention of a preplanned sacrifice and meal by invitation only is made to Saul by the maidens as he approaches the town, during the abortive betrothal scene in v. 12, but its explicit purpose remains unrevealed. As Samuel is on his way to the sanctuary to bless the sacrifice, the narrator informs the audience that Yahweh had pre-announced to Samuel that the following day at about that time, he would send to him a Benjaminite to be anointed as Yahweh's *nāgîd*, 'king-elect'.[1] Two points are noteworthy. As L. Eslinger alone has noted, the maidens characterize the sacrifice as being *lā'ām,* 'for the benefit of the people'. The mention of 'the people' provides a link with ch. 8, where the people requested from Yahweh a king who would work for their benefit.[2] The reader thus is led to wonder what the specific purpose of the sacrifice is and who has arranged it; is it a regular, annual event or a specially arranged event that relates to the temporal stresses and divine purpose noted above? The modern reader is further left to wonder about the significance of the restricted guest list and whether this is a clue to the nature of the sacrifice or

1. For *nāgîd* as 'king-elect' vs. 'leader' see, for example, A. Alt, 'Die Staatenbildung der Israeliten in Palästina', in *Kleine Schriften zur Geschichte des Volkes Israel*, II (3 vols.; ed. A. Alt; Munich: Beck, 1953-1959), pp. 23, 62; J. van der Ploeg, 'Les chefs du peuple d'Israël et leurs titres', *RB* 57 (1950), pp. 45-47; W. Beyerlin, 'Die Königscharisma bei Saul', *ZAW* 75 (1963), pp. 59-60; E. Lipiński, 'Nāgîd, der Kronprinz', *VT* 24 (1974), pp. 497-99; Mettinger, *King and Messiah*, p. 87; Halpern, *Constitution*, pp. 1-11; Edelman, 'Saul's Rescue', p. 197.

2. Eslinger, *Kingship in Crisis*, p. 299.

whether this remains an ambiguous point for the ancient Israelite reader as well.

The second point of note concerns the divinely announced function to be fulfilled by the *nāgîd*, 'king-elect'. The candidate will be appointed to deliver Israel from Philistine oppression in response to the usual 'crying out' (*ṣa'ᵃqātô*) of the people that characterizes the cycle of events in the period of the judges. Although the phrase *na'ᵃqātām* is used in Judg. 2.18 and so does not reflect the identical root as is found in v. 16, the two expressions are homophonous and are probably intended to echo one another. The root *z'q* is used regularly within the body of the judge stories to detail this step of the judge pattern. Its homophoneity with *ṣ'q* similarly calls to mind the earlier events of the premonarchic era, which is still under way until the end of ch. 11 according to the ancient writer's own schematization of Israel's past.

The deliberate link with the larger pattern for the judgeship era should immediately surprise the reader; has Yahweh decided to reject the people's request for a king after all and continue the normative judgeship after Samuel has failed to make a king for them? The question is answered immediately in the following verse. Yahweh informs Samuel as Saul approaches him that he is the man about whom he spoke and adds, 'He is the one who will restrain my people'. The use of the verb *'ṣr* to describe Saul's function in relationship to the people has puzzled many over the years and has generated a number of explanations.[1] In light of developments in ch. 8, there is no need to seek a nonstandard meaning for the verb. Saul's primary function as candidate for the new office of king that is about to be introduced in Israel in response to the people's request will be, in addition to serving as military commander, to restrain the people's tendency to 'become like all the nations' and to adopt foreign practices that will lead them to break the terms of the ongoing Horeb covenant. Like the preceding office of judge, which was depicted to have included judicial as well as military leadership, the king is to spend his lifetime actively holding the people steadfast to the covenant, to prevent the backsliding that

1. For discussions of the sense of *'ṣr*, see P. Dhorme, *Les Livres de Samuel* (Ebib; Paris: Lecoffre, 1910), p. 79; A. Ehrlich, *Randglossen zur hebräischen Bibel*, III (7 vols.; Leipzig: Hinrichs, 1908-1914), p. 198; E. Kutsch, 'Die Wurzel עצר im Hebräischen', *VT* 2 (1952), pp. 57-59; McCarter, *I Samuel*, p. 179.

inevitably was to have occurred after a judge died and left the people without visible leadership. The king is to be a steward of the covenant, which is not a full mediatory role in that he is not to be the spokesperson delivering Yahweh's ongoing revelation; he is to be the guardian of the existing revelation.

During the conversation between Samuel and Saul, Samuel hints to Saul that his trip to the high place where they will eat together will have important ramifications; at the same time, he states that the final unfolding of events will transpire by the next morning. Using a rhetorical question, he asks Saul, *l^e^mî kol-ḥemdat yiśrā'ēl h^a^lô' l^e^kā ûl^e^kol bêt 'ābîkā*—'For whom is all that is desirable in Israel; is it not for you and for your family, your *bêt 'āb* ?' (v. 20). The sense of *ḥemdat* and the initial preposition *l^e^* are ambiguous enough to allow the question also to be construed, 'On whom is the whole desire of Israel (centered)?'[1] While Saul does not immediately grasp the import of the statement and does not seem to realize that it somehow links up to the information supplied by the maidens, the audience, who now know of Saul's designation as king-elect, is led to suspect that the meal is not a normal sacrifice but is specifically tied to Yahweh's plans to designate Saul to the invited guests as his chosen candidate for kingship. Yet is this accurate? Saul subsequently is placed at the head of the guests and served the reserved thigh portion that was kept 'until the appointed time' to be eaten in the company of the invited guests and Samuel. Clearly this indicates that Saul is being specially honored in some way,[2] but we are not told of either the people's reactions to the event, nor Saul's. More importantly, the anticipated anointing that

1. So Mauchline, *1 and 2 Samuel*, p. 96. The decision of McCarter (*1 Samuel*, p. 165) to translate *ḥemdâ* as 'riches' obscures the allusion to the people's 'desire' and request for a king in the preceding chapter.

2. We can presume that the ritual laws concerning the right thigh were in effect in the late monarchic period when the 'Deuteronomistic History' was probably written and that they were meant to serve as background for understanding the significance of the event, even though the story is set in the premonarchic era when such cultic laws may not actually have been in effect. For the suggestion that the event was an installation/investiture meal, see, for example, L. Schmidt, *Menschlicher Erfolg und Jahwes Initiative: Studien zu Tradition, Interpretation und Historie in Uberlieferungen von Gideon, Saul und David* (WMANT, 38; Neukirchen–Vluyn: Neukirchener Verlag, 1970), pp. 84-85; Mettinger, *King and Messiah*, pp. 71-72.

Yahweh ordered Samuel to perform that day in v. 16 has not occurred.

The ritual meal scene is left deliberately unresolved, and because the audience knows of the divine plan, they are left to ponder the intent of Yahweh's command in v. 16 and whether Samuel is again trying to thwart the divine plan out of personal revenge (8.6-7) or whether he has perhaps unintentionally misconstrued the time-frame intended for the process. The sense of the final phrase in v. 19 then becomes clear; Samuel has taken Yahweh's command to indicate that the process will begin on the following day, but need not be completed on the same day. The reader is still not certain about Samuel's purported motivations, however. Why has he not chosen to anoint Saul during the occasion of the sacrifice, which seems to have been called in his honor? Is he still trying to cover up God's move to kingship by secretly designating the candidate? Is the meal a 'test-run' to see how the invited guests will react to Yahweh's candidate, before his actual designation? Has God given Samuel more specific commands that we have not been informed about?

Ambiguity about Samuel's intentions continues in the final two verses of the chapter, vv. 26-27, as he rouses Saul at daybreak the next morning to send him on his way. Again, a sense of temporal immediacy enters the account through an emphasis on a sequence of verbal actions in rapid succession. For some unexplained reason, Samuel seems to be in a great hurry to remove Saul and his weapons-bearer from town. Finally in v. 27, as the three reach the outskirts of town, Samuel is said to reveal to Saul the message of Yahweh in absolute privacy, instructing Saul to 'stand still this day so that I may cause you to know the word of the Lord'. The placement of *hayyôm* on Samuel's lips resonates with the earlier uses of the phrase by Yahweh and the maidens, leaving unresolved the question of Samuel's motives and his successful execution of Yahweh's commands.

Chapter 5

1 SAMUEL 10

The long-awaited moment of purported anointing finally arrives as an anticlimax. Others have already noted the contrast between the *pāk* or vial of oil that Samuel uses to anoint David. In contrast to the small vial, the 'horn' is a typical symbol of royal strength and seems in the contrastive context to echo the statement in v. 10 of the Song of Hannah (1 Sam. 2.10).[1] The same scholars tend to draw attention to the similar use of a vial of oil to anoint Jehu in 2 Kgs 9.1-3, which ends with disastrous results for Israel and Judah. In addition, P. Miscall notes Samuel's use of a question rather than a declaration to state the meaning of the anointing.[2] Since both episodes of anointing with a vial occur within the larger 'Deuteronomistic History', the audience would naturally draw a connection between the two incidents after systematically reading through the Books of Samuel and Kings. At the same time, they would undoubtedly find a deliberate contrast between the two instances of anointing with a vial and David's anointing with the more normative horn.

In a sequential reading of the narrative, where the audience would not have had David's and Jehu's anointing reports for comparative and contrastive purposes, this first account of a purported anointing would probably still have raised audience eyebrows. A late monarchic audience would have known that the king ordinarily was anointed with a horn of oil and that the horn had royal associations. To be told that Samuel anointed the first royal candidate using a vial of oil rather than a horn would have overturned their expectations and raised in their minds questions about the validity and meaning of Samuel's act. These

1. For example, Klein, *1 Samuel*, p. 90, Miscall, *1 Samuel*, p. 59; Polzin, *Samuel*, p. 35.

2. Miscall, *1 Samuel*, pp. 58-59.

questions would then be reinforced by Samuel's use of a question to state the meaning of the anointing rather than a definitive statement. While the question, which is the delayed response to Saul's previous question in 9.21b, is rhetorical and so is not open-ended but has the effect of a declaration, it highlights the ambiguity of the prophet's motivations that has appeared consistently from ch. 8 onward. Samuel's failure to explain to Saul that his twofold task as *nāgîd* is to deliver Israel from Philistine oppression and to restrain the people to maintain the terms of the Horeb covenant recalls in some way his earlier failure to report to the people the *mišpāṭ* of kingship as Yahweh had intended.[1]

The three-part sign in 10.2-7 serves as confirmation of Saul's selection by Yahweh, which has already been revealed by the ritual meal and by the anointing. The use of such signs to establish divine will is known elsewhere in the biblical narratives, as in Judg. 6.36-40 and 1 Sam. 14.8-10, and was a well-attested ancient practice. As already noted by many others, the specific content of the signs serves within the story to recapitulate the key previous events that led up to Saul's anointing and reception of a new status by contrasting 'before' and 'after'. The first part confirms the finding of the symbol of royalty and Saul's own words in 9.5 that his father would begin to worry about him, while the second part recalls Saul's running out of food and his meal with Samuel and the invited guests. The third part of the sign recalls Saul's meeting with Samuel, when he went to the sanctuary and became the guest of honour at an event whose significance was not totally clear.[2]

The third part of the sign predicting an encounter with a group of prophets that would result in the bestowal of divine spirit should not have been necessary. The prior anointing should have resulted in the transferral of some of God's numinous power to his king-elect.[3]

1. Contrast the interpretation of Eslinger, *Kingship in Crisis*, pp. 329-30. The MT is the *lectio difficilior*; the LXX reads as an attempt to remedy a perceived shortcoming.

2. So, for example, H.P. Smith, *A Critical and Exegetical Commentary on the Books of Samuel* (ICC, 9; New York: Charles Scribner's Sons, 1980), p. 67; Buber, 'Die Erzählung', p. 135; Hertzberg, *I & II Samuel*, p. 85; Eslinger, *Kingship in Crisis*, pp. 321-22.

3. For the historical background and meaning of anointing, see, for example, R. de Vaux, 'Le roi d'Israël, vassal de Yahvé', in *Mélanges Eugène Tisserant*, I

However, as depicted, its secret execution had precluded the people at large from recognizing Saul's new status. Only the thirty invited guests who had dined with him the previous evening would have had some indication of his favored status, but not necessarily of his designation as king-elect. His presentation of the priestly portion may have misled them into believing he now had priestly status. Thus, in the narrative recreation of events, Saul's possession by divine spirit during a public religious procession would be necessary to alert the wider public to his new status. The use of the multiple three for the number of steps probably reflects the prevalent custom of threefold repetition or occurrences in narrative plot development.

As might be expected, Saul's reported reception of divine spirit during the religious celebration and as a member of a group of prophets obscures rather than clarifies his new status. Just as the ritual meal the previous evening could have been understood by those present to designate a newly-received priestly status, so his ability to prophesy as a member of the prophetic group would tend to suggest to the eyewitnesses, many of whom would have been his fellow townsmen, that he had become a prophet, not Yahweh's king-elect (10.11-12). Thus, while the three-part sign serves to confirm in Saul's own mind the divine approval of his new status, it creates confusion about his status among the larger populace in the flow of narrative events.

Verse 11 quotes the *māšāl*, 'Is Saul also among the prophets?' and follows it immediately with the question 'Who is their father?', highlighting the issue of the source of authority for king and prophet alike.[1] Within the prophetic sphere, the question focuses audience

(Studi e Testi, 231; Vatican: Biblioteca Apostolica Vaticana, 1964), pp. 129-33; E. Kutsch, *Salbung als Rechtsakt im Alten Testament und im Alten Orient* (BZAW, 87; Berlin: Töpelmann, 1963); Mettinger, *King and Messiah*, pp. 208-32; D.J. McCarthy, 'Compact and Kingship: Stimuli for Hebrew Covenant Thinking', in *Studies in the Period of David and Solomon and Other Essays* (ed. T. Ishida; Winona Lake, IN: Eisenbrauns, 1982), pp. 75-92.

1. For various attempts to analyze the *māšāl* and derive its original context, see, for example, Buber, 'Die Erzählung', p. 140; A. Phillips, 'The Ecstatic's Father', in *Words and Meanings* (ed. P.R. Ackroyd and B. Lindars; Cambridge: Cambridge University Press, 1968), pp. 183-94; V. Eppstein, 'Was Saul Also Among the Prophets?', *ZAW* 81 (1969), pp. 287-304; Schmidt, *Menschlicher Erfolg*, pp. 103-19; B. Birch, 'The Development of the Tradition on the Anointing of Saul in 1 Sam.

attention on the definition of a true prophet, one who serves as the mouthpiece for his god rather than as a self-aggrandizer advancing his own personal interests. In the immediate narrative context, the answer to the question could either be Samuel, the earthly father/leader of the prophetic group, or Yahweh, their ultimate father and source of authority. Within the royal sphere, the question echoes Saul's earlier question in 9.7, 'What is a prophet to mankind?', asking whether the royal office is to function in a mediatory role for ongoing revelation or whether it is to be dependent upon a prophetic 'father' for such revelation.

The fulfillment of the final part of the sign is to be Saul's cue 'to do what your hand finds to do', that is, to perform a military deed under the guidance of the newly received divine spirit as the final event during Saul's reported return home (v. 6).[1] The completion of a military deed forms the second 'testing' step of the tri-partite royal coronation ceremony. The reference in 10.5 to the presence of a Philistine garrison/commander at Gib'at ha'elohim, the site where the prophesying is to take place, strongly hints that the anticipated military deed is to take place immediately after the prophesying. It would also seem to foreshadow the nature of the actual deed Saul is expected to execute: the overthrow/slaying of the Philistine garrison/commander at the 'hill of the gods', a task which links up in turn with Yahweh's command to Samuel in 9.16 to anoint Saul as the one who will deliver Israel from the hand of the Philistines. Yet audience members who have already noted Samuel's generalized declaration to Saul about his specific responsibilities as 'king-elect' in 10.1 will tend to wonder if Saul will indeed be able to decipher and carry out Samuel's vague and cryptic command.

Initial doubts about Saul's ability to understand Samuel's command seem to be intensified by the absence of specific temporal indications in Samuel's closing statement in 10.8. His words are ambiguous: is Saul to proceed immediately to Gilgal, one of the sites of Samuel's annual sanctuary circuit and so within his sphere of control, *after* the

9:1–10:16', *JBL* 90 (1971), pp. 66-67; J. Sturdy, 'The Original Meaning of "Is Saul Also Among the Prophets?" (1 Sam. 10:11, 12; 19:24)', *VT* 20 (1970), pp. 206-13; J. Lindblom, 'Saul Inter Prophetas', *ASTI* 9 (1974), p. 35.

1. The military sense of the phrase 'do what your hand finds to do' was convincingly established by Schmidt (*Menschlicher Erfolg*, pp. 74-80).

completion of the military deed, or is the command meant to qualify further the earlier one and so refer to a sequence of events that is to *precede* the execution of the military deed?[1] Samuel's motivations continue to be unclear and add to the uncertainty of intent. Is Samuel testing Yahweh's choice of candidate and his intended means of communication with the new king by seeing if God will steer Saul along the proper path of action that Saul cannot possibly reach on his own after the conflicting and ambiguous commands from Samuel? Or is Samuel testing Saul's understanding and acceptance of the continuation of prophetically mediated divine command and the existence of a prophetic 'middleman' who will link God and king in the dawning era in which kingship is to serve as the new divinely ordained form of political leadership?

Suspense peaks in v. 13 as Saul arrives at *the* high place (*habbāmâ*). How will he interpret Samuel's vague and potentially confusing commands from vv. 7-8? Will he kill the Philistine commander of Gib'at ha'elohim, and is this his intended test or not? Saul takes no action; instead he is questioned by his *dwd*, who wants to know about his whereabouts over the past few days. Although the term *dwd* is usually translated 'uncle', D.R. Ap-Thomas has made a good case for translating it 'commander' in the present context.[2] The appearance of a military figure is anticipated by the previous mention of the presence of a Philistine *n*[e]*ṣîb* at Gib'at ha'elohim (10.5)[3] while the appearance of Saul's uncle is not; and the man's unfamiliarity and concern with Saul's absence from town is consistent with the *dwd*'s role as a local authority figure trying to head off potential revolt, but not

1. The ambiguity is also noted by Miscall (*1 Samuel*, p. 61), and indirectly by Wénin (*Samuel et l'instauration*, p. 119).

2. D.R. Ap-Thomas, 'Saul's Uncle', *VT* 11 (1961), pp. 241-45. His proposal has been adopted by G.W. Ahlström, *Royal Administration and National Religion in Ancient Palestine* (SHANE, 1; Leiden: Brill, 1982), p. 21. Ap-Thomas does *not* build his argument on the now refuted occurrence of the term in a Mari text in what was originally thought to have the sense of 'commander', so his argument should be given more weight than is usually done. For the refutation of *dwd* as 'commander' at Mari, see J.J. Stamm, 'Der Name des Konigs David', *VTSup* 7 (1960), pp. 165-83.

3. It seems preferable to read the singular form *nṣyb* here instead of the MT *k*[e]*tîb nṣby* as do many of the versions. The MT text would have arisen through the metahesis of *yōd* and *bêt*.

with a relative's ignorance about family business. As noted earlier, the final instances of wordplay on the root *ngd* occur during Saul's exchange with the commander. In response to the commander's order for Saul to 'tell' him what Samuel had said to him, Saul alludes to his confirmed status as king-elect in his report that the she-asses had indeed been found through Samuel's declaration. The *dwd*'s concern over Saul's fraternizing with Samuel, a well-known figure of a neighboring town, again is more consistent in the narrative flow of events with his identification as a commander worried about conspiracy, rather than as Saul's uncle.

Saul's failure to take action against the Philistine *dwd* of Gib'at ha'elohim appears to have been the proper response. Samuel springs into decisive action in 10.7-27 and finally executes Saul's public designation as candidate for king before all the people and under Yahweh's aegis at Mizpah. Acting in his capacity as the existing *šōpēṭ*, he is said to assemble all Israel at Mizpah, one of the four established seats of his 'judging'. There, Saul is reportedly designated as Yahweh's candidate by lot, through the mediation of Samuel.[1] All the people affirm his status as Yahweh's chosen (v. 24), thereby clarifying for the two groups who had shared the ritual meal with him and who had witnessed his prophesying his true status and function. Saul's physical height is used to emphasize his appropriate choice, seeming to confirm the implied destiny already introduced in 9.2. It is to be noted that Saul is not formally installed as king in this scene at Mizpah; the

1. A number of scholars have inferred that the reported lot-casting is intended by the biblical writers to cast a negative tone over Saul's selection by relating the incident to the other two biblical examples of lot-casting, Joshua 7 and 1 Sam. 14.38-46. So, for example, Birch, *Rise of Monarchy*, pp. 48-54; McCarter, *I Samuel*, pp. 191-92, 195; Miscall, *1 Samuel*, p. 64; Polzin, *Samuel*, p. 104. Eslinger (*Kingship in Crisis*, p. 343) suggests that it represents the view of Samuel and not the narrator, while Auzou (*Danse devant l'arche*, p. 197), noting the connection with the other two examples, suggests a possible ironic use here. I believe this is too narrow a construction of the function of lot-casting in ancient Israelite society. Lots were a neutral mechanism by which the divine will was determined. The issue in need of determination need not have always involved legal guilt; it is coincidental that the other two examples of lot-casting, which *are* probably to be interrelated, involve the rendering of a legal decision by God. I would argue that there is a literary tie between the lot-casting that indicated Yahweh's choice of Saul as king-elect and the pronouncement of guilt against Jonathan, thereby indicating indirectly his rejection from potential candidacy, but that it is contrastive in nature, not synonymous.

people accept him as candidate only. The reference to Saul hiding among the baggage reflects the requisite humility of the royal candidate and not Saul's reluctance to assume office.[1]

After the people confirm their acceptance of Saul as Yahweh's chosen candidate for king with the phrase 'may the king live' (*y^{e}ḥî hammélek*),[2] Samuel finally tells them the rights and duties of kingship (*mišpaṭ hamm^{e}lukâ*), which he had been commanded to do by Yahweh in 8.9 under the term *mišpaṭ hammélek*, but which he had avoided doing by misconstruing the sense of *mišpāṭ*. Apparently following the prescription in Deut. 17.18-20, Samuel writes the rules in a book and deposits it before Yahweh. The symbolic sense of the calling of the assembly to Mizpah, 'place of observation', to designate Saul and reveal the requirements of the *mišpāṭ* to be 'observed' by the people, becomes evident. There would also seem to be an intentional link to Samuel's prior convocation of the people at Mizpah in 7.3-6 for the purpose of repenting their breaking of the Horeb covenant by serving other gods.[3]

At the same time, Samuel's motivations throughout the narrative become clearer. It is after Saul's decision to await Samuel's instructions and guidance as Yahweh's mediator before undertaking any military actions, and after his statement to the *dwd* that his new status was only achieved through Samuel's mediation, that Samuel moves

1. *Contra,* for example, R. Good, *Irony in the Old Testament* (London: SPCK, 1965), pp. 63-64; Miscall, *1 Samuel*, p. 64; Wénin, *Samuel et l'instauration*, p. 190; Long, *Reign and Rejection of Saul*, pp. 217-18. To the ancient mind, the reason for Saul's hiding would not have provided a gap, as many modern commentators have found at this point in the narrative. Humility was a requisite characteristic of the royal candidate and its absence would have required explanation, not its presence. Contrast the equally implausible suggestion of Eslinger (*Kingship in Crisis*, p. 347).

2. For the range of meaning associated with this phrase, see, for example, P.A.H. de Boer, 'Vive le roi', *VT* 5 (1955), pp. 225-31; Beyerlin, *Königscharisma*, p. 195; E. Lipiński, *La royauté de Yahwé dans la poésie et le culte de l'ancien Israël* (Verhandelingen van de koninglijke vlaamse Academie voor Wetenschappen, Letteren en schone Kunsten van België-Klasse der Letteren XXVII/55; Brussels: Paleis der Academiën, 1965), pp. 348-52; Mettinger, *King and Messiah*, pp. 133-36.

3. I thus do not agree with Eslinger's anticovenantal reading (*Kingship in Crisis*, pp. 335-43).

forward in fulfilling Yahweh's request to make a king for the people.[1] While Samuel may be depicted to be harboring some degree of resentment about his loss of military leadership and his replacement as *šōpēṭ* by the new office of *nāgîd*, in retrospect, his reported actions appear to have been designed to test Saul's (and to some degree, a portion of the people's) understanding of the ongoing relationship between Israel and Yahweh. They may also have been intended to test the king's and people's understanding of the essential role of prophetic mediation that would continue intact.

The scene ends with the dismissal of the people after the formal designation of Saul as king-elect, with his reception of gifts from most of the citizenry as tokens of their support, but with the doubting of certain men of Saul's suitability as candidate for king (vv. 25-27). Once again in the narrative flow of events, Samuel has ground the process for the installation of a king to a halt, leaving the people with an untested and unconfirmed candidate. While he finally has initiated the installation procedure that Yahweh demanded he should do in 8.7, 9, and 22, he has not yet given Israel the king they requested or the king that Yahweh found acceptable in 9.16-17. The audience is left in suspense as to how the remaining steps of the coronation process will be initiated. Since the denigration of the king (or his stand-in) was a regular feature of the Mesopotamian *akitu* festival,[2] the mention of the group of disapprovers need not be given undue attention; it would seem to be present as part of the kingship topos. Notwithstanding, the questioning of Saul's military capabilities (10.27) provides a lead-in to the ensuing battle account.

1. Eslinger, (*Kingship in Crisis*, p. 336) suggests that the final relative clause modifies the verb 'tell' rather than the noun 'kingdom', so that Saul's elusive answer would represent his obedience to a direct command from Samuel not to reveal information about his anointing.

2. A possible analogous example of royal humility appears in the degradation of the king in the Mesopotamian Akitu festival. For details, see W. Farber, H.M. Kümmel and W.H.Ph. Römer, *Rituale und Beschwörungen*. I. *Texte aus der Umwelt des Alten Testaments*, II/2 (Gütersloh: Mohn, 1987), pp. 222-23.

Chapter 6

1 SAMUEL 11

1 Sam. 11.1-11 recounts Saul's 'testing' as king-elect in his purported rescue of Jabesh-Gilead from the Ammonite threat of disfigurement and servitude. In the unfolding of the narrative's reconstruction of the advent of monarchy in Israel, Saul was formally designated king-elect at the end of ch. 10. According to the expectations of an ancient audience familiar with the royal coronation ceremony, the candidate now would have needed to be tested through the performance of a military deed before being confirmed as king. The story in ch. 11 portrays Saul as a judge-style deliverer who becomes filled with divine spirit (11.6) and under its influence successfully leads a united, twelve-tribe Israel (11.8) to defeat the Ammonites. As is commonly recognized, the dismemberment of the yoke of oxen and their distribution throughout Israel as a threat to those who do not assemble to fight provides a literary echo of the dismemberment and distribution of the Levite's concubine in Judg. 19.29-30. The resulting linkage between the two stories does not appear to be accidental; there are a number of details in Judges 19–21 that are echoed or refracted in ch. 11.[1] Notwithstanding the intertextual play, as noted by G. Wallis, there is an extrabiblical parallel in the Mari texts to the oxen dismemberment and distribution as a summons to war, which lends the present account an air of situational plausibility for any audience

1. For the parallels and their literary significance, see S. Lasine, 'Guest and Host in Judges 19: Lot's Hospitality in an Inverted World', *JSOT* 29 (1984), pp. 41-43; Polzin, *Samuel,* pp. 112-13. Nevertheless, in light of the uncertainty over the direction of compositional dependency and priority, it does not seem wise to accept the proposal made by some that the messengers were sent deliberately to Gibeah because of the pre-existing historical ties between the two groups that are established in Judg. 19-21. So, for example, E. Robertson, 'Samuel and Saul', *BJRL* 28 (1944), p. 194; Auzou, *Danse devant l'arche*, p. 136.

who might have missed the connections with Judges 19–21.[1]

As purported leader of the pan-Israelite host against the Ammonite siege of Jabesh-Gilead, Saul acts as a traditional *šōpēṭ*. His characterization is consistent with his belonging to the end of the era of the Judges in the Deuteronomistic schematization of history. Saul will become the founder of a new era, the era of the United Monarchy, but until he is formally crowned king, he must act in a way consistent with the depicted old political order. Thus, his testing is accomplished under the direction and influence of a benevolent divine spirit in established avenues of acceptable behavior for the era of the *šōpᵉṭîm* that will allow his fellow story characters to witness his fitness for royal office.

The opening scene provides a backdrop for Saul's requisite testing by introducing a new enemy in addition to the Philistines: Nahash of Ammon, who is said to have besieged the Israelite town of Jabesh-Gilead. The additional introductory remarks found in the Greek text provide no vital information that affects the reading of the larger narrative and tend to encumber the otherwise clean and rapid shift of scene. The reference in the Greek expansion to Nahash's failure to allow Israel a deliverer is inconsistent with Samuel's role as Yahweh's designated, successful 'judge' and with the understanding that Yahweh, not foreign kings, controls the course of history. According to the ideology expressed in Judg. 2.11-23, when Israel experiences foreign oppression, it is not because the foreign king is able to prevent the rising up of a deliverer, but because Yahweh is punishing his people. When Yahweh decides to appoint a deliverer, there is nothing the foreign king can do to prevent the deliverer's success. Thus, the longer LXX text would seem to have arisen as a later explanatory gloss to set the scene and is not to be favored over the MT reading.[2]

1. G. Wallis, 'Eine Parallele zu Richter 19, 29ff. und 1 Sam. 11.5ff. aus dem Briefarchiv von Mari', *ZAW* 64 (1952), pp. 57-61.

2. So also, for example, A. Rofé, 'The Acts of Nahash according to 4QSam[a]', *IEJ* 32 (1982), pp. 129-33. *Contra*, for example, T. Eves, 'One Ammonite Invasion or Two? 1 Sam. 10:27–11:2 in the Light of 4QSam[a]', *WTJ* 44 (1982), pp. 306-26; F.M. Cross, 'The Ammonite Oppression of the Tribes of Gad and Reuben: Missing Verses from 1 Sam. 11 Found in 4QSam[a]', in *History, Historiography and Interpretation: Studies in Biblical and Cuneiform Literature* (ed. H. Tadmor and M. Weinfeld; Jerusalem: Magnes Press, 1983), pp. 148-58; McCarter, *I Samuel*, p. 199; Gordon, *I & II Samuel*, p. 122; Long, *Reign and*

In response to Nahash's siege, the citizens of Jabesh-Gilead are reported to offer to make a treaty to serve the Ammonite king. Verses 2-3 further expound the details of the general situation announced in v. 1. The vassal status will entail humiliation of the nation of Israel by the gouging out of the right eyes of the townsmen and will go into effect in seven days unless an Israelite 'deliverer' arrives to fight off the Ammonites. In addition, unless relief is found, a segment of Israel will be forced to enter into a treaty with a foreign nation, which was prohibited by the terms of the Horeb covenant. As L. Eslinger has emphasized, vv. 1-3 portray Israel as a weak, fragmented, and seemingly leaderless political entity.[1]

At first glance, it seems in v. 1 that the Jabesh-Gileadites are being portrayed to have no faith in their king-elect Saul, in their existing judge Samuel, or in Yahweh's faithful action on their behalf. The last time part of Israel had faced an enemy encampment, in 1 Samuel 4, it had resulted in Yahweh's voluntary abandonment of his people. Since Samuel was to have indicated on two previous occasions that the nation's request for a king was a sinful move, the elders' immediate offer to enter into a vassal relationship with Nahash rather than fight would seem to reflect their doubt about Israel's future.[2] Yet, as vv. 2-3 unfold and fill out the details of the situation more fully, the audience is given reason to suspect that the depicted 'quick surrender' is not necessarily to be understood to be an act of desperation, but may rather constitute within the narrative flow of events a stalling tactic to buy some time in order to be able to contact the king-elect in Cisjordan, knowledge of whose recent designation may not have reached Nahash. The elders' motives remain ambiguous, but the audience's attention is piqued.

The change of enemy should provide a signal to the audience that the present episode is a narrative interlude that does not relate directly to Yahweh's stated military purpose for Saul as Israel's first king, which is to save Israel from Philistine oppression. Thus, the military deed that Saul is to perform after being empowered by the divine spirit, after a trip to Gilgal where sacrifices will be offered and where Saul is to await Samuel's arrival for seven days to be shown what he is

Rejection of Saul, p. 219.

1. Eslinger, *Kingship in Crisis*, pp. 360-62.
2. Eslinger, *Kingship in Crisis*, p. 361.

to do (10.6-8), is not to be expected in ch. 11. Nevertheless, it is noteworthy that three links with Samuel's previous predictive commands occur. The Jabesh-Gileadites have seven days to wait for a response from an Israelite savior before being made Ammonite vassals and told by their new overlord what to do, just as Saul is to have a seven-day waiting period for instructions from Samuel. Chapter 11 ends with the people assembling with Samuel at Gilgal to crown Saul as king and to offer *šᵉlāmîm* sacrifices there. Gilgal is the site to which Saul is to precede Samuel and where Samuel will offer *'ōlôt* and *šᵉlāmîm* sacrifices. The appearance in ch. 11 of three details that are anticipated in ch. 10 but not fulfilled in the prescribed manner serves to maintain audience involvement in the plot development and carries on suspense about the arrival of the predicted occasion. It also highlights the importance of the three details, leading the audience to pay close attention to future developments concerning Gilgal, a period of seven days, and the offering of *šᵉlāmîm* sacrifices.[1]

In an interesting play on the standard pattern for judge stories, the men of Jabesh-Gilead send messengers to their fellow Israelites to request aid, rather than appealing directly to Yahweh, or in their circumstances, to the existing judge Samuel. Although they tell Nahash that they will send messengers throughout the territory of Israel, the audience only learns of the messengers' arrival at Gib'at Shaul, 'Saul's hill' or hometown in the context. The narrative reporting of events leaves open the possibility that the Jabesh-Gileadites had intended to enlist the aid of the king-elect from the first but did not want to tip off the Ammonites about his existence.[2] The Jephthah story has a similar

1. Contrast the understanding of intent by Wénin (*Samuel et l'instauration*, pp. 119, 371 n. 91). He has noted the absence of only two details of the command in 10.8, the offering of *'ōlôt* and the seven-day waiting period, and suggests that the narrator intends the audience to think that the command has been more or less carried out by the end of ch. 12, thereby creating an optical illusion to bring his narrative to a close in ch. 12. Then only in ch. 13 does the audience discover that the meeting has not truly taken place.

2. So previously Budde, *Bücher Samuel*, p. 74, although I reject his decision to attribute the single stop to an editorial hand that has inserted it in place of an older description of far-flung travels. Wénin (*Samuel et l'instauration*, pp. 355-56 n. 39) emphasizes that the use of the definite article before 'messengers' in v. 4 indicates that the same group is intended as in v. 3 and so the narrator is deliberately portraying the Jabesh-Gileadites as using a ruse against Nahash to contact directly the king

plot line where the people take their deliverance into their own hands, but only after they have cried out to God for help and have been rebuffed by him (Judg. 10.10–11.11). In their desperation, they are portrayed as choosing an unlikely candidate known for his ruthless but successful razzia abilities, thereby placing Yahweh in the awkward position of normalizing their choice when Jephthah himself acknowledges his need for divine backing for success. Here, the Jabesh-Gileadites seem to be going directly to Yahweh's already designated leader, the king-elect Saul.

The narrative response of 'the people' in Gib'at Shaul is to raise their voices and weep (*wayyibkû*) rather than to 'cry out' to Yahweh for help (*n'q*, *ṣ'q* or *z'q*) in the normal fashion. The implication of the united action and intended context of the weeping is ambiguous; it might represent a communal act of lamentation before Yahweh to gain his attention and favor, or it might, in its contrast to the expected behavior, represent the people's resignation to their circumstances in the face of Samuel's statement in 10.19 that they have rejected Yahweh as their king (cf. 8.7) and their fear that Yahweh's displeasure might result in his re-abandonment of them, as in 1 Samuel 4–7. In the first case, their response would emphasize their intent to have Yahweh continue to serve as their 'king' by guiding the actions of his chosen human agent.

Whatever the intent, Yahweh would seem to have found the weeping acceptable, for he again fills Saul with divine spirit, which this time purportedly causes him to undertake the mustering of all Israel's forces (vv. 6-8). Nevertheless, the depicted bonding between king-elect and the people is based on coercion rather than mutual enterprise: whoever does not assemble will have his oxen dismembered. Acting as Israel's military leader, Saul sends a message to Jabesh–Gilead that they will indeed have deliverance by the following day when the sun has grown hot (v. 9). The besieged men in turn delude Nahash into thinking that the messengers had a negative answer by

whom all Israel had just made at Mizpah in 10.19-20. While I would agree with his understanding of the two groups of messengers, I would dispute his conclusion that they are seeking out the new king; rather, they are seeking out the king-elect who must be tested before he can be installed. Long (*Reign and Rejection of Saul*, pp. 221-23) reaches a similar conclusion to Wénin's, but uses a slightly different line of reasoning.

reporting that they will 'surrender' (*nēṣēʾ*) to Nahash the next day (v. 10). Their use of double entendre in negotiating with Nahash tends to confirm the impression raised by vv. 2-3 and v. 4 that their request for a treaty had been a means of gaining maneuvering space all along.

Saul's reported battle plan demonstrates his cunning as a military commander: he will march all night and mount a surprise, three-prong attack against the unsuspecting Ammonites in the early morning, surrounding the camp and hemming in the enemy for the slaughter (v. 11). The temporal sequence echoes his evening and early morning visit with Samuel, which led to his secret anointing, and may be intended to play off the temporal stresses noted in chs. 9–10 with the emphases on 'today' (v. 13), 'tomorrow' (vv. 9-10), and 'the morrow' (v. 11). If so, they would help stress the divine hand in the unfolding events.

Verse 11 represents a highly distilled use of the battle-report pattern to summarize the account of the battle between Saul and Nahash. All four elements, verbs of movement, verbs of military activity, an indication of the outcome of the battle, and a concluding element indicating the extent of the war are represented, although the last two overlap.[1] What is particularly noteworthy is the almost anticlimactic nature of the actual battle. It is recounted within a single verse, even though the build-up took ten of the chapter's fifteen verses, and immediately after its execution the action shifts to a new setting at Gilgal. The effect is to shift focus from the military encounter itself to its larger purpose: to provide a test for the king-elect and indirectly, a test of the people's understanding of the role of the new king.

The rescue plan is successful, yet leads to a potential misunderstanding of the source of victory by the people. Turning to Samuel, they demand that he set forward those men who at Mizpah had doubted

1. For this outline of the battle report, see W. Richter, *Traditionsgeschichtliche Untersuchungen zum Richterbuch* (BBB, 18; Bonn: Paul Hanstein, 1963), pp. 262-64. He is followed, for example, by J. van Seters, 'The Conquest of Sihon's Kingdom: A Literary Examination', *JBL* 91 (1972) pp. 182-97 and D. Gunn, 'Narrative Patterns and Oral Tradition in Judges and Samuel', *VT* 24 (1974), pp. 286-317. For a slightly different approach, see J. Plöger, *Literarkritische, formgeschichtliche und stilkritische Untersuchungen zum Deuteronium* (BBB, 26; Bonn: Paul Hanstein, 1967), pp. 16-19, adopted by A.F. Campbell, *The Ark Narrative. A Form-Critical and Traditio-Historical Study* (Missoula, MT: Scholars Press, 1975).

Saul's capabilities to be king so that they could be put to death in light of the Ammonite victory. The implication is that Saul's plan has led to victory and that he is personally responsible for saving Jabesh-Gilead. Saul quickly steps in to correct the possible misinterpretation. He credits the victory to Yahweh, the supreme commander, at the same time acting in his capacity as human leader to declare a day of amnesty for wrongdoers (v. 13). Saul's acknowledgment that Yahweh was responsible for Israel's deliverance demonstrates his understanding of the king's subsidiary role to Yahweh as his earthly representative and leads Samuel to initiate the final stage of the kingship ritual, the installation of the candidate as king. Samuel directs the people to assemble at Gilgal to 'inaugurate' (*hiddēš*) the kingship (v. 14).[1] There they officially install Saul as king (*wayyamlīkû šām 'et-šā'ûl lipnê yhwh*) with the appropriate ritual ceremonies and partake of celebrational festivities that include the offering of *šᵉlāmîm* sacrifices (v. 15). In this narrative recreation, Israel finally has its king, and a new era has begun.

1. For this sense of *ḥiddēš*, see, for example, Dhorme, *Livres de Samuel*, p. 95; H. Wiesmann, 'Die Einführung des Königtums in Israel (1 Sam. 8–12)', *ZKT* 34 (1910), p. 137 n. 1; J. Schelhaas, 'De instelling het van koningschap en de troonbestijging van Israëls eerste koning', *Gereformeerd Theologisch Tijdschrift* 44 (1944), p. 268; tentatively, Gunn, *Fate of King Saul*, p. 64; Edelman, 'Saul's Rescue', p. 199; Wénin, *Samuel et l'instauration*, p. 204. The English rendering is not meant to deny *ḥiddēš* its normal sense of 'renewing' something that already exists. In the context of kingship, the ongoing three-step process is being renewed, with the third and final stage of coronation now being undertaken.

Chapter 7

1 SAMUEL 12

1 Samuel 12 is a typical Deuteronomistic summary such as closes each major temporal division within the 'History'. It is put in the mouth of God's current spokesman of that era, Samuel, and its main purpose is to state clearly the role of kingship within Israel. Yahweh has set a king over Israel on the condition that both he and the people remain obedient to his existing commandments spelled out in the Horeb covenant and to any ongoing revealed commands. The chapter represents a speech made to the people at the conclusion of or after the celebrations associated with Saul's coronation. *Contra* R. Vannoy, it is not a detailing of the festivities themselves or the coronation process;[1] it is a summation of the entire process initiated in ch. 8 and a statement of the relationship between the new office of king and the ongoing office of prophet.

The chapter is divided into three segments through the use of the introductory particle *w*^{e}*'attâ* and is further developed through the use of two widely-recognized structuring patterns. Verse 1 introduces the topics to be explored in the remaining verses: the people's request for a king made to Yahweh through Samuel and Samuel's mediatory appointment of a king. The absence of a clear indication of change in setting indicates that Samuel's address is to have taken place at Gilgal, at the conclusion of the celebratory activities associated with Saul's installation.

Verses 2-6 constitute the first section introduced by *w*^{e}*'attâ*, which is loosely organized as a *rîb* or lawsuit proceeding between the people and Samuel, with Yahweh and his anointed king as witnesses. It opens with a reference to Saul's assumption of his role of service in 'walking

1. R. Vannoy, *Covenant Renewal at Gilgal* (Cherry Hill, NJ: Mack, 1978), p. 130.

before' (*mithallēk*) the people. Verses 7-12 form a second section introduced by *w*[e]*'attâ*, which continues the legal pattern, but in a new case between the people and Yahweh. At the same time that the summary of Yahweh's saving deeds on behalf of his people Israel serves as the testimony of proof of Israel's loss of faith in its God, it initiates the covenant pattern by serving as the historical prologue. The section opens with a command to the people to 'stand still' (*hityaṣṣ*[e]*bû*), which contrasts with Saul's motion that begins the first section. Verses 13-25 form the final section, opening again with a reference to Saul and his appointment by Yahweh as king at the people's request and decision. No verbs of motion occur—the situation is static. This section completes the loose application of the covenant pattern, reaffirming Israel's ongoing covenantal relationship with Yahweh and its continuing grounding in obedience by the people and now by their new leader, the king.

As is widely acknowledged, the opening verse refers the audience directly back to ch. 8, where the people initiated their request for a king after experiencing Yahweh's abandonment and reconciliation in 1 Samuel 4–7. Samuel's reference to 'all that you have said to me' should remind the audience of the exchanges in 8.4-9 and 8.19-21, where Yahweh reminded Samuel that he had not listened to all that the people had said and had misconstrued the nature of their rejection: they were not rejecting Samuel's leadership as *šōpēṭ*, but rather Yahweh's kingship (*mélek*). The people's final statement in 8.20 seems to be particularly highlighted by the 'all' in Samuel's statement; there, the people indicated that the new king was to assume the responsibilities of the *šōpēṭ* (*ûš*[e]*pāṭānû malkēnû*) *and* to 'go out before us and fight our battles'. Samuel states that in response to all that the people have said, he has 'caused a king to be appointed over them'. The use of the hiphil conjugation reinforces Samuel's role as mediator; it is Yahweh who is the true appointer and Samuel merely the executor of his will.

P. Dhorme and L. Eslinger have noted the subtle shift in preposition concerning the relationship between the king and people that appears in Samuel's statement. In 8.22, Yahweh commands Samuel to appoint a king 'for' (*l*[e]) them, which would seem to be consistent with their initial request that Samuel appoint 'for' them a king in 8.5 (*śîmâ-lānû mélek*). The use of *lamed* could imply that the king is to benefit the people. By contrast, Samuel states that he has appointed a king 'over' (*'al*) the people, which indicates their subordinate position and perhaps an adversative rather than beneficial relationship.[1] Since the preposition *'al* occurs elsewhere in connection with the role of the king *vis à vis* the people in 8.7, 9, 11, and 19, the last instance in which the people themselves confirm their decision to have a king 'over' them, it seems that there is no intentional message in the change of preposition.

Verse 2 begins a section in which Samuel seeks through legal means to establish that the people's request for a king to replace the office of *šōpēṭ* has not been due to his personal abuse of office. Beginning from the established fact of kingship, Samuel refers to his advanced age and the failure of his sons to succeed him in office, instead remaining among the people. He contrasts himself and his sons to Saul, who now 'walks before them' as king. He then avers, 'but I myself have walked before you from my youth until this day'. With this statement, Samuel begins his self-vindication. He indicates his faithful and long-term servitude as the people's *šōpēṭ* up until the moment of his replacement in favor of the king at Gilgal. His confirmation in v. 3 that 'I am here' echoes his response as a child to Yahweh's call in the temple at Shiloh, where he mistakenly ran to Eli when Yahweh was calling him (1 Sam. 3.4-8, 17) and, while intending to demonstrate his willingness to bear witness in the legal suit, seems to raise a question of his competence as a witness.

Samuel is depicted to set himself over against the people before Yahweh and his anointed, who are to judge the dispute. Here Samuel emphasizes the king's role as Yahweh's earthly representative and spokesman, which would seem to be at odds with his desire to vindicate his own service in that capacity. He asks five questions involving different forms of corruption that could commonly be associated with his service as *šōpēṭ*, which reflect the kind of charges that the people raised against his sons in 8.5 (cf. 8.3). Many have pointed to an intentional reference back to the 'manner of the kingship' in 8.11-17, particularly to v. 16 and the reference to the king taking the best oxen (LXX) and asses for himself, seeing Samuel's statement as a backhanded castigation of practices that will develop under the new regime in contrast to his own integrity and conduct.[2] Since the MT text refers

1. Dhorme, *Livres de Samuel*, p. 100; Eslinger, *Kingship in Crisis*, pp. 384-85.
2. For example, Budde, *Bücher Samuel*, p. 78; H.J. Boecker, *Die Beurteilung*

not to 'oxen' but to strong-bodied youth in 8.16, the parallel is not as firm as possible, and there is no compelling reason to favor the Greek text over the Hebrew here.

Another understanding of the offenses and their victims is suggested by a careful consideration of the three witnessing parties. Samuel is averring his innocence of any wrongdoing before Yahweh, before his anointed, and indirectly before the people. With this in mind, the first two examples involving the taking of an ox or an ass may well have as their intended offended party Yahweh and the king, respectively. A *šôr* was a prime sacrificial offering, and as already noted, the ass was the symbol of royalty. Samuel seems to be stating that he has not preempted any prerogatives of God or king. The remaining three examples involve offenses of office arising from abuses of fellow men. It is noteworthy that the people's responsive witness does not directly mention the taking of animals as a bribe, which was the concern of the first two examples. While their witness that Samuel has not taken anything from anyone could certainly include the animals mentioned in the first two questions, the fact that their response otherwise corresponds sequentially to the topics raised by the last three questions that clearly pertain to them leaves open the possibility that they are only bearing witness to the last three questions. Once again, Samuel's unclear motivations throughout the transition to kingship are highlighted, especially in light of his personal affront in 8.6 and his failure to begin direct proceedings to create a king according to Yahweh's command in 8.22.

The key word *yād* appears in vv. 3 and 5 during Samuel's question-and-answer session. While the first occurrence seems to be a regular idiomatic use of the term in the context of making a bribe by placing money 'in someone's hand', the second use, as a summary question asking what Samuel possesses that is not rightfully his, has overtones of power connected with it. The question suggests an abuse of office

der Anfänge des Königtums in den deuteronomistischen Abschnitten des ersten Samuelisbuches (WMANT, 31; Neukirchen–Vluyn: Neukirchener Verlag, 1969), p. 70; T. Veijola, *Das Königtum in der Beurteilung der deuteronomistischen Historiographie. Eine redaktionsgeschichtliche Untersuchung* (AASF Series B, 198; Helsinki: Suomalainen Tiedakatemia, 1977), p. 95; F. Crüsemann, *Die Widerstand gegen das Königtum* (WMANT, 49; Neukirchen–Vluyn: Neukirchener Verlag, 1978), pp. 64-65; Vannoy, *Covenant Renewal*, p. 12 n. 12a; McCarter, *I Samuel*, p. 213; Eslinger, *Kingship in Crisis*, p. 388.

that allows an official to 'place in his hand' or gain power over things he would not have been entitled to as a regular citizen. The term *yād* has appeared only sparingly in the preceding four chapters, in normal idiomatic usages (so esp. 9.8; 10.4; 11.7). In its three occurrences in 9.16; 10.4; and 10.18, *yād* conveyed the sense of 'power', as it does in v. 5, focusing on Israel's suppression by her enemies. Yahweh's stated role for the king in 9.16 was to have him free Israel from the *yād* or power of the Philistines. According to 10.7, Saul was to complete this task by doing 'what his hand finds to do' as soon as the three-part sign had been fulfilled, effecting a transfer of power from the Philistines to Israel through the completion of a military deed. Samuel's claim in v. 5 not to have abused the power of his office by filling his 'hand' comes in the wake of the transfer of leadership in Israel from himself, the final *šōpēṭ*, to the new king, Saul.

None of the foregoing appearances of the term *yād* stand out in a way that would necessarily lead the audience to suspect that the term is or will become a significant motif. However, having completed my close reading and discovered that this will be the case, I feel compelled to mention occurrences of the term that carry overtones of power, even if they appear as regular idioms, so that their cumulative effect will be evident. Thus, I am bending slightly the procedures I established in the introduction for reading sequentially, in order to help my readers trace *yād*'s slow but steady crescendo to importance.

Verse 6 forms a bridge to the second section introduced by *wᵉʿattâ*, signalling Samuel's move from a defensive to an offensive position. He states that it is Yahweh himself who 'made' (*ʿāśâ*) Moses and Aaron and caused the people's fathers to depart from the land of Egypt. As R. Vannoy and L. Eslinger have argued, the unusual use of the verb *ʿāśâ* is to be linked with a similar use in 11.13 where Yahweh 'has made deliverance' and in the following verse 12.7 in connection with Yahweh's *ṣidqôt*, acts of justification.[1] Thus, Moses and Aaron become examples of actions 'done' or 'made' by Yahweh on Israel's behalf when they are in need of his help. As such, Samuel hints that they are the first examples of divinely appointed mediatory deliverers who served as God's chosen form of political office from Israel's very

1. Vannoy, *Covenant Renewal*, p. 23 nn. 39-41; Eslinger, *Kingship in Crisis*, pp. 391-92.

beginning. His historical notice introduces the topic to be addressed in the following section.

Samuel then commands the people to stand firm so that he may judge 'with them' before Yahweh all the saving actions that Yahweh had done 'with' them and with their fathers (v. 7). Here Samuel has realigned himself with the people, but as one of them, he will nevertheless lead them through a process of judgment about their decision and past behavior. The people have received a king who is to be their new judge, according to their own request. Here, as a private citizen, Samuel launches a countersuit on Yahweh's behalf against the people, serving as prosecutor before the divine tribunal that is now Yahweh alone. There is no mention whatsoever of Yahweh's anointed as either witness or judge in this section. Samuel recites a summary history of Israel's oppression, crying out to God for help, and God's response by sending deliverers, beginning again with Moses and Aaron to clarify what he had only hinted at before. They were the first in a long line of *šōpēṭ* deliverers that Yahweh had used effectively to allow Israel to dwell in safety from the time that it became Yahweh's special people. He names himself as the last of those divinely ordained deliverers to drive home to the people the fact that he is still with them and should still be functioning as their judge according to Yahweh's plan. His recitation of deliverers in v. 11 appears to be deliberately selective and abbreviated; his point can be made without a full list of names and events. The term *yād* is used again in v. 9 to describe the foreign powers whom Yahweh had allowed to oppress Israel in the past as punishment for failure to worship Yahweh.

The second section ends with Samuel's claim that the people requested a king from him in connection with the Nahash incident in 1 Samuel 11, which was an unnecessary move because Yahweh was already their king (v. 12). His apparent quote of the people's earlier request in 8.19 should remind the audience of the whole process that had led to the institution of monarchy and also of Samuel's faulty memory. The people had said, 'Nay, but a king *will be* over us', not that 'a king would *rule* over us', and their original intention was not necessarily to replace Yahweh as their king but rather to have a continuous direct line of communication with him through his appointed royal vice-regent. Similarly, it was not the Ammonite situation that had prompted the people's demand for a king, but rather Samuel's pending death, the unsuitability of his corrupt sons for office, and the need to have a mediator who would prevent them from backsliding and invoking Yahweh's wrath again in such a way as possibly to prompt his temporary abandonment again, as in 1 Samuel 4–7.

Yet, as noted earlier, it seems as though the men of Jabesh-Gilead were to have sent directly to their king-elect for help rather than crying out to Yahweh for deliverance, so Samuel's statement is not entirely misfounded.[1] The Ammonite war was the occasion for the testing of the king-elect, and by enlisting Saul's involvement, the Jabesh-Gileadites jump started the installation process that had again ground to a halt after Samuel had sent everyone home after publicly confirming the candidate for office. Israel did not yet have a king in ch. 10. Thus, the action by the men of Jabesh-Gilead was in some respects a request to have a crowned king who could function fully in his royal capacities as Yahweh's earthly vice-regent.

The final section opens with Samuel's reintroduction of the king, who was not mentioned in the second section, with an emphasis on the people's decision to move to kingship as a new political form, their request for divine approval for such a move, and Yahweh's fulfillment of their request. Although Saul is not named or mentioned directly, he is alluded to by word-play on the root *š'l*. Here is the king for whom you 'asked', *š*ᵉ*'eltem* (vv. 13, 17, 19). The section then details the conditions under which kingship will function within Israel. Obedience by both king and people to the ongoing Horeb covenant and to any other additional commands issued by Yahweh is required to ensure Yahweh's favor and blessing; disobedience by the people will lead to divine punishment of both people and king. The term *yād* is used in v. 15 to characterize the divine power that will be the source of punishment.

A subsection within the final section is introduced by the phrase *gam-'attâ*, where the people are again instructed to stand firm before Yahweh (v. 16). This time, they are to witness a miracle of Yahweh, having last time been called on to review the history of Yahweh's acts of deliverance. Samuel identifies the time of year as the wheat harvest, or late spring, apparently to remind the people of the impossibility of a naturally occurring thunderstorm as well as the potential threat such a storm would make to their crops. Samuel requests that Yahweh send

1. *Contra*, for example, Vannoy, *Covenant Renewal*, pp. 38-39; Eslinger, *Kingship in Crisis*, p. 403; Miscall, *1 Samuel*, p. 75; Polzin, *Samuel*, p. 121.

a thunderstorm to confirm to the people that Yahweh did not approve of their request for a king. The audience already knows of the divine disapproval from Yahweh's statement to Samuel in 8.7-8; the people as characters in the story now have independent divine confirmation of Yahweh's displeasure with their decision, even though he has honored it. They have had reason to suspect Samuel's motivations and interpretation of events up until now, but learn that he is correct in his representation concerning Yahweh's view of their attempt to gain permanent leadership and maintenance from backsliding.

Chapter 12's setting during the wheat harvest has some interesting implications for the nature of the occasion portrayed. The wheat harvest was the second main *ḥag* in the later Israelite monarchic calendar (Exod. 34.22), which came to be known as the Feast of Weeks. Just as the first feast, Maṣṣot, eventually was associated with Israel's deliverance from Egypt, the wheat harvest became associated at some point in time with the covenant at Sinai, since according to Exod. 19.1, Israel reached Sinai in the third month after they left Egypt. The date of this association is unclear, but could conceivably derive from the late monarchic period if it reflects the same process of tying agricultural festivals to saving acts of Yahweh in Israel's foundational past.[1] Samuel's speech is therefore delivered at the occasion that traditionally commemorated the covenant at Sinai, at a sanctuary where the covenant was reportedly reconfirmed through circumcision of the new generation by Joshua after the Israelites first crossed into the land of promise (Joshua 4–5). At the same time, the twelve stones that were to have been erected at Gilgal were to have testified to Yahweh's wondrous deeds on Israel's behalf.[2] The loose structuring of Samuel's speech according to the covenant format also seems to be an intentional association of the chapter with covenantal ideas.

Since there is no stated temporal break between the coronation

1. For the history of the festival, see, for example, R. de Vaux, *Ancient Israel. Religious Institutions*, II (2 vols.; New York: McGraw-Hill, 1965), p. 494.

2. It should be noted, however, that the crossing of the Jordan and the ceremonies at Gilgal take place in spring, at the beginning of a new year, to symbolize the new beginning of Israel's life in the promised land. Thus, even though there are covenantal overtones in the circumcision ceremony, primary place has been given to emphasizing the fresh beginning rather than possible covenantal associations that could have been emphasized by placing the ceremonies at the time of the wheat harvest.

ceremony and festivities in 11.14-15 and Samuel's speech to the people at the wheat harvest in ch. 12, we are left to conclude that the coronation ceremony took place immediately prior to, or perhaps even during the opening days of the wheat harvest. While there is much debate as to whether Israel and Judah annually celebrated the enthronement of Yahweh and concomitantly the reinvestiture of the king as his earthly vice-regent as part of a New Year festival, it is noteworthy that Saul's coronation did not take place at either of the two festivals that might have been New Year celebrations: Peśaḥ/Maṣṣot or Sukkoth. For those who do not accept the existence of any annual enthronement festival, this observation is irrelevant. However, for those who favor the existence of such a festival, the disassociation of Saul's coronation from the festival that traditionally celebrated royal and divine investiture and his association instead with the festival commemorating covenant formation might well have been a deliberate move by the author to stress in a subtle way that the ongoing Horeb covenant was still to be of primary importance in the relationship between God and his people.

In the narrative flow of events, the people's response to the thunderstorm is fear of Yahweh and Samuel, and they immediately request Samuel to pray on their behalf to *his* God from whom they are now alienated to prevent their retributive deaths (v. 19). They admit that their request was the last of a long chain of evils, bringing to final resolution the countersuit initiated by Samuel against the people on Yahweh's behalf. The people's confession heads off the final judgment by the supreme judge Yahweh and an anticipated death sentence. Samuel instantly reassures them that their future obedience to God will result in divine grace, in spite of their sins, because of their special relationship with Yahweh. He avers that he will continue in his intercessory role to instruct the people in the good and right way and that for him to cease would constitute a sin against Yahweh. The section and chapter end with a final warning to the people to obey and serve God because of his great acts and that failure to do so will result in the end of the people and their king (vv. 24-25). Here, the people are aligned with their chosen king over against Samuel and his God.

As noted previously by others, vv. 16-25 broadly echo the assembly at Mizpah in 1 Sam. 7.5-6, thereby reinforcing the ongoing need for prophetic intercession to accomplish reconciliation between

Yahweh and his people.[1] The king will be the representative of his people before Yahweh, but will not be the channel through which communication of the divine will and commandment will be accomplished. As God's earthly representative, the king will fulfill the administrative tasks of military leadership and ensure the observation and maintenance of law and order (9.16-17). Mediation will continue to be carried out by Yahweh's appointment of human intercessors as needed, who in this regard will continue the long-standing, divinely approved method of actualizing Yahweh's rule over his people. They will not assume military or judicial roles as in the past, however; now their role will be limited to prophetic functions. By the end of ch. 12, the people have successfully secured continuous political leadership without compromising Yahweh's kingship.

1. So, for example, Buber, 'Die Erzählung', p. 158; H. Seebass, 'Traditionsgeschichte von 1 Sam. 8, 10:17ff., und 12', *ZAW* 77 (1965), p. 294; Eslinger, *Kingship in Crisis*, p. 408.

Chapter 8

1 SAMUEL 13

Chapter 13 initiates the Deuteronomistic Historian's account of the new era of the United Monarchy, which will last until Solomon's death in 1 Kgs 11.43. The presentation of this era and the succeeding era of the Kingdoms of Israel and Judah will be dominated by the standard regnal account pattern. Verse 1 signals the beginning of the era with its textually corrupt but standard accession and regnal formula. Immediately, v. 2 begins the segment portraying some of the monarch's accomplishments with the account of the battle at the Michmash pass, which extends through 14.46. The presentation of selected deeds from the standard regnal pattern becomes the backdrop for the depiction of Saul's rejection from the office of king for disobedience to divine command and the passing over of his son Jonathan as candidate for the office of king-elect to succeed his rejected father on the throne.

The unity of 13.2–14.46 is indicated by deliberate links between the two chapters. The opening statement in 14.1 that many have found troublesome is a reference back to 13.22, 'the day of the battle', and 14.2 repeats the situation in 13.15, resuming the earlier story line. The Philistines' mistaking of Jonathan and his weapons-bearer as Hebrews in 14.11 plays on 13.6, where the Israelites had deserted into caves and holes, while 14.22 refers back directly to the desertion in 13.6, reporting that these men rejoined the battle. The theme of distress is used in 14.24 to introduce a new episode, carrying forward the unresolved theme from 13.6. These direct literary links between the material in the two chapters demonstrate that they form a single, coherent narrative unit.

The message of 13.2–14.46 is stated clearly in 13.13-14: Saul's failure to obey Yahweh's directives will prevent the establishment of his rulership in Israel, so that he will be replaced by Yahweh's newly chosen *nāgîd*, 'a man after Yahweh's own heart'. The term 'heart' and the contrasting organ 'eyes' will serve as motifs in the search for the new king-elect. Bearing in mind the centrality of 13.13-14, 13.1-12 should explain the circumstances under which Saul will fail to obey Yahweh's command and the ensuing section, 13.15–14.46, should deal with the search for Yahweh's new *nāgîd*.

1 Sam. 13.2 sets the scene and describes for the narrative audience Saul's purported strategy for capturing both Philistine garrisons that were controlling the Michmash pass. He was to have taken two army divisions and circled around north of the Michmash garrison through the hill country of Bethel, while Jonathan was to taken have one and gone to the garrison at Gibeah. As portrayed, the plan was to have the Israelite forces attack both garrisons simultaneously and force the Philistines into the pass, where they could not escape and where they could be killed off by the Israelites closing in from both sides.[1] Jonathan's subsequent premature launching of the attack against Gibeah (v. 3) gave Israel only a partial victory and forced Saul to abort his original plan and go to Gilgal to muster the additional troops that would now be needed to face the Philistine reinforcements that would arrive from the plain (vv. 5-7). In the narrative flow of events, Saul had lost his tactical advantage through his son's rash action.

1 Samuel 13.8-14 finally describes the situation predicted by Samuel back in 10.8 and introduces the long-awaited scene in which Saul is to 'do what his hand finds to do, for Yahweh is with him', but is to wait for seven days for Samuel's arrival to offer sacrifices and to instruct him. With the people beginning to scatter, during the course of the seventh day Saul himself offers the *'ōlôt* and *šᵉlāmîm* offerings that

1. Contrast the understanding of M. Miller that v. 2 describes the situation after the end of the battle ('Saul's Rise to Power: Some Observations Concerning 1 Sam. 9:1-10–10:16; 10:26–11:15 and 13:2–14:46', *CBQ* 36 [1974], p. 161). His proposal has been adopted by Ackroyd, *First Book of Samuel*, p. 104 and Klein, *1 Samuel*, p. 124. For an alternate reconstruction of the stages of the battle, which does not emphasize the crucial role of Gibeah for control over the pass, see C. Herzog and M. Gichon, *Battles of the Bible* (New York: Random House, 1978), pp. 68-71. J. Fokkelman (*Narrative Art and Poetry in the Books of Samuel*. II. *The Crossing Fates* [Assen: Van Gorcum, 1986], p. 32 n. 9) on the other hand, believes the text is not attuned to historical military strategy and so does not reflect such information.

Samuel had announced he was to offer on that occasion, only to have Samuel arrive and appear to declare that Yahweh had rejected Saul for his failure to obey exactly his previous, prophetically-delivered command.[1]

As J. Fokkelman has noted, Samuel's key role as officiator over the sacrifices is highlighted first in 10.8, where it is pronounced as the first action to be associated with events at Gilgal, even though it is not the first chronological event to take place in connection with Gilgal. It is then foregrounded again in 13.10b through the use of *hinnēh* to draw attention to Samuel's arrival to offer the sacrifices.[2] Following A. Berlin's study of the functions of *hinnēh* in narrative writing,[3] the *hinnēh* in v. 10b would most plausibly be construed as a report of Saul's sudden perception of Samuel's arrival, as opposed to Samuel's sudden appearance out of nowhere in a quick succession of events. Notwithstanding, even though Saul remains the center of attention in the narrative, Samuel's arrival, marked by the *hinnēh* construction, and his crucial association with the sacrifices Saul had just offered, is foregrounded.

Taken at face value, Saul's reported rejection would seem to be justified. He has failed to obey God's command to await Samuel's arrival and the prophet's officiation on this specific occasion. After the solemn warning in ch. 12 that the king and people must be obedient or

1. Good (*Irony in the Old Testament*, pp. 67, 70) argues that this initial 'rejection scene' in ch. 13 should be interpreted as Samuel's personal rejection of Saul and that the king's divine rejection only occurs in ch. 15. Although there is no direct indication that Samuel is speaking Yahweh's word in 10.8, the basis for Saul's rejection in 13.13-14, the latter verses make it clear that his rejection is based on disobedience to Yahweh's command, not Samuel's. In addition, Samuel would not have any personal authority to announce that Saul was no longer Yahweh's *nāgîd*. Only Yahweh can elect and reject his candidate for earthly vice-regent. F. Foresti's attempt to assign 1 Samuel 13 to DtrH and 1 Samuel 15 to DtrP, who felt the first rejection story 'was not proportionate to the gravity of the consequence', similarly overlooks the larger function of chs. 13–14 as the testing and rejection of Jonathan as Saul's successor (*The Rejection of Saul in the Perspective of the Deuteronomistic School* [Studia Theologica-Teresianum, 5; Rome: Edizioni del Teresianum, 1984], p. 167). The presence of the two rejection stories seems to have been part of the plot development in the earliest form of the 'History'.

2. Fokkelman, *Crossing Fates*, p. 44

3. A. Berlin, *Poetics and Interpretation of Biblical Narrative* (Bible and Literature Series, 9; Sheffield: Almond Press, 1987), p. 93.

the hand of the Lord will be against people and king and that Yahweh's ongoing mediatory link with his people is to be through his designated prophet, Saul's failure to have complete faith in the word of Yahweh's spokesman and to follow his instructions to the final letter immediately jeopardizes the hard-won kingship. The conditions for the divine acceptance of kingship have been carefully announced, and all actions by the new king will certainly be carefully scrutinized by the deity who was reluctant to grant the people a political form that could facilitate their breaking of the Horeb covenant. The audience should expect that any infraction, however small, will not pass unnoticed.[1]

Nevertheless, in light of the confusing and ambiguous nature of Samuel's command in 10.8, the audience seems to be invited to reflect upon the fairness of Saul's announced rejection and, by extension, to question the fairness of the divine will. While Saul can be held accountable for not clarifying Samuel's prophetic instructions when they were initially delivered in 10.8, Samuel can be held equally responsible for delivering his instructions in a deliberately confusing manner. Such reflection then raises again the question encountered in ch. 10 of how 10.7-8 were to relate to the three-part sign in 10.2-6, and whether the two verses constituted a verbatim relaying of an ambiguously phrased divine message; whether they were a deliberately ambiguous paraphrase of a clearer divine message; or whether they were Samuel's own creation, without divine backing, intended either to confuse and mislead the royal candidate out of spite or envy, or to test Saul's obedience. It seems that the ancient authorial and narrative audiences would have shared with the modern actual audience the same sense of ambiguity about the relationship between the three-part sign and Samuel's subsequent commands to the king in

1. So also Gunn, *Fate of Saul*, pp. 39, 66. Polzin (*Samuel*, pp. 130, 252 n. 12) emphasizes Samuel's guilt in failing to appear in a timely manner, as well as his failure as a prophet that is highlighted by the nonfulfillment of his earlier prediction in 10.8. I think his focus on Samuel's role in 1 Samuel has in this instance led him to miss the main point of the narrative. In addition, 10.8 does not predict that he will offer the sacrifices; it merely states that he will be arriving to do so, which he did, so his part of the prophecy was fulfilled. Saul's failure to have faith in Samuel's prediction by failing to await sunset is portrayed to be the central issue at dispute between the two characters, and the result is Saul's apparent rejection from kingship, not Samuel's rejection from prophetic office.

10.2-8. The opacity of Samuel's motivations throughout the narrative raises the important question of the fairness and severity of the announced divine rejection in light of Samuel's possible contribution to Saul's infraction.

The exact nature of the announced rejection is as ambiguous as the instructions following the three-part sign that were broken. First and foremost, do vv. 13-14 represent a legitimate prophetic pronouncement expressing Yahweh's will, or are they instead Samuel's warning to Saul about his possible future divine rejection in light of his failure to obey the earlier directions from 10.8? The statement can be read either way. Bearing this in mind, the sense to be assigned to the perfect verb form *biqqēš* and the ensuing *wāw* -consecutive form *waysawwēhû* needs to be considered carefully. Should both be construed as uses of the 'prophetic perfect' or the 'perfect of confidence' and translated as future, uncompleted actions or taken at face value as completed acts and translated as perfects?

If vv. 13-14 represent a legitimate prophetic announcement, it is not immediately clear whether Yahweh's decision that Saul's kingdom shall not endure constitutes a rejection of Saul alone or whether it includes a rejection of his entire dynastic house. Had Saul obeyed what are now explicitly stated to have been Samuel's divinely announced commands totally, Yahweh would have established his kingdom over Israel 'forever', *'ad-'ôlām*. All audiences here seem to receive explicit indication that the instructions in 10.7-8, which followed upon the three-part sign in 10.2-6 that was to confirm Saul's divine election as king-elect, were indeed of divine origin. And yet, is the broken command perhaps to be understood to be Saul's failure to constrain (*'ṣr*) the people during the seven-day waiting period, so that they dispersed? Is there perhaps room for the authorial and narrative audiences to conclude that the ambiguous rejection is Yahweh's intentional response to the ambiguous conveyance of his initial command, whether by his own fault or by Samuel's distortion? If so, the fairness of the divine will gets a much-needed boost.

In v. 14, Yahweh's spokesman announces that Saul's kingdom (*mamlakt^{e}kā*) will not be established (*lō' tāqûm*) because of the king's failure to fulfill a divinely mediated command. Yet, the lack of precise temporal limits for the establishment of 'Saul's kingdom' would allow for the possible reign of many Saulides before Yahweh removed it.[1] Verse 14 then goes on to state the central theme for the remaining portion of the battle account, the discovery of the new divinely chosen candidate for the office of king-elect should Saul have been rejected. Any potential candidate would be a man 'after Yahweh's own heart', making 'heart' a key motif in the ensuing search. Verse 15 immediately introduces narrative suspense by having Samuel the kingmaker leave Saul and go up to Gibeah, the site where Jonathan has been positioned since v. 3.[2] Is Jonathan, who is by birth the expected candidate to succeed Saul, the candidate Yahweh will choose/has chosen? Will Yahweh allow any other Saulides to lead Israel, or has/will Saul's mistake led to the immediate rejection of his entire house as well?

The second phase of the battle for control over the Michmash pass serves as the backdrop for exploring Jonathan's status before Yahweh. Verse 16 specifically refers to Jonathan's filial relationship with Saul for the first time in the narrative, highlighting the importance of this link in the coming narrative segment. The narrator devotes vv. 15b-23 to setting the scene. Saul is now reunited with Jonathan on the south side of the Wadi Suweinit at Gibeah, faced with a Philistine horde as great as the sand on the seashore because of his son's rash action. Having begun with 3000 men and the military advantage of a surprise assault, they now have only 600 men and are sitting targets for the Philistines. Saul's appointed task to free Israel from Philistine oppression has not been realized; he and his son, the potential king-elect, have worsened Israel's situation rather than improved it. Raiders are now terrorizing the countryside (v. 17) and many of the

1. Contrast Polzin, *Samuel*, p. 118; Miscall, *1 Samuel*, p. 87; Sternberg, *Poetics*, p. 496; Long, *Reign and Rejection of Saul*, p. 129.

2. *Contra*, for example, Auzou (*Danse devant l'arche*, p. 150), McCarter (*1 Samuel*, p. 227), Klein (*1 Samuel*, p. 123), and Long (*Reign and Rejection of Saul*, p. 95), the course of plot development weighs against the adoption of the fuller LXX reading ('Then Samuel set out from Gilgal and went his way while the remnant of the army went up after Saul to meet the fighting force, going from Gilgal toward Gibeah of Benjamin') in lieu of the MT. The focus is on Samuel's movement away from Saul at Gilgal to Jonathan at Gibeah because Jonathan is the logical replacement as Yahweh's new *nāgîd*. Contrast also the suggestion of Polzin (*Samuel*, p. 131) that Gibeah is here symbolic of the city of sin (cf. Judges 19–21) that stood for Saul's tragic reign.

Israelites have fled across the Jordan or hidden from the bestirred enemy (v. 6). Without swords or spears 'in their hands' (vv. 19-22), the people are more 'hard pressed' (*ṣār*) than ever in face of the increased Philistine presence, punitive raids, and the loss of their strategic military plan that would have allowed them to undertake a surprise attack against small Philistine outposts, without swords or spears, and still expect success. The use of the verb *ṣar* to characterize Israel's situation seems to play off the second task Yahweh had envisioned for the king: to 'constrain' (*'ṣr*) the people within the limits of the Horeb covenant. Instead, Saul, through his son's action, has subjected them to stronger Philistine constraint.

Chapter 13 ends with additional background information that sets the scene for Jonathan's foray in ch. 14. Verse 22 has already indicated that a battle was to follow in its reference to the lack of Israelite arms on 'the day of battle'. In the closing verse, the narrator becomes more specific, telling his audience that the Philistine *maṣṣab* (garrison detail or commander who presumably would head a detail) went out to the Michmash pass. Thus, the upcoming scene is to take place with Philistine troops stationed in the area of the pass itself, having left nearby a relatively unprotected Philistine garrison.

Chapter 9

1 SAMUEL 14

The opening verse begins with a temporal link to 13.22, the day of battle: 'it was *the* day', and introduces the protagonist, Jonathan, the son of Saul. Jonathan's filial relationship to the rejected king is again highlighted, hinting to the audience that the forthcoming battle is to focus on his status as heir-elect to the Saulide throne.[1] The mention of 'son' should take the audience back to the first appearance of the term in 13.16, raising again the question of Samuel's intent or actions after he left the rejected Saul in Gilgal and went up to Jonathan, the heir-elect, in Gibeah. Had he gone to anoint the new man after Yahweh's own heart? Now, the potential *nāgîd* is about to be involved in a military encounter: Jonathan apparently is going to be tested as a suitable candidate for kingship. The royal coronation ceremony appears for the second time to be used as an underlying structuring frame to depict how the author envisions historical events to have unfolded. The reappearance of *hayyôm* to announce the day of battle echoes the use of the same word in chs. 9–10 in connection with the initial designation of Saul as king-elect. Will the battle about to take place result in the appointment of a new king, after the potential candidate has passed his test?

Jonathan initiates a secret foray without the knowledge of his father or the other troops, with the help only of his weapons-bearer. Verses 2-5 then quickly position the Israelites in relationship to the Philistines within the scene, at the same time linking up with the situation

1. Contrast Long (*Reign and Rejection of Saul*, pp. 101-102, 105), who concludes that the emphasis on their filial relationship is intended to be the first overt indication of disunity between father and son, king and crown prince, and that 'the simple juxtaposing and comparing of Saul and Jonathan in ch. 13 evolves in ch. 14 into a rivalry and progressive alienation between them' (p. 105).

described in 13.15-16 to indicate that the upcoming action is to be viewed as part of the ongoing battle for control over the Michmash pass that began back in 13.2. Resuming the opening conversation after the parenthetical interlude, Jonathan expands his original statement of intent in v. 1 to reveal his plan of attack against the Philistines, now derogatorily referred to as 'uncircumcised' to emphasize their non-covenantal status before Yahweh. The mention of circumcision reminds the audience of Israel's covenant with Yahweh and the preceding crisis of the institution of monarchy that Yahweh had seen as a challenge to his direct kingship over his people. Jonathan's plan is to surrender himself totally to Yahweh's leadership, acknowledging that while Israel maybe constrained (*ṣār*) by the Philistines, no constraints exist for Yahweh to bring about Israel's deliverance (*'ên l^e^yhwh ma'ṣôr l^e^hôšî^a^'*) by many or by few, through a saving deed (*'ûlay ya'^a^ śeh yhwh lānû*). Jonathan's language echoes both the task of the political king, who is to *'ṣr* Yahweh's people, and the previous uses of the verb *'āśâ* to describe Yahweh's saving deeds in 11.13, 12.6, 7.

Putting himself totally in the care of Yahweh, Jonathan suggests that the two cross over to the Philistine garrison, which the audience knows is now vulnerable. The stress on the verb *'br* in vv. 1, 6, and 8 brings to mind Saul's earlier crossing into the hill country of Ephraim in search of the symbol of royalty, which may well have occurred through the same pass, providing the audience with a hint that Jonathan's crossing may also lead him to learn about his royal destiny—whether he is to have one or not. Also noteworthy is the narrator's use of the fuller form of Jonathan's name, Jehonathan, in vv. 6 and 8 to emphasize his complete subservience to God and his acknowledgment that only Yahweh can give victory. Jonathan's uncertainty about Yahweh's willingness to use him as an instrument of deliverance, highlighted by the use of *'ûlay* in v. 6 and the subsequent designation of the signs to determine the divine will in vv. 8-10, again focuses attention on the identity of Yahweh's new *nāgîd*. This issue is heightened by the weapons-bearer's reply to Jonathan's proposal in v. 7. He tells Jonathan to do all that his 'heart' moves him to do; he is to follow the inclinations of his heart to learn if he is indeed the man after Yahweh's own heart.

While the focus of the narrative is Jonathan's testing as potential king-elect, a modern reader in particular should not lose track of the underlying battle strategy being portrayed. Greatly outnumbered and facing superior arms, the only chance the Israelites have to capture the Michmash garrison from their position across the wadi in Gibeah is to mount a surprise raid against the garrison itself before the Philistines have arrayed themselves for battle and are prepared. After gaining control of the garrison, the Israelites could then advance across the wadi safely and attempt to push the Philistines back westward. Jonathan's two-man foray certainly was a dangerous undertaking, but was calculated to have the remaining guards at the garrison think that the two were deserting Israelites coming out of hiding who would then be let into the post in order to be questioned about Saul's position, force-strength and battle plan. Once inside, the two hoped to be able to kill off the few remaining guards and then probably signal Saul to cross the pass, kill off the contingent outside, secure the post, and with weapons from the dispatched Philistines, move against the unsuspecting enemy camp north of the fort. Thus, his foray, while daring, was strategically sound and not simply a suicide mission in which his survival would have to demonstrate Yahweh's active protection.

The Philistines tell Jonathan and his weapons-bearer to come to them, seeming to confirm that Yahweh has delivered the garrison into the 'hand' of the two intruders (v. 11). The word *yād* is used in vv. 10 and 12 to designate power. In the account of the ensuing battle between the two groups, Jonathan's inactivity is noteworthy. His actions include only his crawling up to the garrison (v. 13); after his arrival, the enemy simply fall before him, or perhaps over him since he is on his hands and knees, and it is his weapons-bearer who actually kills the twenty odd men, thereby accomplishing the first slaughter (vv. 13-14).[1] Yet in the summary of action in v. 14, both Jonathan

1. Fokkelman (*Crossing Fates*, pp. 50-53) suggests that Jonathan's appearance is a numinous presence of Yahweh, an actualization of the meaning of the name 'Yahweh has given', so that the Philistines 'fall down' or prostrate before Yahweh-the-deliverer, as their idol did in the temple of Dagan in 1 Sam. 5.3-4 and as Goliath will subsequently do before David in 17.49. This appears to be a development of the suggestion of Ackroyd (*First Samuel*, p. 112) that 'the Philistines fell as they suddenly recognized a supernatural power before them'. I think the ambiguity of Jonathan's actions is deliberate, and in light of the use of the larger tri-partite coronation ceremony pattern in which Jonathan, the potential heir-elect, is seemingly being tested but has not yet received any official divine spirit, we cannot refer to him as 'a charismatic hero approved and empowered by Yahweh' as does D. Jobling ('Saul's

and the weapons-bearer are credited with striking down (*hikkâ*) the men. This discrepancy in detail tends to focus attention on Jonathan and his possible identity as Yahweh's new *nāgîd*: must Jonathan personally dispatch the enemy to pass his test, or is his formulation of the plan and participation in it enough?

The divine control over the outcome of the foray is made clear in the ensuing report that universal trembling (*ḥ*ᵃ*rādâ*) struck throughout the Philistine ranks and that the earth quaked. The trembling that had earlier struck the Israelites in the face of the arrival of the Philistine horde in 13.7 now afflicted the Philistine horde in the face of the presence of Israel's god Yahweh.

The resulting commotion in the Philistine ranks was clearly visible to Saul's watchmen across the pass in Gibeah (v. 16), but the reason for Saul's instant surmise that it had been initiated without permission by members of his own ranks is not immediately apparent. Neither is the reason for his request for the ark of God after learning that his son and his weapons-bearer were missing. Nevertheless, both instances serve to demonstrate Saul's failure to act with the cool assurance befitting someone who possessed a benevolent guiding divine spirit. His inaction introduces an element of irony into the narrative when viewed against his earlier possible rejection from the office of king for his decision to take action.[1] As noted earlier, the only way to salvage the situation militarily was for Saul to strike instantly before the Philistines could organize and array for battle. Instead of taking a position of leadership, however, he sat under the pomegranate tree in Migron. It is his son, the heir-elect, who initiates the necessary move, but without his father's knowledge or approval.

In vv. 16-19 the narrator reveals to his audience the first ramifications of Saul's announced rejection at Gilgal: Saul can no longer act with confidence and is uncertain of his divine backing. Now he hesitates to act without oracular consultation with God through an established priestly mediator. He has brought into his camp Ahijah, a descendant of the rejected priestly line of Eli whom Samuel superseded, to serve as his mediatory link with Yahweh, having broken ties with Samuel. In light of the earlier history of the Elide family, the

Fall and Jonathan's Rise: Tradition and Redaction in 1 Sam. 14.1-46', *JBL* 95 [1976], p. 369).

1. The situational irony was noted by S. Lasine in private correspondence.

audience must suspect from the start that nothing profitable can come from such an arrangement.[1]

The growing tumult from the enemy camp finally spurs Saul into long overdue action without awaiting confirmation of Yahweh's will (v. 19). The plot developments leave room for the audience to conclude that the confusion, which Saul now knows has been caused somehow by his son, must have received divine approval to have been as successful and sustained as it was, leaving open the possibility that Yahweh has chosen Jonathan to replace Saul as the new king. This impression would seem to be reinforced as the battle turns miraculously in Israel's favor with the Philistines slaying each other on behalf of the swordless Israelites. Growing awareness of the situation leads the former defectors to rejoin Israel's ranks and once again come under the leadership of Yahweh, pursuing the Philistines who were now retreating westward. The narrator signals the success of the battle in v. 13 by emphasizing both the direct military intervention of Yahweh in the battle and the enemy retreat westward from Beth-Aven.

Verse 24 introduces a new interlude in the story that otherwise seems to have come to a close. All four elements of the standard battle pattern have appeared. Perhaps intending to recall the distress of the people in 13.6 that had resulted from Jonathan's premature assault on Gibeah and the resulting appearance of a Philistine horde and raiding activity, the audience is told that the people had been hard pressed at some point (*ngś*) and that in response, Saul had issued a divinely invoked food ban that day,[2] either prior to or during the battle, to counter or gain revenge for the foreign oppression. Since v. 24 begins with disjunctive syntax, the time frame for the oppression is not clear, nor is the precise moment for the imposition of the ban. Since oppression is not normally a condition that occurs during the course of a pitched battle, it is likely that the oppression in question was to have taken place prior to the Israelite–Philistine confrontation

1. So also, for example, Jobling, 'Saul's Fall', p. 368; Miscall, *1 Samuel*, p. 90; Long, *Reign and Rejection of Saul*, pp. 105-106.

2. As pointed out by H.J. Stoebe (*Das erste Buch Samuelis* [KAT, 8/1; Gütersloh: Mohn, 1973], pp. 265, 271) and followed by Long (*Reign and Rejection of Saul*, p. 114), syntactically the second clause of v. 24, which begins with *wāw* + imperfect, should express an action that is the temporal or logical *sequel* to the one mentioned immediately before.

at the Michmash pass. The apparent reintroduction of the general theme of distress/oppression to carry forward plot development favors the retention of the MT text over against the adoption of the alternate LXX reading, 'Saul made a great blunder that day'.[1]

Saul announces the oath, 'Cursed be the man who eats food until it is evening and I am avenged on my enemies' (v. 24). D. Jobling has pointed out the potential wordplay represented by the Saul's oath action, *wayyō'el*. While meant to reflect the verb *'lh*, 'swear an oath', the expression rings close to the verb *y'l*, 'play the fool',[2] perhaps with the intention instantly to raise doubts in the audience's minds about the appropriateness of the action. The lack of clear indication about when the ban was to have been imposed, coupled with the probable wordplay, should have led the audience to wonder when this ban had been announced and whether Saul is to be understood to be speaking as Yahweh's vice-regent, so that his 'I' represents 'Yahweh' as well, whether his words are as taken to be referring to himself alone after his announced rejection by Yahweh in 13.13-14, or whether he is to be seen to be speaking as the corporate head of the nation Israel.

As commonly acknowledged, the mention of vengeance echoes Joshua's request in Josh. 10.13 that the sun stand still at Gibeon and the moon at Aijalon so that Israel can complete its pursuit of the five Amorite kings who had engaged Gibeon in battle and so that Israel can take vengeance on its enemies. Both instances of vengeance involve an attempt to be able to have as long a period of daylight for visible pursuit and destruction of the routed enemy as possible. Thus, Saul's ban has as its object the complete annihilation of the Philistine horde, which was the task that Yahweh told Samuel he had intended the king to perform. Interestingly, the audience is never told that Samuel ever informed Saul of these words of Yahweh. They may have been the content of Samuel's instructions that Saul was to have received in Gilgal after the sacrifices, but never did. Dramatic irony seems to be at work here to lead the audience to reflect again over the circumstances and fairness of Saul's potential rejection from office and the

1. *Contra*, for example, Dhorme, *Livres de Samuel*, p. 119; Auzou, *Danse devant l'arche*, p. 152; McCarter, *I Samuel*, p. 245; Klein, *1 Samuel*, p. 132.

2. Jobling, 'Saul's Fall', p. 374. He is followed by Long (*Reign and Rejection of Saul*, p. 117).

need to seek a replacement 'after Yahweh's own heart'.

The action continues with the soldiers encountering honey in the forest during their pursuit of the Philistines and Jonathan eating some of it from the tip of his staff, being instantly revived (vv. 25-27).[1] Reference to the use of the staff 'in his hand' as an implement for retrieving the honey seems to foreground this particular item, which would seem to represent a symbol of leadership or office. Thus, Jonathan's authority is being highlighted during his act of eating. Instantly, he is told by one of the men about the curse. The audience now learns that it must have been sworn during Jonathan's absence and so must have been imposed before the battle was joined.

After learning of the ban and his inadvertent breaking of it, Jonathan, still holding his staff of authority, proclaims that his father's curse had 'troubled the land' and that the people should have been allowed to eat freely of their enemy's spoil to ensure a great slaughter among the Philistines (vv. 29-30). 'The land' appears to be a reference to the troops, since v. 25 states that 'all the land' went into the forest. An echo of Achan's 'troubling the land' in Joshua 7 is heard, but with the relationship between troubling and booty reversed. Achan brings trouble by stealing booty; Jonathan claims that Saul has brought trouble by preventing the legitimate taking of booty. Since battle pursuit is still underway when Jonathan speaks and so the time for gathering booty has not yet arrived, the contrast between the two incidents serves to raise suspicion about the legitimacy of Jonathan's statement and to lead the audience to wonder if Saul's action was indeed 'foolish'. Jonathan's suggestion that the troops should be allowed to begin to use the spoils of war to help produce a final victory would seem to break the normal rules of booty-gathering and would have

1. J. Blenkinsopp ('Jonathan's Sacrilege. 1 Sm 14, 1-46: A Study in Literary History', *CBQ* 26 [1964], p. 440) notes the assonance of *rᵉ'û* and *'ōrû* and *ṭā'amtî* and *mᵉ'aṭ* in v. 29, while Gordon (*I & II Samuel*, p. 139) emphasizes the assonance of the key words *'ārar*, 'curse' (vv. 24, 28), and *'ôr*, 'be bright' (vv. 27, 29), which highlights the antithesis between what was to have been and what could have been. Long (*Reign and Rejection of Saul*, p. 120) extends the root-play involving *'ālep* and *rēš* in vv. 24-29 to include the single appearances of *yr'* and *r'h* alongside the twofold uses of *'rr* and *'wr*. He suggests that 'Jonathan's root-play, converting curse to brightening, adds to the developing contrast between himself and his father'. I find its effect to be to raise the question of Jonathan's ability 'to see' according to divine perception, making him a worthy candidate for the kingship.

lost valuable daylight for the enemy pursuit. The final results of Jonathan's plan might well have been a less extensive routing.[1]

Instead of repenting of his action and submitting to the authority of the king and national God who oversaw the ban, Jonathan is said to challenge the royal proclamation, criticizing the decision to impose a ban on the people's inclination to gather spoil before the final elimination of the enemy. His reference to slaughter brings to mind his earlier role in the slaughter of the first twenty guards in the Philistine garrison that had launched the battle that was now a victorious routing, reminding the audience that he might be the new candidate to replace Saul as the nation's authority figure. At the same time, his passive role in the earlier incident should create some hesitancy in the minds of the audience about his military capabilities and his status. Is his insubordination excusable in light of the events of the day or not?

Some scholars have suggested that Saul deliberately invoked the ban in Jonathan's absence after he learned that his son had successfully thrown the enemy into confusion in order to trap him in wrongdoing and have a means of eliminating him as a rival or replacement.[2] In light of the uncertainty in both Saul's mind and the audience's mind over whether Yahweh's potential rejection of Saul in 13.13-14 would have included his entire house and would have been immediately effective or whether it would have allowed room for an unspecified number of successors before being removed, it does not seem likely that Saul would have tried to sabotage his son's chances of following him on the throne. Rather, it would make sense to think that Saul, hoping that Yahweh was indeed favoring his son by allowing him to sneak into the enemy camp and create havoc, imposed the ban just

1. Miscall (*1 Samuel*, pp. 94-95) interprets the Achan–Saul dichotomy to support Jonathan's contention that Saul should have been more flexible in carrying out holy war and should have rescinded his vow in light of the specific course of events that required an extended pursuit. Are we the audience to presume that the Philistines stopped to eat during their retreat? Gordon (*I & II Samuel*, p. 139) suggests that there is a second, intentional parallel being drawn to the 'troubling of the land': the 'troubling Israel' in Ahab's accusation against Elijah in 1 Kgs 18.17-18. Long (*Reign and Rejection of Saul*, p. 118) points to the use of *inclusio* with the phrase *wy'f h'm* in v. 28b and *wy'f h'm m'd* in v. 31b to frame and highlight Jonathan's reaction to the report of his father's ban.

2. For example, Fokkelman, *Crossing Fates*, p. 72; Long, *Reign and Rejection of Saul*, pp. 124-25.

before entering battle as a means of attempting further to please Yahweh, fully intending a swift, victorious outcome in light of the apparent involvement of Yahweh on Israel's side. This way all the spoil could be divided and Yahweh given his fair share before the people began to indulge themselves and failed perhaps to give an accurate accounting of the booty. It probably would never have crossed his mind that his son would not have been told about the ban by someone during the battle or that the routing would have dragged on until nightfall. Following this line of reasoning, Saul's statement 'until *I* am avenged on my enemies' would be intended to include Yahweh, whose earthly vice-regent he was, and might be meant to be an inadvertent slip of the tongue. It would be similar then to the people's statement to Yahweh in 10.8 concerning their desire for a king like all the nations to govern them and go out before them and fight their battles—unwittingly open to misinterpretation.

The narrator provides the audience with information by which to gauge the accuracy of Jonathan's statement in v. 31: Israel struck down the Philistines from Michmash to Aijalon. They were able, without weapons at the beginning of the battle and in spite of their fatigue from the ban, to strike down the enemy and push them back from the central hill country to the western foothills around Aijalon.[1] It would seem then that Jonathan's assessment of the success of the slaughter is wrong and, by implication, that the divinely invoked ban was not a deterrent to success after all. Jonathan's rejection of its efficacy for practical reasons could imply his tendency to underplay the need for ritually prescribed behavior during battle in favor of accomplishing the task at hand, again hinting at his tendency toward insubordination or not giving due weight to the divine involvement in future battles. On the other hand, it is possible that Jonathan felt that Yahweh's active involvement from the very first slaughter was clearly apparent and so no further 'bribery' was necessary to ensure his continued aid. Whatever his reasoning, it seems to have been wrong.[2]

1. Retention of the MT reference to Aijalon, which is lacking in the LXX, seems to be indicated since the extent of the battle is the focus of the verse, *contra* for example, McCarter (*I Samuel*, p. 246). Contrast the conclusion of Long (*Reign and Rejection of Saul*, p. 131) that 14.52 confirms Jonathan's verdict that the victory could have been greater.

2. Contrast the common acceptance of Jonathan's reasoning as correct. Exceptions include Ackroyd, *First Samuel*, p. 115; Stoebe, *Erste Buch Samuelis*, p. 271;

Verse 31 seems to bring the battle to a close at the end of the day, so preparing for the ensuing eating frenzy by the exhausted and famished troops at sundown. Confirmation that night had arrived comes only in v. 34, however, after the report of the people's flying upon the spoil and eating it without allowing the blood to drain adequately. The narrator seems to be trying to create suspense by leading the audience to wonder if the troops had accepted Jonathan's rejection of the ban and were defying Saul by eating before sundown. No clear answer is given to this question. In response to learning about the people's action, Saul establishes a monolithic stone altar, and the audience is told that the people took the oxen 'in their hand' to it *that night* and slew them there (v. 34). The use of *yād* emphasizes that the people have appropriated the spoil for themselves. Does v. 34's reference to 'that night' mean that the people's previous slaying of sheep, oxen and calves on the ground took place during daylight hours? Equally ambiguous is the underlying act that prompts Saul to declare that the people have acted treacherously or faithlessly (*b^e^gadtem*) in v. 33. Ostensibly, it is a reaction to the report that the people are eating flesh with undrained blood, but the open question as to the timing of their eating remains lurking as an additional, prior act of treachery in the breaking of the divinely invoked ban.[1]

Ironically, the imposition of the ban, which was intended to win divine favor, results in the people's infraction of blood laws, a sin against Yahweh that can only bring divine displeasure. In contrast to his earlier hesitation to engage the Philistines in battle, Saul springs into action instantly in order to 'constrain' the people to observe what were to have been existing laws forming part of the Horeb covenant (Lev. 19.26; Deut. 12.23-27). He seems to be back on track fulfilling his royal duties as announced by Yahweh in 9.17.

Saul now pursues the completion of his royal duty: the deliverance of Israel from the hand of the Philistines. He proposes the night-time pursuit and killing of the still retreating Philistines–'let us not leave a man of them alive' (v. 36). The men's response, 'all that is good *in your eyes*, do', is ominous. The reference to Saul's 'doing' in accordance with his eyes rather than his heart, the seat of judgment of the

Jobling, 'Saul's Fall', p. 368.

1. Fokkelman (*Crossing Fates*, p. 67) and Polzin (*Samuel*, p. 137) conclude that the people fell on the spoil prematurely at Jonathan's suggestion.

one whom Yahweh has chosen, brings to mind Saul's potential rejection by Yahweh and the quest for the new king, the man after Yahweh's own heart. The use of *'āśâ* to describe Saul's action also brings to mind the connection of this term with Yahweh's acts of deliverance. We are reminded that Saul may not be that man any more; the men have wittingly or unwittingly emphasized that point—but when will Yahweh remove his favor from Saul? Has he already, or does he still stand behind the king?

The priest's request that they should draw near to God (v. 36) heightens the sense of uncertainty about Saul's status before God—is Saul's judgment inadequate? The failure to receive an answer from the oracular consultation (v. 37) leads Saul to conclude that a sin has been committed 'today'. The repetition of *hayyôm* links up with its previous appearances in 14.1 and in chs. 9–10 in connection with the king-making process, hinting that the sin may have halted the coronation procedure. The king gathers the cornerstone leaders of the people to determine the nature of the sin. Before the proceeding begins, he issues an oath condemning the culprit(s) to death, even if it be his son Jonathan, in light of his inability to achieve total annihilation of the Philistines because of the withdrawal of support by Yahweh, the 'deliverer of Israel', on account of the sin.

Saul is aware of one sin—the people's failure to drain the blood properly from the meat, and of a second potential sin in their failure to await sundown to eat, breaking his divinely backed ban. His averral that even his son is to be killed if found to be the culprit is an assurance of his seriousness and the gravity of the loss of divine support to finish off the Philistine slaughter. His perception that Jonathan must have had Yahweh's support in his successful launching of the battle under adverse odds seems to have allowed him to state that there would be no exceptions to the rule to drive home the point, while feeling confident that nothing was really at risk since his son clearly had been shown divine favor. The dramatic irony introduced through his statement now brings the issue of Jonathan's response after inadvertently eating the honey to a head, along with the larger issue of whether Jonathan, Saul's son and the heir-elect to the throne, is the man after Yahweh's own heart. Has Jonathan successfully passed his test to become Saul's successor? Was he ever really Yahweh's *nāgîd*?

The people's silence in response to Saul's ultimatum contrasts with their earlier willingness to go along with Saul's judgment—they know of Jonathan's sin earlier 'that day'. Saul confidently places his family against the people in the ensuing public lot-casting, thereby highlighting for the audience the identification of his son's fate with his own. Again, the people tell Saul to do 'what his eyes' consider to be good, driving home the contrast with the motif, heart (v. 40).[1]

Jonathan is quickly determined by lot to be the guilty party. In this scene there is a reversal of the public announcement of Saul's choice as *nāgîd* in 1 Sam. 10.20-24. Here, the lot-casting before the nation leads to the public proclamation of the divine rejection of the heir-elect as potential *nāgîd*. The emphasis on the filial relationship between Jonathan and the rejected Saul now is explained: son, like father, has transgressed divine precepts. Yahweh pronounces Jonathan guilty of sin, thereby passing negative judgment on his earlier insubordination and failure to be contrite when told of his unintentional sin. A king is to be humble and atone for his sins and those of his people, not to challenge the fairness of the circumstances under which the sins arise. Now assuming the role played earlier by Samuel at Gilgal (13.11), Saul demands to be told what his son has done (v. 43)[2] and condemns him to death (v. 44). Jonathan accepts his guilt and with it, his rejection as the man whom Yahweh might have chosen to succeed his father on the throne of Israel. He indicates his understanding through his submissive reply, 'I am here; I will die', even before Saul condemns him to certain death (v. 43).

The people have not comprehended the larger issue under evaluation, Jonathan's possible suitability for candidacy as king-elect, and on the basis of their partial perceptions, they ransom Jonathan from death. They state that Jonathan has 'brought about' (*'āśâ*) this great deliverance in Israel and then vow to spare him from death, adding thereafter that the deliverance was done 'with God' (v. 45). They thus stress Jonathan's accomplishment and the primacy of the human agent

1. Long (*Reign and Rejection of Saul*, p. 125) notes the omission of the word 'all' from the otherwise identical response in v. 36a, emphasizing in his opinion growing popular resistance to Saul's initiative.

2. As noted by Miscall (*1 Samuel*, p. 96). Long (*Reign and Rejection of Saul*, p. 124) points to the contrast between Saul's 'untroubled' response to learning his son is about to die because of a vow he made and Jephthah's troubled response in Judg. 11.35. However, the underlying reasons for making the vow do not seem to be identical (personal insecurity for Jephthah vs. the troops' insecurity for Saul), so I am not convinced that there is intentional narrative analogy at work here.

as central to the battle, but eventually acknowledge the divine agency as well. The audience knows it is just the opposite: it is Yahweh who was in control of the entire situation and Jonathan's 'feat' was not even single-handed; his weapons-bearer did the actual killing. The people ransom Jonathan, now playing the role that Saul did at the end of the victory over Ammon in overturning a pending death sentence.[1] The verb used to describe the ransoming is *pdh*, which refers to a legal redemption for an assessed price. In light of Jonathan's infraction of a divinely overseen ban that constituted his commitment of a ritual sin and the guilty verdict rendered by Yahweh himself, one would have expected the need for his ritual redemption, indicated by the verb *g'l*. The people believe they have adequately released Jonathan from the civil death sentence imposed by the king, but the audience is left to ponder whether their action has been adequate to release him from the divine sentence pronounced against him.

As a result of Jonathan's insubordination and the time required to adjudicate the matter, Saul is forced to break off any further pursuit of the Philistines, having to rest content with the extensive, but incomplete routing of the enemy (v. 46). Jonathan, who began the battle sequence in 13.3 with a rash and untimely deed that eliminated the Israelite advantage in battle, seems to have made up for his initial mistake by undertaking an equally rash and daring deed that managed to succeed in turning the tide back in favor of the Israelites (14.6-15), only to become an obstacle that blocked the total defeat of the enemy though an inadvertent mistake that was wrongly defended (14.26-30). Because of the actions of the heir-elect, Saul was not able to deliver Israel completely from the hand of the Philistines, which was one of his prime directives as king. The audience is forced to ask whether hereditary kingship has indeed provided the people with a better form of political leadership than the lifetime office of *šōpēṭ*. At the same time, Jonathan's questionable behavior, once fully reviewed, leads the audience back to the central issue raised by 13.13-14: who is the man Yahweh may have chosen as a new *nāgîd* after his own heart? It is not Jonathan.

The question is, was it ever Jonathan? The preceding narrative leaves open the possibility that Jonathan was the intended candidate,

1. So also, for example, Miscall, *1 Samuel*, p. 97; Fokkelman, *Crossing Fates*, p. 76.

since Yahweh seems to have used him as an agent of deliverance in 14.6-15. In this case, Jonathan's subsequent insubordination would have led Yahweh to change his mind and declare Jonathan's testing as candidate for office a failure. Yet, the course of events in chs. 13–14 also allows room for the conclusion that Jonathan never was Yahweh's candidate. The audience is not told that Yahweh regretted his choice or changed his mind. If one presumes that God chooses his candidates on the basis of their inherent personality traits, which may or may not reach their full potential, one could conclude that Jonathan would never have been Yahweh's choice because of his rash nature that was subsequently revealed on the battle field when he was put in a position of leadership. From this viewpoint, Yahweh's passing over of Jonathan in favor of another more suitable candidate would seem to be a justified and wise decision. Either way, the section of the narrative presenting a selection of Saul's deeds as king (13.2–14.46), the third step in the regnal account pattern, ends with a military victory for Israel and an ongoing search for the identity of Yahweh's new *nāgîd* who will replace Saul if he has indeed been rejected from the kingship.

Verses 47-48 immediately summarize Saul's accomplishments as king, presenting the third step in the regnal account pattern but not employing the customary formula that appears in the subsequent era of the Kingdoms of Israel and Judah. Instead of the standard phrase, 'Now the rest of the acts of Saul, and all he did, are they not written in the Book of the Chronicles of Israel (or Judah)', we are supplied with a list of Saul's extensive military victories against his surrounding enemies. Nevertheless, the summary nature of the list of military deeds is clear. Within the kingship regnal pattern, the summary of deeds signals the end of the monarch's active career and immediately precedes notice of his death. In the account of Saul's career, then, the appearance of the summary at this particular point in the larger narrative must be a deliberate move by the narrator to inform his audience that Saul's active career as king has effectively drawn to a close.[1]

1. Contrast the view of S. Yonick (*The Rejection of Saul as King of Israel* [Jerusalem: Franciscan Printing, 1970], p. 59), M. Sternberg ('The Bible's Art of Persuasion: Ideology, Rhetoric and Poetics in Samuel's Fall', *HUCA* 54 [1983], p. 51), and Long (*Reign and Rejection of Saul*, p. 130) that it signals the era of rest predicted in Deut. 25.17-19 and so the arrival of the time for revenge.

The reported victories are said to have taken place after Saul had captured (*lkd*) the kingship (*hamm*^{e}*lûkâ*) over Israel, a phrase that is highlighted by Samuel's earlier pronouncement that Yahweh had decided not to establish (*hēkîn*) Saul's kingship (*mamlakt*^{e}*kā*) to Israel forever in 13.13. The implication of the narrator's statement is that Saul was able actively to secure his position on the throne through force of arms[1] in spite of his apparent announced divine rejection. Perhaps the intention is that his ability to secure Israel from its surrounding enemies through astute military strategy, of which two examples are given in 1 Samuel 11 and 1 Sam. 13.2–14.46, led to his popularity and willing acceptance by the people. Since Saul went out to meet Samuel as he approached in 13.10, it would seem that the potential rejection was announced privately to Saul and so was not common knowledge. Just as the people failed to understand Yahweh's verdict against Jonathan, they also have failed to perceive any possible break between Yahweh and Saul. Indeed, Saul's impressive list of military victories would seem to demonstrate Yahweh's continuing favor and assistance in battle. This in turn raises the question in the audience's mind as to whether God might not have rescinded his earlier rejection of Saul, or whether the announced rejection was backed by divine authority after all, or was merely a warning by Samuel. Would a rejected king be able to accomplish such a long list of victories without divine support? This question once more raises the specter of the temporal ambiguity of Saul's rejection in 13.13-14 and the issue of Saul's guilt in light of the ambiguity of Samuel's commands in 10.8.

A parenthetical explanatory note naming Saul's children, wife, and uncle who served as his military commander then follows, along with a notice of continued fighting against the Philistines (vv. 49-52), serving as a bridge to the ensuing narrative of the battle against Amalek in ch. 15. Verse 48 ends the summary of deeds with a reference to Saul's successful deliverance of Israel from plundering Amalekites, which is the topic of ch. 15. The genealogical information details the potential heirs to the Saulide throne, which, in light of the

1. So, for example, Fokkelman, *Crossing Fates*, p. 81 n. 84. Long (*Reign and Rejection of Saul*, p. 130) notes the lack of mention of Yahweh's involvement in the victories in contrast to his naming in the summaries of David's accomplishments in 2 Sam. 8.6, 14, suggesting that the summary thereby 'is not without dark shadows'.

possible change in divine stance toward Saul, provides a list of candidates in addition to Jonathan who might now be eligible to become 'the man after Yahweh's own heart'.

Noteworthy is the absence from the list of heirs of Abinadab, who appears in 1 Sam. 31.2; 1 Chron. 8.33; 9.39; and 10.2, and possibly also of Eshbaal/Ishbosheth, who was Saul's youngest son (1 Chron. 8.33; 9.39). Some have equated him with Ishvi in v. 49, but the absence of Abinadab as well could indicate that the list in v. 49 reflects a Saulide genealogy dating from before the birth of the two youngest male children. Nor is any mention made here of Saul's concubine Rizpah or her children by Saul, Armoni and Mephibosheth (2 Sam. 21.8). Were it not for the absence of Abinadab, it would be plausible to conclude that the main function of the list is to introduce the Saulides who will play a role in the remaining narrative episodes.[1] This could still be maintained by equating Ishvi with Eshbaal and either restoring Abinadab to the list in v. 49, or seeing his presence in 1 Sam. 31.2 to be a late gloss influenced by his appearance in the Saulide genealogies in 1 Chronicles 8 and 9 and his noted absence from the Samuel narratives.

The concluding verse 52 has a dual function. On one level, it refocuses attention on military matters in its reference to continued fighting against the Philistines for all of Saul's days. On the other hand, it reminds the audience that in spite of Saul's valiant military successes that have been presented in a summary form implying that Saul's active military career has now ended, he had not yet fulfilled his intended task of delivering Israel from Philistine oppression. This comment then highlights again the question of Saul's status *vis à vis* Yahweh as continuing king of Israel, this time putting a negative cast on his potential rapprochement with God.

1. So, for example, Auzou, *Danse devant l'arche*, p. 155 n. 55; Miscall, *1 Samuel*, p. 97; Fokkelman, *Crossing Fates*, p. 83.

Chapter 10

1 SAMUEL 15

Verse 1 takes up the key theme of royal dependency upon prophetically mediated ongoing divine revelation that was established by the end of ch. 12, sounding the important thematic root *šm'* as the condition of Yahweh's tolerance of the people's assumption of the additional burden of kingship. *šm'* was used heavily in chs. 8–12 to stress the roles and relationships between Israel, Yahweh, king and prophet, particularly to establish the need to be obedient to the Horeb covenant and to ongoing divine revelation in the new monarchic era.[1] Saul is commanded by Yahweh's spokesman, Samuel, whose status is foregrounded by positioning the preposition *'ōtî* first in Samuel's statement, to 'obey' Yahweh's words and execute his military will, as Yahweh's earthly vice-regent. Saul is personally to smite Amalek, and he and the people are to destroy utterly every living thing associated with it, down to the youngest human and animal. There seems to be a deliberate distinction expressed in the command through the use of the 2nd person masculine singular verbal form to describe the act of smiting as opposed to the use of the 2nd masculine plural verbal form for the act of consecrating to sacred ban. King and people will be held accountable for the execution of the ban.

The acts are to execute divine punishment on Amalek for what they did to Israel during its journey out of Egypt (Exod. 17.7-13; Deut. 25.17-19). As noted by S. Yonik and M. Sternberg, the list of animals to be devoted to the ban corresponds exactly to those mentioned in

1. Polzin (*Samuel*, p. 49) stresses its use as a *Leitwort* in 1 Sam. 1–7 as well. Alter (*Art of Biblical Narrative*, p. 93) identifies *šm'*, *qwl*, and *dbr* as *Leitwörter* in ch. 15, while Long (*Reign and Rejection of Saul*, p. 136) names *šm'* and *qwl* as keywords.

Judg. 6.3-5 as the victims of Midianite and Amalekite raids.[1] The specification that the war is to involve *ḥērem* apparently is made because Amalek is not located in the land of Canaan and so would not normally fall under such treatment (Deut. 20.10-18).

The recitation of past events contrasts with the presentation of Yahweh's 'saving deeds' (*ṣidqôt*) found in 1 Sam. 10.17-19; 12.6-12 and specifically highlights the claim made in 10.18 that Yahweh delivered Israel from the hand of *all* the kingdoms that were oppressing it. The contrast also brings to mind Yahweh's previous voluntary abandonment of his people in 1 Samuel 4–6, seeming to lead the audience to wonder if perhaps Yahweh has decided to make amends for his past lapses in fulfilling his covenantal duties toward Israel by bringing to justice the group whose earlier harrassments went unpunished.

Saul is said to comply immediately with the prophetically mediated command, to 'make the people to hear' (*wayšamma' 'et-hā'ām*), to muster troops representing all Israel (v. 4), and to lie in wait[2] in the wadi near the city of Amalek. The king's first act reportedly is to inform the people of Yahweh's command, its reasons and its restrictions, so the entire Israelite citizenry knows the terms under which the battle is to proceed. Having positioned himself for launching an attack, he pauses to remove the Kenites from the midst of the Amalekites (cf. Judg. 1.16)[3] because of their aid to Israel on its journey out of Egypt (v. 6). Saul's action seems intended to demonstrate his knowledge of Israel's past history, his desire to fulfill the spirit of Yahweh's command in accordance with that history, and indirectly, to establish his lack of ignorance as an alibi for any failure to execute his assigned mission fully. Since the Kenites were not technically part of Amalek, Saul's purported act does not constitute an exempting of a portion of

1. Yonick, *Rejection of Saul*, p. 51 and Sternberg, 'Bible's Art', p. 50. By contrast, Long (*Reign and Rejection of Saul*, p. 138) finds the closest parallel to be the list of Saul's victims at Nob in 1 Sam. 22.19. He notes that only the camels are missing.

2. I follow the almost universal adoption of the Greek text that presumes an underlying Hebrew verb *'rb* rather than the MT's *yrb*, but favor the retention of the *qal* stem rather than trying to restore a defective *hiphil* stem, as does McCarter (*I Samuel*, p. 261).

3. So McCarter (*1 Samuel*, p. 266), adopting the proposed emendation of *h'm* to *h'mlq* at the end of the sentence.

the enemy from the ban by royal prerogative, as P. Miscall suggests.[1] A summary report of the engagement of battle, the widespread smiting of the enemy, and the taking of booty ensues, cursorily covering all four steps to be expected in a battle report. The minimal amount of space 'backgrounds' rather than foregrounds the battle itself, whose victory is not an issue in light of Yahweh's assured backing.

The first indication of a potential failure in execution of the divine command occurs in v. 8 in the midst of the report of the successful completion of the smiting and total *ḥērem*: although Saul smote Amalek from Havilah to Shur and devoted to *ḥērem* all the people as he was commanded, he spared the Amalekite king, Agag. The divine command did not stipulate the fate of the enemy king over against the fate of the people. In light of the previous sparing of the king of Ai in Josh. 8.23-29 during a battle involving *ḥērem*, the modern audience at least is left to wonder whether the taking of the enemy king alive for humiliation and subsequent execution was a standard ancient practice; whether Saul has exercised his royal prerogative here and allowed an exemption to the ban, such as Joshua made for Rahab and her family in Josh. 6.17;[2] or whether he has spared the enemy king because he was not given a specific command about his disposal. Has Saul followed the prophetically mediated instructions for this war so literally, in order to complete his assigned task successfully, that he has failed to consider the clear intent of the command to wipe out Amalek utterly from existence? Has his sparing of Agag resulted from his desire to follow divine commands to the letter or has he done so out of other motivations? The narrator does not provide the ancient or modern audience with a clear understanding of Saul's motives, although at the same time, he does not suggest a possible alternative motive for Saul's action.

What of the animals that also were included in the ban? The narrator goes on to state that they became a source of disobedience for the

1. Miscall, *1 Samuel*, p. 100.

2. So Miscall, *1 Samuel*. Building on the prior discussion of R. Polzin (*Moses and the Deuteronomist* [New York: Seabury Press, 1980], pp. 74-80), he argues that within the 'Deuteronomistic History', diligent observance of the law allows room for interpretation and adaptation to circumstances, rather than a literalistic adherence to stipulated conditions.

people; just as Saul had spared Agag, breaking the divine command, the people spared the best of the animals (v. 9). The people, apparently just like Saul, have taken Yahweh's command concerning the *ḥērem* literally too; they have spared the best of the small flocks, large herds, the fatlings and the rams. Their selective preservation technically falls within the boundaries of the command that Saul proclaimed to them to kill the suckling, ox, sheep, camel and ass: the specified animals were indeed killed. Yet, in contrast to Saul's action, the narrator provides a motive for the people's action: they destroyed what was despised and worthless (v. 9). They have deliberately adhered to a literal interpretation of the law in order to use the resulting loophole to their own advantage. The linking of Saul's sparing of Agag with that done by the people in v. 9 leaves the issue of Saul's underlying motives unresolved. Nevertheless, it emphasizes his guilt alongside that of the people's, regardless of his motivations. Whether he was acting out of personal interest like the people, or out of extreme deference to Yahweh, he is equally guilty of not carrying out the spirit of the divine command, which was evident in light of the supporting quotation of historical motive.

Saul's failure leads to Yahweh's repentance for having caused Saul to be crowned king because of Saul's turning away (root *šwb*) from God and his failure to establish (*hēkîn*) his words. The root *šwb* will serve as a *Leitwort* for the balance of the chapter.[1] As noted by J. Fokkelman, Yahweh's announcement to Samuel of his repentance as the beginning of his revelation, prior to providing reasons for the decision, has great shock value, contrasting with his earlier persuasive tactics in dealing with Samuel and the acceptance of the people's request for a king in ch. 8.[2] The use of *hēkîn* recalls the earlier statement in 13.13 that Yahweh would not 'establish' Saul's rulership because of his failure to 'obey' (*šmʿ*), linking *šwb* with the larger theme of obedience. 'Turning' from Yahweh is, by definition, an act of disobedience to the Horeb covenant or his ongoing revealed commands. It is noteworthy that the plural form, 'words', is used rather than the singular, suggesting that Saul has failed to comply with more than one divine command.[3] Typically, prophetically mediated divine

1. As also noted by Polzin (*Samuel*, p. 141).
2. *Crossing Fates*, p. 92.
3. Sternberg (*Poetics*, p. 496) emphasizes that Saul's second sin here combines

revelations are introduced as 'the word of Yahweh', regardless of the length of their content. Yahweh's direct speech will be restated by the narrator in the third person in the closing verse of the chapter, making vv. 12-35a a long *inclusio* explaining the background to Yahweh's repentence.

Yahweh's first-person announcement to Samuel that he has repented that he made Saul king now allows the audience to resolve the ambiguity concerning the source and force of the previous announcement of rejection in 13.13-14. It is only in the wake of the events in the war against Amalek that God regrets his appointment of Saul. Only now has he formally made a decision in light of Saul's failure to obey commands. In retrospect then, Samuel's announcement in 13.13-14 was a warning to Saul about the consequences he could expect for disobedience. Also in retrospect, the audience learns that Jonathan was neither selected nor rejected as 'the man after Yahweh's heart' to replace Saul in ch. 14; it is only now that Yahweh has resolved to remove Saul from the kingship.

Yahweh's repenting (*nḥm*)[1] caused by Saul's turning (*šwb*), which in turn leads to Samuel's anger (*ḥrh*) and crying out (*z'q*), introduces into the story a direct play on the pattern for ideal judgeship found in Judg. 2.11-23. Here, however, Yahweh's repentance is negative in force rather than positive (2.18), caused by the 'turning' of the king instead of the 'crying out' of the people after their previous turning away from Yahweh (2.18, 19). The effect is to identify king and people closely and to emphasize Saul's role as corporate head of Israel. Samuel then assumes the roles of both Yahweh and the people by becoming angry (2.20) and crying out to God for the king's (and people's?) deliverance. The pattern-play ends with two possible outcomes: Yahweh's punishment of the offender(s) or his having pity and forgiving the transgressor(s) once again, creating momentary suspense in the story line.

with the first one in 1 Sam. 13 to give him an image of a habitual offender. He believes the writer uses the double rejection to improve the moral proportion between cause and effect: Saul's sin here looms larger since he has not learned from his previous aberration. Yet at the same time, Sternberg feels his punishment looks milder since his dynasty has already been doomed. I read the text differently.

1. Gordon (*I & II Samuel*, p. 144) notes that Gen. 6.6-7 provides a rare parallel to the present repentance that functions to reverse what is intended for good instead of the more usual function of repentance to withhold or mitigate judgment.

Samuel's arousal early in the morning to meet with Saul (v. 12) recalls the early morning meeting of the two in 1 Sam. 9.26–10.8 that led to Saul's secret anointing as king-elect, setting the stage either for the reaffirmation of Saul's kingship or for the reversal of the earlier scene and Saul's rejection. The meeting between the two is to take place at Gilgal, the site of Saul's coronation after Saul's 'crossing over' (v. 13), recalling his crossing into Mt Ephraim in search of the symbolic asses. As Samuel prepares to meet Saul, he is informed that the king has erected a victory stela (*yād*) for himself at Carmel before circling around (*wayyissōb*) to Gilgal (v. 12). The use of the verb *sbb* to characterize Saul's route serves two purposes: it indicates that the stela required extra effort to set up because it was located off the planned course of march to Gilgal, and it brings to mind the almost homophonous imperfect verbal form of the root *šwb*. In the latter case, the intention is ambiguous; is the audience to consider it to serve as a condemning commentary, through homophonous association, on the *yād*-building, tantamount to 'turning' from Yahweh by claiming personal victory, or is it rather to imply the opposite sense—that Saul has gone out of his way to erect a memorial honoring Yahweh as the grantor of victory over the Amalekites, as a deliberate act of 'turning' *to* God?

During the confrontation at Gilgal between king and prophet, Samuel's former warning in 13.13-14 becomes a divinely decreed reality. Upon Samuel's arrival at Gilgal, Saul greets him with the announcement that he has done the Lord's commandment (v. 13), ironically using the same phrasing that Yahweh had used to Samuel in v. 11 to substantiate his warranted repentance over Saul's appointment.[1] There is no reason to adopt the expanded LXX reading in v. 13 that Samuel arrived in Gilgal just as Saul was making burnt offerings to Yahweh from the best of the spoil he had taken from Amalek.[2] The MT text provides a more sensitive intertextual reading in its allusion to Samuel's command in 10.8 and to Saul's initial warning in 13.13 for

1. So noted by Klein, *1 Samuel*, p. 151; Fokkelman, *Crossing Fates*, p. 95; Long, *Reign and Rejection of Saul*, p. 144.

2. For example, Dhorme, *Livres de Samuel*, p. 133: McCarter, *I Samuel*, pp. 262-63; Klein, *1 Samuel*, p. 151. Contrast, for example, Hertzberg, *I & II Samuel*, p. 121; Sternberg, 'Bible's Art', p. 72; Long, *Reign and Rejection of Saul*, p. 143.

his failure to await Samuel's arrival to offer the sacrifices. It suggests that Saul has gone to Gilgal once again to offer sacrifices, but this time he will await Samuel's arrival and his officiation to try to right his previous wrong, even though his decision to sacrifice the animals has made them an exemption from the commanded ban.

Samuel immediately refutes Saul's statement, referring to the voices of the still-living sheep and oxen he 'hears' (*šm'*), in contrast to the words that Yahweh had told Saul to 'obey' (*šm'*) in vv. 1-3. In his reply, Saul immediately establishes that the animals are part of the Amalekite flocks and herds that *the people* spared from the ban to sacrifice to Yahweh, Samuel's God, but that *we*, the people and king together, have devoted to the ban everything else, implying the proper performance of Yahweh's command that both king and people were to execute the ban.[1] His statement agrees with the narrator's presentation of the situation concerning the animals in v. 9 except in his understanding of the people's motives. Saul, who himself spared Agag in what appears to have been a desperate desire to fulfill the divine command to its last iota, has presumed that the people have acted under similar altruistic motivations, or has been lied to by them about their specious piety. His willingness to align himself with the people's actions in otherwise executing the *ḥérem* in the last part of v. 9 emphasizes the purity of his own motives, but at the same time provides a deliberate contrast to the similar linking of king and people by the narrator in v. 9 in a condemnatory bond. Saul believes he and the people have acted in good faith; the audience has already been told by the narrator that Saul has been deceived by the people and that he himself has been overscrupulous and stands condemned along with the people for disobedience.

Samuel the king-maker then cuts off Saul from further explanation, telling him what Yahweh had said to him 'that night'.[2] The temporal reference seems to point back to v. 11, which had taken place the previous night. Yet the expanded argument that ensues contrasts dramatically with Yahweh's directly quoted statement in v. 11, leaving

1. *Contra* McCarter (*I Samuel*, p. 259), who alters the pronouns of the MT text in favor of the LXX.

2. Polzin (*Samuel*, p. 146) suggests that Samuel's association with the nighttime consultation of God in this chapter binds him to Saul, who was similarly associated in ch. 14.

the audience to question whether Samuel's comments in v. 17 are his own elaboration and interpretation of Yahweh's message or part of an additional, unreported message that accompanied the quoted statement. Once again, the issue of the reliability of a prophet's words is raised and more specifically, Samuel's motivations.

Either temporarily stepping out of his mediatory role as divine mouthpiece to clarify for Saul the apparent situation or continuing to act as Yahweh's spokesman to force Saul to realize the error of his ways, Samuel begins a long question-and-answer session that will lead to Saul's rejection from kingship. Structurally, this section has been associated with the judgment speech to an individual[1] and with the *rîb* condemnation pattern.[2] Beginning with a question as he did when he initially anointed Saul to be king-elect in 10.1, Samuel recalls Saul's own words in 9.21. At the same time, he stresses Saul's loss of divine support by referring to his use of his 'eyes' as his faculty of perception rather than his 'heart', the seat of divinely guided perception. Samuel then refers to Saul's status as Yahweh's *anointed*, Yahweh's earthly vice-regent, and to his failure to obey (*šm'*) Yahweh's mediated command. The command is summarized again, apparently to remind the audience that its original intent was clear to its human audience, even though the specific terms were capable of deliberate or misdirected misconstruing.

Samuel continues with another question intended to apprise Saul that he has committed disobedience (*lō'-šāma'tā*) by swooping on the spoil, thereby doing what God viewed as evil. The question recalls Saul's accusation against the people in 14.32 during the battle at the Michmash pass, where the troops may well have been guilty of transgressing Saul's eating ban that had been designed to safeguard Yahweh's due from the spoils, but where Saul moved immediately to 'constrain' the people's actions by building the altar. The reference to doing evil in Yahweh's eyes echoes the use of the same phrase in 12.17 to describe the people's request for a king and its use

1. So, for example, C. Westermann, *Grundformen prophetische Rede* (BEvT, 31; Munich: Kaiser Verlag, 1960), pp. 92-119; Birch, *Rise of Monarchy*, p. 98, who thinks it has shaped the entire chapter; McCarter, *I Samuel*, p. 270; Fokkelman, *Crossing Fates*, p. 96.

2. So S. Yonick, 'The Rejection of Saul: A Study of Sources', *AJBA* 1 (1971), pp. 36-37; Klein, *1 Samuel*, p. 152.

elsewhere in the Book of Judges to describe the people's acts of turning away (*šwb*) from Yahweh. Samuel's statement that Saul has personally swooped on the spoils is meant to make Saul realize that as king and corporate head of Israel, he is responsible for the actions of the people in accordance with Yahweh's announced royal task of constraining the people (9.17). It resounds with the implications already noted in v. 11.

Saul slowly grasps the import of Samuel's view of the king as steward of his people and now separates himself from his earlier alignment with the people. He unwittingly continues to condemn himself by referring to his sparing of Agag, whom he has taken to Gilgal to Yahweh as testimony that he has observed the exact words of the divine command delivered to him by Samuel, which did not specify that he was to kill the king. As H.W. Hertzberg notes, Saul's mention of Agag's sparing allows Samuel to realize for the first time that the enemy king is still alive and needs to be executed.[1] At the same time, Saul continues to extend his own pure motives to the people's actions, or to accept their lie to him at face value. Yet, by separating himself from them in his second response, he has signalled his dawning realization that his presumptions about their behavior being identical to his or his acceptance of their own explanation of their motives may be incorrect.[2] He now claims no responsibility for the sparing of the animals for sacrificial purposes, thereby highlighting Yahweh's previous command that both he and the people were to be held responsible for executing the complete ban (v. 3).

Samuel, in his role as prophetic spokesman, pronounces in psalmic format that obedience (*šmʿ*) to Yahweh's direct command is of primary importance for king and people; normal avenues of communication through cultic sacrifice are of secondary importance. His contrast of obedience and sacrifice would seem to indicate that he has at least conceded the possibility that the animals could have been exempted from the ban for subsequent cultic sacrifice, which may in turn hint that vv. 17-23 are meant to be Samuel's personal interpretation of Yahweh's short pronouncement in v. 11 rather than the

1. Hertzberg, *I & II Samuel*, p. 127.

2. Contrast the reading of the two responses by Sternberg ('Bible's Art', pp. 76-82) and Fokkelman (*Crossing Fates*, p. 98).

summary of further pronouncements made the same evening.[1] Speaking on behalf of Yahweh, Samuel then pronounces Saul's rejection because of his rejection (*m's*) of God's word, reversing his earlier role as king-maker in chs. 9–10 and Saul's choice by Yahweh to be his anointed one. As the representative of the people, Saul stands condemned before Yahweh for their deliberate disobedience to Yahweh's command and for his own failure to constrain them (*'ṣr*) as their king; as an individual and as king, Saul also stands condemned for having spared Agag and not having grasped the intent of Yahweh's *ḥérem* against Amalek, being instead a literalist in his approach to the interpretation of revealed divine will.

Saul confesses his guilt immediately to Yahweh's mediator, Samuel, and asks for Samuel's mediatory help in re-establishing his personal communication with God (vv. 24-25). His instant action contrasts with Jonathan's earlier act of defiance when told of his infraction by the troops (14.29-30), yet recalls Jonathan's immediate acceptance of Yahweh's guilty verdict in 14.43.[2] In stating his realization of the source of his sin, Saul emphasizes Samuel's mediatory role as divine mouthpiece by linking Samuel's words with the 'mouth of Yahweh' that has been 'transgressed' (*'br*) (v. 24). Saul has 'crossed over' his bounds as king, hinting that his crossing over to Gilgal will now end in a reversal of the result of his initial crossing over into Mt Ephraim. Saul states that his transgression has resulted from his misplaced respect for the people and his listening to their voice (*šm'*).

The king now understands that his source of authority comes from above, not from the *vox populi* who have allowed him to take the kingship (14.47) that has not yet been firmly established by God (13.13). He has presumed or has been persuaded of the good intentions of the people instead of suspecting their greed and underlying motivations and has accepted their interpretation of events instead of Yahweh's. Recalling Yahweh's repentance over making Saul king because of his failure to establish Yahweh's words issued on

1. Such an understanding would be consistent with Miscall's view that Samuel denounces Saul for daring to interpret the command against the Amalekites in a way that does not fully agree with Samuel's interpretation (*1 Samuel*, p. 107). Miscall seems to develop ideas previously expressed by Gunn (*Fate of Saul*, pp. 48-49).

2. Sternberg (*Poetics*, p. 509) also notes the similarity to 14.43. In addition, he adduces Achan's immediate confession of sin, seeing a deliberate continuation here of the Achan–Saul parallel from v. 19.

more than one occasion, Saul's confessed hearkening to the voice of the people may be meant to include his allowing them to ransom Jonathan in 14.45 as well as his failure to prevent them from eating 'with the blood' in 14.43-45. As noted by others,[1] there is a sense of completion in the fact that the king who was appointed at the request of the people should meet with his rejection through his listening further to the voice of the people. The same individual who was characterized as one who would expressly oppress the people rather than listen to their voice (8.10-18) has been removed from office for listening to the *vox populi* and being misled by it.

His expressed desire to 'return' (*šwb*) to Yahweh's worship through Samuel's mediation recalls the people's return to Yahweh in 7.3-11. As H.W. Hertzberg notes, Saul considers his sin to be a minor or moderate transgression (*'br)* that is reparable through Samuel's intervention, rather than an irreparable rejection (*m's*).[2] Samuel's refusal to 'return' with Saul would seem then to re-emphasize the irreparability of Saul's rejection. Yet Samuel's failure to include God's reasons for rejecting Saul in his reiteration of Yahweh's pronouncement raises again the specter of Samuel's self-serving interests. Has Samuel refused because all mediation is useless in light of Yahweh's final decision, or has he refused because he does not want to allow Saul a rapprochement with the Lord? The ambiguity is not quickly resolved.

Saul's inadvertent tearing of Samuel's robe as he grabs it in an act of desperate supplication[3] to forestall Samuel's departure becomes a symbolic occasion for Samuel's final communication of Yahweh's decision and plan. Samuel announces that the kingdom of Israel has been torn from Saul 'this day' and has been given to a more deserving

1. For example, Gunn, *Fate of Saul*, p. 74; McCarter, *I Samuel*, p. 270. Long (*Reign and Rejection of Saul*, p. 156) sees Saul's confession as recalling Samuel's solemn exposition in 12.14-15.

2. Hertzberg, *I & II Samuel*, p. 128.

3. For this meaning of Saul's act, see R.A. Brauner, '"To Grasp the Hem" and 1 Sam 15.27', *JANESCU* 6 (1974), pp. 35-38. The suggestion of McKane (*I and II Samuel*, pp. 102-103) and Ackroyd (*First Samuel*, p. 128) that in order for the symbolism to work, Samuel must tear Saul's robe is unnecessarily literalistic, especially in light of the clear textual statements. For another understanding of Saul's act, see D. Conrad, 'Samuel und die Mari-"Propheten". Bemerkungen zu 1 Sam. 15.27', *ZDMG*Sup. 1 (1969), pp. 273-80.

neighbor (v. 28). The temporal phrase *hayyôm* resounds with the earlier uses of the phrase in chs. 9–10 during Saul's appointment as king and with uses in the battle at the Michmash pass, particularly in connection with the sin that halted the pursuit. Does this mean Saul will now die, or does it mean that Yahweh will allow him to live out his natural life (as the judges of the preceding era who also had received divine spirit had done after they had fulfilled their task of military deliverance), but without further divine support?

The reference in v. 28 to 'another who is "better" (*ṭôb*) than you' plays on two previous passages. In the more immediate context, it reverberates with the people's sparing of all that was good (*ṭôb*) and their destroying the rest. So, too, will Yahweh destroy Saul in favor of one who is 'better'.[1] In addition, it recalls the initial description of Saul in 9.2 that stated that there was no man in all Israel who was 'better' in the sense of being comparable in physical stature to Saul (*w^{e}'ên 'îš mibb^{e}nê yiśrā'ēl ṭôb mimmennû miššikmô wāma'lâ gābō'^{a}h mikkol-hā'ām*). While Saul was said to have been unsurpassed in outward physical stature, according to the narrative flow of events he has proven to be only average in inward judgment, matters of the 'heart', which were the primary criterion of acceptability to Yahweh. He has now been rejected in favor of someone who is 'better' in matters of judgment.

Samuel's additional statement to Saul that Yahweh, the overseer or everlasting one of Israel, will not repent because he is not a man that he should repent allows both options concerning his motives to be possible, but tends to favor the first upon reflection. On the one hand, the audience knows that the Lord does indeed repent because of his direct statement to that effect in v. 11 and its summary restatement in v. 34, in addition to the examples provided from past history, particularly in the Book of Judges. Thus, seen in this light, Samuel's statement can be interpreted as a personal move to cut Saul off from any potential rapprochement with Yahweh, who indeed might yet repent and reinstate Saul.[2] On the other hand, Samuel's statement may be intended to be an explicit citation of the well-known phrase from Num. 23.19-20, which Balaam uses to proclaim his inability to alter

1. The play is also noted by Fokkelman (*Crossing Fates*, p. 106), but developed differently.

2. So, for example, Polzin, *Samuel*, p. 140.

the divine plan once set in motion. Such a view would seem to be consistent with Samuel's crying out to Yahweh all night on Saul's behalf in response to the announcement of repentance, to no avail. His quotation would then signal his tired resignation to the divine plan that has been announced.

Saul seems to grasp the import of the quotation by requesting that Samuel now accompany him back to the sacrificial worship to honor him before the people, abandoning any hope now of having his sin pardoned but continuing in his outward worship of Yahweh.[1] Samuel's willingness to accede to this request results in the realignment of king and people. Saul visibly affirms his role as steward of the people after his confession of sin on their behalf as their corporate head. By outward appearances, he remains king, but he knows in his heart that he has been judged unworthy of the position by God and so will no longer truly be king.

After Samuel reportedly ritually executes the enemy king whom Saul had exempted from the ban, Samuel and Saul part company until the day of Saul's death, an apparent allusion to an approaching meeting of the two. The reference to Saul's death anticipates the expected death notice that will formally complete the structural frame of the account of Saul's career as king, while Samuel's mourning over him (*'bl*) symbolically indicates that Yahweh's rejection has led to his 'death' as active monarch. Both remarks remind the audience that the summary of his career has already appeared in 14.47-48 and so reinforce the finality of Saul's rejection and the virtual termination of his active career as king. Saul apparently is now king only in name and by virtue of the inability of divine spirit to be completely removed from a human once it has been bestowed (cf. Judg. 2.18).

1. Contrast the interpretation of Polzin, *Samuel*, p. 144.

Chapter 11

1 SAMUEL 16

The chapter centers on direct character revelation and the unfolding of events through the use of direct discourse, building on the key theme of *ṭôb* and the statement in 15.28 that Yahweh has given the kingdom of Israel to a man who is 'better' than Saul. The speeches by various individuals will explore the way in which David is 'better' than the first king while portraying David's anointing as the new *nāgîd* in circumstances that directly compare and contrast with Saul's designation and anointing.[1] As is commonly recognized, the root *r'h* appears as another *Leitwort* within the chapter,[2] though its function in helping to develop the *ṭôb* theme has not been widely understood. The heavy concentration of direct speech tends to highlight the few statements made by the narrator, which allow some means for the audience to evaluate the opinions expressed by the other speakers and to permit the introduction of suspense concerning Saul's knowledge or ignorance of David's anointing, which is not finally resolved until v. 19.

In contrast to Saul's situation in chs. 9–10 where Yahweh led Saul to Samuel to be anointed, Samuel is dispatched as the Lord's mediatory king-maker to designate by anointing the new king-elect, who is a

1. A. Rose ('The "Principles" of Divine Election. Wisdom in 1 Samuel, 16', in *Rhetorical Criticism* [ed. J.J. Jackson and M. Kessler; Pittsburgh Theological Monograph Series, 1; Pittsburgh: Pickwick, 1974], p. 57), building on comments by M. Kessler ('Narrative Technique in 1 Sm 16.11-13', *CBQ* 32 [1970], pp. 548-50), argues that the narrative is constructed as a series of didactic utterances followed by responses to the teachings by their intended audiences.

2. Fokkelman (*Crossing Fates*, p. 119) suggests that *bw'* is an additional *Leitwort* in the narrative. He is followed by Polzin (*Samuel*, pp. 159-61, 257 n. 4). I find its emphasis less pronounced and crucial in this chapter, although it will have a more central role in ch. 17.

son of Jesse the Bethlehemite.[1] The contrast in procedure between appointing the new king-elect and the old one immediately hints that the new candidate will not follow the same course as the old one has. The significance of Yahweh's reported initiative in replacing the rejected candidate immediately to prevent a break in leadership is enormous. It signals his understanding and acceptance of the people's motivations for demanding a king in ch. 8, which were seen to be open to misinterpretation because of the unfortunate choice of words to present and characterize the request.[2] The problem of leadership by an intermittent judgeship has been successfully overcome.

Yahweh is to have 'seen' for himself a king among Jesse's sons (v. 1). The *Leitwort r'h* makes its first appearance as a description of Yahweh's process of choosing a new candidate for king. It plays off earlier sight–blindness imagery in the Book of Samuel, as well as contrastive imagery concerning 'hearing' (*šmʿ*).[3] As noted in connection with Saul's anointing, David will be anointed with oil carried in the normative 'horn' instead of a vial, also echoing Hannah's Song in 1 Sam. 2.11.[4] In response to Samuel's reply that Saul will kill him if he 'hears' (*šmʿ*) of his mission, Yahweh must lay out a plan of action, a ruse, for Samuel to use to accomplish his prescribed task.[5] Samuel's lethargy and 'blindness' that have been characteristic throughout the preceding chapters continue, although now out of fear of human reprisal. God must lead the blind mediator along a course of action in order to have his will enacted.[6]

1. So noted by Miscall, *1 Samuel*, p. 115.

2. Contrast Kessler ('Narrative Technique', p. 548 n. 25), who contrasts the choice of the old king by popular demand with Yahweh's personal choice of the new king. But Yahweh chose Saul also.

3. Especially emphasized is a connection with Samuel the 'seer' in ch. 9. So, for example, Alter, *Art of Narrative*, pp. 93, 149-50; Miscall, *1 Samuel*, p. 118; Fokkelman, *Crossing Fates*, p. 130.

4. See Polzin, *Samuel*, p. 153.

5. As noted by Fokkelman (*Crossing Fates*, p. 119), no *zěbaḥ* involving the heifer is recounted. Contrast Hertzberg, *I & II Samuel*, p. 137. There is a widespread association of Samuel's fear of death/objection to divine commissioning with similar passages involving Moses in Exod. 3–4, Jeremiah in Jer. 1.7, and even with Gideon. So, for example, Kessler, 'Narrative Technique', p. 548 n. 23; Schmidt, *Menschlicher Erfolg*, pp. 38-40, 49; Rose, '"Principles" of Election', p. 45; Miscall, *1 Samuel*, p. 116; Klein, *1 Samuel*, p. 160.

6. Sternberg (*Poetics*, pp. 96-97) sees the use of the *Leitwort r'h* here to

The chosen ruse parallels the sacrificial meal in 9.11-14[1] at which Saul was made the guest of honor by Samuel before the invited guests. In the first instance, it was unclear whether Samuel had arranged the sacrifice 'for the benefit of the people' to announce Saul's selection as candidate for king in response to Yahweh's announcement that he was to anoint the young Benjaminite who would arrive the following day in 9.11-14, or whether it was a prearranged regular feast honoring the local townspeople, to which Saul was also issued a special invitation by the prophet, as Jesse's family would be in this case. In either case, the use of parallel cultic contexts for recounting the act of anointing must be a deliberate move by the biblical writer to invite his audience to compare and contrast the two incidents. A similar ruse is used by Absalom to proclaim his kingship at Hebron (2 Sam. 15; cf. 1 Kgs 22.24-27).

The reference to the trembling attitude of the elders who go out to meet Samuel functions as a reinforcement of Samuel's announced fear concerning Saul's learning of his trip, highlighting it in the minds of the narrative audience as a point to be reckoned with in the ensuing episode. As noted by K. Gros-Louis and D. Gunn, the tense atmosphere conveys the critical importance of the visit.[2] After Samuel's announcement of Saul's final rejection and Yahweh's choice of a 'better' man to be king, the king and the narrative audience should be vigilant for any movement by Samuel the king-maker toward the new candidate. The elders' trembling contrasts nicely with the lighthearted, friendly reception of Saul as he approached Ramah, the site of his anointing, in 9.11-14.

David, who must be sought out from among the sheep, a metaphor for Yahweh's people, is anointed as king-elect during the sacrifice. His family and possibly also the invited guests served as witnesses. By contrast, Saul was honored by being placed at the head of the invited guests and given a priestly portion, but was anointed in private, without witnesses, the following day. The mention of Samuel's consecra-

resume the negative portrayal initiated in 1 Sam. 9.6-10.

1. Gordon (*I & II Samuel*, p. 150) suggests that the reference to the sacrificial meal is meant to be ironic in light of 15.15, 21.

2. So K. Gros-Louis, 'The Difficulty of Ruling Well: King David of Israel', *Semeia* 8 (1977), pp. 18-19, and Gunn, *Fate of Saul*, p. 148 n. 2. Kessler ('Narrative Technique', p. 549) focuses on the contrastive sense of *šālōm* as it is used here vs. in earlier speeches in chs. 7, 8, 12 and 15.

tion of Jesse's family separately from the town elders (v. 5) and the reference to the act of anointing having taken place among the brothers (v. 13) is ambiguous in its import. Does it indicate that the elders were only aware that Jesse's entire family was somehow being honored by Samuel's presence but were not privy to the actual act of anointing, or were they witnesses to the entire proceeding? Either way, David's family knew of the anointing, which contrasts dramatically with Saul's anointing in absolute privacy[1] and creates the possibility of word of the action reaching Saul, who already would have been monitoring Samuel's movements suspiciously.

Verses 6-7 take up the *Leitwort r'h* as Yahweh commands Samuel not to be deceived by appearances; Samuel is not to consider (*nbṭ*) Eliab's physical presence (*mar'ēhû*) or his height to determine his fitness for office, for in fact Yahweh has rejected (*m's*) him. Yahweh's reprimand recalls Samuel's earlier comments to the people at Mizpah in which he confirmed the logic of Yahweh's choice of Saul as candidate by noting how he stood a full head above the people when he was 'among them' (10.23-24).[2] As noted by many, the 'blind' Samuel is following the track used to choose Saul, the now-rejected king, by wrongly presuming that Eliab must be the new *nāgîd*.[3] The reprimand also takes the audience back to the first description of Saul in 9.2 as 'better' than any Israelite by virtue of his extra head in height. In Saul's case, the author and narrator have led their audiences to conclude that physical appearance was a false indication of unusual natural ability. In deliberate contrast, David, the youngest of Jesse's sons, would have been the shortest as he stood among his brothers for anointing (v. 13). The *Leitwort r'h* returns in Yahweh's critical statement that he sees in accordance with the heart, whereas man sees in accordance with the eyes (v. 7). The sentiment recalls Saul's first rejection in 13.13, Yahweh's announcement that he had chosen a new

1. *Contra* Hertzberg (*I & II Samuel*, p. 136) and Klein (*1 Samuel*, p. 159), who state that the anointings both take place in private.

2. I believe the intentional contrast with Saul's designation at Mizpah favors the normal sense for *b^{e}qéreb* in v. 5, *contra* Hertzberg, who renders it 'from the midst' to try to make the scene parallel to 9.27–10.1 (*I & II Samuel*, p. 139).

3. Ackroyd (*First Samuel*, p. 132) points out that a slight emendation would turn *neged*, 'before', into *nāgîd*, 'king-elect'. I suspect that the choice of *neged* for preposition rather than the more common *lipnê* was deliberate, precisely to call to mind the term *nāgîd*.

man 'after his own heart', and the use of the contrasting key words 'heart' and 'eyes' in the ensuing narrative to highlight Saul's failure to judge according to his heart.

In light of Yahweh's statement in v. 7 about the source of judgment, its recollection of Saul's physical 'goodness', and the developing indications that the new candidate will be different than Saul, the narrator's description of David in v. 12 should be given particular attention. As one of the statements of non-direct speech in the story, it is highlighted structurally. David is described by three phrases: he is *'admônî 'im-y*^{e}*pēh 'ênáyim w*^{e}*ṭôb rō'î*. It is almost universally accepted that the three attributes are all positive and that David is here ironically presented as a handsome youth. 'Ruddiness' or the possession of red hair is an infrequent characteristic in the Bible and so tends to represent an unusual quality that sets David apart from others, making him distinctive. The grammatical force of the particle *'m*[1] that occurs after the first adjective is somewhat unclear, as is the exact sense of the immediately following abstract noun *yāpēh*. One would have expected an adjective to appear in parallel with the first one. For the third attribute, the motif *ṭôb* reappears as a quality of the noun *ro'î*, whose sense must be considered carefully in the context and, I believe, contrasted with the previous use of the related noun *mar'eh* in v. 7.

Grammatically, David's description would seem to require a close association of the last two attributes, both of which would appear to be governed by the *'im*. In addition to being ruddy in physical appearance, David was endowed 'with beauty of vision and good insight' or judgment. In Gen. 16.13, the noun *ro'î* has the sense of 'perception, insight', where it refers to 'a God of seeing'. I believe that this is its intended meaning here as well. In contrast then to Saul who was *ṭôb* only in the physical sense, David apparently is *ṭôb* in another, more important sense—inwardly handsome, or astute in judgment. The use

1. The MT text *'im* can stand with its regular prepositional force. The reappearance of the closely related phrase in 17.42 tends to weigh against the emendation to *'élem* (so, for example, M. Krenkel, 'Einige Emendation zu den Büchern Samuels', *ZAW* 2 [1882], pp. 309-10), to *śē'ār* as in Gen. 25.25 (for example, A. Klostermann, *Die Bücher Samuelis und der Könige* [Kurzgefasster Kommentar zu den heiligen Schriften Alten und Neuen Testamentes, 3; Nördlingen: Beck, 1887], p. 61) or to *'éṣem* (so T.K. Cheyne, 'Critical Gleanings from Samuel', *ExpTim* 10 [1899], p. 521).

of *ṭôb* in v. 12 is to be seen as a reference back to Samuel's statement in 15.28 that the kingdom has been given to another who is 'better' than Saul.[1]

The anointing results in David's reception of Yahweh's benevolent guiding spirit, transferred from Saul (vv. 12-13). Once divine spirit is bestowed upon a human, it apparently cannot be totally removed. Therefore, the transferral of 'good spirit' from the rejected king to the king-elect requires its replacement with some form of divine spirit. Saul, the disobedient king, now purportedly receives a malevolent guiding spirit that will prevent him from effectively carrying out his role as king, thereby punishing both king and people in accordance with the pronouncement in 12.13-15.[2] Specifically, 12.15 states that if the people disobey God's commandment, then 'the hand of the Lord' will be against both people *and* king. Since in the narrative flow of events it was the people's disobedience in deliberately misconstruing the *ḥērem* command against Amalek in ch. 15 that spurred Saul's final rejection from the office of king for failing to 'constrain' their action, it is fitting that the malevolent spirit be issued as a form of prolonged punishment of the nation and its king to teach Israel the need for ongoing obedience. Had the writer had Yahweh simply strike Saul dead, his fellow characters, the people of Israel, would not have suffered misfortune for their guilt and the narrative and authorial audiences would not have had an opportunity to learn a vicarious lesson from the narrative history. In the episode in progress, the entire nation, with their leader and guardian being deliberately misled in his judgments by the evil guiding spirit, will suffer from his decisions and actions until David is crowned king and can effectively govern according to the benevolent guiding spirit. Samuel's withdrawal home to Ramah (v. 13) emphasizes Saul's total abandonment

1. Sternberg (*Poetics*, p. 356) notes the interrelation of the three uses of *ṭôb*, but translates *ṭôb rō'î* as 'good-looking', in the sense of physical beauty, shifting away from the more ambiguous *ṭôb* used in 9.2 to describe Saul, which can mean either 'good' or 'handsome'.

2. Contrast Klein (*1 Samuel*, p. 162), who believes the author has presented a deliberate contrast between the permanent spirit of David and the temporary spirit of Saul. Slightly differently, Rose ('"Principles" of Election', p. 52) contrasts the different qualities of the two spirits, emphasizing that Saul's was common to prophetic guilds, while David's was for royal leadership. This overlooks Saul's original reception of divine spirit in 10.1 during his private anointing.

to the force of the new malevolent spirit.

Continuing the theme of deceptive outward appearances and the inward and outward sense of *ṭôb*, Saul's courtiers perceive that their lord has been overtaken by an evil 'divine' spirit (*rûaḥ 'elōhîm*) and suggest as a remedy for the present and any future incidents of temporary tormenting that he secure the services of a lyre player who can make it 'good for him' (*ṭôb lāk*) (vv. 15-16). Do the courtiers understand that the evil spirit has been sent by Yahweh specifically and is to be continually present, replacing the benevolent spirit that has been passed to David, or are they presupposing that some temporary evil spirit has befallen Saul and may return in the future? In ironic contrast to Saul's reception of a *divine spirit* in 10.5 in a situation that involved lyre music, here the lyre's music is supposed to drive away the evil divine spirit and make Saul inwardly 'better'.

Saul commands them to 'look for' (*re'û*) a man who 'does well to play' (*mêṭîb lenaggēn*) and to bring him to him. Saul's phrasing is deliberately two-sided; outwardly, he is requesting a person who plays the lyre well in accordance with the courtiers' suggestion. However, the two words need not be linked in meaning, so that his statement also carries the double entendre, 'look for a man who does well, to play', where the emphasis is on finding a man who *mêṭîb*, who can then secondarily play or learn to play the lyre. In this case the use of the verb *r'h* to characterize the search becomes particularly loaded for the narrative audience in light of the previous discussion of the term in vv. 1 and 6-7. Yahweh has 'espied' a king among Jesse's sons (v. 1 who is 'good' in an inward sense and who therefore should 'do well' because he is guided by good instincts and judgment. Saul has requested his servants to 'espy' the man who is 'better' than he (15.28) in 'doing well'. Is the audience to understand Saul's choice of words to be intentional or unintentional? Must he now rely upon others to 'see' for him and not be deceived by outward appearances because of his possession of the malevolent spirit, or has word of David's anointing reached his ears from Bethlehem, as Samuel and the elders feared would happen? The courtiers comply with his request by bringing David, the anointed king-elect, to the court. Do they do so unwittingly, in a scene filled with dramatic irony,[1] or have they understood

1. So, for example, Gunn, *Fate of Saul*, p. 78; Hertzberg, *I & II Samuel*, p. 141.

the undertones of Saul's request, themselves having heard of David's anointing?

David's introduction to Saul comes first as hearsay in the form of his reputation from one of the king's military personnel. It is a *ná'ar*, not simply an *'ébed*, who states in words almost reiterating Yahweh's statement in v. 1 that he has 'seen' a son of 'Jesse the Bethlehemite'.[1] In describing David, the *ná'ar* begins with his knowledge of playing, the overt focus of Saul's request, but significantly, does not specify that David does that activity particularly 'well' as one would expect in light of the king's apparent request for an expert lyre player. The informer then proceeds to reel off an unsolicited and extensive list of Davidic attributes, which are highlighted by virtue of their unrequested character. The first two additional attributes relate the the speaker's own military interests and needs. David has prowess as a *gibbôr ḥáyil*, 'strong warrior', and as an *'îš milḥāmâ*, 'man of war'. His military capabilities recall the final statement in ch. 14 about Saul's instant attachment to himself of any *'îš gibbôr* or *ben-ḥáyil* he encountered because of the hard fighting against the Philistines[2] and echo Saul's appointment as king to deliver Israel from the hand of the Philistines in 9.16. In light of the narrative links, these additional qualities of David's should ensure his attachment to the court by Saul, regardless of his musical abilities, and would seem to be the cause of his dual appointment as weapons-bearer as well as musician in v. 21. The slight change in phrasing to characterize able military men between 14.52 and v. 18 may be a deliberate move by the author to hint to the audience that David will not turn out to be the type of warrior that Saul anticipated or wanted (cf. 2 Sam. 3.1).

The remaining additional traits of David include his being 'discerning of speech' (*n^e^bôn dābār*) and 'a man of form' (*'îš tṓ'ar*). The former attribute emphasizes David's possession of good judgment and intellectual faculties, which have already been presented in v. 12 as the qualities that make him a man who is 'better' than Saul. The use

1. Rose ('"Principles" of Election', p. 51) thinks the repetition serves to emphasize the different purposes for David's choice: 'the divine and human choices converge on David for reasons proper to their own environment'.

2. As correctly noted by Hertzberg (*I & II Samuel*, p. 141); *contra*, for example, J.T. Willis, 'The Function of Comprehensive Anticipatory Redactional Joints in 1 Samuel 16–18', *ZAW* 85 (1973), pp. 300-302; Rose, '"Principles" of Election', p. 63; and Alter, *Art of Biblical Narrative*, p. 150.

of the phrase 'man of form', apparently to suggest an attractive physical build, seems to reflect a deliberate avoidance of the more common adjective *ṭôb* (cf. 1 Kgs 1.6) to drive home the dichotomy between inward and outward beauty and once again indicate indirectly that David's 'beauty' is first and foremost inward. The placing of his physical appearance as the last item in the list devalues the importance of this criterion, suggesting that the speaker shares Yahweh's stress on the inward before the outward. Nevertheless, it satisfies the expectation of the audience that David, like all good heroes, has been blessed with attractive physical attributes in addition to inward beauty.[1] As a fitting summary of David's character, the *náʿar* states, 'Yahweh is with him', apparently meaning to imply that his numerous positive qualities are manifestations of divine gifts and therefore of divine favor. Does he know, as the audience does, that Yahweh is indeed with David in the form of the benevolent guiding spirit bestowed at his familial anointing to be king-elect, or is his comment coincidental?

Since Saul sends messengers to Jesse requesting that he send his son David, whose name has not been supplied by the military spokesman, the audience's growing suspicions that word of David's anointing somehow reached Saul as Samuel feared would happen are finally addressed. Verse 19 contains direct speech by Saul and so is not a statement by the narrator providing background information on plot development. The earlier scene of David's anointing 'among his brothers' is perhaps to be understood to have been witnessed by the elders of the town who were present at the sacrifice after all, allowing for word to leak out and eventually reach Saul. If the audience now can presume Saul's knowledge of the anointing, then the double entendre of his command in v. 17 can also be construed as deliberate rather than inadvertent. The command would then be a test of the loyalty of Saul's servants, who must also have heard of David's anointing. This reassessment of the previous flow of narrative events

1. Contrast Fokkelman (*Crossing Fates*, p. 137), who sees David's physical attractiveness to be the opposite of Saul's rejected state. Miscall (*1 Samuel*, p. 119) says the characterization *'îš tōʾar* serves no obvious function but will be alluded to in 16.12 and 17.42. Biblical writing technique does not ordinarily include gratuitous description. Kessler ('Narrative Technique', p. 551) suggests that the entire description of Saul in v. 18 may be either a polemic against the values of the heroic age or a criticism of man's blindness in overlooking the candidate whose physical beauty is apparent to the beholder.

seems inescapable in light of the specific naming of David in both the MT and the LXX.[1]

Saul does not specify his reasons to Jesse for wanting David at his court, but implies that he wants him because of his abilities as a shepherd. The narrative audience knows that they were made privy to David's location 'among the sheep' by the narrator in connection with David's summons to be anointed in v. 11, but that this information was not hinted at in any way by the *ná'ar* to Saul in v. 18. That Saul should seek out David for his 'shepherding' qualities rather than for any of the five attributes listed in the previous verse, clearly signals Saul's acquired knowledge of David's new status as king-elect and his identity as the man who is 'better' than he. At the same time, Saul's reference to David's status as a shepherd indicates precisely his reason for wanting him at the court: shepherd is a metaphor for the office of king. Saul wants to 'see' for himself and gain control over the new king-elect.[2]

Saul's characterization of David as a shepherd therefore encapsulates the last four highlighted attributes listed about David in v. 18. The first two indicate David's fitness to assume the king's task as the military leader who will deliver Israel from the hand of the Philistines, while the last two stress directly and indirectly his possession of inward judgment that should allow him to 'constrain' the nation to obedience as guardian of the existing terms of the Horeb covenant (9.16-20). All four are royal qualities, possessed by a man who has been favored by Yahweh by the bestowal of divine spirit through anointing. Saul as well as his courtiers has learned that Yahweh is indeed with David.

Leading an ass, the symbol of royalty, laden with gifts that duplicate the items Saul was to receive as the second part of the sign confirming his selection as *nāgîd* in 10.3,[3] David the obedient son went to Saul, 'stood before him, loved him greatly, and became his weapons-bearer' (v. 21). Verses 21-22 contain clear reminders of Saul's rise to

1. I find the attempts to explain it away by, for example, Rose ('"Principles" of Election', p. 55) and Fokkelman (*Crossing Fates*, p. 137) totally unconvincing.

2. Fokkelman (*Crossing Fates*, p. 138) emphasizes how Saul's request for his courtiers to 'see' the man who 'does well' in v. 17 makes him God's competitor and raises a question about which master David will really serve.

3. Contrast Fokkelman (*Crossing Fates*, p. 138), who sees the gifts as specimens of the flocks associated with David's occupation as shepherd.

kingship in the symbol of royalty, the gifts, and the comparison of the two obedient sons being sent off by their fathers to seek their destiny. Yet the end result is different, by virtue of the new set of circumstances. Saul stands before the people and Yahweh as king, while David stands before the king as his servant, awaiting the king's death before he can become king himself. As a servant, David must swear an oath of loyalty to his liege-majesty, Saul, before becoming his weapons-bearer who is bound to preserve the life of the king.

While it is commonly assumed by following the LXX interpretive additions that the ambiguous phrase 'he loved him' in v. 21 has Saul as its subject, grammatically, David is the subject of the entire sentence. The failure of Saul's name to appear in the MT after the verb 'loved' in order to signal a change in subject should, therefore, be taken as an indication that David is the intended subject of the phrase in question and that his 'love' for Saul reflects the idiomatic use of love language to express treaty obligation.[1] In this way, David ironically swears to protect and preserve the life of the predecessor whose continuing existence will prevent him from attaining the throne himself while Saul, his overlord, need not promise any reciprocal protection to his vassal servant.

David's new role as weapons-bearer should remind the narrative audience of the incident between Jonathan and his weapons-bearer at the Michmash pass, where the heir-apparent was inactive before the enemy and dependent upon the weapons-bearer to kill the Philistines at the outpost. David is now to assume the same role on Saul's behalf, killing the Philistines in place of the inactive, fallen king.

By binding David to him through an oath of loyalty, Saul has ensured David's inability to kill him without suffering death himself. Knowing that David has been anointed as his successor, Saul has 'neutralized' him by moving him to the court for constant surveillance and by making him personally responsible for protecting the life of the existing king. Since Saul's request to Jesse that David be allowed to serve the king follows David's appointment as weapons-bearer but

1. Esp. J.A. Thompson, 'The Significance of the Verb "Love" in the David–Jonathan Narratives in 1 Samuel', *VT* 24 (1974), pp. 334-38, *contra*, for example, Gordon, *I & II Samuel*, p. 153. His argument builds on the prior work of W. Moran, 'The Ancient Near Eastern Background of the Love of God in Deuteronomy', *CBQ* 25 (1963), pp. 77-84.

precedes his role as musician (v. 23),[1] the narrator appears to be stressing David's primary role as the king's weapons-bearer. As the new *nāgîd* who has received God's grace, Saul's placement of David in his court will allow him and the nation of Israel to benefit indirectly from the divine blessings that will flow from God's favored man.

Saul's reference to David's having found 'grace' in the king's eyes (v. 22) has layers of meaning. On the one hand, it states Saul's knowledge or opinion (*b*ᵉ*'ênāy*) that David has found 'grace'—divine grace. On another level, it indicates Saul's decision to try to benefit indirectly from the grace by associating himself with David instead of killing his successor immediately, which was a viable option open to him. In this case, David has been the recipient of royal grace in having his life spared by the apparently jealous king.

1. Note the use of *yād* in v. 23 to allude to David's power over Saul.

Chapter 12

1 SAMUEL 17

As officially anointed *nāgîd*, David must now be tested to prove his suitability for coronation to Yahweh and Israel. His slaying of Goliath serves to fulfill the requisite second step of the coronation ceremony[1] and is deliberately framed to contrast with what was potentially Jonathan's previous unsuccessful testing during the battle at the Michmash pass in chs. 13–14.[2] In the narrative flow of events, Israel again faces its primal enemy the Philistines across an intervening

1. Thus, it is not an alternative account to ch. 16 of David's arrival at Saul's court, as is almost universally agreed. See among close literary readers, for example, Gros-Louis, 'Difficulty', pp. 22-23; Alter, *Art of Biblical Narrative*, pp. 147-48, 152-53; Fokkelman, *Crossing Fates*, p. 202. D. Damrosch (*The Narrative Covenant* [San Francisco: Harper & Row, 1987], pp. 198-99) considers it an addition to the HDR meant to create a frame in which David's rise begins with an initial skirmish against the Philistines and concludes with their decisive vanquishing in 2 Sam. 5. This overlooks the clear parallels and contrasts drawn to chs. 13–14 within the story and its primary function to depict David's testing as king-elect. By contrast, Sternberg (*Poetics*, p. 231) takes a more moderate stance, suggesting that chs. 16 and 17 might be intended to express a sequential development of the relationship between Saul and David demonstrating David's launching of his public career with the blessing of both humanity in peacetime (ch. 16) and God in wartime (ch. 17). The study by H. Jason ('The Story of David and Goliath: A Folk Epic?', *Bib* 60 [1979], pp. 36-70) fails to attempt to deal with the relationship between chs. 16 and 17 and is generally not useful for the task of close reading.

2. The existence of some connection with chs. 13–14 has been noted by Miscall (*1 Samuel*, p. 124) and Fokkelman (*Crossing Fates*, p. 143), but not for the specific reasons noted here. Gunn (*Fate of Saul*, p. 79) compares the chapter with Saul's deed at Jabesh-Gilead. He has correctly sensed the story's role as a testing for the king-elect, but has overlooked the more germane and deliberate parallels drawn with chs. 13–14 to Jonathan. Herzog and Gichon comment on the occurrence of single-handed feats in both battles, but do not draw any conclusions about the function of the parallel in the development of the narrative (*Battles of the Bible*, p. 72).

'chasm', this time the more open Valley of Elah instead of the steep Wadi Suweinit (vv. 1-3). In face of the direct challenge by Goliath to an individual representative combat, Saul again becomes unable to assume his leadership role as deliverer (14.2, 18; v. 11). The battle is undertaken on his behalf by the king-elect, David, just as the previous battle was launched by the heir-elect and potential *nāgîd*, Jonathan. After an initial flight by the Israelites (13.6-7; v. 24), the enemy is engaged and is itself put to flight (14.23; v. 51). Both battles result in victories in which the enemy has been killed by their own swords (v. 51; 14.20).[1]

Having established a roughly similar battle situation, the narrator focuses on the contrasts between the actions of Jonathan and Saul in the two encounters in order to highlight David's clear possession of divine spirit and to show retrospectively that Jonathan lacked it. Jonathan mounts a surprise attack on an undermanned garrison with the aid of his weapons-bearer in a dangerous but potentially successful plan that allows him to dictate the outcome. David, on the other hand, accepts the challenge offered by Goliath, going into the individual contest in which Goliath has taken the initiative and in which, by virtue of his armor and weapons, the Philistine stands as a fully protected 'garrison' on the alert, putting David at a major disadvantage. Jonathan undertakes his attack armed with a sword and spear and with the aid of another skilled warrior, whereas David enters with the less conventional though lethal weapon, the slingshot (v. 49), and without a back-up sword (v. 50) or human aid. Jonathan enters combat without the firm knowledge that Yahweh will perform a saving deed for him (14.6) and needs to confirm the divine will through the proposal of a sign (14.8-12). David, by contrast, states confidently to Saul that Yahweh will snatch him away (*nṣl*) from the Philistine's grasp. Unlike Jonathan, he knows that he possesses Yahweh's guiding spirit (16.13). Finally, Jonathan relies on his weapons-bearer to kill the twenty Philistine guards (14.13) but David kills Goliath himself (v. 49). As a result of the instant victory, Israel is able to despoil the Philistine camp quickly (vv. 52-53) instead of undertaking a lengthy pursuit under a ban.

1. I find unconvincing Polzin's proposed parallel between 17.55–18.2 and the trial scene in 14.36-46 where Abner is to play the role of Ahijah, David of Jonathan, Jonathan of the people who ransomed him, and Saul, himself (*Samuel*, pp. 175-77).

The narrator begins by establishing the battle scene (vv. 1-3) and highlighting Goliath's apparent invulnerability (vv. 4-7). Reference to his extraordinary height should remind the narrative audience of Eliab and Saul who shared the same trait, their rejection by Yahweh, and God's statement to Samuel that man judges by outward appearances instead of by inward perceptions, as he does. Although Saul and his troops are shattered (*ḥtt*) and afraid because of Goliath's appearance, David, who possesses divine spirit and so is able to perceive according to Yahweh's criteria (*ṭôb rō'î*, 16.12), reassures Saul that no man's 'heart', the correct seat of judgment, should fail on Goliath's account (v. 32). The Philistine is vulnerable and will himself 'fall' before David in v. 49.[1]

The narrator uses Goliath's speech to emphasize further David's possession of inward perception and to develop a theme introduced at the end of ch. 16 with David's appointed status as Saul's servant, the levels of mastership within Israel. Goliath characterizes the Israelite troops as 'servants of Saul' (v. 8) and defies the ranks of Israel to produce *a man* so that the two may fight together (v. 10). The loser and his people will become the servants of the winner's nation (vv. 9-10). David's response to Goliath's challenge immediately clarifies the nature of Goliath's taunt: the 'uncircumcised' Philistine who lacks membership in the covenant community (cf. 14.6) has actually defied the ranks of the living God, who is Israel's true master, not Saul. He has unknowingly issued a challenge to Yahweh, who is not a man at all and who will be able to overcome any mortal through his chosen human agent, as David emphasizes in vv. 46-47.[2] Saul and the troops have been so set back by Goliath's physical appearance that they have not heard the real import of Goliath's speech or they would have realized that he had sealed his own fate by defying Yahweh. Goliath's failure to grasp the true situation of Israel's relationship with Yahweh recalls the previous Philistine misunderstanding in 4.5-9.

Verses 12-15 form a parenthetical aside concerning David and his

1. Sternberg (*Poetics*, pp. 339-40) emphasizes that Goliath's deliberate portrayal as a totally self-confident character is a strategy that guarantees his defeat for the narrative audience.

2. Klein (*1 Samuel*, p. 178) points to the stress placed on *'îš* through repetition in these verses as an attempt to indicate that the killing of Goliath is a man-sized job to establish a contrast with the youth who will actually prevail.

family, specifically recalling events in ch. 16. They remind the audience of the names of David's father and three eldest brothers, thereby calling to mind the previous anointing scene in which the family all appeared together, the rejection of the three eldest sons as Yahweh's new king-elect, David's anointing, and the family's bearing witness to the event. The reminder seems to have been included to set the stage for the forthcoming exchanges between David and Eliab, and David and Saul.[1]

At the same time, vv. 12-15 supply new information that would seem to indicate the passage of some time between the present battle and previous events in ch. 16. Jesse is now described as old, a detail not stated before. His three eldest sons now serve Saul, a new development, while David has returned home from Saul's service to care for the family's flocks. The phrasing of v. 12 allows room for the possibility that David's return home was a temporary measure because of the departure of the three eldest sons to be part of the troops rallied to fight the Philistines, requiring the father to relieve them of their shepherding duties temporarily and replace them with the youngest son. The informational gap leads the narrative audience to wonder about the reasons for David's return home from the court, the length of time he was away, and then reminds them that no response from Jesse was given to Saul's request that David be allowed to 'stand before' him in 16.22. I believe the two verbs *hlk* and *šwb* in v. 15 are best repointed as perfect forms rather than as participles, making them consistent with the perfect form used in v. 14 to describe the contrasting action of the brothers: the three older ones had followed (*hālᵉkû*) Saul, but David had departed (*hālak*) and turned aside (*šāb*) from attendance on Saul to take care of his father's flocks in Bethlehem.[2]

After a forty-day span with the older sons absent (v. 16), Jesse begins to worry about their welfare, just as Kish did about Saul in 10.2, and sends David, another son, with provisions and orders to

1. So noted also by P. Miscall, *The Workings of Old Testament Narrative* (Semeia Studies: Chico, CA: Scholars Press, 1983), p. 58; Fokkelman, *Crossing Fates*, p. 163; D. Gooding, 'An Approach to the Literary and Textual Problems in the David–Goliath Story: 1 Sam. 16–18', in D. Barthélemy *et al.*, *The Story of David and Goliath* (OBO, 73; Göttingen: Vandenhoeck & Ruprecht, 1986), p. 59.

2. The noniterative sense of the two verbs is also accepted by Fokkelman (*Crossing Fates*, p. 154 n. 16).

return with a token indicating their safety. The expression 'forty days' is a conventional indicator of the passage of a considerable period of time. The obedient son David sets off early in the morning, having entrusted the flocks to a caretaker, arrives at the battle as the troops have drawn up to fight, deposits the provisions with the mess captain, and arrives 'empty-handed' among the ranks to greet his brothers (vv. 20-22). He then witnesses and hears for the first time what his brothers and the Israelite troops had already witnessed and heard for forty days: Goliath's lone stand and challenge to individual combat. David's response contrasts greatly with that of his fellow Israelites after Goliath's first appearance and now, after forty days, he merely listens, or, given the overtones of the verb *šm'*, he 'obeys', in contrast to the others who feared greatly and were shattered after the first encounter and even now flee, after forty days of the challenge. The contrast is heightened grammatically by placing the subject in v. 24, 'all the men of Israel', in first position before the verb to contrast with Saul's action. The implication is that they have been fleeing for forty days, twice a day, in response to the challenge.

The source of authority for the statement made by the terrified soldier in v. 25 about the rewards forthcoming from the king for dispatching Goliath, while initially ambiguous, is confirmed to be Saul. The narrative audience is not told that Saul has actually issued such a promise and the phrasing of the Israelite soldier leaves open the question whether an official royal decree has been issued or whether the rewards are presumed to be forthcoming because of the gravity of the situation and the normal types of rewards under the circumstances. David's request for confirmation concerning the royal rewards for the slaying of Goliath then seems to clarify the ambiguity. Many people now confirm the first words, repeating them verbatim with formulaic language typical of a decree, 'so shall it be done' (v. 27). In response to the official Philistine edict that has stated that the winner will become the master of the loser, Saul has issued a counteredict to his own nation: the winner will be freed from serving the master. What at first glance appeared to be an interest by David in one or all of the rewards that motivated his request for repetition proves instead to be a desire to clarify the source of the edict in an attempt to discern the king's true state of mind. Both the narrative and authorial audiences, on the other hand, should be aware that David's question has another dimension, asking about the reward that God will give to his chosen champion who successfully destroys his enemy: what reward will David receive for passing his test as king-elect?

Ironically, in contrast to David's perception of Goliath and Saul, Eliab is unable to discern David's true state of mind. He answers his own question to David about the younger brother's motivations without letting David speak, charging him with evil intentions in coming to see the battle. On the most basic level, he seems to imply that David has sneaked away without permission to watch the battle, shirking his family duties as shepherd. As mentioned before, v. 15 may imply that Eliab normally had responsibility for the flock, so his words on one level may be an attempt to chide David for seeking excitement so quickly and a return to the court-related life of which Eliab and his brothers were only now getting a taste, in contrast to their usual dreary job. On a deeper level, however, in light of previous events in ch. 16, Eliab may be accusing the king-elect of coming to watch Saul's destruction at the hand of the Philistine, since he knows that Saul has been rejected by Yahweh and so is defenseless.[1] David's response mirrors Eliab's; he asks a question and instantly answers it himself with a rhetorical question that emphasizes their joint knowledge of his status as *nāgîd*. The two questions, 'What have I done now? Isn't this the matter/problem?', counter Eliab's insinuation that David planned not to help Saul with his affirmation that he will indeed 'do' as Yahweh's agent. The use of the verb *'śh* stresses the need for a divine act of deliverance, being the normal verb used to describe Yahweh's saving deeds on behalf of Israel.

To ensure his ability to become God's agent, David repeats his question concerning the rewards for the victor to the troops so that they will mark his apparent interest and convey it to the king, gaining Saul a formal audience (v. 31). The strategy works, and David is once again summoned before the king, as in 16.19. Without need of a formal introduction because of his previous service in ch. 16, he reassures Saul that appearances are deceiving, hinting that the men would have no reason to fear if they would only follow their hearts instead of their eyes. He then states that he will fight the Philistine as Saul's

1. Contrast the discussion of Fokkelman (*Crossing Fates*, pp. 162-65), who focuses on psychological motivations, and that of Gooding ('Approach to David–Goliath Story', p. 59), who focuses on sibling jealousy as the primary cause of friction.

servant. While his self-characterization before the king as 'your servant' reflects normal protocol, it also raises again the issue of mastership from vv. 8-9 and 16.21. The former weapons-bearer has now returned to defend the life of the king, but as the servant of Yahweh. Saul, continuing to be deceived by appearances, protests that David may be a *ná'ar*, a status that David received upon his appointment as weapons-bearer in 16.21, but lacks the amount of experience of the Philistine *ná'ar*, who truly ranks as an *'îš milḥāmâ*. Saul's words recall the description of David by a *ná'ar* of Saul's court in 16.18 as an *'îš milḥāmâ*. The term *ná'ar* seems to be used in v. 33 in a way that exploits its dual sense of 'youth' and 'retainer, attendant'.[1] David is both a youth and a retainer.

David's response in vv. 34-37 is designed to reassure the king that he is capable of one-to-one combat, but highlights for the king the true factor that will determine the battle: Yahweh's presence with David. His speech to Saul contains allusions that intentionally or unintentionally remind the king of who David is. While the reference to events that had befallen him as a shepherd since his departure from Saul apparently are meant to bring the king up to date on his activities since they last parted (cf. v. 15), they also bring to the mind of the audience and, by implication, to the mind of Saul, David's familial occupation before he was anointed by Samuel and became Saul's servant (ch. 16). David's assurance that Yahweh will rescue him from the 'hand of' the Philistine, just as he has from wild animals since he returned home, which the audience knows is due to his possession of Yahweh's spirit, should also remind Saul of the reason that he sought him out in the first place: his hearsay knowledge that David had been anointed as Yahweh's new *nāgîd*.

Saul's blessing at the end of v. 37, 'go, for Yahweh himself will be with you', indicates his understanding of the import of David's offer. It signals his acceptance of David as Goliath's challenger and his hope that the less qualified youth before him can succeed in his Herculean task. At the same time, it conveys Saul's pre-existing knowledge that David is Yahweh's new *nāgîd* and so will be able to succeed at the task because of his possession of divine spirit.[2] David's fight against

1. For the different nuances of *ná'ar*, see J. MacDonald, 'The Status and Role of the Na'ar in Israelite Society', *JNES* 35 (1976), pp. 147-70.

2. Klein (*1 Samuel*, p. 179) has correctly understood this, but has not realized

Goliath will only confirm publicly the rumor that Saul has already accepted to be true.

In a reversal of roles, Saul now arms David, his appointed weapons-bearer, for battle (vv. 38-39). David assumes the place of the king in taking on responsibility for battle. However, he is not yet king, but only king-elect, who has not proven himself worthy of the office of kingship by successfully being tested in human battle. Thus, his statement to Saul that he is not able to go forward in the symbols of royal office because he has not been tested or proven (*lō' nissîtî*) in v. 39, repeating and confirming the narrator's statement that he was unable to proceed for the same reason, highlights his own understanding of the situation and his status. He removes the royal weaponry to which he is not yet entitled[1] and uses instead the weapons associated with his existing threefold status as a shepherd, a *ná'ar* or member of the army, and untried *nāgîd*, the one which he has mastered, the slingshot (v. 40).[2] With shepherd's staff and slingshot 'in hands', he goes forward to to battle with Goliath. The narrator's mention of David's possession of a common *maqqēl* (v. 40) seems intended to recall to the audience's minds by way of contrastive analogy Jonathan's royal *maṭṭeh* in 14.27, thereby highlighting the dissimilarity between the heir-elect and Yahweh's chosen candidate, David.

David squares up to Goliath, who is now preceded by his shield-bearer in customary fashion, but whose invulnerability at the same time weakens in light of the need for an attendant. Goliath, like the Israelites, focuses on outward appearances rather than inward strengths. He 'sees' David (*r'h*, v. 42), but not in the sense in which

that Saul, as well as the court retainer, has already indicated his knowledge of David's anointing in 16.19.

1. Contrast the suggestions by Gunn (*Fate of Saul*, p. 79) that 'Saul's way is not David's way'; by Fokkelman (*Crossing Fates*, p. 176) that David cannot use the weapons because they belong to Yahweh's rejected king; and by Gordon (*I & II Samuel*, p. 158) that 'David's eschewing of conventional armor will ensure that the glory goes to Yahweh to whom it belongs'.

2. Contrast the usual understanding of David as an unskilled shepherd by, for example, Alter (*Art of Biblical Narrative*, p. 81) and Fokkelman (*Crossing Fates*, p. 172). For the slingshot as a regular infantry weapon in the army, see, for example, Y. Yadin, *The Art of Biblical Warfare in Biblical Lands* (trans. M. Pearlman; New York: McGraw–Hill, 1963), pp. 9-10; J. Sasson, *The Military Establishments at Mari* (Studia Pohl, 3; Rome: Pontifical Biblical Institute, 1969), p. 26.

Yahweh sees in 16.1. He focuses on David's outward appearance, describing him in terms echoing the *ná'ar*'s initial description of David at 16.12, but with notable differences. While David remains 'ruddy', he now appears to the Philistine as a youth who is beautiful in physical appearance, *y^e^pēh mar'eh*, an expression that almost mixes elements from both halves of the previous description's final two traits, *y^e^pēh 'ênáyim w^e^ṭôb rō'î*, but contains the important substitution of *mar'eh*, appearance, for *ro'î*, perception. Goliath's perception of David misses his central strength, his inward beauty and strength of judgment that mirrors Yahweh's criteria. Goliath considers David worthless (*bzh*) because of his apparent lack of fighting qualities and views his presence as a degradation of his own military skill. His cursing of David by his gods would have been a customary procedure, but in the context, becomes a significant pitting of the Philistine gods against Yahweh in a rematch recalling the events of ch. 4–6.[1]

After the traditional exchange of taunts by the warriors (vv. 44-47),[2] the long-awaited battle is engaged and draws to its expected result. David's response to Goliath's taunt repeats Goliath's own threat of defeat but now publicly announces what the Israelites should have been able to understand at Goliath's first appearance, had they listened with their 'hearts' to his words and not focused on his outward appearance. Yahweh, the true object of Goliath's defiance, will fight Goliath through a human agent (*hayyôm hazzeh y^e^sagger^e^kā yhwh b^e^yādî*) (v. 46), so that superior skill or weaponry will not be necessary to fell the enemy. The battle is over in the space of two verses. With the first shot, David strikes Goliath in the *mṣḥ*, an apparently vulnerable spot.[3] The stone then sinks in, causing the Philistine

1. Parallels with chs. 4–6 have been noted previously by, for example, Klein (*1 Samuel*, p. 180) and Fokkelman (*Crossing Fates*, p. 186).

2. Such taunt matches were standard practice in the *Iliad*, but are also known from the *Tale of Sinuhe*. For the acknowledgment that the exchanges between Goliath and David are a regular precursor to single combat, see, for example, R. de Vaux, 'Single Combat in the Old Testament', in *The Bible and the Ancient Near East* (ed. G.E. Wright; Garden City, NY: Doubleday, 1961), pp. 122-35; Hertzberg, *I & II Samuel*, p. 152; Auzou, *Danse devant l'arche*, pp. 178-80; Gooding, 'Approach to David–Goliath Story', p. 67.

3. For the suggestion that the *maṣḥâ* is a greave, see A. Deem, 'And the Stone Sank into his Forehead. A Note on 1 Samuel xvii 49', *VT* 28 (1978), pp. 349-51. For its identity as a codpiece, see J. Sasson, 'Reflection on an Unusual Practice

to fall down face forward (in pain?), finishing up in a position identical to that of his god Dagon before Yahweh's ark in 5.4. He is subsequently beheaded, just like the god whose champion he is (v. 51; 5.4). Since David, as untested king-elect, did not have a sword 'in his hand', he is forced to appropriate Goliath's and behead the enemy with his own weapon. The resultant suggestion that the Philistine had committed a form of suicide would not be lost on the narrative audience in light of Goliath's failure to understand that his challenge to Israel had constituted a defiance of Yahweh. At the same time, the narrator's report that Goliath's head finished up 'in David's hand' (v. 57) drives home the transfer of Israel's fate from the Philistine to David, the newly proven *nāgîd*.

The duel comes as an anticlimax, since its outcome has already been announced by David in his previous speeches. The narrator steps in to draw an analogy to 13.22 and at the same time, to contrast the actions of Jonathan and Saul (v. 50). Goliath is killed by his own sword and the Philistines are routed, paralleling their fate after Yahweh's intervention in 14.20 (v. 51).

The chapter ends with a scene that serves as a bridge between past and forthcoming narrative action, vv. 55-58. As Saul's 'sees' David go off to his test as king-elect, he asks his general Abner the loaded question, 'The son of this whom is the youth/retainer?', *ben-mî-zeh hanná'ar*. The king's use of the demonstrative may in part reflect a derisive tone, as it does frequently in the story.[1] However, it may also be a deliberate link to the somewhat enigmatic *zeh* in v. 12 that describes Jesse as the son of 'this Ephrathite'. His reference to David as *the* youth instead of by name could also derive from an attempt to denigrate him by refusing to call him by name, implying he is a nobody. In this case, it would not indicate his ignorance of David's identity, as is commonly presumed. Had Saul intended his question to cast aspersion on David, one would have expected him to ask *ben-mî-hanná'ar hazzeh*. On the other hand, the present wording of the question may simply be an attempt by the narrator to focus attention on the main purpose of Saul's question by putting David in the background and not drawing attention to him by using a neutral

Reported in ARM X:4', *Orientalia* 43 (1974), pp. 409-10.

1. So Polzin, *Samuel*, pp. 172-73.

descriptive term, foregrounding instead the main issue, the identity of his father.

In either case, the introductory temporal phrase places the question in the wake of Saul's conversation with David in vv. 32-37, so Saul should recognize David. R. Polzin's creative attempt to harmonize the two conversations by suggesting that Saul thought David had backed out of the challenge by refusing the armor and so would not have presumed that he was the figure in the distance does not seem necessary to explain this final exchange of dialogue.[1] What then is in his mind as he sees the person whom he knows is Yahweh's *nāgîd*? The question is highlighted by its threefold repetition in vv. 55-58.

On the immediate level, the question links up to his prior decree that the family of the slayer of Goliath will be made free in Israel; Saul is asking Abner about the identity of David's father who is a 'nobody' but who will now become a 'somebody' through his son's heroics.[2] In this respect, the question develops the theme introduced earlier in vv. 25, 27 and 30. David's failure to name his father in the preceding conversation (v. 34) now leads Saul to try to remember this information, which was told to him in the past (16.19) but had slipped his mind, not being as crucial as David's identity as Yahweh's probable *nāgîd*. Saul's use of the term *'élem* in his second posing of the question in v. 56 instead of the term *ná'ar* tends to emphasize his promise that Goliath's slayer would marry a princess, since the word designates a sexually ripe young man.

On another level, however, the question echoes the one asked about Saul in 10.12 by his fellow townspeople after he prophesied among the prophetic band. They became confused by appearances after Saul's reception of divine spirit. In both cases, the implied identity of the father in question would appear to be Yahweh. Saul's hearsay knowledge of Yahweh's choice of David to be the new king-elect is about to be confirmed or denied by David's test and will reveal whether David has a new adoptive divine father, Yahweh, as Saul already believes—

1. Polzin, *Samuel*, p. 173.

2. As emphasized by Gooding ('Approaches to David–Goliath Story', p. 60). A creative but implausible alternative explanation is offered by Miscall (*Workings of OT Narrative*, p. 71). He suggests that the question to Abner may be an implied rebuke for not fighting Goliath himself, raising the issue of Abner's whereabouts during the chapter by linking it to the later encounter between Saul, Abner and David in ch. 26.

Yahweh himself will be with you (v. 37, cf. Ps. 2.7).

Both question levels are answered in vv. 57-58 by David himself. He appears before Saul with Goliath's head, indicating that Yahweh is his new adoptive father, and he confirms this status in his response to the question's more mundane level by naming Jesse the Bethlehemite and characterizing him as Saul's servant. The chapter ends with a return of the theme of servantship. Jesse remains a servant of the human king Saul, but David has demonstrated that his true master is Yahweh.

Chapter 13

1 SAMUEL 18

The foregoing narrative continues through vv. 1-5 of ch. 18. Saul makes David a permanent court resident, refusing to let him return to his father's house (v. 2). His action brings to mind his first request to Jesse to allow David to remain at court (16.22), which went unanswered and which subsequently was revealed to have been denied (17.15). With the public confirmation of the rumor of David's anointing by Samuel to be *nāgîd,* Saul moves quickly to secure the indirect blessing that David will bring to Israel through his possession of Yahweh's benevolent guiding spirit by making him a regular part of his staff. At the same time, he can monitor closely any attempts to launch a *coup d'état* centered around the son of Jesse by having his 'rival' more or less under 'house arrest' where his every action can be closely monitored.

Jonathan, the heir-elect to the throne by birth who had accepted Yahweh's decree of guilt in 14.43, now symbolically relinquishes his office to Yahweh's chosen *nāgîd,* David (vv. 1-4).[1] Presumably having learned like his father and other courtiers that David had been anointed by Samuel and having witnessed David's felling of Goliath, he seems to accept his passing over by Yahweh graciously. He enters into a formal pact (*b^erît*) based on loyalty (verb *'hb*) with the new king-elect. By giving David his own robe, armor, and weaponry, he effectively transfers to him the office of *king-elect.* Having successfully passed his test of suitability for kingship, David is able to accept

1. So noted previously by, for example, J. Morgenstern, 'David and Jonathan', *JBL* 78 (1959), p. 322; Hertzberg, *I & II Samuel*, p. 155; Blenkinsopp, '1 and 2 Samuel', p. 315; Ackroyd, *First Samuel*, p. 147; Mettinger, *King and Messiah*, pp. 34, 39; Gunn, *Fate of Saul*, p. 80; Jobling, *Sense of Biblical Narrative*, I, pp. 19-20; Klein, *1 Samuel*, p. 182; Gordon, *I & II Samuel*, p. 159.

the official representative symbols of office of *nāgîd*. He still may not receive Saul's royal armor and weaponry (17.38-39) until the reigning king's death, when he will officially be crowned king.

Verse 5 serves both as a summary of the consequence of Saul's decision to enlist David's service permanently and as a chronological indicator. David, Yahweh's designated king-elect, is able indirectly to bestow upon Israel the blessing that Saul, the rejected king, could not give it: military victory gained through Yahweh's help and guiding spirit. David now assumes the role of the king by fighting his battles for him. The statement that David was successful wherever Saul sent him echoes Saul's valiant military career summarized in 14.47-48, reminding the audience of Saul's loss of effective leadership abilities and the end of his career at that point. David, who began his military career as the king's weapons-bearer (16.21), has now become king in all but name. His repeated military successes over time result in his promotion by Saul to the rank of general (v. 5). They also cause him to win the favor of the populace at large, including the 'servants of Saul' or other courtiers. He is viewed as 'good' (*wayyîṭab*) by both of the latter groups, thereby indirectly signalling that the man who is 'better' than Saul and to whom Yahweh has given Israel (15.29) has been accepted by the nation, concluding the search that has been connected with that motif. By the end of v. 5, the story has moved forward in time by many years.[1]

With v. 6 the narrator immediately goes back to the aftermath of the Goliath incident to fill in specifics about how David came to earn his eventual promotion. The victory song that is sung by the women to the king in v. 7 credits Saul and David with equal military honor in a couplet employing synonymous parallelism.[2] The reference to the cel-

1. Willis ('Redactional Joints', pp. 306-308) argues that v. 5 is an anticipatory redactional joint alluding to events in 18.13–20.33, and is widely followed. Auzou (*Danse devant l'arche*, p. 186) has understood the verse more accurately: it is a summary meant to end the preceding tradition, but one which covers a long period of time. The succeeding chapters then go back in time and zero in on specific events that take place within that span of time.

2. So noted by, for example, Hertzberg (*I & II Samuel*, p. 157), but argued at length by S. Gevirtz, *Patterns in the Early Poetry of Israel* (Studies in Ancient Oriental Civilization, 32; Chicago: University of Chicago Press, 1963), pp. 14-24. Gevirtz is quoted by McCarter (*I Samuel*, p. 312) and Fokkelman (*Crossing Fates*, p. 214).

ebrational festivities with music faintly echoes the prophetic train that Saul had joined in 10.5-13 and the accompanying *māšāl* that emphasized his first public manifestation of divine spirit that had created confusion about his status in the minds of those present. Here, by contrast, there is no confusion among the witnesses as to the significance of events: while Saul is the king of Israel and so must be credited with the victory, David is the true source of victory and new military leader.[1] Saul, too, realizes the people's perception; his final statement in v. 8, 'there remains only the kingship for him', is an accurate summary of the situation; the anointed *nāgîd* has suc-cessfully passed his test and now only needs to be crowned to assume the throne. The king's statement reveals to the narrative audience that in the wake of developments, he feels an urgent need to keep an eye on David to prevent his premature loss of the throne.

Again recalling Saul's prophesying in 10.5-13 under the influence of a divine spirit, now Saul is overpowered by an *evil* divine spirit that causes him to rant rather than prophesy and to attempt to kill David twice unsuccessfully with his spear (vv. 10-11). The term *yād* is used in the descriptions of both king and king-elect to help establish a sense of rivalry and conflict. Saul's royal power is symbolized by his holding his spear in his hand, while David's power as king-elect is symbolized by his holding in his hand a lyre, an instrument that produces harmony of spirit. In this first instance of direct and open conflict between the king and king-elect, it is an evil divine spirit that specifically is said to motivate the attack. The implication is that an outside force is attempting to thwart the divine plan by killing Yahweh's chosen *nāgîd*.

Upon gaining self-control again, Saul has two very different reasons to fear David. Realizing that he has lost Yahweh's benevolent guiding spirit to David (v. 12), the king fears David's attempt to dethrone him prematurely by killing him, even though David had sworn an oath of loyalty to protect his life when he had become his royal servant (16.21). However, Saul has equal reason to fear for David's safety at his own hand because of his sporadic but uncontrollable possession by a malevolent divine spirit that has now revealed its desire to thwart

1. Thus, observations by D.N. Freedman (review of *Patterns in the Early Poetry of Israel*, by S. Gevirtz, *JBL* [1964], pp. 201-202), quoted by McCarter (*I Samuel*, p. 312), are also germane.

Yahweh's plan for Israel's history by killing the divinely appointed *nāgîd*. Saul, whose actions in the past chapters have revealed him to be consistently pious and respectful of Yahweh's will, would not seem to want to do anything that would challenge the will of his God. Since David has been officially anointed as Yahweh's *nāgîd* and has passed his military testing, Saul's deliberate or inadvertent killing of the king-elect would result in the thwarting of God's plan, with grave consequences.

The reason for Saul's removal of David from the court, from his own presence where either party might be killed by the hand of the other, remains a mystery to the audience. It may reflect a twofold, contradictory motivation: self-preservation and obedience to Yahweh's will, or it may reflect either one of the options. The informational gap creates narrative suspense. Saul appoints David as a commander of a thousand before the people. Does he do this in the hope of having David die in battle, or does he do it to avoid his possible thwarting of God's plan while benefitting his nation, knowing that it would not pose any risk to David's life because 'Yahweh was with him' (vv. 12-14)? The audience is not told. Nevertheless, Saul's decision only aggravates the initial situation, for it gains David the respect and loyal support ('love', *'hb*) of the entire citizenry of Israel and Judah,[1] fuelling Saul's first fear of assassination. At the same time, it makes his own potential assassination of David under the influence of an evil spirit a graver problem, adding negative popular reaction to the more important negative divine reaction. Should David die now by his hand, he in turn would almost certainly be assassinated by a Davidic supporter. The narrator has the audience's full attention.

Finally, Saul's motivations are revealed in v. 17. Saul's personal solution to his double bind is to try to have David killed in battle by the enemy, shifting responsibility for the thwarting of Yahweh's plan on to Yahweh's own enemies and so avoiding any threat to his own life. He wants to eliminate David by having him killed. Self-preservation has taken precedence over his royal duties as nation-preserver. Picking up on the marriage theme announced in 17.25, Saul now offers to David the reward to which he was entitled after slaying Goliath: a promise of marriage to his daughter. It comes belatedly and

1. The political sense of *'hb* in v. 16 has been noted previously by Thompson, 'Significance', p. 337; McCarter, *I Samuel*, p. 313; and Klein, *1 Samuel*, p. 189.

conditionally. David must become a professional soldier, a *ben-ḥáyil*, and fight Yahweh's battles while awaiting the actual ceremony. A delay between betrothal and marriage would have been customary, allowing both partners to reach the acceptable age of wedlock and allowing the prospective son-in-law to generate the necessary bride-price.

The irony of Saul's statement and his self-motivation–'let not my hand be upon him but the hand of the Philistines'—is readily apparent to the audience. David has already been fighting Yahweh's battles in the place of Saul and will have neither the adverse 'hand' of Saul or the Philistines upon him because of his protection from the 'hand' of Yahweh. As widely acknowledged, David's expression of humility conveys the kind of polite deference expected of a commoner to the king. It echoes Saul's earlier expression of humility in 9.21, but at the same time, reminds the narrative audience of David's entitlement to the status of royal son-in-law or adoptive royal son because of his slaying of Goliath and because of his choice by Yahweh to succeed Saul as king. Saul unwittingly has created the means by which David can become an official member of his family.

For an initially undisclosed reason, Saul marries the promised Merab off to another, but enters into a subsequent agreement with David for the hand of his other daughter Michal (vv. 20-29). What is at first presented as an informational gap, the reason for the failure of David's marriage to Merab to take place (v. 19), is subsequently explained indirectly through character dialogue. As soon as Saul extends the second marriage offer to David, this time involving his younger daughter Michal (vv. 20-21), he commands his servants to try to persuade David in private to accept the offer (vv. 22-23). The narrative audience is thereby led to suspect it was David, not Saul, who broke the first marriage agreement. Confirmation of the suspicion follows immediately in v. 23b, where David confides to his fellow courtiers that his primary obstacle to accepting Michal's hand is the bride-price (*'ānôkî 'îš-rāš*).[1] David was unable to marry Merab

1. Contrast the standard view that Saul reneged on the deal: for example, Hertzberg, *I & II Samuel*, p. 161; Ackroyd, *First Samuel*, p. 153; Gunn, *Fate of Saul*, p. 81; Klein, *1 Samuel*, p. 186; Gordon, *I & II Samuel*, p. 161. Fokkelman (*Crossing Fates*, p. 233) correctly notes the use of passive forms to express Merab's marriage to another, so avoiding the explicit naming of Saul as the responsible party,

because he could not pay the requisite bride-price in time! His lack of wealth once again highlights Saul's failure to back up his previously issued edict in connection with Goliath's challenge in 17.25. David has received neither royal bride or personal wealth. The status of his father's house remains unconfirmed, although upon audience reflection, it would seem not to have been altered to that of *ḥopšî*. Since David apparently could not turn to them to gain the requisite financial support to produce the bride-price, he must have been helping support his family, who remained 'unfreed'.[1]

Learning of the reason for David's hesitation from the courtiers, Saul offers him the unconventional bride-price of one hundred Philistine foreskins in the hopes of David's meeting his death while collecting them. The prize is paid in double, and David becomes Saul's son-in-law and adoptive royal son, to the king's dismay and growing fear (vv. 27-29). David's delivery of 'double' the required foreskins reminds the audience of the other incidents involving 'doubles'. Saul has failed in both of his doubled attempts to kill David, first by his own hand under the influence of an evil spirit and then by the hand of the Philistines on his own initiative.

As noted by R. Alter and followed by R. Polzin,[2] the narrator deliberately avoids informing the audience of most of David's motivations within the chapter, in contrast to his spelling out of Saul's thoughts explicitly. Nevertheless, by having David's response to Saul's bride-price offer repeat Saul's reaction to learning that Michal loved David, he offers indirect commentary through analogy. 'The matter was pleasing in the eyes of PN' occurs first in v. 20, where it is connected with Saul's realization that he can now attempt to fell David by the hand of the Philistines, and a second time with a new marriage proposal. It thus has a negative association. When the same phrase is used about David's reaction in v. 26, it is connected with his realization that he can now become the king's son-in-law. The narrative

but concludes that the passive forms intentionally reveal how 'Saul shirks responsibility'. Polzin (*Samuel*, p. 177) goes so far as to claim that Merab had already been given to Adriel when the offer was made to David!

1. Fokkelman (*Crossing Fates*, p. 232) has seen David's declining of the marriage offer in v. 18 as an allusion to 17.25. But it is only with David's confiding of his poverty, *rāš*, in this second discussion of the new marriage proposal that the link with 17.25 becomes explicit.

2. Alter, *Art of Biblical Narrative*, pp. 114-19; Polzin, *Samuel*, pp. 176-80.

audience would consider such an opportunity to be *yāšār* in light of the king-elect's victory over Goliath and his status as *nāgîd*, but David's specific thoughts about why it would be *yāšār* to become Saul's son-in-law are deliberately withheld from the audience. Instead, we are informed only of David's actions; he eagerly moves to acquire the bride-price and does so before the allotted length of time has expired.

Why is David so eager to marry royalty? Because of the established analogy, a veil of suspicion is cast over his motivations for joining the royal family. Are Saul's suspicions about his possible assassination at the hand of the king-elect or one of his supporters totally unfounded, or are David's motivations pure and honorable?

The full weight of Yahweh's being with David is evident: Saul, like Balaam or like Joseph's brothers, is unable to make a move that would be harmful to Yahweh's chosen one. Regardless of his own personal intentions, his actions result in the furthering of Yahweh's divine plan and will. Saul's plan for David to die at the hand of the Philistines results instead in the man's marriage into the royal family and a string of victories over the Philistines because of his leadership, bringing instead of death for David, the great national honor and esteem that was fitting for the king-elect (v. 30).

Chapter 14

1 SAMUEL 19

Having had his personal plan for David to be killed by the Philistines fail twice and having Yahweh's chosen *nāgîd* as his son-in-law, Saul now moves to kill David from within his own ranks. He gives an order for his servants and his own son Jonathan to kill him (v. 1). Jonathan's status as Saul's son is emphasized through repetition in v. 1, seeming to suggest that Saul has become very concerned for the security of his son's future in face of David's popularity among the people and with God. Saul's ongoing attempts to eliminate David highlight the ambiguity already noted in the previous chapter concerning his underlying motivations. The narrator has refrained from disclosing his motives, and the only clue the narrative audience has received from his own lips about his motives was his fear that all David could have in the future that would go beyond his current accomplishments or possessions would be the kingdom (18.8).

With Saul's renewed attempt to have David killed, the audience is once again invited to speculate about the source of his fear concerning David's taking over of the kingdom that Yahweh has already declared he has lost: is he concerned for his personal safety and the possibility of assassination, or is he concerned about the possible continuation of his descendants on the throne?[1] In theory, his personal rejection by Yahweh has not precluded Jonathan's succession to the throne, even though he apparently is aware that David has been anointed as Yahweh's intended successor by Samuel. In either case, Saul's decision to try to kill off Yahweh's anointed and tested king-elect constitutes a

1. Jobling (*Sense of Biblical Narrative*, I, p. 20) suggests that the repetition signals that the identity of the father–son relationship is endangered. He suggests further that the repetition of Jonathan's name in vv. 6-7 is done to emphasize his mediatory role.

deliberate attempt to thwart the divine plan for the future of the monarchy in Israel.

In contrast to Saul however, Jonathan has accepted the divine plan for David's succession to the throne (18.1-4) and now must attempt to thwart his father's own plans, whatever their underlying motivation, in order to ensure the enactment of the divine will. His 'delight' in David in v. 1 (root *ḥpṣ*) mirrors Yahweh's purpose and plan for the young man and contrasts with his father's prior facetious use of the same verb to describe his stance toward David in 18.22.[1] He tells David of his father's death order, warns him to hide, and then offers to 'see' (verb *r'h*) whatever he can about Saul's thoughts concerning David and report them to him (v. 3). The unusual use of the expression *lᵉyād* in v. 3 to signify 'beside', when viewed in light of the prior uses of *yād* to represent 'power', portrays Jonathan as volun-teering to 'stand up' to his father's power on behalf of David, with whom he shares oneness of spirit (18.1). H.W. Hertzberg's suggestion that the troublesome phrase *'ᵃšer 'attâ šām* in the same verse refers not to the field but to the location 'by the hand of' Saul, expressing Jonathan's offer to serve as David's substitute, clearly captures the sense of the ensuing developments, even if it requires one to charge the author with having produced a dangling modifier.[2]

The identity between Jonathan and David appears again in v. 4 in Jonathan's statement to Saul, 'Do not sin against your servant, against David', where 'your servant', upon initial utterance, would refer to Jonathan. With the subsequent addition of the phrase 'against David', there is a semantic identification of Jonathan, 'your servant', with David, the new referent of 'your servant'. At the same time, Jonathan's blood-link to Saul is emphasized repeatedly through the repetition of the terms 'father' and 'son' in the narrative. By combining the two sets of identifications, David becomes Saul's son through syllogism.

Verses 4-5 reintroduce a number of motifs from previous episodes, using Jonathan's speech to Saul as a kind of résumé of past events for the audience as well as for Saul. The return of the motif *r'h* on Jonathan's lips suggests that he will be able to discern Saul's inward thoughts, seeing in the manner of Yahweh, rather than having to rely

1. So also Fokkelman, *Crossing Fates*, p. 250.
2. *I & II Samuel*, p. 163.

on clues about the king's intentions from his outward facade. Jonathan proceeds to speak 'well' (*ṭôb*) of David, reminding Saul that David's recent 'deeds' (root *'śh*) in which he risked his life to slay the Philistine had been very 'good' (*ṭôb*) for the king. Continuing, Jonathan states that through David, Yahweh 'made' (*'śh*) a great deliverance for all Israel that Saul himself 'saw' (*r'h*) and rejoiced over. Ending with a rhetorical question, Jonathan reminds his father that killing David without cause by shedding innocent blood would result in his committing sin (v. 5).

The prince's reference to the great victory Yahweh had wrought through David should recall to the minds of the narrative audience the people's perception of the great victory that Yahweh had wrought through Jonathan at the Michmash pass. Their perception had been incorrect and had been followed by Jonathan's realization that Yahweh had condemned him for breaking his father's divinely invoked ban (14.45-46). By affirming that David's slaying of Goliath was indeed a saving deed by Yahweh on Israel's behalf, Jonathan seems to be indirectly confessing his knowledge that David, not he, is Yahweh's confirmed *nāgîd* who will follow Saul to the throne of Israel.

Jonathan's entire address to his father seems to be carefully constructed to remind the king of his rejection by Yahweh and of David's designation and successful testing as his divinely chosen successor. His twofold application of the term *ṭôb* to describe David is followed by the closing rhetorical question. The mention of 'sin' in the question should have reminded Saul of his personal rejection in ch. 15 for his commitment of sin against Yahweh in his failure to shed guilty Amalekite blood completely and of Yahweh's announced choice of a man who was 'better' (*ṭôb*) than him to become the new king.[1] Yahweh's use of the expression *ṭôb* to characterize Saul's chosen successor should then have resonated with Jonathan's twofold use of the same term to describe David, reminding the king of his knowledge that David was indeed Yahweh's chosen *nāgîd*. At the same time, Jonathan's singling out of David's slaying of Goliath among his many 'deeds' that had benefitted the king apparently was calculated to drive home to Saul his knowledge that David's confidence going into that

1. The link with ch. 15 has also been noted by Fokkelman (*Crossing Fates*, p. 257) and Miscall (*1 Samuel*, p. 126). Both stress the occurrence of the term 'sin' in the two chapters.

duel stemmed from his possession of divine spirit (17.37).

Being persuaded by Jonathan's discerning words, a trait associated with David in 16.18 and now being illustrated by his soul mate or alter ego, Saul swears an oath not to have David killed (v. 6). D. Jobling and J. Fokkelman have noted the close parallels in vv. 6-7 to Jonathan's trial at the end of the battle at the Michmash pass in 14.36-46. In each case, the apparent king-elect is under Saul's death sentence but is saved by external mediation to which Saul acquiesces.[1] I believe they are correct to note the presence of echoes from 14.36-46, but that the echoes are intended to lead the narrative audience to contrast Jonathan's earlier situation with the one David is now experiencing, rather than to recapitulate it. Jonathan had broken a divinely invoked food ban and was designated guilty by Yahweh himself. He was subject to the divinely invoked death sentence of the king. Although his life was ransomed by the troops, it was done in a way that apparently was ineffectual in removing his guilt before Yahweh. By contrast, David has done nothing wrong, but has been sentenced to death by the king's personal decree without Yahweh's backing. Jonathan's 'ransoming' speech is an attempt to make his father recognize the lack of legitimate grounds for killing David by contrastively alluding to his own situation in the past, where the ransoming should not have taken place, but did—all the more reason to halt the looming unjustifiable death sentence.[2] Jonathan then repeats the whole exchange to David and institutes David's restoration to Saul's service.

While peaceful relations between the king and king-elect last for a while, they are broken as a result of another war with the Philistines, in which the *nāgîd* brings home a victory (v. 8). Saul is then reposses-

1. Jobling, *Sense of Biblical Narrative*, I, p. 20; Fokkelman, *Crossing Fates*, pp. 256-57.

2. Miscall (*1 Samuel*, p. 127) has drawn attention to the link between the lifting of a death sentence and Yahweh's making of victory found here and elsewhere in 11.12-13 and 14.45. In the latter two instances, the two are drawn into a cause-and-effect chain, whereas in Jonathan's speech, they are juxtaposed as part of a larger speech to dissuade Saul from David's death sentence, but are only one of many possible cause-and-effect chains that are presented by Jonathan. Since Saul's reasons for lifting the sentence are not revealed, the audience is left to ponder whether this otherwise effective chain has been the decisive point for Saul, or something else—hence Miscall's characterization of the text as 'opaque'.

sed by an evil spirit, this time one sent by Yahweh, and for a third time tries to kill David under its influence as the latter played his lyre (vv. 9-10).[1] In the previous two instances, David evaded Saul through action associated with the verb *sbb*, remaining in his presence. This time, he flees (*nws*) from Saul's presence, escaping unaided, at night. As a result, Saul pursues him, sending messengers to stand guard outside his house and kill him in the morning.

His wife Michal, who also was Saul's daughter, but whose relationship as spouse to David is emphasized in her identification (v. 11), warns David that he must escape himself that very night or be killed in the morning. Her words put the burden of managing to escape on David personally: *'im-'ên^{e}kā, m^{e}mallēṭ 'et-napš^{e}ka hallaylâ*, 'if *you* will not save your (own) life tonight', you will be dead (v. 11). They seem to belie a double bind she is in by virtue of her status as royal princess and wife to David: the bind of conflicting loyalty to father and to husband. The precise meaning of her statement to David remains highlighted as the narrator avoids telling or simply fails to tell the narrative audience whether Michal's ensuing actions are part of her self-made plan to save the husband she is said to love (18.20) or whether they are a plan put together by David in response to her initial announcement that he must work out his own escape plan.[2] As a result, additional suspicion about David's motivations and character seem to be raised.

As a dutiful and loving wife, Michal has notified her spouse of the danger he is in from the king. However, as a presumably dutiful daughter, she cannot in good conscience actively plan her husband's escape from her father's decree. Thus, her emphasis that David must save his own life that same night, implying that he must formulate his own plan for escape and she, as an obedient wife, will then have to do whatever he orders her to, seems to reveal her master plan for satisfy-

1. The significance of the elapsed time between 19.7 and 19.8, with the restored status quo only being breached by the combination of war and the evil spirit, was emphasized by Stuart Lasine in correspondence.

2. Contrast the common acceptance that Michal is lying to her father and has acted on her own: for example, Auzou, *Danse devant l'arche*, p. 189; Hertzberg, *I & II Samuel*, p. 166; Ackroyd, *First Samuel*, p. 157; McCarter, *I Samuel*, p. 326; Alter, *Art of Biblical Narrative*, p. 120; Berlin, *Poetics of Biblical Narrative*, p. 25; Klein, *1 Samuel*, p. 197; Sternberg, *Poetics*, p. 244; Fokkelman, *Crossing Fates*, p. 269; Miscall, *1 Samuel*, p. 127.

ing both parties and remaining in the good graces of each. The narrator states that Michal caused David to be lowered out of the window to effect his escape, just as Rahab did to help the Israelite spies escape from Jericho in Josh. 2.15, 18, and that she pretended he was sick in order to buy him extra lead time in his flight. The audience is thus initially led to believe that she herself formulated the entire plan for escape as part of her own solution to her bind, playing husband off against father in her attempt to salvage her situation. She appears to have been personally responsible for thwarting the three sets of messengers sent by Saul with different orders designed to remove him from his home and deliver him to Saul for killing (vv. 11, 14, 15).

Michal's responsibility for the escape plan seems to be reinforced by her position as the subject of the reported actions in vv. 12-14. As was noted in the previous chapter, the use of passive verbs to describe Merab's marriage to another turned out to be an accurate reflection of responsibility: it was David, not Saul, who broke the marriage contract. Here then, Michal's active participation in David's escape would seem to imply that the plan was her own. If the incident with the teraphim in vv. 13-16 is intended to be a deliberate recollection of Rachel's deceiving her father in connection with teraphim,[1] then Michal's active role in formulating the plan would also be emphasized.

However, Michal's response to Saul's angry accusation that she has sent his enemy away so that he has escaped introduces the alternative possibility that David was responsible for the plan after all, as she had told him he must be, and that she was merely an obedient player. She states, 'He himself said to me, "Send me away; why should I kill you?"' (v. 17), emphasizing that she was only following the orders of her husband and so was not personally responsible for his departure. When her statement is put beside her opening statement to David that he must escape *himself*, it is no longer certain that she has acted on her own initiative; her claim to have followed orders becomes a real possibility.

It is noteworthy that Saul does not identify Michal as his daughter in their conversation; this would appear to be a deliberate attempt by

1. So esp. Alter, *Art of Biblical Narrative*, p. 120. Fokkelman (*Crossing Fates*, p. 276), followed by Polzin (*Samuel*, p. 182), suggests that the incident anticipates the scene with the medium of Endor in 18.12.

him to indicate that he intends to 'disown' her for her loyalty to her husband. Is the second part of Michal's response, then, the revelation of the alleged threat to her life, a lie geared to gain sympathy from her father by reminding him of their blood-bond in the hopes of regaining his fatherly support and escaping any possible reprisal he might impose in his anger? Or, is it merely a statement of the actual course of events that evening?

Neither parallels with the immediately preceding incident with Jonathan nor prior information concerning the relationship between David and Michal allow the audience to decide whether or not Michal has lied to her father. Although the scene between Michal and David resembles the one between Jonathan and David in that both involve the formulation of a plan at night between David and one of Saul's children to spare David's life against the command of the king, there are subtle, though important differences. Whereas Jonathan's identity as Saul's son is stressed, here Michal's identity as David's wife is stressed.[1] Whereas Jonathan clearly announces to David his plan to act as mediator to learn of his father's intentions, Michal announces to David his need to escape on his own initiative, implying his need to formulate his own plan. Michal's previously revealed love for David would allow either interpretation of her actions to be plausible and does not help the audience choose one over the other. Since the audience has not been informed of David's reciprocal love for Michal, his possible threat to her life should she not help him is not inconsistent with any known character trait. David's questionable motivations now seem to appear a second time (cf. 18.26) in connection with his marriage into the royal family.

The ruse used by Michal to buy David time by pretending he was sick and performing a healing ceremony over him (vv. 13-16) would have had many overtones for the ancient audience. First, sickness was often associated with affliction by an evil spirit in the ancient world. Saul's attempt to have David killed while himself under the influence of the malevolent spirit was therefore an ironic reversal of the true state of affairs: it was Saul, not David, who was truly sick and needed to be healed by the magical rite that Michal appeared to be applying to David. The situation plays with the idea of appearance versus reality,

1. Berlin (*Poetics of Biblical Narrative*, pp. 24-25) emphasizes the masculinity of Michal's traits in contrast to the femininity of Jonathan's traits *vis-à-vis* Saul.

'seeing' and 'truly seeing', which was stressed in ch. 17. Another irony centers on Michal's use of a ceremony of healing that ordinarily was used to protect a person from death or the menace of evil supernatural spirits to protect her husband from death at the hand of her own human father.[1] A third irony involves the presumed use of Saul's ancestral gods by Michal to protect David from their living descendant, which results in a turning of the family gods against their own kin.

Although all the literary twists on the ancient healing ritual that are employed in vv. 13-16 are beyond the ken of the modern audience, certain implications are clear. As described by H. Rouillard and J. Tropper,[2] ordinarily two approaches could be taken to healing a sick person through substitution. Both involved the creation of a substitute representing the sick person, which was put beside that person so that the sickness would transfer to it. The substitute was then destroyed, taking with it the malady, and the family teraphim or ancestral gods were feasted in appreciation for their assistance. The substitute figure could either be an effigy of straw or mud, or an animal, usually a goat or a sheep. The substitute was dressed in clothes belonging to the sick person, and a piece of the person's hair was attached to it. In the case of the figure, it was placed inside the bed alongside the sick person; the animal was tied up beside the bed.

Michal appears to have feigned David's sickness by creating a substitute figure that was in bed where it was supposed to be, blocking the messengers' view of the allegedly ailing David on its other side.[3] Her use of goat hair to simulate a lock of David's hair played off the acceptable use of a goat as a substitute figure in the healing ritual. When the messengers went over to the bed on their return trip under Saul's orders, they discovered that the substitute had indeed 'stood in'

1. H. Rouillard and J. Tropper, '*trpym*, rituels de guérison et culte des ancêtres d'après 1 Samuel xix 11-17 et les textes parallèles d'Assur et de Nuzi', *VT* 37 (1987), p. 347.

2. Rouillard and Tropper, '*trpym*'. In a similar vein, see Auzou, *Danse devant l'arche*, p. 190.

3. The interesting suggestion by Ackroyd (*First Samuel*, p. 158) that Rachel put the teraphim beside the bed rather than in the bed for a protective function has correctly sensed the ritualistic context in the scene, but has not fully grasped its specifics. Fokkelman's attempt to assign the teraphim a fertility role seems to overlook the clear healing context (*Crossing Fates*, p. 273).

for the absent David, who had fled long ago, and that one of the ancestral figurines of Saul's family had been used to ward off the evil spirit for whom they served as messenger, its kinsman Saul, at the same time protecting David, the adopted family member, from certain death.

David's escape is not totally successful; Saul is informed that he is in Naioth in Ramah. The audience has been told that David has fled there to meet with Samuel, his anointer (v. 18), but Saul does not seem to have this same information, even though he has been given enough clues to deduce it for himself. The scene at Ramah has structural parallels to the preceding scene involving David's feigned illness. Both scenes focus on Saul's pursuit of David and his attempt to kill him. Both involve the unsuccessful sending of three sets of messengers to apprehend the fugitive. Saul's stripping under ecstatic influence (v. 24) produces a reverse image of the dressing up of the teraphim in David's clothes (v. 13).[1]

Verse 20 depicts a situation where Samuel is standing as presider over an assembly of ecstatic prophets. The LXX version of v. 20 must be adopted over the corrupted, nonsensical MT reading, as is widely acknowledged. By implication, David has joined the band of prophets, since he is with Samuel. Yet he does not catch the contagious prophetic spirit that afflicts the outsiders. As noted by others,[2] the repetition of the phrase *gam-hēmmâ/hû'* six times, after each affected party prophesies, highlights the spreading divine power.

The situation of a group of ecstatic prophets recalls Saul's joining of the prophetic band after his anointing by Samuel in 10.5-12. There, he appeared to onlookers to catch their 'fever' when he began to prophesy among them, even though the narrative audience knew that this was part of a pre-arranged sign to prove to Saul that his anointing was from Yahweh. His possession by the prophesying spirit made him a part of the divine sphere, an insider who possessed divine favor. By contrast, in this scene the king-elect seems to remain 'uninfected' by the prophetic spirit, in contrast to everyone else around him,

1. So previously, for example, Fokkelman (*Crossing Fates*, p. 285), who states that the stripping also anticipates Saul's death and stripping by the Philistines in 31.9, and Polzin (*Samuel*, p. 181).

2. For example, Auzou, *Danse devant l'arche*, p. 190 n. 34; Fokkelman, *Crossing Fates*, p. 278; Polzin, *Samuel*, p. 182.

including Saul, although this point is only made indirectly by the narrator.[1] Yet, the circle of insiders and outsiders has been reversed: now David is part of the inside circle that is being protected from harm by rendering outsiders harmless through spirit possession. The prophetic power is creating a kind of 'force field' to protect Yahweh's *nāgîd* from harm. Before, Saul was included among the insiders by virtue of his prophetic power, which set him apart from the unaffected world at large. Now he is left naked, symbolically stripped of his dignity and royal symbols of authority.[2] The ambiguous nature of prophetic possession is ably demonstrated through the contrastive use of the *māšāl*, 'Is Saul also among the prophets?' in chs. 10 and 19. The entire incident, with its focus on Saul, highlights the king's fate as one who has been rejected for disobedience to divine command: he has become the victim of the dark side of the divine spirit.

1. Polzin's suggestion (*Samuel*, pp. 184-86) that the deliberate contrast highlights David's escape from the evils resulting from the 'illicit commingling' of prophecy with kingship and is the central concern of the scene does not seem warranted in light of the failure of the narrator to draw specific attention to David's lack of possession. This is merely implied in the scene, where the focus is rather on Saul and his subsequent encounter with the prophetic spirit after his rejection.

2. So noted by Gordon, *I & II Samuel*, p. 165.

Chapter 15

1 SAMUEL 20

The chapter relates a second encounter between David and Jonathan over Saul's intentions to kill David, building upon the first encounter in 19.1-7. David is said to flee from the prophetic frenzy at Naioth to Jonathan and to ask him in accusing tones why Saul still seeks his life. The narrator has artfully aligned Jonathan and Saul as father and son in v. 1 by stating that David's speech took place *lipnê y*[e]*hônātān*, 'before Jonathan', and then by having David ask what his sin is, what he has done (verb *'śh*) before Jonathan's father, *lipnê 'ābîkā*. Father and son stand united, with David as their petitioner, reminding the audience of their positions side by side in 19.3.[1] The reappearance of the term 'sin' and the verb *'śh* similarly recall the key terms of Jonathan's prior speech to Saul that resulted in the king's oath that David would not die.

Jonathan's reply in v. 2, *ḥālîlâ lō' tāmût*, plays off Saul's formal oath in 19.6, but at the same time does not bear the same weight of authority, containing *lō'* instead of the prohibitive *'al* and *ḥālîlâ* instead of the divine invocation, *ḥay yhwh*. The implication that Jonathan may not be able to guarantee David's safety or his father's honoring of his oath by playing a mediatory role is expounded in the following discourse.[2] He feels he can protect David because Saul has made him his confidant and does not 'act' without 'baring his son's ear'. The verb *'śh* is repeated, contrasting David's 'doing' of military

1. Contrast the interpretation of the parallel phrases by Fokkelman (*Crossing Fates*, p. 296). Jobling (*Sense of Biblical Narrative*, I, p. 21) extends the imagery identifying Saul and Jonathan into v. 2 with Jonathan's speech.

2. Contrast Gunn (*Fate of Saul*, p. 84), who sees the statement as a naïve reference to Saul's oath. Miscall (*Workings of OT Narrative*, p. 108) has seen the parallel, but offers a different interpretation.

deeds as Yahweh's new *nāgîd* with Saul's inability to *do* without consulting his son Jonathan, emphasizing the tension resulting from the situation. The question and answer recall David's question-and-answer response to Eliab's accusation in 17.29, which also hinted at David's need to 'do' a military deed as Yahweh's representative.[1]

The use of the phrase *yigleh 'et-'oznî* deliberately echoes the use of a similar phrase in 8.21 to describe Samuel's prophetic consultation of Yahweh and the use of the identical phrase in 9.15 to describe Yahweh's revelation to Samuel of his choice of Saul as king-elect to deliver Israel from the hand of the Philistines and maintain Israel's fidelity to the covenant. Since the idiom can have overtones of divine revelation, the contrast between David, who now is the receiver of Yahweh's revelations and doer of his will, and Saul, who can no longer receive divine revelations and so must seek the advice of his son for military matters, is heightened. The resulting picture emphasizes Saul's loss of divine support once again, but at the same time implies that he feels that his son may not yet have been totally rejected from the throne by Yahweh. He is misguidedly looking to his son to receive indirect divine support, instead of to David, whose repeatedly successful 'doings' illustrate his clear possession of divine favor, in contrast to Jonathan.[2]

David's response to Jonathan's reassurance seems designed to stress his close link to Yahweh and so to secure the help of the passed-over heir-elect in ensuring the realization of the divine will. He begins by setting Jonathan over against his father, shattering the image created in his opening words. His reference to his present 'favor' in Jonathan's eyes should recall for the narrative audience Saul's ominous use of the same phrase to describe David and persuade Jesse, unsuccessfully, to release him for service at the court in 16.22, creating a contrast between the stance of the two royal figures towards David. It also should establish for all concerned that Jonathan's acceptance of David's status as king-elect has become public knowledge. David's oath couples his own life with Yahweh's (*ḥay yhwh wᵉḥê napšᵉkā*),

1. Miscall (*Workings of OT Narrative*, p. 106) similarly links the question to David's response to Eliab as well as to his future questions in 16.1 and 29.8.

2. Contrast, for example, Fokkelman (*Crossing Fates*, p. 306) and Polzin (*Samuel*, p. 189), who see it to stress Jonathan's ignorance/self-deceit concerning his true relationship with his father.

thereby subtly impressing upon Jonathan his need to forego family loyalty once again in order to ensure that Yahweh's will for succession is not thwarted, by implying that the royal son is the only 'step' separating David from death.[1]

Jonathan's counterresponse signals his understanding of the true stakes. He tells David he will enact (*'e'eśeh*) for David's benefit whatever David's 'soul' (*népeš*) commands (v. 4). In light of David's equation of his *népeš* with Yahweh's life-force, Jonathan's response indicates to David his acceptance of the divine will that has chosen him as Saul's successor and his readiness to work actively toward making the divine plan a reality. His words are reminiscent of those spoken to him by his weapons-bearer in 14.7; he now symbolically becomes David's weapons-bearer, having already turned over to him the weapons of the office of king-elect. His new symbolic duty is to defend the life of his superior with his own life. The narrator's use throughout the chapter of the full form of Jonathan's name *yehônātān*, thereby stressing Yahweh's action in giving, should be seen as another deliberate move to symbolize Jonathan's acceptance of the divine will and his readiness to serve as a vehicle for its implementation.

David then lays out the plan he has formulated to Jonathan. As before, it involves David's hiding in the open field while Jonathan ascertains his father's intentions toward David. Unlike the first time, though, David instead of Jonathan takes the initiative to work out the strategy and chooses one that cannot but remind Saul of the rumored circumstances of his anointing in Bethlehem at a sacrifice, as well as the king's own prohibition made in v. 2 that forbade David to return home again.[2] David's role as initiator should remind the narrative audience about the ambiguity of who was responsible for the plan in the intervening scene between Michal and David and leaves it still unresolved. David's taking of initiative here tends to reinforce the plausibility of his action with Michal earlier, although it does not rule out her own initiative, which seemed during the opening portion of

1. McCarter (*I Samuel*, p. 341) restores an underlying Hebrew text *kî nišba'* for the MT text *kepésa'* on the basis of LXX, reading 'he has sworn between me and death'. If he is correct, the choice of words would deliberately contrast David's pact with Jonathan with Saul's alleged pact between David and death, again separating father and son in their stance towards David.

2. The connection with 18.2 was previously noted by Gunn (*Fate of Saul*, p. 85) and adopted by Polzin (*Samuel*, p. 189).

the story to be more plausible. Again recalling the exchange between Jonathan and his weapons-bearer, David, having assumed Jonathan's position, lays out a two-option scenario that is designed to reveal Saul's will, just as earlier it was designed to reveal Yahweh's will (vv. 5-7; cf. 14.8-10).

Having laid out the plan, David appeals directly to the pact that Jonathan had sworn with David in 18.3, the pact initiated by Jonathan, which is now more fully described as a *b*ᵉ*rît yhwh*. He urges Jonathan to uphold the pact by observing its accompanying *ḥésed* or loyalty obligations. David's twofold self-description in v. 8 as 'your servant' when referring to the pact must be understood to convey more than the normal form of politeness owed to a member of the royal family. Unfortunately, the modern audience cannot be certain of the overtones intended because the precise meaning of 'a covenant of Yahweh' is no longer clear. It would seem to be an agreement to which Yahweh was made witness; whether it could be a contract that made the parties equal in responsibility or made one superior to the other is not clear, although the appeal to *ḥésed* might suggest that a vassal-style pact was envisioned.

David's request that Jonathan slay him directly if he has found him 'guilty' (*'āwôn*) instead of delivering him to Saul to be killed (v. 8) now challenges Jonathan to declare his stand concerning loyalty—will he honor family ties or his 'covenant of Yahweh' first? David's use of the term *'āwôn* instead of *ḥaṭṭā'* to describe possible charges of wrongdoing may be a deliberate attempt to separate Jonathan from Saul on a semantic level.

Jonathan's reply in v. 9 avers his primary loyalty to David, Yahweh's anointed. Yet his closing words form a rhetorical question to which David needs an absolutely unambiguous answer. David therefore forces Jonathan into a clarification of his decision by taking up an apparent 'loophole' in the proposed plan: 'who will tell me if your father answers you harshly?' (v. 10). The question once again zeroes in on the key issue of loyalty—what if Jonathan has a change of heart in response to his father's negative attitude and sides with family after all? In the instance with Michal, her statement that David had threatened her with bodily harm unless she co-operated seems to have been specifically designed by herself or by David to allow her back into her family's graces. Here, David is afraid that Jonathan will back out of his plan with him because of the inevitable fall from family grace that the prince will encounter. David awaits Jonathan's definitive answer.

Taking David out to the field, where the narrative audience can imagine the two standing side by side just as Saul and Jonathan had stood in ch. 19 (*wayyēṣᵉ'û šᵉnêhem*, v. 11), Jonathan swears by Yahweh, the God of Israel, that he will reveal (*gālâ 'et-'ōzen*) to David whatever his father's intentions are and allow him to escape if they are evil (vv. 12-13). Jonathan's use of the title 'Yahweh God of Israel' seems designed to indicate that his action has national ramifications,[1] while his use of the phrase 'uncover the ear' should remind the audience of his prior use of the phrase to characterize his position as his father's confidant. It is his privileged position as inside family member that will allow him to serve as mediating go-between to prove his loyalty to David by betraying his father's confidence. His closing prayer, 'May Yahweh be with you, as he *was* with my father', reveals his motivating consideration: he knows that Yahweh has abandoned Saul and now has bestowed his favor upon David, his 'king-elect'. Jonathan's 'prayer' is rhetorical in its request, echoing the more certain averral by Saul that Yahweh is with David in 17.37. The prayer again conveys to the audience Jonathan's consistent desire to implement the divine will, at the same time highlighting Saul's initial acceptance of the divine will, but his subsequent decision to try to thwart it by killing David.[2]

Before answering the procedural aspect of David's question, Jonathan lays out the obligations that David must fulfill under the terms of their pact. If the royal son survives his mission and is not killed by his own father because of his loyalty to David, David is to uphold the 'loyalty of Yahweh' and not kill Jonathan or any of his family (*bêtî*) at any time in the future (vv. 14-15). The loyalty extends to Jonathan's immediate family—wives, children, parents, and siblings, and thus is a long-term pact to be honored for generations between the house of Jonathan and the house of David (v. 16a). Jonathan then makes David reconfirm the pact by swearing an oath stating his covenantal love, thereby binding the lives of the two

1. So too, Fokkelman, *Crossing Fates*, p. 310.

2. Miscall (*Workings of OT Narrative*, p. 114) raises a question concerning the intention of Jonathan's wish that David receive Yahweh's support, which had proven to be disastrous for Saul.

together as one. As widely recognized, this loyalty will be executed in 2 Samuel 19.

The final phrase of v. 17 recalls the onset of Jonathan's 'love' in 18.1. At that point, his 'affection' seemed to be one more unfortunate, ironic blow to the royal house and seemed to characterize Jonathan as a naïve, unsuspecting youth. However, in retrospect, he seems to have understood the import of the duel with Goliath completely and acted with quick shrewdness. He seems to have recognized that David had passed his test as *nāgîd* by killing Goliath and, while willing to accept the divine decision for David to follow Saul on the throne, he apparently recognized the potential danger he and his family would be in should David attempt to take the throne by force. By purportedly establishing his pact with David on the spot, he was able to secure the favor and future obligatory action of the king-elect.[1]

His wise move has now paid off. In the narrative flow of events, he has just secured his personal safety and that of his immediate family against the typical blood-baths that accompanied changes of dynasty by appealing to the pact. He has been willing to sacrifice his crown in exchange for the guarantee of the lives of his family, showing himself to be a pragmatist.[2] When Jonathan lays out the final signal that will let David know if he should return to court or flee (vv. 18-22), it comes only as an afterthought to the main exchange, whose purpose has already been accomplished. A young boy will serve as the unknowing messenger between the two. The meeting ends with a reminder of the covenantally guaranteed plan that has just been established, the main focus of the conversation.

The remaining verses (23-42) narrate the execution of the plan. Saul becomes suspicious of David's absence on the second day and questions Jonathan. Jonathan uses the excuse suggested by David, his need to attend an annual sacrifice for his extended family or lineage (*mišpāḥâ*), but elaborates the details. The narrative audience should be alert to the importance of the additional information. Jonathan states

1. Miscall (*Workings of OT Narrative*, p. 115) also recognized the deliberate manipulation undertaken by Jonathan. Contrast Gunn, *Fate of Saul*, pp. 84-85; Fokkelman, *Crossing Fates*, p. 312; Polzin, *Samuel*, pp. 188-89.

2. This is particularly true if v. 16b was originally a curse, as was proposed by Smith (*Books of Samuel*, p. 189) and has been followed by Klein (*1 Samuel*, p. 208). I find this a strong possibility.

that David asked him to grant him leave 'because he commanded me, my brother. Now then, if I have found favor in your eyes, let me escape (*mlṭ*) and see my brothers.' The prince's words yield a double entendre, since David and Jonathan have now become 'brothers' through their pact and David has indeed requested that the king's son, his 'brother', permit him to 'escape' to safety and so preserve his own family.[1] The verb *mlṭ* was used repeatedly in the preceding chapter to describe David's flight from Saul (vv. 10, 11, 12, 17, 18) and so is deliberately loaded in its use by Jonathan to Saul.[2]

Jonathan's words provoke Saul's anger, as would be expected, particularly since David's prior escape (*mlṭ*) was through the assistance of Jonathan's sister; the royal family is aiding and abetting a declared enemy of the crown. In addition, David's supposed return home to participate in a sacrifice cannot help but remind Saul of David's rumored anointing by Samuel under similar circumstances.[3] Saul's response confirms the implications of Jonathan's earlier statement in v. 2 that the king believes or hopes that Jonathan might yet be able to become his successor to the throne. He stresses Jonathan's 'choice' to forego blood ties ('your mother's nakedness'), using the same verb that was used in 16.8-10 to describe the process of selection of the new anointed among Jesse's sons and reminding the audience that in contrast to Samuel, Jonathan has made the correct choice.[4] He then states directly that Jonathan and his kingdom (*malkûtekā*) will not be established (verb *hēkîn*) as long as the insignificant 'son of Jesse' is alive (v. 31). His words ironically recall Samuel's words of warning to Saul in 13.13: Yahweh would have established your kingship to Israel but now your kingship will not be established. They should remind the audience of the former ambiguity in 13.13 concerning Jonathan's ability to sit on the throne before the cutting off of the house, caused by the temporal phrase 'forever'.

Saul's command that Jonathan bring David to him 'because he is a

1. Contrast Miscall (*Workings of OT Narrative*, p. 106), who links 'brother' to Eliab in 17.28-29 and 'brothers' to the coming scene at the cave of Adullam in 22.1. Sternberg (*Poetics*, p. 435) concludes that Jonathan's misquote is non-deliberate and that the narrator did not intend to reveal anything about his character through it.

2. So too, Fokkelman, *Crossing Fates*, p. 332.

3. So previously, Fokkelman, *Crossing Fates*, p. 337.

4. Similarly, Fokkelman, *Crossing Fates*, p. 335. There is no need to adopt the implied LXX text *ḥbr*.

son of death' is a direct order to the heir-elect to conspire with him to thwart the divine plan by killing Yahweh's designated and tested 'king-elect'. Saul's words reveal that he knows the divine plan, which calls for David to succeed him on the throne instead of Jonathan, but that he intends to thwart it so that Jonathan may be given a chance to rule in spite of Yahweh's rejection. It is still unclear whether Saul has understood the import of the divine guilty verdict against Jonathan in 14.42. He may be falsely hoping that his personal rejection has not affected Jonathan's chances to succeed him, failing to recognize that the heir-elect has sealed his own fate with Yahweh through his insubordination at Michmash. Alternatively, he may well be aware of Jonathan's guilt before Yahweh, but may have decided that the heir-elect will still be able to gain the throne through natural succession and the support of the citizenry (who have not understood the import of the guilty verdict), if only David can be eliminated.

Ironically, Saul's characterization of Jonathan in v. 31 as 'the son of one twisted by rebellion', retaining the MT consonantal text over the LXX, echoes David's prior question to Jonathan in v. 1 'what is my *'āwôn*?', emphasizing that both parties are indeed guiltless before Yahweh. At the same time, Saul's characterization of his wife proves to be a misplaced self-characterization, since it is he who has become twisted by his rebellious obsession to thwart the divine plan. Just as the repetition of the root *'wh* tends to link David and Jonathan, so does Saul's use of the semantic construction 'son of' to describe both.

Jonathan's second attempt to dissuade his father from his useless attempt to thwart the divine plan and lift his newly pronounced death sentence against David that breaks his own divinely sworn oath from 19.6 results in his father's attempt to kill him. Jonathan's two questions in v. 32 try to make Saul recognize what he already knows, that David's 'deeds' (verb *'śh*) are done with Yahweh's support, so that to kill him would be to thwart the divine plan and bring disaster upon himself and the nation. They only provoke the king further (he has already declared his intent to thwart the plan in v. 31), leading him to strike out with his spear at his own son in blind rage, just as he had against David on three prior occasions. Jonathan's clearly declared alignment with David leads to his momentary sharing of the same declared royal death sentence before his father, a possibility that the heir had anticipated in v. 14. Notwithstanding, Saul's action almost thwarts his own twisted, rebellious plan to place his son on the throne by killing the heir-elect himself. As a result of Saul's action, Jonathan 'feels pain' for David (v. 34), recalling David's earlier use of *'ṣb* in v. 3 to suggest why Saul might not disclose all of his plans concerning the chosen *nāgîd* to Jonathan.[1]

The final scene recounts Jonathan's modified enactment of the prearranged signal to David. After shooting an unspecified number of arrows and sending the youth to retrieve them, he shoots one arrow behind the youth and says the appropriate words, instead of the prearranged shooting of three arrows behind the youth. Jonathan then sends the lad back into the town with his weapons and initiates a final personal exchange with David. The reintroduction of the theme of weapons-bearer should remind the audience of Jonathan's earlier symbolic assumption of this role on David's behalf in 18.4 and v. 4, which now is reinstated. His act allows the two to talk in privacy, but at the same time demonstrates his nonaggressive stance toward David and his continuing loyalty, even after the encounter with his father.[2] The narrator's twofold use of the phrase *'îš 'et-rē'ēhû* in v. 41 to describe the exchange between the two seems to be a deliberate attempt to remind the audience of Samuel's declaration to Saul in 15.28 that Yahweh had given the kingdom of Israel to Saul's *rē'â*. His use of the somewhat awkward *higdîl*, 'to magnify', to describe the end result of David's experience similarly stresses David's ascendancy.

The scene concludes with Jonathan's reminder to David of the divinely overseen eternal pact between the two and their descendants (*zéra'*), which was the reason for his desire to speak to David once more before his flight. The preservation of Jonathan's progeny is the price David has paid for Jonathan's serving as the 'step' between himself and death (v. 3). Jonathan's threefold repetition of the terms of the pact in vv. 14-17, 23 and 42 stress that the eternal pact between the two houses of David and Jonathan was the central focus of the chapter and reveal the active and skillful self-preservation abilities of the passed over heir-elect.

1. So also, for example, Miscall, *Workings of OT Narrative*, pp. 109, 116; Fokkelman, *Crossing Fates*, p. 298.

2. Fokkelman (*Crossing Fates*, pp. 324, 248-49) also notes the connection with 18.4. I find no need to go so far as to posit an identification between the youth and David, however.

Chapter 16

1 SAMUEL 21

With Saul's new pronouncement that David is a 'son of death' (20.31), David has become an official fugitive of the state in the narrative flow of events. Leaving Jonathan, who returns to town where the New Moon feast was observed, presumably to the capital, David goes to Nob, specifically to Ahimelech the priest (v. 1). His destination is a person, just as when he had fled to Samuel at Ramah in 19.18. Ahimelech's identification as a priest immediately raises the possibility that David has sought asylum in order to protect his life, particularly when he has not been accused of a particular crime by the king who has issued his death warrant.

Ahimelech's trembling response (v. 2) quickly rules out this option, however, since he should not be afraid of one seeking asylum. He trembles because the person who has arrived is David and because David is alone, with no man with him (v. 2). David's solitude is emphasized by the priest's reference to it with two consecutive phrases, *'attâ l^e^baddekā w^e^'îš 'ên 'ittāk*. What has Ahimelech heard of the recent New Moon incident; does he know that David has fallen from royal favor again? Ahimelech's trembling introduces suspense into the plot line.

The priest's statement reminds the narrative audience that David must now protect himself, without the help of members of the royal family or other human intermediaries. The king-elect will be in potential danger for the balance of the story. At the same time, it reminds us that David has Yahweh with him and so does not need human assistance to avoid whatever danger he will encounter. Ahimelech's 'trembling' recalls the trembling of the elders of Bethlehem in 16.4 at Samuel's arrival. Both instances of fear result from the arrival of a public figure who has fallen from favor with the king—a royal 'enemy'. It is possible that distant echoes of the

Israelites trembling at the Michmash pass before the superior enemy forces are also meant to be heard.[1]

David frames a response that will allay Ahimelech's fears but simultaneously allow him to move forward in realizing his purpose in seeking out this particular priest. As noted by J. Fokkelman, the number of words spoken by David and Ahimelech are inversely proportional to the level of fear. After Ahimelech's brief greeting David makes long explanations that gradually conquer Ahimelech's suspicions. As the priest becomes more calm, he begins to answer David in longer and longer statements, while David cuts his words back to a minimum, allowing the priest to take over and work for him.[2] David assures Ahimelech that he is on a secret mission from the king himself and only temporarily lacking human support; he will link up with the other *nᵉʿārîm* at the appointed place.[3] The priest apparently knows David from his official capacity as army commander (18.13) since he recognizes him and expects him to be accompanied by others. He finds David's explanation reassuring and in character.

J. Fokkelman, followed by R. Polzin, has noted the double entendre in David's statement that 'the king' has appointed him to a certain matter and sent him in secret (v. 3). While he intends Ahimelech to presume that he is referring to Saul and is clearly fabricating a false cover story—there is no rendezvous with other personnel—the narrative audience is able to recognize the dramatic irony in his words. Unbeknown to Ahimelech, they can been seen to refer to the divine king Yahweh, who has anointed him to be king-elect, thereby sending him on a special mission that must remain unconfirmed public information until Saul's death.[4] The use of *ṣwh* reflects Yahweh's appointment of a new *nāgîd* in 13.14, while *šlḥ* links up with Jonathan's statement that Yahweh has sent David away in 10.22. David also uses

1. So, for example, Miscall, *Workings of OT Narrative*, p. 127; Fokkelman, *Crossing Fates*, p. 353; Polzin, *Samuel*, p. 196.

2. Fokkelman, *Crossing Fates*, p. 354.

3. Alter (*Art of Biblical Narrative*, p. 71) explains the phrase *pᵉlōnî ʾalmōnî* as an authorial abstraction intended to hint that the entire story is made up by the crafty David. By contrast, Berlin (*Poetics of Biblical Narrative*, p. 100) argues that the phrase functions to enhance the mysteriousness of the purported mission: 'The refusal of David to give away the name of the location fits in with the general urgency and secrecy that he is trying to communicate'.

4. Fokkelman, *Crossing Fates*, p. 355; Polzin, *Samuel*, p. 195.

the verb *yd'* twice in his explanation, introducing the theme of knowledge or human versus divine perception that was already explored previously in chs. 16 and 17 and will be a central focus of ch. 21 as well.

David then moves on to beginning to reveal his primary purpose for visiting Ahimelech with his question, 'What is there under your hand?' (v. 4). The prepositional phrase *taḥat yādᵉkā* indicates that David is interested in something that has been entrusted to the charge of the priest, introducing once again the theme of power in the use of the term *yād*. He then quickly deflects any suspicion his comment may have aroused by demanding five loaves of bread into 'his hand' or 'that which can be found', *hannimṣā'*, another double-edged term that suggests he is after something more significant than food, the transfer of some form of power from the priest to himself, even though his need for food for his mission would have been natural. The unavailability of common bread leads to his being given five sanctified loaves of bread of Presence from the offering table (vv. 4-6). Ahimelech's statement that there is only sanctified bread 'under his hands', repeating David's previously uttered weighty phrase, reminds the audience that the bread is not the main objective of David's quest, at the same time reinforcing his interest in some sort of sanctified object that is in Ahimelech's charge.

As noted by P. Ackroyd and followed by P. Miscall, David's reception of bread destined for Yahweh recalls Saul's reception of bread from men *en route* to Bethel to worship in 10.4.[1] In both instances, Yahweh's anointed are able to partake of his own food. The echoes of 10.4 seem more germane than J. Fokkelman's attempt to link the bread with Jesse's gifts to Saul in 16.20 or his sending of supplies to his sons in 17.17,[2] both of which involved ordinary foodstuffs. R. Polzin's proposed link between the bread and Jonathan's eating of forbidden honey in 14.27, suggesting that both deal with ritually questionable food,[3] may be more legitimate. The narrator may intend

1. Ackroyd, *First Samuel*, p. 171; Miscall, *Workings of OT Narrative*, p. 128.

2. Fokkelman, *Crossing Fates*, p. 356.

3. Polzin, *Samuel*, p. 195. Gunn (*Fate of Saul*, p. 151 n. 18) compares David's action with Saul's impiety at Gilgal, emphasizing that David's impiety in breaking religious rules and receiving the consecrated bread by a lie brings no rebuff, but should do.

the audience to contrast the two situations in order to realize that David, as the anointed *nāgîd*, is entitled to eat food that has been ritually separated, while Jonathan, the passed-over heir-apparent, is not. It is important to bear in mind, however, that the honey was not sanctified for purposes of serving as food for Yahweh as the bread was; it was made taboo in order to keep the troops focused on their pursuit and on the destruction of the enemy.

The narrator now introduces a new character into the scene, a servant of Saul who has been 'constrained' before Yahweh. The appearance of a courtier immediately raises questions for David's safety, while the reappearance of the verb *'ṣr* recalls Yahweh's statement that as his king, Saul was to *'ṣr* his people in 9.17.[1] Here is an example of one 'constrained' by Saul. The specifics of his constraint are unimportant to the narrator; his mere state of being constrained is the central point to be conveyed. Saul's control over this particular servant is asserted accordingly by the information, creating a threat to David. The potential threat grows and diminishes at the same time as the servant's full identity is given. He is Doeg the Edomite, who is chief shepherd for Saul.

Doeg's Edomite origin drives home Saul's failure as king on two fronts. It indirectly reminds the audience of his failure to carry out total *ḥérem* against Yahweh's declared enemy in ch. 15 in the association between Amalek and the region of Edom. At the same time, it highlights the king's willfull audacity or stupidity in appointing someone who is not of Yahweh's people and one who is among Yahweh's enemies (14.47) to a national post. Doeg's position as head shepherd of Israel parodies the use of this occupation to describe the office of kingship; a foreigner has been put in charge of 'minding the flock' instead of Yahweh's chosen candidate, the trained shepherd David (16.11; 17.15).[2] The frequently adopted emendation altering *hr'ym* to

1. Alter (*Art of Biblical Narrative*, p. 66) emphasizes that the lack of a verb in v. 8 is a deliberate move by the narrator to focus on the man rather than anything he might have done, which offers further support for my suggestion that the specifics are not as important as the mere claim that Doeg is *n'ṣr*. He goes on to suggest that the verse, an interruption in the dialogue exchange that dominates the chapter, is aptly placed as foreshadowing, prior to the discussion of weapons, in light of events in ch. 22. The audience does not learn this except in retrospect, however.

2. So also Miscall, *Workings of OT Narrative*, p. 128.

hrṣym on the basis of 22.17 lacks textual support and misses the clearly intended irony.[1]

Doeg's Edomite origin similarly highlights Saul's failure as a king in his constraint of one who is not a member of Yahweh's people—he has carried out his divinely intended royal function on an enemy instead of a fellow Israelite! Saul's loss of divine support and royal credibility is once again demonstrated. The use of *'ṣr* has a more immediate link in David's assertion in v. 6 that he and his fictitious companions have been 'constrained' from sexual relations with women following usual custom before a battle assignment.[2] This initial appearance of the key root *'ṣr* in the chapter serves to illustrate the correct functioning of the royal constraint of Yahweh's people to uphold covenantal law, thereby preparing the audience for the contrastive misuse of royal constraint with Doeg. Doeg's stance 'before Yahweh' recalls Samuel's hewing of Agag 'before Yahweh' in 15.33, hinting that his neighboring countryman is deserving of the same fate.

In spite of the obvious royal blunders that Doeg embodies, which tend to temper the threat he poses to David by highlighting Saul's incompetence, Doeg's Edomite associations make him an untrustworthy entity who could easily thwart the divine plan by killing Yahweh's anointed. As is widely acknowledged, the audience cannot help but anticipate treachery from this individual. Will he expose David's own treachery?

With Doeg now lurking in the vicinity but Ahimelech's confidence gained, David presses forward with his main purpose for visiting the priest. He asks a new question whose wording picks up on his opening request in v. 4 but adds the important adverb *pōh* and nouns *ḥ^{a}nît* and *ḥéreb*: 'Isn't there *here* under your hand *a spear* or *sword*?' (v. 9). J. Fokkelman has noted David's subtle reversal of the usual order of 'sword and spear' to 'spear and sword' that would immediately catch

1. So, for example, Budde, *Bücher Samuel*, p. 149; S.R. Driver, *Notes on the Hebrew Text of the Books of Samuel* (2nd rev. edn; Oxford: Clarendon Press, 1913), p. 176; Blenkinsopp, '1 and 2 Samuel', p. 315; McCarter, *I Samuel*, p. 348; Klein, *1 Samuel*, p. 213. H. Graetz may have inspired the suggestion by his identity of Doeg as 'head of the bodyguard' (*Geschichte der Jüden von de altesten Zeiten bis auf die Gegenwart*, I [11 vols.; Leipzig: Leiner, 1874-1911], p. 209), but did not initiate it, as McCarter claims.

2. So, for example, Miscall, *Workings of OT Narrative*, p. 128; Fokkelman, *Crossing Fates*, p. 359.

the audience's attention.[1] Finally, David has revealed the object of his quest: a dedicated weapon that is in the sanctuary of Nob under Ahimelech's charge. Again David quickly tries to allay any suspicion that might arise about his request by assuring the priest that he was sent off so urgently that he did not have time to get his sword or weapons.[2] His specific mention of his lack of a sword provides the two final clues that the audience should need to be able to identify the object of his quest. First, he is after a particular dedicated sword rather than a spear. Secondly, his professed lack of a sword echoes the narrator's statement in 17.50 after David killed Goliath: *w^{e}ḥéreb 'ên b^{e}yad-dāwīd*.

Ahimelech confirms that he has charge of Goliath's sword, reminding David and the audience that it was war-booty personally secured by David when he killed the Philistine (v. 10). His statement to David, 'If *it* you will take for yourself, take it, for there is not another except this one', hints through double entendre that David is the only one entitled to use of the unique sword because he won it and it is rightfully his. David's reply addresses the implied level of Ahimelech's words directly: 'There is none like it; give it to me'. He has secured the object of his quest, the unique sword of Goliath, which was his victory spoil from his successful testing as king-elect. His description of the sword recalls Samuel's statement concerning Saul at his public designation as *nāgîd* in 10.24 ('There is none like him among the people'),[3] and the psalmic refrain about Yahweh ('There is none like you among the gods'), highlighting through the associations his status as Yahweh's *nāgîd* as he strikes out on his own, cut loose from ties to the Saulide court. He is armed with the weapon he won on his own rather than those given him by Jonathan in 18.4, the weapon that demonstrates his ability to carry out Yahweh's assigned royal task to deliver Israel from the hand of the Philistines (9.16). The object of power has now been removed from Yahweh's custody and bestowed by the national priest upon Yahweh's chosen earthly vice-regent-elect,

1. Fokkelman, *Crossing Fates*, p. 360.

2. The modern audience's lack of knowledge about protocol for bearing arms in ancient Israel precludes a clear decision about whether or not David's comments are plausible. Is it likely that an army commander would routinely carry a weapon, so that David's lack of arms is a signal to Ahimelech that something is awry, or would a commander have been unarmed when on leave?

3. So also Polzin, *Samuel*, p. 197.

who will use it to execute the divine will, ironically killing the Philistines with their own weapon.

David's subsequent flight the same day from Saul to Achish, king of Gath (v. 10), adds a new dimension to David's interest in securing Goliath's sword. Goliath was himself from Gath. It would now seem that he had planned to escape from Saul's death sentence by fleeing outside Israel's borders and that he felt he needed the sword as bargaining power with Achish. David's intentions, which have never been revealed since his introduction in ch. 16, once again come to the fore. Does he plan to join with the enemy? Will he truly betray his country, or only appear to do so?

Achish's servants recognize David by unspecified characteristics or traits and warn their king of his identity with a rhetorical question that quotes the victory song that the women of Israel were to have sung after David slew Goliath. Specific reference to the David and Goliath incident, as opposed to the many other battles that David was to have won for Saul over the Philistines (18.27, 30; 19.8), implies that the unique sword in David's hand, which would have been familiar to the courtiers of Gath, may have been a clue to his identity. One might expect such a trophy to be claimed by the king himself.

Ironically, the courtiers are reported to have concluded from the quoted song that David must now be 'king of the land' because of his superior military prowess, drawing the very conclusion that Saul was dismayed could be extracted from the words (18.8).[1] In typical fashion, they have not got their facts straight concerning the political make-up of Israel,[2] but they nonetheless have perceived for the wrong reasons the truth of the situation in Israel: David is not king of the land—there is no such title for the Israelite king—but he is the king-elect of Israel who now possesses Yahweh's guiding spirit and has been the country's military leader and source of success ever since his anointing. He is unofficial king, lacking only a crown. Thus, the courtiers 'unknowingly know'.

For the first time, David experiences fear (v. 12). He takes the words of the courtiers 'to heart', the seat of divine judgment that links

1. So previously, Fokkelman, *Crossing Fates*, p. 365. Ackroyd (*First Samuel*, p. 172) notes that a slight emendation in v. 11 yields 'one who smites the land'. Perhaps the closeness was deliberate, to imply a pun.

2. So noted previously by McCarter, *I Samuel*, p. 356.

him closely to Yahweh in his status as the one after Yahweh's own heart (13.14), and senses that he is in danger from Achish, king of Gath. The king may decide to act upon the unwitting knowledge of his 'wise' courtiers. David has left the territory of Yahweh and placed himself in the very position that Saul had hoped to put him in—within reach of the hand of the Philistines, who could be the agents of his death (18.17, 21). By implication, his flight to Achish, while carefully planned, had not been done in consultation with Yahweh, since it is only now, for the first time, that he is listening to 'his heart'. Quickly formulating a plan for self-preservation, he changes his judgment while in the hands of the courtiers so that in their eyes he appears to be mad (v. 13-14).[1]

The narrator contrasts David's 'heart' with the courtiers' 'eyes' in order to highlight his deliberate deception of the Philistines and to inform the audience that he is in full control of his actions. David's feigned madness then offers a stark contrast to Saul's uncontrolled fits of madness in 16.14, 23; 18.10-11; 19.9-10, 22-24. David, who possesses Yahweh's benevolent spirit, can use it for self-protection by appearing to be possessed by an evil spirit while Saul, who has lost the benevolent divine spirit, cannot escape fits of madness caused by an evil spirit sent by Yahweh.[2]

Achish is fooled by the deception and his comments to his courtiers introduce dramatic irony for the audience. He states that they can plainly 'see' (*r'h*) that David is a madman (*'îš mištaggēaʿ*), so why have they brought him into his royal presence (v. 15)? The use of the hithpael conjugation to describe David's madness carries possible connotations of self-induced madness that the audience knows is exactly the case. At the same time, the ancient belief concerning madmen renders Achish's statement to say ironically that David is clearly under the protective care of a god, so why has he been brought before the king? Achish has unwittingly confessed that he cannot touch David because of his divine protection! His rhetorical question stating

1. Hertzberg (*I & II Samuel*, pp. 182-83) interprets David's change to result from the direct intervention of God, who has cut short his inappropriate thoughts to rebuild life among the Philistines. I would suggest rather that David is responsible for the belated initiative to consult his heart to learn God's intentions.

2. So too, Ackroyd, *First Samuel*, p. 173: Gunn, *Fate of Saul*, p. 86; Klein, *1 Samuel*, p. 217.

that such a protected one will not enter his house (v. 16) brings to mind David's entry into the house of Saul and the resulting problems that Saul had experienced. On one level, Achish himself has foolishly let slip from his grasp his most dangerous enemy because of his inability to discern David's true identity. On another level, the Philistine king has wisely refused to let Yahweh's protected king-elect enter his house and be given the opportunity to harm him and his people, God's declared enemies.[1]

1. Miscall (*Workings of OT Narrative*, p. 130) sees v. 16 to be an ironic forecast of David's return to Achish and suggests that the larger episode demonstrates that the Philistines are no threat to David since they are easily tricked. In retrospect from ch. 27, the saying is ironic. I believe the episode demonstrates the potential danger the Philistines pose, even if the danger arises from misconceptions, and David's need to conceal his identity and intentions if he is to seek refuge among them.

Chapter 17

1 SAMUEL 22

As the narrative continues, David now escapes (*mlṭ*) from his true enemy, the Philistines, to the cave of Adullam (v. 1). Rumor of his return reaches his family, who join him there (v. 1), and reaches at least 400 others, who also join him and accept him as their leader (v. 2). Reference to some of the men who join him being 'distressed' (*māṣôq*) calls to mind the distress of the Israelites on two occasions in ch. 14, although there the verb used was *ngś*. As noted by R. Klein, the adjective is used in Deut. 28.53, 55, 57 and Jer. 19.19 to describe those experiencing siege warfare.[1] Others are men who have creditors after them or men who are embittered in soul. All are implied to be citizens of Saul's state who have learned at first hand the problems that can accompany a king who has been abandoned by his God. David becomes a commander of a unit of 'disloyals', in contrast to his former role as commander over a regular army division of soldiers loyal to Saul (18.13). As noted by D. Gunn, after his establishment of his new support group, the narrator uses less urgent verbs of motion to describe David's actions, *hlk* and *bw'* rather than *mlṭ* and *brḥ*,[2] subtly indicating that David's position is now more secure.

Claiming to the king of Moab to be uncertain of knowing what saving deeds God/the gods will do (*'śh*) on his behalf, David seeks political asylum for his parents at 'the lookout of Moab' (vv. 3-4). His family-ties to Moab have been previously developed in Ruth 4.17-22, and Moab's purported defeat by Saul (14.47) would have earned sympathy for the declared Israelite state enemy.[3] Since the audience

1. Klein, *1 Samuel*, p. 222.
2. Gunn, *Fate of Saul*, p. 86.
3. So also for example, Hertzberg, *I & II Samuel*, p. 184; McCarter, *I Samuel*, p. 359; Fokkelman, *Crossing Fates*, p. 373. Fokkelman also points to the contrast

has not been told that David feels he has lost Yahweh's support, it is likely that his words are meant to be understood as a ruse to secure his parents from reprisal by Saul, now that he is a declared royal enemy. As anointed *nāgîd* he can be certain of Yahweh's support; perhaps he is alluding to his uncertainty about challenges that other national gods will make to Yahweh.

David's use of the verb *yd'* picks up a thread introduced in the previous chapter, the theme of human versus divine knowledge, for further development. He then returns to 'the stronghold' (*hamm*[e]*ṣûdâ*) and remains there for an unspecified length of time until the prophet Gad tells him to go to the land of Judah, giving him divine direction (vv. 3-4). David enters the forest of Hereth (v. 5). His ability to receive communication from Yahweh through prophetic channels contrasts with Saul's inability to communicate with Yahweh, who has abandoned him, highlighting for the audience the effect of Yahweh's benevolent spirit.

Finally, Saul is informed that 'David is known and men who are with him' (v. 6). As noted by J. Fokkelman, the report conveys two pieces of information to Saul: that David now has some sort of support group, and that the band 'is known'.[1] Their 'discovery' apparently takes place only after David's return to Judah, even though many others had learned of his earlier presence at the cave of Adullam.[2] The use of the phrase *nôda' dāwīd* to describe David's discovery deliberately reintroduces the verb *yd'* but uses it ambiguously. What exactly has Saul learned about David and his group? The narrator's reference to 'some' men who are with David reminds the audience that David now has men loyal to him who were once loyal to Saul.

In a parenthetical aside, the scene is moved back to 'the hill' (*baggib'â*) where Saul is sitting beneath the tamarisk tree on the height, spear in hand, surrounded by his attendants (v. 6). His situation recalls his station in 14.2 on the outskirts of 'the hill' under the pomegranate tree at the threshing-floor at the Michmash pass,[3] which

with the Philistine king, Achish, who was not receptive to David, though an enemy of Saul's also.

1. Fokkelman, *Crossing Fates*, p. 381.

2. Contrast Fokkelman, *Crossing Fates*, pp. 376-77, who sees v. 4 as a synopsis of chs. 22–26 and thus, that David's stay at Adullam takes place *later* than Saul's execution of the priests of Nob.

3. Fokkelman (*Crossing Fates*, p. 380) extends the situation analogy from

was the first instance where he had been hesitant to lead his troops after his warning of possible divine rejection by Samuel. Mention of his spear echoes David's reference to a 'spear or sword' in his negotiations with Ahimelech in 21.8 and contrasts with David's possession of Goliath's sword. The king and king-elect now both have a corps of loyal men, but are distinguished by their weapons as well as their possession of divine favor. The spear also recalls the previous incidents involving the same weapon that had taken place at court, in which the king had tried to kill David and his own son Jonathan, hinting that a new attempt to kill someone may be coming.[1]

Turning to his attendants, Saul accuses them of treason and conspiracy with the rebel 'son of Jesse' (vv. 7-8). The servants are addressed by Saul as Benjaminites, members of Saul's own home tribe. The king proceeds to accuse all the Benjaminite servants of conspiracy, asking sarcastically if the son of Jesse will give all of them fields and all of them vineyards and make them commanders of military divisions of one thousand and one hundred. His threefold use of *kull*^{e} *kem* highlights his self-separation and alignment over against his alleged servants, who have in his opinion all deserted him, while, as noted by J. Fokkelman, his use of the term *bēn* to describe his attendants, David and Jonathan in vv. 7-8 further emphasize his self-separation from the rest of those around him.[2]

Saul's comments, introduced by *gam-lekull*^{e}*kem*, imply that he has himself bestowed the lands and ranks mentioned upon members of his home tribe as special favors. His words ironically illustrate the introduction of the practices cited as negative aspects of kingship by Samuel in 8.12-14 before all the tribes. Saul is citing them as positive advantages of kingship to impress upon those loyal to him how they have benefitted from their loyalty to the crown. He intends to imply that the rebel David, contemptuously called the son of Jesse, cannot possibly offer similar benefits to his ragtag corps, who are debtors and misfits.[3]

ch. 14 to include the disappearance of a member of the ranks—now David instead of Jonathan, his alter ego—the eventual pronouncement of a death sentence, and the appearance of members of the Elide priesthood.

1. Fokkelman, *Crossing Fates*, p. 380; Gordon, *I & II Samuel*, p. 173.
2. Fokkelman, *Crossing Fates*, pp. 382-83.
3. The direct reference to 8.12-14 is commonly pointed out. Contrast the understanding of the sense of the statement by, for example, Klein (*1 Samuel*,

Finally revealing his 'knowledge' about David, Saul specifically accuses his servants of conspiracy in failing to 'disclose' (*gālâ 'et-'oznî*) that Jonathan had made a pact with David, even though none among them had suffered ill-effects in the form of reprisals from the king. He then goes on to expound further his understanding of the pact, repeating his opening phrase 'no one discloses to men', stating that his own son had 'confirmed' or 'established [root *qwm*] his servant', a reference to David, against him, or perhaps, 'in his place', as 'an ambusher' (*l*^{e}*'ōrēb*), on this very day. Saul's words repeat key phrases from earlier chapters, creating interlocking chains of significance for the perceptive narrative audience. First, the expression 'disclose' links Saul's speech with the previous occurrences of this idiom in 8.21; 9.15; and 20.2. The first two involved prophetic revelation while the last described Jonathan's special role as his father's confidant. Saul publicly admonishes his servants, all of whom have sworn an oath of loyalty to the king, for failing to convey to him any 'revelations' they may have received directly or indirectly. His words remind the audience of his abandonment by God and his personal inability to receive divine communications, leaving him dependent upon others for his information.

Next, Saul's use of *qûm* recalls its utterance by Samuel in 13.13 in his warning to Saul of possible future rejection by Yahweh that would result in the failure of his kingship to be 'established'. Saul knows that Jonathan, the heir-elect, has 'established' the terms of Samuel's warning by refusing to kill David, Yahweh's chosen successor to Saul. Finally, his description of David as 'an ambusher' recalls his own setting of an ambush against the city of Amalek in 15.5, raising the specter of his final rejection in favor of David for his failure to carry out total *ḥérem* against the Amalekites. This apparent deliberate echo favors a retention of the MT text over the LXX presumed reading *'yb*.[1] In his mind, David has become his enemy who is actively seeking to claim the throne that has been promised to him by Yahweh. With its many echoes to earlier scenes, Saul's accusation against his loyal

p. 224) and Polzin (*Samuel*, pp. 198-99), who believe David has promised payoffs for conspiracy.

1. Hertzberg's conclusion that David has decided to stage an armed revolt at home is too literalistic a reading of the text (*I & II Samuel*, p. 187).

courtiers expresses undercurrents of self-accusation for personal failure.

The silence is broken by Doeg the Edomite, whom the audience now learns is in Gibeah, standing *'al* ('against') the servants of Saul (v. 7). The preposition conveys a sense of both physical and psychological opposition. Doeg is standing apart from the other servants, which is logical in light of his previous introduction in 21.7 as a head royal shepherd, a position that would not have made him a regular attendant on the king at the court. More importantly, however, he is separated from the Benjaminite attendants by virtue of his Edomite origin; he is an outsider whose judgment is not to be trusted.[1] His appearance immediately recalls his 'constraint' at the sanctuary at Nob during the exchange between Ahimelech and David and the uncertainty it generated about David's safety and ability to get away with his ruse. A dark cloud now looms on the horizon.

Picking up on Saul's own derogatory tone, Doeg reports that he 'saw' (*r'h*) the 'son of Jesse' go to Nob, to Ahimelech, the son of Ahitub. For the first time, Ahimelech's patronymic appears: he is the son of Ahitub, and thus, the brother of Saul's priest Abiathar who bore the ephod at the battle at the Michmash pass in 14.3 and a member of the Elide dynasty whose doom was announced in 2.30-36. The narrative audience should now become very apprehensive about Ahimelech's fate in light of the certain doom awaiting his house and his unknowing aiding and abetting of the fugitive David. By referring to Ahimelech's status as Ahitub's son, Doeg has also picked up on Saul's earlier principle of alignment through the use of the term 'son' and has closely linked David and Ahimelech over against the king.

In his immediately ensuing accusation, Doeg builds as damaging a case against Ahimelech as possible. Using the verb *š'l* that reflects the king's own name, Doeg claims that Ahimelech 'inquired of Yahweh' on David's behalf and that he also gave him provisions and the sword of Goliath the Philistine. His words are carefully chosen. He begins with an act that would feed Saul's anger the most, deliberately using the verb *š'l* to remind the king of his inability to consult Yahweh because of his fall from grace and David's tenure of grace in his stead. He then converts what for the audience and narrator was the most

1. Contrast McCarter (*I Samuel*, p. 364) and Fokkelman (*Crossing Fates*, p. 403), who think that Doeg is presiding over Saul's entire retinue.

potentially unlawful action Ahimelech performed, his bending of the cultic rules by giving David consecrated bread to eat, into what he feels will be an even more incriminating charge for the king, the priest's supplying David with official provisions for a military mission. He thus links the provisions with the third charge, the supplying of the sword, to imply that Ahimelech has abetted David in preparing for armed revolt. In so doing, he has eliminated the only truly questionable legal infraction that could have been brought against the priest.

Doeg's emphasis in his final accusation on the nationality of the former owner of the sword that Ahimelech gave to David—not merely Goliath, whose name alone would have been enough to establish identity, but Goliath the Philistine—seems designed to drive home to the king his personal failure to deliver Israel from the hand of the Philistines in contrast to David's successes in this area. At the same time, his emphasis on David's possession of the sword indirectly leads the king to believe that David is now an armed and dangerous enemy of the state rather than a mere fugitive as before, who poses a direct threat and must be actively eradicated.

Doeg's first accusation lacks confirmation from the unfolding of dialogue and action in ch. 21, immediately raising a question of the reliability of the outsider's testimony. Even though the next two charges correspond to known actions and so lead the narrative audience to concede that Ahimelech *could* have consulted Yahweh for David, David's apparent failure to consult Yahweh before his flight to Achish was duly noted in connection with his reported 'fear' in 21.13 and his consultation of his 'heart' for the first time on that occasion. Is Doeg's most damaging charge a lie or not?

Acting on Doeg's charges, Saul summons Ahimelech and his entire *bêt 'āb* to Gibeah and accuses the priest of conspiracy. The narrator's report that 'all of them' went to the king (v. 11) resonates with the use of *kōl* in vv. 6-9, establishing the priests as a united body against the king, while at the same time preparing the audience for the execution of the pending doom awaiting the Elide house. Ahimelech's submissive response, *hin^{e}nî '^{a}dōnî* (v. 12), echoes Samuel's reponse to Yahweh's call as a child in 3.4-10 and also seems to play off David's earlier words to him concerning 'the matter of the king' in the dual nature of the title lord here. Ahimelech is willing to answer any charges put to him before his true Lord, Yahweh.

More significant in terms of situational parallels is the echo with Jonathan's response to Saul's inquisition in 14.43 immediately before his sentencing to death. The king's accusation repeats phrases from his previous blanket accusation of his Benjaminite attendants in vv. 7-8, thereby highlighting them.[1] Included are 'Hear now, oh son of PN', 'Why have you conspired against me', and 'to establish him against/instead of me as an ambusher this very day'. The conspiracy consists of 'the son of Ahitub' supplying provisions and a weapon to the rebel 'son of Jesse' and consulting Yahweh for him—a reversal in order of the charges that were laid out by Doeg. J. Fokkelman has suggested that the repetitions are intended to depict Saul as a man so caught up in his fixations that he is not interested in facts so much as 'revolving his own pathology'—he cannot escape his own warped illusory reality.[2]

Ahimelech's response in vv. 14-15, in contrast to that made by Doeg to the king's accusations, seals his doom. Unlike Doeg, he immediately launches into what he believes is his strongest defense rather than his strongest offense, but his words in fact turn out to be the most damaging evidence against himself, thereby ironically making his statement parallel to Doeg's in its effect. Ahimelech appeals to David's unparalleled trustworthiness among Saul's servants, his status as the king's son-in-law, leader of the royal bodyguard, and his honor among the royal family. He calls David by name, showing him respect, in contrast to the use of the derogatory 'son of Jesse' by the king and Doeg. All of the traits he lists would ring as treasonous attributes to the king who has already decided that David has left his circle of servants and is actively plotting a *coup d'état*, using his former positions of authority as leverage to gain support. Saul's status as both plaintiff and judge in the legal suit being tried in vv. 12-16[3] leaves no hope for a fair defense.

Continuing with his futile defense, Ahimelech now moves on to the specific charges, addressing only the last charge, that of consulting

1. So noted previously by, for example, Gunn, *Fate of Saul*, p. 87; McCarter, *I Samuel*, p. 364; Klein, *1 Samuel*, p. 222; Miscall, *Workings of OT Narrative*, p. 132; Fokkelman, *Crossing Fates*, p. 397.

2. Fokkelman, *Crossing Fates*, p. 386. By contrast, Sternberg sees the arrangement as a deliberate expression of an ascending order of treason (*Poetics*, pp. 421-22).

3. Fokkelman, *Crossing Fates*, p. 394.

Yahweh for David, which is one that was unverified from ch. 21 and thus the only one of questionable veracity. He asks rhetorically if he only began today to inquire of God for David, or alternatively, if the occasion in question would have been his beginning of inquiry. The lack of a morphologically defined conditional tense in Hebrew makes both translations possible. He quickly answers the question himself with an emphatic no, *ḥālîlâ lî*, and an appeal to the king not to hold the matter against himself or his entire house because he knew (*yd'*) nothing great or small about all of this (v. 15). His final words ironically echo Jonathan's claim to David in 20.2 that his father discloses all things great and small to him,[1] highlighting through the parallel the gullibility of both men.

The priest's opening two words in v. 15, *hayyôm haḥillōtî*, need to be construed idiomatically rather than literally to preserve the narrative's chronological coherence. The accusation cannot take place on the same day as David's visit to Nob or else the report concerning David 'and men with him' in 22.6 would be impossible. Verse 6 presumes that enough time has passed that David has begun to form his band at Adullam.

Ahimelech's response leaves the ambiguity of Doeg's charge concerning his consultation of Yahweh on David's behalf unresolved. Has he chosen to begin his answer with that charge simply because it was the final one and he plans to deal with the charges in reverse order, somewhat as Saul did in framing his accusation from the information presented by Doeg? Or has he deliberately focused on that charge because it is the only one that he knows to be untrue and to be the least damning of the three now that he has found out the truth of the situation? His role as priest entitles him to consult Yahweh; it does not entitle him to give out provisions or dedicated weapons to non-temple personnel. His opening words stress his established role as oracle-giver and his performance of that role for David in the past. He then moves on to stress his loyalty to Saul, identifying himself as 'your servant', and appeals to the king not to hold 'anything' (*dābār*) of the entire situation against him or his family. The use of the indefinite *dābār* continues the ambiguity concerning his performance of the consultation. It seems as though he was planning a longer self-defense that would have dealt with specific details of the charges, but was

1. Also noted by Polzin, *Samuel*, p. 199.

interrupted by Saul and his premature pronouncement of the death sentence before he could even finish (v. 16).

The king's death sentence echoes the one pronounced against Jonathan before the Elide priest Abiathar in 14.44[1] and ironically contrasts with the one concerning David in 19.6. Here, however, the entire house is sentenced to death for Ahimelech's act because of associative guilt. The king claims that the 'hand' (*yād*) of the priests of Yahweh is also with David since they failed to 'disclose' (*gālâ 'et-'ōzen*) their knowledge (*yd'*) of David's flight to him (v. 17). Once again the motif associated with power appears, and the reappearance of the thematic expression 'disclose' highlights Saul's abandonment by God and his inability to consult or receive indication of the divine will through established priestly and prophetic channels. The runners who are attending him refuse to carry out the royal command directed at them to execute the priests by 'putting forth their hand' against the priests of Yahweh. They respect the sacredness and inviolability of the priests and know the inappropriateness of trying to overcome the power of the divine.

The narrator's use of *pg'* to describe the commanded execution reminds the audience of Saul's earlier 'encounter' with the band of prophets in 10.5, where he was filled with benevolent divine spirit and became part of their group. Here, he wants to destroy a group who possess divine spirit. As loyal servants of the king, they try to protect their lord from committing a gross blunder against his Lord, Yahweh. Their refusal to kill also echoes the people's refusal to execute Jonathan in 14.14-45.[2]

As Saul orders the non-Israelite Doeg, his informant, to fall upon (*pg'*) the priests (v. 18), the audience knows that their doom is sealed. Doeg has already been separated physically and psychologically from the loyal servants at his introduction in v. 9. His non-Israelite status makes him capable of disregarding Yahweh's sanctity, so that the ensuing report that he slew 85 men wearing the linen ephod is no surprise. The reference to the linen ephod recalls Samuel's service under the Elides in 2.18 and the announcement of the downfall of the Elide

1. So too, Polzin, *Samuel*, p. 199. However, the issue leading to Ahimelech's condemnation is not ritually questionable food, as Polzin suggests, since Saul knows nothing of this incident; Doeg has not reported that the provisions were holy bread.

2. So noted by Fokkelman, *Crossing Fates*, p. 404; Polzin, *Samuel*, p. 199.

house in the same chapter, which has now been carried out through the agency of an enemy of the state, an Edomite. The narrator goes on to inform his audience that Doeg struck Nob, the settlement of the priests, with the edge of his sword, carrying out what amounted to *ḥérem* against the very list of living items that Saul had been commanded by God to exterminate at the city of Amalek in 15.3.[1] The subject of 'smote' (*hikkâ*) in v. 19 is somewhat ambiguous, but would seem grammatically to refer to Doeg, the last-named precedent in v. 18. The audience is left to wonder whether Doeg acted on his own initiative, carrying out 'blood revenge' for Saul's action against the city of Amalek in Edom,[2] or whether he carried out a subsequent order made by Saul that ironically would have involved the misapplication of *ḥérem* to his own people, mirroring his misapplication of *'ṣr* to the non-Israelite Doeg (21.8).[3]

Abiathar's escape from the bloodbath signals the fulfillment of 2.30-36, especially v. 33. As a declared enemy of the state, he joins forces with David, the other declared enemy of the state (v. 20), who, ironically, is the reason for the massacre of Abiathar's lineage. The narrator's decision not to present Abiathar's own words of report to David concerning the events that had taken place at Gibeah in v. 21, but merely to summarize them in terms of Saul's killing of the priests of Yahweh sets an ambiguous stage for David's ensuing confession in v. 22. David specifically states that he 'knew' (*yd'*) on the very day he was at Nob that Doeg would certainly inform Saul, thereby introducing details concerning the court scene that were not necessarily

1. So noted previously by, for example, Ackroyd, *First Samuel*, p. 179 (indirectly); Hertzberg, *I & II Samuel*, p. 188; Gunn, *Fate of Saul*, p. 88; Klein, *1 Samuel*, pp. 222, 225; Fokkelman, *Crossing Fates*, p. 406.

2. The equation drawn here between Amalek and Edom almost certainly provides clues about the situation of the intended audience. Amalek appears as a historical entity in narratives dealing with the periods before the 7th century BCE. Edom, by contrast, became a symbol of treachery in the closing years of the Judahite monarchy when it sided with neo-Babylonia during the two attacks on Jerusalem and refused to give asylum to Judahite refugees. Both are associated with the same geographical region, allowing their equation. The audience reacting to Doeg must be late monarchic, exilic or post-exilic.

3. So noted by Fokkelman (*Crossing Fates*, p. 404), who sees Saul as the subject of *hikkâ* and his action as an attempt by the king to take vengeance on Yahweh himself by destroying his priests.

told to him by Abiathar. Is the audience to presume that Abiathar had advised him of all the details of the slaughter before he made his reply, or are we to conclude that David's 'confession' expresses his own suspicion as to why the priests would have been slain, revealing his sense of responsibility for the ensuing slaughter?

David now confesses to Abiathar that he personally has turned against or changed (*sabbōtî b*ᵉ) every soul of Abiathar's lineage. His use of *sbb* echoes or plays upon Saul's command to his servants and to Doeg to turn against the priests in vv. 17 and 18 and so need not be emended on the basis of LXX to presume an underlying consonantal text *ḥbt*.[1] The confusion of *sāmek* and *ḥēt* would not be usual in any script. On analogy to the use of the root in 1 Kgs 12.15, David's use of *sbb* may convey overtones that his failure to take action against Doeg when he realized the looming danger was a result of his 'knowledge' of Yahweh's plan to execute his announced punishment on the Elides.

Appealing to Saul as their common enemy, David commands Abiathar to remain with him, reassuring him that he will be well-guarded if he stays (v. 23). He thereby reinforces the image of Saul as Abiathar's foe, even though he has just confessed his ultimate responsibility for the death of Abiathar's kin. As others have already noted, Abiathar's escape introduces into the narrative the motif of divine blessing continuing through a survivor.[2] David's close linking of his *népeš* with Abiathar's recalls Jonathan's similar linking of his *népeš* with David's in chs. 18 and 20, highlighting the fact that here, David is the one actively seeking to gain the favor of the other. Is he concerned that his lying to Ahimelech, which has occasioned the death of many innocent people, may have cost him some of Yahweh's support, so that he needs to be assured of his continued ability to communicate with Yahweh through established channels? This seems to be a valid deduction from the narrative developments.

1. *Contra*, for example, Driver, *Notes*, p. 182; McCarter, *I Samuel*, p. 363.

2. For example, Ackroyd, *First Samuel*, p. 179; Hertzberg, *I & II Samuel*, p. 189.

Chapter 18

1 SAMUEL 23

The ambiguity of Doeg's charge concerning David's priestly consultation of Yahweh at Nob continues as the narrative audience is now specifically told of David's oracular consultation of Yahweh after receiving word that the Philistines were fighting against Keilah and robbing their threshing floors (vv. 1-2). How has he been able to accomplish this consultation? The question is prolonged by the narrator's report that David's men express their fear over being located within Judah, let alone going to Keilah 'to the forces of the Philistines' (v. 3).[1] The use of the preposition *'el* rather than *'al* or *b^e^*, the latter two of which convey a clear adversative sense, suggests that the men may not have not understood David's plan and may think that he has suggested that they join forces with the Philistines against Keilah, rather than fighting against Philistines to rescue Keilah.

Keilah's status as an Israelite or non-Israelite town is not clear from the facts presented. On the one hand, Yahweh's directive that David is to cause the settlement to be 'delivered' (*hôša'tā*) from the Philistines (v. 2; cf. v. 5) would seem to imply that the town is Israelite and that David is being commanded to assume the task that Yahweh intended for Saul in 9.16.[2] However, David's derogatory reference to

1. *Contra* McCarter (*I Samuel*, p. 369), there is no need to emend the MT text to parallel the geographical reference to Judah in the first half of the verse.

2. This is the common view. See, for example, Hertzberg, *I & II Samuel*, p. 190; Ackroyd, *First Samuel*, p. 181; Gunn, *Fate of Saul*, p. 89; McCarter, *I Samuel*, p. 372; Klein, *1 Samuel*, p. 233; Miscall, *1 Samuel*, p. 139; Fokkelman, *Crossing Fates*, p. 426. Blenkinsopp ('1 and 2 Samuel', p. 316) seems to be a lone dissenter, suggesting that Keilah may have been considered *at that time* to have been within the Philistine sphere of influence. If the Philistines were to have attacked it, perhaps it is more plausible to presume that the town was neither Israelite nor Philistine, but simply independent. Gunn (*Fate of Saul*, p. 89) sees a deliberate

Yahweh's main enemy as 'these Philistines' in his initial divine consultation in v. 2 highlights his primary interest in fighting off Yahweh's declared enemies under any circumstances, rather than his fighting them only on Israelite soil. Is it possible that Yahweh has given him permission to deliver a non-Israelite settlement that will eventually become Israelite through David's influence? His men's responsive comments in v. 3 allow room for the conclusion that the city lay outside Judah, as does David's interest in preserving the contents of their harvest against Philistine seizure; did he plan to take the food himself at some later date if he needed extra supplies for his band of refugees?

The men do not seem to have known that David consulted an oracle about his plan or they would not have questioned its decision or misunderstood its directive. David's second oracular consultation confirms for all involved the divine backing of their enterprise; Yahweh himself is giving the Philistines into their hand (v. 4). The motif *yād* appears again as an indication of the seat of power. In a brief, bare-bones battle report, David's delivery of Keilah from the Philistines is summarized (v. 5). Should Keilah be meant to be understood to have been Israelite, the narrator would be portraying David as once again taking on the first task that Yahweh intended the king of Israel to perform, the delivery of his property from Philistine oppression (9.16). As noted, however, Keilah's Israelite status is not certain in the scene.

The mention of David's leading away cattle in v. 5 is highlighted as one of the few details presented about the battle. Although it is commonly thought to refer to David's strategy to disperse the means by which the Philistines had planned to carry the grain back home as a preliminary step in the battle plan,[1] its reporting after the summary phrase 'he fought against them' would seem to suggest that it refers to his taking of booty after the battle. It is then followed by the requisite

contrast with Saul's deliverance of Jabesh-Gilead in ch. 11 because of the use of the verb *yṣʿ*.

1. So esp. Hertzberg, *I & II Samuel*, p. 191. He is followed by, for example, Stoebe, *Erste Buch Samuelis*, p. 418; Klein, *1 Samuel*, p. 231. McCarter (*I Samuel*, p. 371) offers a less plausible variation on the theme: the cattle were taken to forage on the threshing floor remains. This option seems also to be adopted by Gordon (*I & II Samuel*, p. 176): 'the Philistines evidently had been availing themselves of the local grazing facilities'.

summary of the extent of the victory. Such an understanding would be most consistent with the normative use of *nhg* to refer to booty collection. The booty represents the beginning of his establishment of an economic base, the securement of the wealth to which he was entitled as the slayer of Goliath (17.25) but which he never received from Saul.

The answer to the lingering question concerning David's ability to consult Yahweh twice about Keilah comes in the narrator's statement in v. 6 that Abiathar had fled to David 'and an ephod descended in his hand'. The priest had arrived with control over an instrument for the determination of the divine will, which he has now put at David's disposal in order to strengthen David's power and defeat his enemy. The term *yād* continues to serve as a symbol of shifting power in this chapter.[1] The indefiniteness of the opening temporal clause 'when Abiathar had fled to David at Keilah' seems to denote chronological matters in favor of priestly ones, while leaving the precise moment of Abiathar's arrival of no consequence for the ensuing action. J. Fokkelman's argument that Abiathar had not yet reached Keilah at the time of David's attack, so that the narrator is deliberately synchronizing Saul's slaughter of the priests at Nob with David's slaughter of the Philistines at Keilah to contrast the proper and improper use of the sword, seems to have read much more into the text than its writer intended.[2]

Ironically, Saul claims that God has alienated David into 'his hand' upon hearing of David's entering Keilah, stating that the fugitive has trapped himself by entering into a settlement with bars and gates (v. 7). The meaning of the verb *nikkar* is disputed. In the MT it is pointed as a piel of the root *nkr*, 'to be foreign', suggesting a sense of becoming a foreigner, or perhaps, of 'being alienated'.[3] Alternatively,

1. So noted also by Miscall (*1 Samuel*, p. 139), who emphasizes the prominence of the theme in ch. 22 onwards. Fokkelman (*Crossing Fates*, p. 424) indicates its use as key theme in ch. 23.

2. Fokkelman, *Crossing Fates*, p. 427. Picking up on a suggestion of Fokkelman on p. 423, R. Polzin suggests that the first two inquiries sound more prophetic in their pronouncement and are to be deliberately contrasted with the two that take place after Abiathar's arrival with the ephod (*Samuel*, p. 201).

3. G.R. Driver, 'Some Hebrew Words', *JTS* (1927-28), pp. 395-96; A.M. Honeyman, Review of *Lexicon in Veteris Testamenti Libros*, edited by L. Koehler, *VT* 5 (1955), p. 222; Stoebe, *Erste Buch Samuelis*, pp. 417, 419.

the consonants could represent a corruption of a niphal conjugation of the root *msr*, 'to hand over', as presumed by the Latin text. The LXX reading presumes a niphal stem of an underlying Hebrew root *mkr*, 'to sell', which is commonly followed,[1] while the context would allow for a corruption of an original consonantal text *skr*, 'shut up', as in Isa. 19.14.[2] If the MT text is accepted as it stands, it would have Saul express his ability to gain power over David even though he has fled to a settlement outside the boundaries of Saul's domain, so becoming an alien, because of the king's ability to lay siege to the foreign city and capture him. Such a meaning would be consistent with the earlier ambiguity concerning Keilah's Israelite status already discussed. Has Saul received accurate information about David's whereabouts; did David enter the town after defending it against the Philistines, or did he take his Philistine booty and leave, having earned the town's future support?

On the basis of his scouting reports, Saul assembles his troops and goes against Keilah with the express purpose of hemming in David and his men (v. 9). The narrator's use of the verb *ṣwr* to describe Saul's intended action against David and company echoes the Israelites' being hemmed in by the Philistines at the Michmash pass in 13.6. Saul wants to turn the tables on his declared enemy, David; by implication, he should be trying to hem in his true enemy, the Philistines.

The narrator reports that David 'knew' (*yd'*) that Saul would be plotting evil against him, apparently in the same way that he 'knew' Doeg would inform Saul in 22.22, and summons Abiathar to bring the ephod so he can consult Yahweh (v. 10). R. Polzin emphasizes that knowledge is a key theme within chs. 20–23, with over one third of the uses of the root *yd'* within 1 Samuel occurring in these four chapters.[3] David's command echoes the one which was given by Saul to Abiathar's kinsman, Ahijah, at the Michmash pass in 14.18

1. For example, Budde, *Bücher Samuel*, p. 156; Smith, *Books of Samuel*, p. 212; Dhorme, *Livres de Samuel*, p. 209; Ehrlich, *Randglossen zur hebräischen Bibel*, III, p. 247; Hertzberg, *I & II Samuel*, p. 189; Ackroyd, *First Samuel*, p. 181.

2. S.R. Driver, *Notes*, p. 184, quoting N. Krochmal; McCarter, *I Samuel*, p. 369; Klein, *1 Samuel*, p. 228.

3. Polzin, *Samuel*, p. 200.

concerning the ark of God.[1] David's prayer is addressed before the ephod to Yahweh, God of Israel, implying the matter at hand is one concerning national security.[2] This need not imply that Keilah is an Israelite city about to be attacked by its own king; the threat against David's life is a matter of national security since he is the divinely anointed and tested king-elect whose kingship will bring Israel prosperity.

David states that he has been firmly informed that Saul intends to slay the city of Keilah *ba'ᵃbûrî* (v. 10). The last term carries its normal sense of 'on my account', but has additional overtones deriving from the homophonous noun *'ābûr*, 'produce, yield', and the underlying root *'br*, 'cross over, transgress'. Saul intends to slay the city because of David's successful 'yield' against the Philistines that has produced booty and new supporters, and because of David's 'crossing over' to Keilah.

Yahweh answers affirmatively both of David's questions about whether the lords of Keilah will 'cause him to be closed up' (hiphil of *sgr*) into Saul's hand and whether Saul will go against the town as he has heard (vv. 11-12). David's self-characterization as Yahweh's servant seems to be a deliberate move by the author to highlight his special relationship with Yahweh over against his status as Saul's servant and to remind the audience of Saul's loss of servantship status to Yahweh. The verbatim reporting of David's inquiries to Yahweh and Yahweh's response similarly emphasizes David's ability to communicate with Yahweh and determine the divine will, over against Saul's inability to do so. Upon learning of his certain betrayal, he leaves Keilah with his band of men that has now swelled to 600 and roams from place to place, keeping on the move (v. 12). Saul aborts his planned pursuit after being informed that David had fled (*mlṭ*) from Keilah. He no longer is able to capture him by siege.

For those who favor the view of Keilah as an Israelite town, Saul's attack against his own people in order to capture David would emphasize his misplaced priorities as he attempts to thwart the divine plan. At the same time, it would depict the larger Israelite citizenry as remaining loyal to their king, so contrasting with Saul's earlier accusations in ch. 22 about the treachery of various segments of his con-

1. So also Fokkelman, *Crossing Fates*, p. 427.
2. Fokkelman, *Crossing Fates*, p. 429.

stituency. However, such a view would seem to contradict the repeated reports in 18.16, 30; 22.2; and 23.13 concerning David's expanding support within Israel. David's departure from the town would emphasize his desire to avoid risking the lives of his fellow Israelites once again, as had happened at Nob, or their incurrence of guilt by harming the anointed king-elect,[1] at the same time stressing that it would not be treachery but the will of God that would defeat Saul.[2]

David's wanderings take place while he remains in the general vicinity of the wilderness, in the natural 'hunting grounds' (*m*ᵉ*ṣādôt*) there and in the mountain in the wilderness of Ziph, with Saul constantly seeking him (v. 14). The narrator tells the audience that God did not give David into Saul's 'hand' or power in order to emphasize that David continues to receive divine protection. Two words in v. 14 seems to have overtones worth exploring. First, the use of the verb *yšb* to describe David's status while in the wilderness, while conveying the more immediate sense of 'tarrying' or 'remaining', may also have implied overtones associated with 'ruling'; David's initial 'kingdom' is the wilderness realm, with his subjects his band of 600 misfits.[3] Secondly, the noun *m*ᵉ *ṣādôt* has a primary sense associated with natural hunting grounds out in the wild rather than as a 'stronghold', which is entirely appropriate in the given context. Saul is the hunter and David the prey in a game of cat and mouse taking place in the wilderness south of Judah. The narrative audience is reassured, however, that God is in control of the entire situation and that Saul is doomed to failure as a hunter; he may no more harm his anointed successor than can David, the anointed successor, harm the ruling anointed one.

David's second instance of fear occurs when Saul actually sallies forth to seek his life (v. 15) while he is in the wilderness of Ziph at Horesh. Mention of his fear reminds the audience that he first experienced fear after hearing the words of the Gittite courtiers who unknowingly had accurately diagnosed his royal status in 21.12. In both instances, David's fear stemmed from a king who was actively

1. So Ackroyd, *First Samuel*, p. 182.

2. So Gunn, *Fate of Saul*, p. 90; similarly Klein, *1 Samuel*, p. 233.

3. Contrast Fokkelman (*Crossing Fates*, p. 438), who thinks that the verb signals the end of David's period of fleeing through God's permanent protection. Since David continues to flee from Saul and is forced to seek refuge among the Philistines in subsequent chapters, this suggestion is unlikely.

seeking, or who would probably seek to kill him. At Gath, David was alone and unable to control his situation among the enemy, being at their mercy; here, he is in control of a band of men and knows the terrain well, being able to move about to elude capture. Saul's reported advance highlights David's continuing fugitive status and his fear of being surrounded and cornered by Saul's superior forces. He appears to have lost his confidence for the moment and to have forgotten his guaranteed divine backing as *nāgîd*.

Ironically, it is Jonathan who 'strengthens David's hand in God' by going to David at Horesh and reassuring him that 'the hand' of his father Saul will not find him and that he will be king over Israel (vv. 16-17). Jonathan's relationship to Saul is stressed by his identification as Saul's son once and his dual reference to Saul 'my father' within the two verses.[1] Jonathan is able to locate David easily and gain access to his hiding place, presumably because of their pre-existing covenant. Jonathan takes on the role of a priest here, pronouncing the cultic phrase 'fear not' and reassuring the king-elect of the divine plan that calls for him to be king, which will not allow him to fall into Saul's destructive power. He then adds that he will be second in rank to David and that Saul his father also knows this (v. 17).

Saul's knowledge of the divine plan that calls for David rather than Jonathan to succeed him on the throne has already been revealed to the audience back in 17.37 and so is not news to David or the audience. Jonathan's future status as second in rank to the king is a new piece of information to the audience, however, whose origin becomes a focus of attention. Is Jonathan now revealing something that was worked out in their prior meetings in chs. 18, 19, or 20 but which was deliberately withheld from the audience at one of those times to come as a surprise here? Is this a consequent detail of David's loyalty to Jonathan's house sworn in 20.14-17? Is Jonathan taking advantage of David's weakness here to 'up the ante', so to speak, firming up his specific position *vis-à-vis* the king-elect now that he has survived the encounter with his father in ch. 20? Is Jonathan moving to secure his family's royal future by inserting David as a kind of interloper into

1. Fokkelman (*Crossing Fates*, p. 441) suggests that Jonathan's emphasis on his filial status to Saul is intended to indicate that the crown prince sees the possibility of a future rapprochement between David and Saul. Does this idea not read too much into the text?

the Saulide line but maintaining himself as next in line to the throne after David? The narrator's report in v. 18 that the two of them made a covenant before Yahweh after Jonathan's words suggests that the new item, Jonathan's position as second to David, was a new arrangement that required formal stipulation expressed in the updated pact.[1]

The Ziphites now supply Saul with the explicit information he needs to capture David, but David is rescued by a messenger whose sender is unidentified. Saul apparently has broken off his sally against David or has given up temporarily, for the Ziphites go to him at 'the hill' with specific details pinpointing David's location in the hunting grounds at Horesh on the hill of Hachilah south of Jeshimon. Has Jonathan convinced Saul to stay home after his return from David as his unspecified payment for his position as second to David (v. 17)? The Ziphites promise to shut David up (*sgr*) in the king's hand, so fulfilling all the king's human desire to go down to capture David (v. 20). The Ziphites' use of *sgr* and *yrd* echo the use of these terms by David in his inquiry to Yahweh concerning the actions of the lords of Keilah in vv. 11-12. The author seems to have deliberately repeated the verbs in order to establish a contrastive parallel between David's ability to seek and receive divine information and Saul's inability to do so, which leads him to have to depend upon less reliable human sources for his information. By their words the Ziphites equate themselves with the lords of Keilah in their stance toward David and at the same time fan the misguided flames of Saul's lust for David's death and his deliberate attempt to thwart the divine plan.

The Ziphites' status as Israelite citizens needs to be considered carefully in light of their parallel position to the lords of Keilah. By their own admission, David is hiding among them 'in the wilderness', or outside Judah proper, and their magnanimity in capturing David and delivering him to Saul may stem from the same situation that transpired at Keilah: they want to remove from their midst a potential raider of their threshing floors and, at the same time, earn the favor

1. Contrast the usual view that it is not a new updating, but a restatement of the terms of the existing pact: Hertzberg, *I & II Samuel*, p. 193; Ackroyd, *First Samuel*, p. 184; McCarter, *I Samuel*, p. 375, who also sees it as preparatory to 24.17-22. A notable dissenter is Miscall (*1 Samuel*, p. 142) whose position is close to the one espoused here.

of the king to their north who might prove to be a helpful future ally against the Philistines.

Saul's blessing upon the Ziphites for having 'spared' him (*ḥ^a^maltem 'ālāy*) by providing information concerning David's whereabouts (v. 21) contrasts with his previous tirade against his fellow Benjaminites and strengthens the impression that Ziph is to be considered non-Israelite. The root *ḥml* was used in 15.3, 9, 15 in connection with the divine command to Saul to enact *ḥérem* against Yahweh's enemy Amalek. Here, Saul states that the Ziphites have spared his life by revealing David's hideout. By implication, he believes that David has become his enemy who is actively seeking to kill him. By linking the use of *ḥml* in this chapter with the three uses in ch. 15, the audience is led to conclude that Saul's statement is meant to be a deliberate ironic reversal of the situation from ch. 15.[1] There, Saul spared the life of the foreign king of Amalek; here, foreigners from the southern region are sparing his life in a figurative way. While a direct equation between Amalek and Ziph does not seem to be implied, as was the case with Amalek and Edom in the narrative segments dealing with Doeg (21.7; 22.9, 18-23), a loose association between the two based on a common southerly location and shared foreign status seems deliberate.

Once again, Saul has confused his sense of loyalties and definition of friend and foe: David is a fellow Israelite who is his friend, while the Ziphites are foreigners who should be his foes. His words to the Ziphites also contrast with his earlier accusations against his fellow Benjaminite courtiers in 22.6-8, again emphasizing his misplaced perceptions.[2] His loss of bearings is further revealed by his statement in v. 23 that if David is in the land, he will seek him out among the thousands of Judah, echoing the 'thousands' of the victory song sung after David slew Goliath in 18.7.[3] Instead of continuing to slay his true enemy, the Philistines, Saul is seeking to slay Yahweh's chosen king-elect within his own territory and among his own people.

The audience knows that David is not in mortal danger from Saul's

1. Polzin (*Samuel*, p. 204) draws the same connection, but a different conclusion; for him, the linking 'joins Agag's fate and Samuel's rejection'. Fokkelman (*Crossing Fates*, p. 444) considers it an echo of Saul's self-pity in 22.8.

2. So previously, Gunn, *Fate of Saul*, p. 90.

3. Similarly, Fokkelman, *Crossing Fates*, p. 446.

pursuit because the king has lost his divine backing and Yahweh has repeatedly protected David from Saul's attacks. Now, however, a foreign people have offered to betray David and deliver him into Saul's hand. For the first time since David's visit to Achish at Gath, David is in a position of real danger. The suspense mounts as Saul commands the Ziphites to spy on David for a while to learn all of his haunts in the area (vv. 22-23). Will Saul be able to trap David during his next sortie thanks to the aid of the foreigners? Saul leaves with his men to seek David (v. 25). When David hears of Saul's advance, he moves his group to another hiding place, the cliff, in the wilderness of Maon. Saul learns of his move, however, and pursues (v. 25). Thanks to the Ziphites, he now has explicit information concerning the exact location of David's hideouts. Saul closes in on the correct mountain, but fortunately for David, from the opposite side (v. 26). He continues to close in on David and his men, gaining ground as the latter group try to escape, and is on the verge of capturing them when a messenger arrives, drawing Saul off to deal with a Philistine raid that has been mounted on the land (vv. 27-28).

As noted by J. Fokkelman, the messenger's sender is not specified in the story, but is implied to be Yahweh.[1] The messenger arrives in the nick of time to deliver David from Saul's capture and sends Saul off to execute his intended task, Israel's deliverance from its true enemy, the Philistines. Yahweh has demonstrated his ability to protect his anointed one even from foreign intervention and threat, ironically using the Philistines as the indirect agent of David's 'deliverance'.[2] The mention of 'the land' in v. 27 resonates with Saul's use of the phrase in v. 23. It reminds the audience of one of Yahweh's two intended purposes for Israel's king: the protection of his landed property (*nāḥălâ*) within the land from foreign oppression and attack. At the same time, it once again highlights Saul's inability to distinguish between 'insider' and 'outsider' in his dogged pursuit of the future Israelite king (cf. Doeg the Edomite), whose death would result in the suffering and misfortune of his own land and people.

1. Fokkelman, *Crossing Fates*, p. 449.
2. So too, Miscall, *I Samuel*, p. 143.

Chapter 19

1 SAMUEL 24

Continuing the previous episode, v. 1 (23.29, English text) reports that David left the Rock of Escape in the wilderness of Maon and went to the hunting grounds of En-Gedi, seeming to end the incident of Saul's pursuit. Yet, reference to the 'hunting grounds' bears the potential of continued cat-and-mouse play, which is borne out in the ensuing verses. After Saul returns from fighting the Philistines, he is informed of David's location in the wilderness of En-Gedi (v. 2) and he once again pursues David and his men, this time with three divisions of highly trained soldiers (v. 3). As J. Fokkelman notes, the author deliberately omits the final steps from the battle report, the statement of the outcome, its extent, and the gathering of booty and instead has Saul rush back to his pursuit of David.[1] His omission is a subtle signal to the audience that the forthcoming verses will resume focus on the theme of Saul's pursuit of David. Saul proceeds to Ibexes' Rocks (v. 3), a specific landmark whose mention implies that Saul's informants have been careful to pinpoint the fugitive band's location for the king. Once again, tension mounts as Saul closes in on David through the help of a third party; will he be able to thwart the divine plan after all?

Continuing to set the scene, the narrator informs the audience that Saul enters a cave in the vicinity of the animal enclosures to relieve himself, the very cave in whose innermost recesses David and his men are sitting (v. 4)! David is now cornered by the unsuspecting Saul and the scene suspense reaches its peak. Will he be caught? No—the tables are turned and the cat becomes the mouse. Saul's lack of knowledge becomes David's advantage and his men urge him to kill the king, quoting what appears to be a prophetic announcement that had been

1. Fokkelman, *Crossing Fates*, p. 451.

made to David some time in the past (v. 5).[1] The divine message was that Yahweh is giving David's enemies 'into his hand' to do with as he sees fit, or according to what is 'good in his eyes'. David's men have identified Saul as David's enemy by equating him with the prophetic pronouncement. They have assumed that David should take the same stance that Saul has taken toward him and declare him an enemy. The men's comment forces two decisions upon David: to determine who his true enemy is and to act in a way that aligns his human seat of judgment, the eyes, with Yahweh's seat of judgment, the heart. Will he let his human jealousy and rage over Saul's unjust pursuit blind him to the larger truth of the situation?

David's act of secretly cutting off the corner of the robe belonging to Saul (v. 5) rather than killing the king reveals his rejection of his men's suggestion. Yet, even this harmless act leads David's heart, the seat of divine judgment, to smite him (v. 6), demonstrating to the audience the inappropriateness of any action against Yahweh's anointed one. David then confirms the message in his direct speech to his men in v. 7, in which he identifies Saul once as his lord and twice as the Lord's anointed one and avers that he should not 'send forth his hand' against such an individual. His words express the view that once bestowed, divine spirit cannot be revoked, so that even though Saul has fallen from Yahweh's favor and has received an evil spirit in place of the former benevolent guiding spirit, he remains in possession of some form of divine spirit until his death and is to be treated as sacrosanct.

Others have seen in vv. 4-6 a self-serving interest on David's part; in evaluating the situation, they believe he has shrewdly decided that it would be in his best interest to set an example by refusing to harm the person of the king by treating him as sacrosanct, thereby establishing a precedent for his own future reign.[2] However, in light of the decisions with which David is faced, and especially in light of the exploration of the theme of human judgment by sight versus divine judgment by the heart, the focus of the verses would seem rather to be on David's use of his heart to discern appropriate behavior and the

1. Gordon (*I & II Samuel*, p. 179) concludes that men have fabricated an oracle to drive home their point.

2. For example, Miscall, *1 Samuel*, p. 149; Fokkelman, *Crossing Fates*, p. 458; Polzin, *Samuel*, p. 210.

divine will. David begins by cutting the royal robe, but could well have gone on to kill Saul himself had his heart not indicated that any violation of the Lord's anointed is wrong. Thus, the influence of the heart, the seat of divine judgment, becomes the turning point in vv. 4-6,[1] leading David to express his realization aloud to his men as an oath and to his subsequent restraint of those with him from violating the king as well. The verses do not seem to have as their primary function the exploration of the origin of the doctrine of royal inviolability. Rather, they seem to presume the audience's familiarity with and acceptance of this ideology, which David then himself upholds in his personal struggleto discern and act in accordance with the divine will in the given situation.

The motif *yād* is used in David's statement to highlight the inappropriateness of the use of power against one's king. His words lead to a division among the men, apparently winning some of them over to his position, and he prevents any of them from rising 'to' Saul, either with good or bad intentions (v. 8). Saul then rises and leaves the cave to pursue his original path, without knowledge that anything had transpired inside the cave (v. 8). The king remains blinded by his divine rejection and his quest to thwart Yahweh's plan to have David ascend the throne of Israel, even though David's earlier pronouncement concerning the inviolability of one anointed at Yahweh's command applies equally to his own person, the anointed king-elect, emphasizing the inappropriateness of Saul's determination to eliminate David.

David's subsequent confrontation of Saul in the remaining verses of the chapter are intended to make the message stated to the men explicit to Saul, thereby highlighting the invalidity of Saul's stance toward David and the inappropriateness of his resolve to kill the anointed *nāgîd*. David leaves the cave and calls out after Saul. Identifying him as 'my lord, the king' (v. 9), he signals his submissive, loyal status as Saul's servant and Saul's implied status as Yahweh's anointed one. He continues to demonstrate his submission, bowing to the ground and doing obeisance in the king's view (v. 9). David then confronts Saul

1. The heart is David's own and represents his inner struggle for recognition of the divine will. It is not the agent for an imposition of the divine will from without, as suggested by Hertzberg (*I & II Samuel*, p. 198) and Fokkelman (*Crossing Fates*, p. 464).

with his actions, carefully avoiding a direct accusation against Saul by shifting the blame for his belief that David is seeking to harm him to unnamed human 'misinformers' (v. 10).

Creating a situation where he becomes a self-represented plaintiff before the king, who is to serve as the highest human magistrate, he lays out his case against his nameless opposers, citing his interpretation of the facts and the evidence that he believes proves his innocence.[1] David reminds the 'judge' Saul that his own royal eyes, the seat of human perception, have witnessed how Yahweh that day placed him into David's hand inside the cave. Informing Saul that some of his men urged him to kill the king, he repeats his key statement he made to his men to the king himself: I will not stretch forth my hand against my lord because he is the Lord's anointed (v. 11). The motif *yād* appears twice in David's speech, emphasizing his potential physical power over Saul but indicating his acknowledgment that such power must be exercised properly, even when the opportunity for improper use arises, as it had in the cave.

Continuing, David tries to win Saul's favor and the decision of the fictitious court by citing the evidence of the piece of royal cloak in his hand. In addressing Saul as 'my father', David is making a two-fronted appeal to the judge/king. In the immediate context of the court scene, he is showing his respect for the king's authority as judge by addressing him with a title of respect that reflects his lesser, dependent position. On a more personal level, however, he is stressing his familial tie to Saul as Michal's husband and his subservient position as 'son' within the royal family as a subtle form of additional self-justification. By reminding Saul that the mock case before him is in some respects a family matter, since it concerns legally related individuals, he is hinting to Saul that as an involved party, he cannot serve as an impartial judge in the situation and should disqualify himself from sitting as judge over the dispute. This is a masterful way of leading Saul to realize that their dispute, which involves the king and king-elect, can only

1. The judicial aspect of vv. 8-15 has been noted previously by Miscall (*1 Samuel*, p. 147), and Fokkelman (*Crossing Fates*, p. 466). It tends to contradict the interpretation of David's bowing to the king as an acting out in great abandon of his role as Yahweh's chosen one, mocking Saul, as suggested by Polzin (*Samuel*, p. 207).

be fairly heard and decided by the highest court and its judge, Yahweh.

To drive home to Saul the lack of evil intent and rebellion (*péša'*) 'in his hand', David shows Saul the corner of the royal cloak that he had cut off, holding it out 'in his hand' and commanding Saul, still the presumed judge, to 'know' and 'see' how he could have gained control over Saul's entire person had he wanted (v. 12). Saul is to assess the truth of David's statement by using his 'eyes', the seat of human judgment, to evaluate the proffered evidence.[1] David's use of the two verbs 'to see' and 'to know' echo Saul's earlier commands to the Ziphites in 23.22-23 concerning their certain establishment of David's hideouts, suggesting that David knows Saul's criteria for judging the accuracy of an argument or sizing up a situation and is now using them to persuade the king to his own position.

The piece of royal robe displayed firmly in David's hand in v. 11 cannot help but call to mind for both the audience and Saul the earlier robe-rending incident in 15.27-28 through which Samuel symbolized the removal of the kingdom from Saul and its transferral to 'your neighbor/companion who is better (*ṭôb*) than you'.[2] Thus, while on a literal level it demonstrates David's restraint and failure to kill Saul even though he had the opportunity, on another level it graphically illustrates for all concerned Samuel's earlier prediction. David now literally holds within his hand a piece of the royal cloak, a symbol of the kingdom itself. Having rejected Saul's royal armor and weaponry in 17.38-39 because he had not yet passed his test as king-elect, but having subsequently received the cloak and weaponry of the office of king-elect upon his slaying of Goliath (18.4), he now is able to claim a piece of what is rightfully to become his at Saul's death: the royal robe itself. He is clearly the intended 'companion' who is better than Saul, to whom Yahweh will transfer the kingdom.

David then mounts a direct attack against the behavior of the judge who now becomes the opponent in the suit. He contrasts his own lack of sinning in respect to Saul with Saul's continued, active lying in wait

1. Miscall (*1 Samuel*, p. 146) notes the centrality of 'hearing' and 'seeing' here as in chs. 1–3, but the reversal of order. Now 'seeing', not 'hearing', is to lead to knowledge.

2. So, for example, Ackroyd, *First Samuel*, p. 188; Gunn, *Fate of Saul*, p. 95; Klein, *1 Samuel*, p. 239; Fokkelman, *Crossing Fates*, p. 458; Miscall, *1 Samuel*, p. 148; Polzin, *Samuel*, p. 209.

to seize his own person to highlight the inappropriateness of the king's behavior and its nonprovocation by David's actions (v. 12). The audience is invited to reflect upon the accuracy of David's self-characterization and to recall that Saul's desire to kill David derives from his awareness that Yahweh has chosen the Bethlehemite to be the next king. It is not David's personal actions that have provoked the royal death sentence against him, but rather, his status as Yahweh's anointed, a situation over which David had no control. Unlike David, Saul refuses to honor the sacrosanct status of Yahweh's anointed.

Having now effectively removed Saul from the position of judge in his original defense suit to that of a defendant in a countersuit, David makes an appeal to the new judge, Yahweh. He indirectly petitions Yahweh through the use of jussive constructions to judge between them and avenge him upon Saul (v. 12). He emphasizes that his own hand will not be against the king, once again driving home to Saul the inappropriateness of the use of physical force against Yahweh's anointed. His appeal to divine punishment of the infractions by the existing king highlights the only appropriate means of recourse for dealing with an unjust king: God himself must punish his chosen vice-regent.

David's quotation of what is probably the first half of an old proverb and his accompanying comments in vv. 13-14 are designed to drive home to Saul the indefensibility of his death sentence against the king-elect and the wrongness of his dogged pursuit. Proverbs tend to be comprised of two three-word statements joined by *wāw*, and J. Fokkelman is probably correct in his suggestion that a contrasting, positive statement with which the audience would have been familiar has been left unspoken.[1] David's averral that his hand will not be against Saul seems to argue that the spoken negative half of the proverb cannot be applied to him personally, but that the unspoken positive part can. His failure to commit an unlawful or unethical action against the king by killing him has demonstrated that he is not a wicked person. The unspoken implication of David's statement, however, is that Saul is a wicked person, as indicated by his unjustified pursuit and attempt to kill the Lord's other anointed that reveal him to be guilty in ethical, civil and religious spheres. David's vow in the second half of v. 13 would then express his decision not to retaliate,

1. Fokkelman, *Crossing Fates*, p. 465.

returning wickedness with wickedness, thereby contrasting his innocence with Saul's implied guilt.

The ensuing question in v. 14, 'after whom has the king of Israel gone out?', reiterates the verb *yṣ'* from the proverb, linking the two statements. By analogy to the proverb, where a characteristic (wickedness) begets its own qualities, David's question would seem to imply that a king's actions should always exhibit appropriate royal behavior but that Saul's current 'going out' after his person breaks the expected norm. By drawing a very tight analogy to the proverb, David's question could be taken to imply that the king of Israel should only engender another king, reminding both the audience and Saul that the *mî* in question, David, is indeed the king-elect toward whom Saul ought to be acting in an appropriately royal manner, but is not. Instead, the king is pursuing (*rdp*) his divinely appointed royal successor with malicious intent, as David's second question emphasizes.

By answering his own two questions with self-humbling identifications as a dead dog and a flea,[1] David appears to be trying to use gross understatement to jolt Saul into recognizing the truth of the situation and the error of his attempt to thwart the divine plan by killing Yahweh's chosen royal successor. Saul and the audience are well aware that David is not an insignificant nobody easily dismissed and forgotten. At the same time, David's self-abasement and voluntary subservient stance before the reigning king highlights his lack of malice toward Saul and Saul's concomitant guilt in maintaining undeserved malice toward David.

Completing his judicial case and appeal for a just decision, David affirms to Saul his belief that Yahweh will become a judge in their dispute and will act as judge between the two (v. 16). He goes on to reiterate his hope that Yahweh will consider (the evidence) and then find for his side, again appealing indirectly to Yahweh through the use of jussive constructions. He seeks a verdict outside of the normal judicial jurisdiction of the royal court (*miyyādekā*), where he knows he cannot find a partial judge. The motif *yād* appears again, this time to symbolize the human sphere of authority and power.

David's entire address to Saul in vv. 8-16 is a masterful example of

1. For biblical and extrabiblical uses of the expression as a form of self-humility or, when applied to another, of castigation, see the convenient discussion in McCarter, *I Samuel*, pp. 384-85.

discerning speech, demonstrating his possession of the characteristic attributed to him by a Saulide courtier in 16.18. It is a persuasive piece of dramatic rhetoric with multiple levels of meaning, designed to make Saul realize the error of his ways and break off his continued pursuit of the Lord's other anointed. Following the allusion to the tearing of Saul's robe and the announcement that the kingdom was to be given to 'a better one' in 15.27-28, the speech illustrates for the audience David's possession of acuity in speech and judgment as characteristics through which he surpasses or 'bests' Saul, confirming the dimensions of his *ṭôb* that were explored in ch. 16.

Saul's reply to David's mock trial and self-defense is carefully designed to build to a crescendo in an anticlimactic failure to be diverted from his chosen path of action. As noted by R. Polzin, his initial response, 'Is this your voice, my son David?', (v. 16) faintly echoes Samuel's accusing rhetorical question to Saul in 15.14, just before he announces Yahweh's reconfirmed rejection of Saul from the kingship.[1] With it he signals his assumption of his appointed role of judge, designating David's status as petitioner by calling him 'my son' and asking rhetorically if David has chosen to bring his case before him by referring to David's 'voice'. His immediate raising of his own voice to render a verdict results in an unexpected display of tears instead of words to announce his final decision (v. 16c), leaving the audience uncertain about his underlying motivations and conclusions. Has David's masterful speech so moved him that he has realized the error of his ways and is repentant, or has David's speech confirmed for him his belief that Yahweh is now actively seeking to remove him from the office of king by delivering him to the power of the king-elect, who will kill him? The second option includes within it an allusion to the familial dimension of the father–son terminology, which, as discussed above, tends to emphasize the king–king-elect relationship between the two and the need for divine judgment to settle their dispute.

Saul then proceeds to clarify his verdict by delivering a more traditional judicial pronouncement. His response is carefully constructed, laying out a verdict with accompanying argument (vv. 18-19) and then a second argument leading to a second verdict (v. 20) in an

1. *Samuel*, p. 109. Contrast the sense applied to the phrase by Alter (*Art of Biblical Narrative*, p. 73).

AB–B′A′ structure.[1] He finds in favor of the defendant-turned-plaintiff, David, against himself, stating that David is the more righteous (*ṣaddîq*) of the two because he has done good acts (*g*^e^*maltanî haṭṭôbâ*) toward him while he has done evil acts toward David (*g*^e^*maltîkā hārā'â*) (v. 18). Saul goes on to explain that his verdict stems from his acceptance of the veracity of David's immediately preceding declaration concerning the events that had taken place within the cave. He specifically accepts not only David's reporting of the events that were to have transpired, but also his interpretation of them: you did good acts toward me today in that you did not kill me when Yahweh 'closed me up' (*sgr*) in your hand (v. 19). He repeats the terms *rā'â* and *hrg* from David's speech, as well as the latter's assessment that their meeting in the cave was the result of divine providence and was to have benefitted David to Saul's detriment. However, it is noteworthy that Saul refers to his seeming divine deliverance into David's power (*yād*) not with the neutral verb *ntn* that David used, but with the verb *sgr*, which he himself used earlier in 23.7 to describe his anticipated overpowering of David at Keilah. The same verb was also used subsequently by David and Yahweh to characterize David's anticipated betrayal by the citizens of Keilah (23.12) and by the Ziphites to offer David's betrayal to Saul in 23.20.[2]

This subtle shift in terms suggests that Saul has reflected on the events himself and has decided not only that David's assessment of Yahweh's involvement in their meeting was accurate, but further, that Yahweh is actively seeking to betray him to David and so accomplish his elimination, the very task he is desperately seeking to accomplish against David. It betrays his conviction that God is conspiring to remove him prematurely from the throne and place David in his stead. Thus, his shift in key terminology reveals that the recent events have not altered his understanding of the larger picture at all; it

1. J. Fokkelman (*Crossing Fates*, p. 469) argues that the response in vv. 18-22 is structured as three motivational statements introduced by *kî* (18b; 19a implied; 20a) followed by two conclusions introduced by *w*^e^*'attâ* (vv. 21-22). He thus implies that the speech is governed by an 'if, if, if. . . then, then' constructional principle. In light of the judicial context and the implied 'then. . . if' construction of vv. 18b-19 and 'if. . . then' construction of v. 20, it would appear that the *w*^e^*'attâ* clauses are not linked directly to the *kî* arguments, but are intended to be summaries of the entire event, as noted by Miscall (*1 Samuel*, p. 147).

2. So also Fokkelman, *Crossing Fates*, p. 469.

expresses his belief that David's magnanimity has merely forestalled the divine plan temporarily.

Moving on to render a second verdict, Saul continues to present argumentation by countering David's quotation of a proverb with a rhetorical question that sounds proverbial in its phrasing: 'If a man finds his enemy, will he send him on a good path?' (v. 20). While possibly a known proverb,[1] the reference to 'path' goes back directly to v. 8, so that the entire question seems to reflect Saul's recent experience and his evaluation of the events that transpired. It is noteworthy that Saul presumes that David shares his hostility and considers the king to be his enemy. The reappearance of the term 'enemy' takes the audience back to the statement in v. 5 by David's men concerning the divine promise to deliver David's enemies into his hand and their similar presumption that Saul must be David's enemy because he has been seeking his life. The events that have transpired have demonstrated David's belief that Saul is not his enemy; Saul, by contrast, has signalled his inability to change his own stance toward David while confirming that David does not share his hostility, thereby highlighting the irrationality and untenability of his own position.

Moving to the level of divine judgment as David had in his earlier discourse and using the same jussive construction, Saul invokes Yahweh to reward (*šlm*)David with goodness for his actions towards the king that day (v. 20). His statement confirms the inability of a citizen to receive adequate redress against the king in a regular law suit and the need for all punishment of royal misdeeds to come from the divine sphere. As reigning king, Saul hopes for the bestowal of divine blessing upon the injured party instead of self-punishment as the guilty party. However, on another level, his comments reflect irony and a hope for David's loss of divine favor because of his actions that day. Since Saul has indicated his continuing belief that Yahweh is actively seeking to destroy him and thinks that David has probably overturned the divine plan that day by failing to kill him, his statement carries overtones of a possible bitter reward for David from Yahweh for the sparing of Saul's life. At the same time, his appeal for restoration at the divine level alerts both David and the narrative audience to his decision not to resolve the dispute on a human level and, therefore, of his failure to alter his position or

1. So suggests Klein, *1 Samuel*, p. 241.

course of action against David, irrational as it might be.

Having fulfilled his role as judge at the mock trial, Saul concludes his reply to David on a more personal level, summarizing the knowledge he has gained from their encounter in two statements each introduced by *w*^{e}*'attâ* (vv. 21-22). First, he avers to David and the audience his certain knowledge that David will become king and that the kingdom of Israel will be established 'in his hand' or under his power, using the familiar motif *yād* (v. 21). His statement confirms the implications of his comment to David before his combat with Goliath in 16.18 that 'Yahweh is with you' and his comment to Jonathan in 20.31, 'For as long as the son of Jesse lives upon the earth, neither you nor your kingdom shall be established'. Like the latter comment, it takes the audience back to Samuel's warning to Saul at Gilgal in 13.13 that Yahweh would establish (*qwm*) his kingdom to Israel forever if he would obey Samuel's prophetically delivered divine commands but otherwise, would appoint another to be *nāgîd* over his people.[1] Saul is here announcing the certain fulfillment of Samuel's proclamation in 13.13-14, thereby indirectly acknowledging his awareness that David is Yahweh's anointed *nāgîd*. At the same time, he is confirming at least part of Jonathan's statement to David at Horesh in 23.17.[2] Thus, David's previous mock trial has made Saul publicly concede his knowledge of David's status as king-elect.

What has prompted Saul's announcement of his knowledge of David's status as *nāgîd*? Although there have been hints in the narrative beginning as early as ch. 16 of his knowledge of David's destiny, it would seem that his statement has been prompted by his immediately preceding encounter with David. In that context, it was apparently the common belief of David, his men, and Saul alike that Yahweh had delivered Saul into David's hand for destruction that led to Saul's announcement of David's certain destiny to be king. Once again, then, it is Saul's belief in his active persecution by Yahweh that has motivated his confession, rather than David's words and mock trial *per se*.

It would seem to be the same belief that leads Saul to his second statement in v. 22, which takes the form of a command that David

1. So also Fokkelman, *Crossing Fates*, p. 471; Miscall, *1 Samuel*, p. 148.

2. So previously Hertzberg, *I & II Samuel*, p. 197; Ackroyd, *First Samuel*, p. 189; Klein, *1 Samuel*, p. 241; Fokkelman, *Crossing Fates*, p. 471.

take an oath overseen by Yahweh not to cut off his seed after him or to destroy his name from his father's house. Knowing himself to be doomed and believing that Yahweh has appointed David to be his executioner, Saul seeks to extract an oath from David not to undertake a bloody dynastic purge when he acts as Yahweh's agent to gain the throne. By implication, he wants the anticipated killing to be restricted to his own person. His extraction of the oath seems motivated by his additional, unfounded belief revealed earlier in the narrative that Yahweh has not necessarily rejected Jonathan or other sons from eventually assuming the throne, after David's reign. The same hope seems to have been expressed by Jonathan in his similiar oath-bound negotiations with David in 20.14-17[1] and 23.17. The parallel oath scenes establish in retrospect a realignment of Jonathan and Saul as father and son, both of whom share as their top priority the securing of the welfare and perpetuation of the Saulide royal house. At the same time, they tend to emphasize in retrospect Jonathan's keen diplomatic skill, political awareness and self-serving interests in his dealings with David.

After David swears not to undertake a bloody royal purge, Saul breaks off his dogged pursuit and returns home. David and his men, however, do not accompany the king; instead, they return to the hunting grounds in the wilderness. The confrontation has not led to a rapprochement between the king and king-elect, only to an acknowledgment by Saul of the destiny of each, a reassurance from David of his nonhostile intentions toward Saul personally, and an oath by David not to eliminate the Saulide royal house entirely. The relocation of David and his men in the hunting grounds leaves open the possibility that further pursuit will ensue and thus, the possible testing of both men's claims and decisions.

1. The parallels are widely acknowledged. See, for example, Ackroyd, *First Samuel*, p. 189; Fokkelman, *Crossing Fates*, p. 472; Miscall, *1 Samuel*, p. 147; Polzin, *Samuel*, p. 210.

Chapter 20

1 SAMUEL 25

The chapter opens with the report of the death of the king-maker Samuel and his mourning and burial by all of Israel. The placement of the notice at this point in the story seems to have been motivated by the previous confrontation between the king and king-elect, both of whom were anointed on Yahweh's behalf by the prophet. Saul's closing statements in ch. 24 reveal his acceptance of his own fate and David's destiny as his immediate successor to the throne. By reporting Samuel's death at this juncture, the audience is led to feel that no further developments in the divine plan can or will occur because of the removal of Yahweh's designated prophetic agent. The balance of the story should therefore merely relate the inevitable unfolding of Saul's death and David's accession to the throne.

Nevertheless, both men will now have to rely upon their own resources to actualize their destinies. Samuel's death removes from David his most important supporter. David will no longer be able to look to Samuel the king-maker for protection or guidance, as he had in 19.18-24. Although he now has with him the Elide, Abiathar, through whom he can ascertain the divine will in individual instances via the priestly ephod, he no longer has a direct link to Yahweh via his chosen prophetic messenger, through whom he can communicate directly with God and receive divine communications directly. Similarly, with Samuel dead, Saul is free to pursue his plans to try and eliminate the divinely designated king-elect without any possible fear of prophetic intervention or condemnation. Even though Samuel has kept his distance since his announcement of Saul's rejection in 15.34-35, his reappearance in the narrative flow of events has always remained a possibility hanging over Saul's head. Thus, although the audience has not been specifically informed that Saul had developed a fear of prophetic intervention, the possibility seems to be raised upon reflection over the significance of Samuel's death for Saul's ongoing career. Samuel's removal leaves both king and king-elect on their own to establish their destiny without divine intervention or direction. David must seek to attune his heart to God's and learn the type of behavior fitting for a future king.

Whether or not David was among the 'all Israel' who assembled to honor and bury Samuel, in the wake of the funeral David and his men once more change location and move to the wilderness of Paran, according to the MT text, or of Maon, according to the LXX text (v. 1).[1] In favoring the LXX reading, which is not the *lectio difficilior*, David would be returning to the region where he had been a mountain away from capture by Saul (23.24-28). The audience should immediately wonder whether he will now be free from danger, in light of Saul's confession, or whether he will still be the object of pursuit. Even if the MT reading 'Paran' is followed and understood to reflect David's fear of Saul's action in light of Samuel's passing and his retreat very far south, as the story unfolds David will return to the region of Maon, the sight of his near capture by Saul, thereby raising the same question. Saul's failure to invite David to return to the court as the rightful king-elect at the end of ch. 24 has set the audience up for David's retreat. By implication, the future king has understood Saul's unaltered position toward him, in spite of his confession.

A new episode begins in v. 2 with the introduction of a wealthy herdsman who resides in Maon but whose 'doings' are in neighboring Carmel, where at the moment he is shearing his extensive flocks. Carmel was last encounterd as the sight where Saul erected his victory *yād* after defeating the Amalekites in 15.12 and where his rejection by Yahweh was reconfirmed by Samuel. As already noted, Maon was the sight of Saul's nearly successful capture of David as the two chased each other around the base of the mountain (23.24-28). Thus, the new geography should remind the audience of Saul's status as Yahweh's rejected king and of his past attempts to thwart the divine plan by killing the designated king-elect.

1. The LXX reading is adopted, for instance, by Wellhausen, *Text der Bücher Samuelis* (Göttingen: Vandenhoeck & Ruprecht, 1871), p. 131; Driver, *Notes*, p. 195; Dhorme, *Livres de Samuel*, p. 220; Blenkinsopp, '1 and 2 Samuel', p. 316; J. Levenson, 'I Samuel 25 as Literature and History', *CBQ* 40 (1978), p. 12; McCarter, *I Samuel*, p. 388; Klein, *1 Samuel*, p. 245; Gordon, *I & II Samuel*, p. 182.

The man is identified as Nabal, a name meaning 'foolish', and he is instantly contrasted with his wife Abigail (v. 3). She is characterized as *ṭôbat-śékel* and *yᵉpat tō'ar*, 'good in respect to insight' and 'pretty in respect to physical appearance', both traits that resonate with David's description to Saul by a courtier in 16.18 (*nᵉbôn dābār* and *'iš tṓ'ar*; cf. *yᵉpēh mar'eh* in 17.42).[1] By contrast, Nabal is characterized as *qāšeh* and *ra'ma' ᵃlālîm*, 'severe' or 'crude', and 'bad in respect to practices'. David's previous use of the adjective *qāšeh* to describe Saul's potential actions in 20.10 would seem to create for the audience a link between Nabal and Saul, whether or not David's characterization in 20.10 was to be viewed as reliable. The link gains further reinforcement in light of Samuel's use of the verb *śkl*, 'to act foolishly', to describe Saul's deeds in 13.13, making Saul and Nabal fellow 'fools'. Thus, from initial characterization, Nabal seems to become something of a surrogate Saul, and Abigail something of a surrogate David.[2]

By selecting the order of character traits carefully, the narrator hints to the audience that Abigail's central trait in the ensuing story will be her insight, while her natural beauty will play some sort of important role. In Nabal's case, his crudity or severity will be the primary characteristic that guides his behavior, with his misdeeds playing a secondary role. Nabal's final identification as a 'Calebite',[3] a member of the southern clan of Caleb, seems to also carry with it the deliberately negative overtones of its more literal meaning 'doggy' and provides an ironic link to David's self-deprecating characterization as a 'dead dog' in the previous episode (24.14).

Drawing a link to v. 1, the audience learns that David hears of Nabal's shearing while he is still in the wilderness (v. 4) and sends ten of his soldiers (*nᵉ'ārîm*) to Carmel on his behalf to ask Nabal for peace (v. 5). More specifically, they are to offer friendship (*kōh leḥāy*) and peace in respect to Nabal himself, his house, and all that he has. They are also to inform him that David has heard that he has

1. So noted also, for example, Levenson, '1 Samuel 25', p. 18; Miscall, *1 Samuel*, p. 151.

2. Levenson ('1 Samuel 25', p. 22) concludes that Nabal and Abigail are personifications of the fool and the virtuous wife in wisdom literature.

3. So reads the *qᵉrê*. The *kᵉtîb klbw*, 'like his heart', would anticipate Nabal's fate in v. 37, but would eliminate the known connection of the Calebite clan with this region in 1 Chron. 2.42-49 and the nice pun.

shearers and wants him to know that some of his shepherds had spent time with David and his men and had not experienced humiliation at their hands or had not missed anything all the time David had lived in Carmel (vv. 6-7). Nabal is to ask his own attendants/soldiers for verification of the facts (v. 8). The messengers are finally to end with a request that they find favor in Nabal's eyes in light of their arrival on a 'good' day and to ask him to give whatever his hand finds (*t^enâ-nā' 'ēt 'ᵃšer timṣā' yād^ekā*) to his servants and to his son, to David.

David's message is carefully structured to lay a logical groundwork for his final request for food and supplies from the unknown Nabal. The greeting is to be directed not merely to Nabal, but to his whole house and all that he has, seeming to hint that David's interest concerns Nabal's wider possessions.[1] He then moves on to the rumor concerning Nabal's shearing activity as an indication that the Calebite has had a successful season of sheep-raising and indicates that he has directly contributed to Nabal's present ability to harvest the wool by taking care of his shepherds who spent time with him and his men in Carmel. The wording of David's actions toward the shepherds is deliberately vague, leaving open the possibility that hostile threats may have been forthcoming from David's group itself and that his magnanimity concerned his restraint of his own men from harming them, rather than his offer of protection from outside attack. His suggestion that Nabal's own men would verify the 'facts' could reflect a 'godfather' situation where no one would dare say anything bad about David for fear of reprisal.[2]

David is now requesting belated payment for his services at a time when such requests should be honored and humbly identifies himself as Nabal's 'son' or servant (v. 8), recalling his use of the same filial expression of servantship to Saul in the preceding episode (24.11,

1. Levenson ('1 Samuel 25', p. 15) emphasizes that the close association drawn here between Nabal and his possessions is a key theme in the story, which will tell how the fool and his property come to be parted. 'It is precisely Nabal's attitude toward his holdings which destroys the potential for the *šālôm* with David which the latter seeks.'

2. David's request has been characterized as a 'protection racket' by, for example, Ackroyd, *First Samuel*, p. 195; Levenson, '1 Samuel 25', p. 19; Gunn, *Fate of Saul*, p. 98; and J. Rosenberg, *King and Kin* (Indiana Studies in Biblical Literature; Bloomington, IN: Indiana University Press, 1986), pp. 149-50. Rosenberg makes the verse the first narrative protest against Davidic taxation!

16).[1] In this case, however, no official agreement had preceded that had established David's status as Nabal's 'son' or servant, so that the identification is a voluntary one on David's behalf, as indicated by the *lāmed* before both *son* and *David.* It is David himself who is alleging that he is Nabal's 'son'.

David's request that Nabal give 'what his hand finds' seems to echo other pregnant uses of this phrase in the preceding narrative. Specifically, it appears to recall Yahweh's command to Saul 'to do what your hand finds to do' in 10.7, where the motif *yād* had explicit military overtones. It also seems to recall the exchange David had with Ahimelech at the sanctuary of Nob in 21.4 concerning supplies, where David overtly asked for food and weapons, but was really seeking to secure Goliath's sword. In the latter case, *yād* served as a source of authority, but was indirectly linked with control over a weapon. Bearing in mind these two passages and the use of *yād* as a motif throughout the Saulide narrative as a symbol of power,[2] it seems reasonable for the narrative audience to believe that David's request to Nabal bears undertones of a threatened power conflict if the request is not honored.

Having delivered the message to Nabal, David's men await a response (v. 9). Nabal answers unfavorably, denigrating David by saying in two rhetorical questions that he is an unknown entity as well as a 'son of nobody', unworthy of serious attention or consideration (v. 10). The double question may be intended to echo Saul's triple question to Abner concerning David's identity in 17.55-58[3] and his later outburst in 22.7-8 where he derogatorily characterizes David as the 'son of Jesse'.[4] Continuing, Nabal seems to let the men know that he in fact does know something about David. He brushes aside David's appeal to be considered a legitimate servant by stating 'today, servants abound', perhaps implying that with the impending celebration of the sheep-shearing and bestowal of rewards for good service, many will

1. So noted previously by R. Gordon, 'David's Rise and Saul's Demise: Narrative Analogy in 1 Samuel 24-26', *TynBul* 31 (1980), p. 48.

2. Miscall (*1 Samuel*, p. 150) notes that the exercise of power or restraint is at issue in the chapter, where the play between *yād* as 'hand' and as 'power' continues.

3. So also Polzin, *Samuel*, p. 211.

4. So also Gunn, *Fate of Saul*, p. 97. Connections forward to Sheba's rebellion cry in 2 Sam. 20.1 are drawn by Levenson ('1 Samuel 25', p. 24) and Gordon ('David's Rise', p. 45).

come looking for gifts, whether they have legitimate claims or not. Nabal then continues, however, by adding the statement, '(including) those who are breaking away, each on account of his lord', perhaps hinting at his knowledge of David's breach with his official liege majesty, Saul (v. 10).

Nabal's use of *prṣ* seems to pick up on the threatening overtones of David's request, acknowledging his understanding that David or his envoys are prepared to fight for the supplies they need. Nevertheless, he rejects the request, again using a rhetorical question to indicate that his food is for his official employees, his shearers, and will not be given to outsiders with unproven claims (v. 11). The phrasing of the rejection seems to imply his questioning of the ten men's legitimate ties with David. The resulting ambiguity of intent leaves the audience to wonder in turn whether Nabal's earlier reference to men breaking away from their lords was really a reference to David and Saul or a suspicion that the ten men before him were fleeing from their lord, David, but using him as an excuse to gain food for their flight. Echoes of David's flight from Saul and his claim to Ahimelech at Nob to be on a secret assignment surface again. Now Nabal's knowledge concerning David's identity and status is highlighted.

Meanwhile, the ten men return to David and recount their exchange with Nabal (v. 12). David's response is a command that every one of his men gird on their swords (v. 13), initiating the move toward armed conflict already hinted at twice in the preceding narrative. The act of arming is foregrounded by its threefold repetition in the space of v. 13, contrasting nicely with the earlier threefold offer of peace in v. 6.[1] The mention of the force of 600 associated with David is consistent with the last count given for his ranks after he had left Keilah in 22.13. His decision to leave 200 to watch the belongings while he goes to deal with Nabal seems to hint at his possession of a large amount of goods, which would have included the cattle captured at Keilah (23.4).[2] By implication then, David is not desperate for the food he

1. So noted also by Miscall, *1 Samuel*, p. 151. Rosenberg (*King and Kin*, p. 150) sees David's rushing headlong into a disaster of his own making to be a deliberate 'parry in the confederate-style politics of retaliation'.

2. Ackroyd (*First Samuel*, p. 196) sees in the reference to the 200 left with the baggage an anticipation of the legal decision by David in ch. 30. Fokkelman (*Crossing Fates*, p. 490) points to the contrastive connection with 17.39, where David now girds on his sword.

has requested from Nabal. His motives concerning Nabal now become suspect. Has he deliberately forced a confrontation in order to seem to have a legitimate grievance and basis for gaining control over Nabal's flocks and wool? Has this been a long-standing plan, formulated months ago in Carmel when Nabal's shepherds first appeared on the scene? Has David set up Nabal?

The narrator quickly switches scenes to Abigail, who has not been heard of since her initial introduction in v. 4. She is informed by one of the soldiers/attendants of her husband that David has sent messengers from the wilderness to 'bless' their lord, but that Nabal has 'flown' (root *'wṭ*) against them (v. 14). Three points are immediately of note. The attendant feels no need to introduce David to Abigail by more than his first name, implying that David was already known to her by reputation. Secondly, he characterizes David's message as one of 'blessing', while David characterized it as one of 'peace'. He therefore reveals himself to be favorably disposed toward David. Thirdly, by seeking out Abigail, the attendant has in effect, 'broken away from his lord', Nabal, in his attempt to have Abigail overturn her husband's unfortunate decision. He has revealed his lack of respect for his lord's decisions and his unwillingness to accept them. The irony of Nabal's earlier words of rejection of David's request in v. 10 are thereby highlighted.[1]

The attendant proceeds to tell Abigail that David's men were exceedingly good to them and, repeating the exact phrasing of David's message in v. 7, states that 'we were not humiliated or deprived of anything the whole time we went with them, while we were in the field' (v. 15). His use of David's own words tells the audience that the attendant must have been present at the exchange between Nabal and the ten men sent by David. Instead of speaking up at the time the claim was being made to confirm its truth to Nabal, or of confirming it secondarily after Nabal's reply, the attendant has chosen to confirm its truth indirectly by informing Abigail of the situation.

While David's phrasing allowed room for speculation as to the source of the threat to the shepherds and the amount of active assistance or restraint involved, the attendant now clears the air in his continuing, self-styled testimony: a wall they were to us, all night and day, all the time we were with them shepherding the flocks (v. 16).

1. So noted by Levenson, '1 Samuel 25', p. 16 and Klein, *1 Samuel*, p. 249.

Members of the audience who are sympathetic to David's cause should be relieved to learn that David's protection was a legitimate and active thwarting of outside hostile threats and not a restraint of his own men from harming Nabal's shepherds. By implication then, his request for food and payment from Nabal is legitimate after all. However, is his planned armed attack in reprisal for Nabal's denial a legitimate response to Nabal's 'foolish' decision?

The attendant now warns Abigail of the imminent military threat that has resulted from Nabal's failure to grant David's legitimate request for 'blessing'. Picking up on the overtones explored in vv. 8 and 10, he tells her that she must 'know' (*yd'*) and 'see' (*r'h*) what she must do, for 'evil' (*rā'â*) has been determined or has become the end result for their lord and all his house[1] since he is son of a good-for-nothing, talking to David (that way) (v. 17). Nabal's description as a *ben-bᵉliyyá'al*[2] tends to link him with those who had despised Saul after his initial public designation as king-elect at Mizpah in 10.27 and had refused to pay him tribute, adding a new dimension to Nabal's refusal of David. Like his cohorts, the foolish Nabal has refused to acknowledge the appointed king-elect and supply him with the appropriate gifts of tribute.[3] The apparent link with 10.27 tends to confirm

1. Gordon ('David's Rise', p. 46), apparently followed by Polzin (*Samuel*, p. 211), suggests that the reference to evil is a hint of the future fate of the Saulide house since Nabal is an alter ego of Saul. Polzin suggests in addition that David's request for food from someone whose life is subsequently put in jeopardy by the request creates a parallel between the present situation and the incident at Nob in chs. 21–22. I find the differences more compelling than the similarities, although he is perhaps justified in drawing attention to Saul's involvement in blood-guilt after his rejection as king, which contrasts with his earlier avoidance of such an act in 11.12-13, and the potential dire consequences that might await David should he engage in a similar act of vengeance.

2. For discussions of the meaning of this term, see, for example, D.W. Thomas, '*bᵉliyya'al* in the Old Testament', in *Biblical and Patristic Studies in Memory of Pierce Casey* (ed. J.N. Birdsall and R.W. Thomsen; New York, 1963), pp. 11-19; J. Emerton, 'Sheol and the Sons of Belial', *VT* 37 (1987), pp. 214-17.

3. So noted also by Klein, *1 Samuel*, p. 249. Gordon (*I & II Samuel*, p. 183) sees the alienation of master and servant that is demonstrated by the servant's use of the phrase *bᵉliyyá'al* to describe Nabal to be a feature of the relationship between Saul and his staff and one more indication of the way in which Saul and Nabal are psychologically 'twinned'.

for the audience their suspicion that Nabal knew of David's status and relationship to Saul.

The attendant indicates that the only hope of averting the imminent confrontation lies with Abigail. In light of her description in v. 3 as beautiful and discerning, the attendant's words imply that she must use her natural gifts to defuse the situation. By implication, neither David nor Nabal will budge; David's legitimate request has been dishonored and Nabal is too crude and unscrupulous in his dealings to change his position. Abigail must mediate if either Nabal or his house is to be spared. It is noteworthy that the attendant names two of the three items listed by David as sources of peace in his initial greeting to Nabal in v. 6 as targets of David's pending evil intentions. The omitted item is 'all that you have', which has become the point of contention between the two men.

The spotlight focuses on Abigail; will she be able to act appropriately to avert the impending attack? She quickly loads provisions on asses, the mount of royalty, and directs her male attendants to cross over before her; she is following after them. The woman is all action; she deduces that the only way to head off the disaster is to satisfy David's request for provisions immediately and sends the goods off instantly, with the promise to follow personally (vv. 18-19).[1] The narrator explicitly informs the audience that Abigail does not apprise Nabal, her husband, of the events that have transpired or her actions (v. 19), making her an independent agent in the scene. Her motives for not approaching Nabal are thereby highlighted; is she afraid of his response? Does she consider it hopeless to change his mind? Or perhaps, is she moving to avert evil from befalling Nabal's house, which includes herself, leaving Nabal to deal with the personal evil he has earned from David?

Attention is quickly shifted back to Abigail as she rides her ass toward David (v. 20). Having ascended a hill, she now is descending the other side, out of view presumably of Nabal, but also of David and his men, who are coming to intercept her. The circumstances are very reminiscent of Saul's pursuit of David in the same neighborhood

1. Parallels to Jacob's sending of gifts to Esau to soften presumed hostility in Gen. 32.14-22 are drawn by, for example, Hertzberg, *I & II Samuel*, p. 203; Fokkelman, *Crossing Fates*, p. 493; and Gordon, *I & II Samuel*, p. 183.

around a similar, if not identical mountain.[1] Abigail, however, has taken the more direct route over the mountain, which has allowed her not to miss her 'prey' in the same way that Saul did. She then surprises David, meeting him unexpectedly. The situation now recalls David's surprise confrontation of Saul outside the cave near Ibexes' Rock in the preceding episode (24.8-22).

Before describing the encounter and reactions of both parties in more detail, the narrator digresses to inform the audience of a vow David had made to destroy every last 'wall-pisser' from all that belonged to Nabal by morning for his having returned David's good deeds of protecting his belongings with evil (and ingratitude) (vv. 21-22). His words echo Saul's reply to his legal petition outside the cave in 24.17-20, where the king/judge confessed his guilt for having returned David's good deeds with evil and petitioned Yahweh to reward David with good (*y*ᵉ*šallemkā ṭôbâ*).[2] His response also contrasts markedly with Saul's earlier failure to punish the worthless fellows who had despised him, recognizing that Yahweh directly kills the enemies of Israel (11.12-13). The audience may be intended to link David's derogatory characterization of male members of Nabal's household with the narrator's description of Nabal as a 'doggy' Calebite in v. 3.[3] The correctness of Saul's behavior and his decision to look to God to punish his enemies is emphasized by his immediate confirmation and coronation as king. By contrastive implication, David's vow is wrong; even if David has been wronged by an 'enemy', he must look to God to carry out the punishment and not initiate it himself. The implications of Samuel's death now looms large: will David be able to align his heart with God's?

Now the audience should realize that Abigail's mediatory task is even more urgent and has become much more difficult, if not hopeless. The circumstances have changed. She seemed originally to have acted on the belief that David would have been the more reasonable of the two men and the most likely to be placated. Now the audience should understand that David will not be easily dissuaded

1. So noted also by Gunn, *Fate of Saul*, p. 98 and Klein, *1 Samuel*, p. 249.

2. So, for example, Miscall, *1 Samuel*, p. 151; Klein, *1 Samuel*, 249; R. Gordon, *I & II Samuel*, p. 184.

3. This suggestion was made by Stuart Lasine in private correspondence. It would also apply to the use of the phrase 'wall-pissers' in v. 34.

from his position, having uttered an oath to his men.

The scene returns to the unsuspecting Abigail, who spies David before he sees her, hurries forward, and dismounts from her ass, falling upon her face before David and bowing to the ground in a gesture of humility and servitude (v. 23) that directly recalls David's actions before Saul in 24.8. Falling upon his feet in supplication, she tells David to lay full punishment for the iniquity upon her and then, calling him her 'lord' and herself his 'maidservant' (*'āmâ*), she begs him to hear her out (v. 24). Her self-characterization as a maidservant is overtly one of self-deprecation and humility,[1] aimed at expressing her position of dependence and mercy before David, who has the upper hand in the situation and who is now being cast in the role of judge, as David had done previously with Saul in 24.9-15. Through narrative analogy, Abigail becomes a surrogate David and David a surrogate Saul in a court-plea proceeding in which David now becomes the appointed judge who is to learn a lesson through the petitioner's plea.

Nevertheless, Abigail's self-characterization also carries with it deliberate sexual overtones associated with being a mistress or concubine, which, in light of Abigail's earlier description as physically beautiful, would seem to imply an invitation to David to settle any remaining debt or 'punishment' through sexual favors.[2] This is without knowledge of David's oath to his men. In light of the earlier unflattering description of her husband, the audience is left to wonder whether the shrewd Abigail has sized up David physically and decided to take advantage of her husband's blunder to get some self-satisfaction. Is there a possible word-play intended between *'ᵃmāṯᵉkā*, 'your maidservant', and *'ᵃmittᵉkā*, 'your truth', where the truth of the situation is her desire to become David's mistress?

Continuing her appeal in v. 25, Abigail tells David not to 'set his heart' or focus his attention on 'this good-for-nothing man', Nabal, because he epitomizes the literal meaning of his name while she, his maidservant, did not see the men whom he sent arrive. J. Levenson

1. McCarter (*I Samuel*, p. 398) especially emphasizes how Abigail's statements and actions represent conventional courteous and respectful behavior.

2. Gunn (*Fate of Saul*, p. 101) picks up on the sexual overtones and is followed by Miscall (*1 Samuel*, p. 152). Levenson ('1 Samuel 25', p. 19) highlights the romantic quality of the intimate encounter between David and Abigail, each of whom has shed attendants.

suggests that Abigail's pun on her husband's name may be a deliberate depiction of her applying to the situation at hand an old proverb whose variant can be seen in Isa. 32.5-8.[1] Whether she was familiar with a particular proverbial formulation concerning 'folly' or not, the pun is a logical one. For the first time, Abigail reveals her feelings about her husband. Her contempt leads the audience back to her earlier failure to notify Nabal of her plan in v. 19 and tends to favor her desire to avert danger from the house but to leave Nabal to fend for himself as her primary motive for action.[2]

In using the loaded phrase 'do not set your heart' to characterize David's decision-making process, Abigail unwittingly reminds the audience that David has been anointed king-elect because he is 'the man after Yahweh's own heart' (13.14). At the same time, his decision to seek personal revenge against Nabal seems to have been shown by contrastive narrative analogy with Saul's treatment of worthless men in 11.12-13 to be contrary to Yahweh's heart. The audience is left to wonder if David's planned course of action will lead to his rejection by Yahweh, just as Saul's earlier military undertakings in this very same neighborhood against Amalek had led to his rejection for disobedience or failing to be of one heart with Yahweh. Indeed, Saul's erection of the victory stele (*yād*) on Mt Carmel 'for himself' in 15.12, which seemed to be an act claiming personal victory for the defeat of Amalek instead of crediting it to Yahweh, the true victor, raised the identical issue of the need for the king to rely upon Yahweh to kill Israel's enemies instead of taking personal responsibility (or credit) for the task. Abigail's words also raise a question about her direct knowledge of David's status as king-elect. Has she learned something through the local grapevine, or are her words merely coincidental?

Although unaware of David's oath, Abigail appears to have understood from encountering David and his men *en route* over the mountain that David has resolved to seek revenge. David and his party were advancing toward Nabal's household in spite of her delivery of the supplies initially requested. Her characteristic insight has allowed her to evaluate the situation correctly. Her petition to David is, therefore, an attempt to make him realize that his planned course of action is wrong and should be aborted, just as David's petition to Saul was

1. Levenson, '1 Samuel 25', p. 14.
2. *Contra* Berlin, *Poetics of Biblical Narrative*, pp. 30-31.

aimed at having the king realize the error of his continued pursuit of the king-elect with intent to kill and his need to abort his attempt to thwart the divine plan. Abigail's motives for seeking to divert David's wrath are still not clear, but seem to stem from self-preservation.[1] Yet is there more? Is she also seeking to divert the king-elect from a potentially suicidal course of unkingly action?[2]

Abigail now ironically utters an oath that the audience realizes is a counteroath to David's (v. 26).[3] She emphasizes that Yahweh has personally withheld David's soul from associating with or entering into bloodshed and from using his 'hand' to deliver himself, and she wills that his enemies and those who are seeking evil for him become like Nabal. Her statement indirectly acknowledges that Nabal is a true enemy of David, but also iterates the divine displeasure over self-deliverance found elsewhere in Deuteronomistic writings (esp. Judg. 7.2). Her reference to Yahweh's personal protection of David provides the audience with their first certain clue that she may know about David's status as king-elect. Its exact meaning is uncertain, however; is she alluding to her knowledge of David's refusal to kill Saul that was narrated in the preceding chapter or to the present situation, where she hopes that her speech will result in David's not committing illegitimate bloodshed? The motif 'hand' is used to describe the use of power for one's benefit.

Abigail continues by urging David to give the 'blessing' that she, his 'marriageable maidservant' (*šipḥâ*) has brought, to the soldiers/men who follow him. She specifically refers to her food supplies as the 'blessing' that her husband's attendant had told her David had requested in v. 14 and states that she has 'caused them to come', thereby picking up on her previous use of the verb *bw'* (to characterize David's failure to 'enter into' bloodshed by Yahweh's restraint) to indicate her mediatory role. Her subtle shift from self-characterization as a mere *'āmâ* to a more menial and available *šipḥâ* highlights her sexual overtures to David as part of the bargain. The goods can be used to appease the men and serve as 'booty' from the aborted

1. Levenson ('1 Samuel 25', p. 19) sees her to be overtly interceding on Nabal's behalf, but covertly disassociating herself from him.

2. This is the understanding of, for example, Hertzberg, *I & II Samuel*, p. 203; Gordon, 'David's Rise', p. 46; and Klein, *1 Samuel*, p. 251.

3. Fokkelman (*Crossing Fates*, p. 501) contrasts the two speeches.

campaign; David can be free from any accusations of bribery by not personally accepting any of the goods,[1] but can have a separate reward from his maidservant.

The audience is finally apprised of Abigail's full knowledge about David's status as Yahweh's anointed *nāgîd* in vv. 28-31, the remaining part of her petition. She asks David to show consideration for her sin, because Yahweh will certainly make for her lord an established house in light of his fighting the wars of Yahweh and in light of the fact that evil will not be found in him all of his life. David's lack of evil (*rā'â*) deliberately contrasts with Nabal's stated evil in regard to his dealings, setting David over against Abigail's husband as a virtuous and worthwhile man who is destined for success. Abigail confirms her hearsay knowledge that David is Yahweh's appointed *nāgîd* in her reference to him as leader of Yahweh's wars and to his destiny to be the founder of a sure dynasty. She goes on in v. 29 to allude to her knowledge of David's slaying of Goliath, which was narrated in ch. 17,[2] and possibly to her knowledge of his dogged pursuit by Saul as narrated in chs. 22–24, stating that David's pursuers and enemies will be 'slung out' by Yahweh while his own soul will be tied inside the pouch of life[3] with Yahweh his God. She ends with a statement assuring David that Yahweh will 'do' on his behalf all (the good) that he spoke concerning him and will guide him as official *nāgîd* over Israel so that

1. The gift seems to serve more as a booty pay-off than as tribute paid to the future king, *contra*, for example, Ackroyd, *First Samuel*, p. 197, and Klein, *1 Samuel*, p. 250. Its destination for the men and not for David has been emphasized as an explicit attempt to clear David of any potential charges of bribery by Levenson ('1 Samuel 25', p. 19) and Klein (*1 Samuel*, p. 250).

2. So noted also by, for example, Gunn, *Fate of Saul*, p. 100; Miscall, *1 Samuel*, p. 154; Fokkelman, *Crossing Fates*, p. 508; and Polzin, *Samuel*, p. 211. McCarter (*I Samuel*, p. 399) denies the connection because of the use of the generic term for man, but it is likely that Abigail is deliberately attempting to generalize her allusions to David's past and future deeds so as not to seem too pushy or too anxious to become his future queen.

3. N.H. Tur-Sinai (*The Book of Job: A New Commentary* [rev. edn; Jerusalem: Kiryath Sepher, 1967], pp. 240-41) argues that *ṣ^e^rôr* refers to a tied document, as in Job 14.17. He is followed by McCarter, *I Samuel*, p. 399. By contrast, Gordon (*I & II Samuel*, p. 186), claiming to build on the work of A.L. Oppenheim but citing a discussion that has no relevance to the issue at hand, associates the phrase with the string of the shepherd's bag. The latter option is more plausible in light of the echoes with 17.40-50.

this shedding of blood without cause and self-delivery must not become for him a tottering or a stumbling block of the heart. Mention of the heart again reiterates the message that David needs to align his perceptions and actions with those of God and raises a threat to his already existing status as *nāgîd* should he not await Yahweh's direct command or initiative but take matters into his own hands.[1]

In closing, Abigail asks her lord David to 'remember (*zkr*) his maidservant' when Yahweh will have done well for him. Her speech confirms her extensive knowledge of David's exploits and speculation concerning his future as king that she must have learned from rumors, but at the same time, suggests that David's anointing by Samuel to be *nāgîd* might not have been common knowledge. It appears that his heroic feats have earned him a reputation and speculation about a bright royal future among the citizenry of Israel and Judah—or does it? Does Abigail also know about the anointing, to which she appears to allude in her reference to the words Yahweh has spoken and the making of a sure house? It seems that she is perhaps trying to pretend she does not by phrasing her knowledge of David's exploits and status in veiled and futuristic terms so she will not appear to be ingratiating herself with the future king and making a bid to become a royal mistress. Her petition ends with an appeal to the appointed judge, David, to rule leniently in the case of her infraction in view of the extenuating circumstances that affect him directly.

Like David's plea to Saul, Abigail's plea meets receptive and thankful ears in David, who now has been made fully aware of the larger issues at stake in his self-serving decision to avenge Nabal's personal insult. Following Abigail's lead, David credits Yahweh with sending her as a mediating agent and with heading off certain blood-guilt, now directly confessing to her his oath for revenge that she had surmised earlier (vv. 32-34). David accepts the provisions Abigail had sent to him as full settlement of her debt and sends her to her home 'in peace'.[2] She has successfully averted David's wrath against Nabal's

1. The sense of *ṣwh* as 'appoint' or 'give orders to' is probably deliberately ambiguous in the context, forcing the audience to consider more carefully the gist of Abigail's larger speech. As a converted perfect implying future action, the sense 'will appoint' seems less likely in light of her apparent familiarity with much of David's career and her strong hints that she already knows that he is in fact Yahweh's duly appointed and acting *nāgîd*.

2. Gordon ('David's Rise', p. 48) notes the occurrence of *rîb* terminology in

house, her primary mission from the outset. But what of Nabal himself, or Abigail's sexual overtures? Now that it is clear that Abigail knew of David's reputation even before her husband's attendant approached her with the crisis precipitated by Nabal's refusal to send David provisions, can we be sure that preservation of her own house was all that Abigail was after from David from the start?

Fortunately, the audience is not left hanging; answers to the first two questions and an inference concerning the third follow in the remaining verses of ch. 25. Abigail returns home as she is instructed to find her husband in the midst of a feast fit for a king, with his 'heart good' from his heavy intoxication (v. 36). The references to Nabal's feasting on food that should have been given to the 'king-elect' David, and his possession of a heart that could be made 'good' only through intoxication or by being rendered senseless prepare the audience for the arrival of long-anticipated poetic justice. Abigail reacts by telling her husband nothing until 'the light of morning', the time appointed by David for completion of the now-aborted extermination of all males from Nabal's house (v. 34). In the morning, 'when all the wine had left Nabal' so that he could experience the full weight of her deeds, she told him everything. There is a deliberate play on *nābāl* and *nēbel*, 'wineskin', in the verse,[1] resulting in an insinuation that Nabal had become a limp, deflated, useless sack of skin. Her announcement has its desired impact; Nabal's now-normal heart dies inside him and he becomes a stone, unable to react or move. The audience is left to decide whether his condition resulted from fear over what he had narrowly escaped at David's hands, reaction to loss of his wife's support and guidance, or reaction to the loss of a small fraction of his vast possessions.[2] In ten days, Nabal becomes ammunition for Yahweh's slingshot (v. 38), fulfilling Abigail's desired fate for all of David's enemies from v. 29. Yahweh has vindicated the insult to his anointed.

David's reaction to the news of Nabal's death is to acknowledge Yahweh's intervention on his behalf to remove his disgrace and his

1 Samuel only in 24.15-16 and 25.39. He seems to have overlooked the narrative analogy provided by the petitioner–judge conversational exchanges that precede the verdicts in both chapters.

1. So also, for example, Gordon, 'David's Rise', p. 51.
2. The last option is developed especially by Levenson, '1 Samuel 25', p. 17.

active restraint of the king-elect from evildoing, confirming the truth of Abigail's earlier assessment of the situation. The term *ḥerpâ*, 'disgrace', was last encountered in 17.10, 25-26, 45,[1] where Goliath had defied Israel, Saul, and Yahweh and had been killed by Yahweh through the agency of David. David has now relearned the lesson he already knew but had forgotten. Yahweh will personally avenge the evildoer and blood-guilt is unacceptable.

David then immediately sends messengers to Abigail to ask her to become his wife. As usual, no motives for his actions are given. The audience is left to wonder whether he was intrigued by Abigail's repeated sexual overtures in her petition to him and her actual beauty, whether he might have been most interested in her powers of insight, or whether her recent inheritance of Nabal's holdings might have been an important, influencing factor in his marriage invitation. Did he want to have her as a wealthy and influential bedmate, or as a conscience to help him steer clear of future nonkingly and potentially self-defeating behavior? Did he perhaps want both qualities?

In this new set of negotiations between David and the house of Nabal there is no rebuff of the initial request. Dealing directly now with the lady of the house who has proven herself to be shrewd and quick-actioned, the audience sees a repeat in reverse of Abigail's initial encounter with David after she descended the mountain. She bows her face to the ground, willingly makes herself David's servant rather than master, as Nabal had done,[2] then hurries to mount her ass. In between, she accepts the marriage offer by characterizing herself by the two sexually suggestive terms she had used previously when talking directly to David, *'āmâ* and *šipḥâ*. Her earlier overtures had not fallen on deaf ears; she has got what she wanted after all: she has become David's wife. Her knowledge of rumors concerning David's destiny loom large in the background, implying that she had planned for this eventuality carefully.

The writer concludes this episode with a brief review of David's marital history. He begins by stating that David also took Ahinoam from Jezreel and that both of the women became his wives, seeming to

1. So noted by Miscall, *1 Samuel*, p. 154.

2. The contrast between Nabal's response to David's request and Abigail's is noted also by, for example, Fokkelman, *Crossing Fates*, p. 156; Miscall, *1 Samuel*, p. 156; and Klein, *1 Samuel*, p. 252.

imply from his phrasing that David married both women at about the same time (v. 43).[1] In an aside, he tells us that Saul had given David's first wife Michal to Palti ben Laish of Gallim (v. 44). Is the writer attempting to provide indirect commentary on David's motives concerning Ahinoam after all? No details are provided about how David came to meet Ahinoam, unless the audience is to intimate from the particular attention paid to the five female attendants who accompanied Abigail that she was Abigail's attendant-turned-fellow-wife. Perhaps the audience is to conclude that David would have married Ahinoam for the common reasons of physical attraction, so that by implication, Abigail was married primarily for her influence, insight and wealth as the widow of Nabal, and secondarily for her beauty.

1. Fokkelman (*Crossing Fates*, p. 525) concludes that the notice concerning Ahinoam is meant to be pluperfect in tense. The emphasis on David's marrying 'both' seems to belie such a chronological assumption. The suggestion by Levenson ('1 Samuel 25', p. 27) that Ahinoam is Saul's queen is impossible in light of the established time frame, her ability to still bear children, and David's subsequent request for Michal's reinstatement after Eshbaal's death in order to gain an heir with Saulide legitimacy. Had he been married to Saul's queen, he would have had a legitimate claim through her, without Michal.

Chapter 21

1 Samuel 26

The preceding episode of David, Nabal and Abigail served as an instructive interlude in the David–Saul conflict, teaching the king-elect his need to rely upon Yahweh rather than on self-help to deal not only with the rejected sacrosanct king, but also with other enemies. This chapter takes up the ongoing conflict between king and king-elect to test the extent to which David has learned a lesson from his near massacre of Nabal's house out of personal revenge.

Continuing the narrative flow of events, the Ziphites once again send messengers to Saul in Gibeah with detailed information about David's exact hiding place: he has returned to the hill of Hachilah on the east of Jeshimon (v. 1). Repeating the situation in 23.19, Saul has been supplied with the explicit information he needs to capture David. Will he act upon the tip-off, or has he accepted David's destiny to succeed him on the throne? In light of his confession in 24.20 and the oath David swore to him not to kill the royal heirs to secure the throne that would be his (24.21), will he break off his persistent pursuit and his attempt to thwart the divine plan? As noted at the beginning of ch. 24, David's retreat to the wilderness and Saul's failure to invite him back to court after their confrontation tends to imply that the rejected king will not give up his attempt to kill the king-elect so that his son Jonathan may follow him on the throne.

Not unexpectedly then, Saul acts on the information from the Ziphites, taking 3,000 of his most elite troops with him to the wilderness of Ziph 'to seek David' (v. 2), as he had done in 24.2. In the first instance, he had resumed his pursuit of David after he had had to go and fight the Philistines just when he had been closing in on David at Maon. Once again, he has taken his best fighting force, which was five times as large as David's, to eliminate his successor. He camps at the hill of Hachilah beside the road to Jeshimon, apparently so as not to miss David (v. 3).

However, David is not at the hill; he is in the wilderness, from where he sends out spies to locate Saul's exact position. All of a sudden, the tables are turned and David has become the hunter, luring Saul, his prey, to him. Whereas previously Saul had sent the Ziphites back to make certain of David's exact position and his various haunts (23.22-23), now David has used the king's spies, the Ziphites, to lure Saul down to him (by supplying them with false information?) and has sent out his own spies to uncover the exact location of the opposing camp (v. 4). David then personally scouts out the Saulide camp and pinpoints the sleeping spot of the king, beside the army commander Abner (v. 5). While Saul was unable to capitalize on his spies' information, David is able to walk right into the enemy camp (*wayyāqām dāwīd wayyābō' el-hammāqôm 'ašer ḥānâ-šām šā'ûl*) and personally ascertain the sleeping spot of his target![1] Does this mean none of his former comrades recognized him (18.12-16), or does it imply that their respect for him led them to fail to report his presence to Saul, thereby committing conspiracy (22.7-8)? The audience is not given enough information to decide between the two possibilities.

Apparently returning to his own base of operations, David asks two of his men, Ahimelech the Hittite and Abishai, the son of Zeruiah and brother of Joab, his nephew, to go with him to the enemy camp, to Saul. Only Abishai volunteers; the Hittite seems to have considered the mission too dangerous (v. 6), although David's solo trip to the camp would seem to belie his fear.[2] By contrastive analogy, Ahimelech's refusal emphasizes Abishai's willingness to lay down his life for his lord, which in turn hints that this is the very characteristic that David is seeking in his choice of man for the mission he has in mind.[3] What is his plan? Does he intend to kill Saul through his proxy Abishai?

1. *Contra*, for example, Hertzberg (*I & II Samuel*, p. 208), and Ackroyd (*First Samuel*, p. 202), who state that he surveys the camp from above, on an adjoining hilltop. David's ease of access during this trip tends to go against the conclusion of Gunn (*Fate of Saul*, p. 102) and Klein (*1 Samuel*, p. 257) that the description in v. 3 highlights the inaccessability of Saul and the heroic feat planned by David.

2. His failure to carry through a Davidic request may be meant to foreshadow Uriah's later failure to comply with David's entire command in 2 Sam. 11.6-13.

3. Gordon (*I & II Samuel*, p. 188) compares the situation with the visit by Gideon and Purah to the Midianite camp in Judg. 7.9-14.

Under cover of night, David and Abishai enter Saul's camp to find the king sleeping in the center of the camp, surrounded by Abner and his men, his place marked by his spear that is thrust into the ground at his head (v. 7).[1]

The description in v. 7 almost parallels that of David's initial visit to the camp in v. 5, but with two important changes. During the first incident, David saw the spot (*māqôm*) where Saul was sleeping or would sleep, while during the second trip, he sees Saul himself, who is sleeping. This slight shift in description is further elucidated by the other change in detail between the two scenes: the reference to Saul's spear stuck in the ground at his head in v. 7. Apparently, the spear was the key element that had allowed David to determine Saul's intended sleeping spot during his initial trip. It has served as a predetermined marker for the return trip in the dark.[2]

Although the incident near Ibexes' Rock in ch. 24 involved a chance meeting between Saul and David while the current meeting with Saul has resulted from David's own initiative, Abishai concludes that both reveal the involvement of Yahweh. He paraphrases the refrain previously uttered by David's men in 24.5 (MT). However, instead of using the more neutral verb *ntn* that the men used, he employs the loaded verb *sgr* that featured in the episodes involving Keilah (23.11-12), the Ziphites (23.20), and David's confrontation of Saul at the cave (24.19): God has 'closed up' your enemy in your hand this day (v. 8).[3] The subtle shift tends to emphasize the active role and initiative on the part of Yahweh, whom Abishai believes is working on behalf of his *nāgîd* to the detriment of the rejected king. He is suggesting that Yahweh has intentionally delivered Saul into David's power (motif *yād*) for execution. How will David react, having just walked away from the incident with Nabal where he learned that Yahweh will deal directly with his enemies?

In contrast to the previous occasion where the men strongly implied that David should personally deal with Saul, Abishai now volunteers to kill Saul with a single thrust of his own royal spear (v. 8). Abishai's

1. For an alternative proposal, see Miscall, *1 Samuel*, p. 158.

2. *Contra* Klein, *1 Samuel*, p. 257. Blenkinsopp ('1 and 2 Samuel', p. 317) notes that among modern Arabs, a lance stuck in the ground indicates the sheik's tent.

3. The deliberate use of *sgr* is also noted by Fokkelman (*Crossing Fates*, p. 534).

phrasing seems deliberately worded to remind David of the twofold attempt Saul had made on his life at court with the very same spear in 18.11 and the subsequent third attempt on a second occasion in 19.10.[1] The loyal servant is volunteering to assume responsibility for killing the sacrosanct person of the king to avenge his lord. He is living up to the character trait for which he seems to have been chosen for the mission. Is this what David intended to happen all along? Is he trying to rid himself of Saul and claim the throne to which he has been anointed by forcing a loyal follower to take on blood-guilt rather than waiting for Yahweh to deal with the rejected king?

David's response to Abishai's offer diffuses the suspense. He commands Abishai not to kill the king, using a rhetorical question to emphasize that no one can use self-help (*šālaḥ yād*) against the Lord's anointed without being subject to punishment (v. 9). It is noteworthy that David phrases his prohibition using *'al* + imperfect verb to express an immediate, specific command rather than by using *lō'* + imperfect verb to emphasize the durative nature of the prohibition against killing the Lord's anointed. Is he trying to leave room for Abishai to exercise his free will and deliberately incur the blood-guilt anyway? Probably not; continuing, David finally reveals his understanding of the means by which Saul will be eliminated from the throne. Swearing an oath by Yahweh, he states that Yahweh himself will deal with the rejected king in one of three ways: he will personally smite Saul (*ngp*), he will die of natural causes, or he will perish in battle at the hand of an enemy (v. 10). David's phrasing of his prohibition apparently was based on the urgency of the moment.

The first option for Saul's death iterates the lesson he had just learned from his encounter with Nabal, who was personally 'smitten' by Yahweh (25.38).[2] The second reflects the situation that was normal during the preceding era of the judges, after an individual had received divine spirit. The third option represents the means by which Yahweh punished Israel in the premonarchic period: he delivered them 'into the hand' of their enemies, foreign nations who oppressed

1. So also Hertzberg, *I & II Samuel*, p. 206; Fokkelman, *Crossing Fates*, p. 535; Gordon, *I & II Samuel*, p. 188. The irony of the proposal to kill Saul in the way he tried to kill David earlier is pointed out by Gunn (*Fate of Saul*, p. 102) and Klein (*1 Samuel*, p. 257).

2. So also, for example, Gunn, *Fate of Saul*, p. 103; Fokkelman, *Crossing Fates*, p. 536; Miscall, *1 Samuel*, p. 159.

them after defeating them militarily. As the new corporate representative of the people, the king's death in battle against a foreign army would represent his divine punishment.[1]

David once again reiterates that *he* must not 'put forth his hand' against the Lord's anointed and then orders Abishai to take the royal spear at Saul's head and the water jug so that they may be gone (v. 11). The two objects, which will serve as the corner of Saul's cloak did in 24.4, 11 as evidence corroborating his failure to kill Saul even when given the opportunity, symbolize Saul's royal office and his life.[2] However, David proceeds to remove the two items himself, taking full responsibility for the act, even though no one among Saul's men could have seen him or known of his actions because they remained in a deep divine sleep (*tardēmat yhwh*; cf. Gen. 2.21; 15.12; Isa. 29.10; Prov. 19.15; Job 4.13; 33.15) that had fallen upon them (v. 12). Although David's motives remain hidden, perhaps he takes charge of the situation and personally removes the spear to avert any potential move by Abishai to kill the king in spite of the blood-guilt he would thereby incur.[3] The audience is left to reflect upon David's earlier prohibition to Abishai in v. 9 and to wonder whether he was intentionally suggesting such an action to his nephew or not and why he chose this particular individual to accompany him in the first place. Did he simply need a dependable witness for the return trip who would report the events that would transpire to his own men, who would not be present? No clear answer to this question is forthcoming.

Reference to Yahweh's divinely induced sleep confirms in part Abishai's earlier assessment of the situation; apparently Yahweh has indeed given Saul 'into David's hand', but in order to test his king-elect to see if he has fully digested the lessons he should have learned

1. In retrospect, it will be seen to anticipate Saul's actual death, as noted by Ackroyd, *First Samuel*, p. 203; Gunn, *Fate of Saul*, p. 103; McCarter, *I Samuel*, p. 408; Miscall, *1 Samuel*, p. 160.

2. For the water jug as a staple and symbol of life, see Gunn, *Fate of Saul*, p. 103. Fokkelman (*Crossing Fates*, p. 537) sees the spear as a symbol of death and power and the water jug as a symbol of life. The suggestion by Polzin (*Samuel*, p. 212) that the author intends a contrastive analogy to the Nob incident where David 'takes' a sword and bread seems far-fetched to me.

3. So also Sternberg, *Poetics*, p. 244. For an alternative possibility, see Klein, *1 Samuel*, p. 258, who sees it as a contrastive analogy to 24.6.

from the preceding two episodes. Yahweh gives David the opportunity to kill Saul by allowing him to move unhampered into the Saulide camp and to have access to the defenseless, sleeping king and to a conveniently placed weapon. David was able to understand that he must not resort to self-help to eliminate the existing king; he must rely upon Yahweh, his heavenly lord, to deal with him in an appropriate way.

Crossing over to the top of a hill opposite Saul's camp, possibly the hill of Hachilah, David confronts Abner and Saul's men from a distance beyond that where visual recognition was possible (v. 13), unlike his confrontation of Saul at the cave near Ibexes' Rock (24.8) at close range. In calling down to the Saulide troops in the valley (v. 14), David becomes a kind of surrogate Goliath (cf. 17.8-11). His specific target, however, is Abner, who responds on behalf of the army by asking who is calling out or challenging the king (v. 14). Just as in 17.55, Abner is unable to identify David; he cannot recognize the king-elect.

David then chides Abner with two rhetorical questions and a third question that accuses him of failing to carry out his duty of protecting his lord the king against a member of 'the people' or the army who entered to destroy the king (v. 15). Is he referring to himself or to Abishai? Abishai is the one who resolved to kill Saul upon finding him defenseless, but was deterred by David, Saul's former commander of a thousand (18.13) who had sworn an oath of allegiance and loyalty to the king as a member of 'the people'. The audience has no evidence that Abishai had ever served in Saul's army before joining David's force. Yet Abishai did not clearly enter the camp with the intention of slaying Saul. He entered at David's request as his attendant, awaiting further orders, without knowledge of an explicit plan of action. In this regard he functions as Jonathan's attendant did in ch. 14. Is David deliberately characterizing Abishai as one of 'the people' in order to drive home to Saul the fact that David and his men are not self-made rebels, but loyal citizens who have been forced into exile?[1] Again, the

1. Fokkelman (*Crossing Fates*, p. 543) renders the phrase 'one of our troops', referring to David's men, which is possible, but not clearly indicated by the presence of a 1st person plural possessive suffix. The situation is not as clear-cut as in v. 22, where the young man is, by implication, one of Saul's attendants.

audience is not given any clues that allow them to resolve the resulting ambiguity.

In a stylized trial scene[1] that provides a structural parallel to the trial scene in 24.8-19, David accuses Abner of failing to carry through his obligations as a sworn servant of the king, using the technical treaty terminology *'āśâ haṭṭôbâ*, 'do good',[2] to emphasize that Abner has breached his oath to Saul. Invoking Yahweh, who undoubtedly was to oversee the punishment of the disloyal servant, he pronounces those who were assigned duty as official oath-bound royal bodyguards to be 'sons of death' (v. 16), recalling the fate pronounced by Saul against him in 20.31. As evidence for Abner's failure to perform his duty, David challenges Abner to locate the king's spear and water jug.[3]

Although Abner has not identified his accuser, Saul recognizes David's voice and asks him the identical question he did in their confrontation outside the cave at Ibexes' Rock (v. 17; 14.16): 'Is this your voice my son David?'[4] Whereas in ch. 24 the question came after David's long self-defense-turned-accusation against Saul, here Saul

1. So noted also by Fokkelman, *Crossing Fates*, p. 542.

2. For the phrase in treaties, see W.L. Moran, 'A Note on Some Treaty Terminology of the Sefire Treaties', *JNES* 22 (1963), pp. 173-76; M. Weinfeld, 'Covenant Terminology in the Ancient Near East and its Influence on the West', *JAOS* 93 (1973), p. 192; M. Fox, '*Ṭôb* as Covenant Terminology', *BASOR* 209 (1973), p. 41.

3. Gordon suggests that Abner's appearance in this chapter, 'which has a distinctively forward thrust (cf. vv. 19f.), can justifiably be read as an oblique commentary on events after Saul's death. Just as Abner could not secure Ishboshet's position on the throne indefinitely, so he cannot now guard Saul against David's advance' (*I & II Samuel*, p. 188).

4. The repetition is also noted by, for example, Miscall, *1 Samuel*, p. 160; Gordon, *I & II Samuel*, p. 189. Rosenberg (*King and Kin*, p. 136) emphasizes David's role as royal ombudsman of royal custom, laying the foundation for the throne he will occupy in declaring the sacredness of the king's person as the anointed of Yahweh and the need for aides to protect the person and the political neutrality of office. According to Rosenberg, David teaches the servants the art of obeisance and kings the art of rule at the moment of his greatest and most ideal victimship. He believes that the author is deliberately portraying David not to have open designs on the throne, but to be designing the *constitution* of the throne to which he pays obeisance. 'It is the semantic of sovereignty that comprises the true arena of political struggle' (p. 139). I find his suggestions to go beyond the intent of the text.

begins by acknowledging David's loyal status as 'son'. David's status as the 'son of Saul' forms a deliberate contrast to Abner and the other royal bodyguards who have just been pronounced 'sons of death' for their disloyal service. Confirming his identity, David launches into a second attempt to divert the king from his chosen obstinacy in trying to thwart the divine plan by killing the king-elect, asking Saul what wrong (*rā'â*) is in his 'hand'.

Once again as in ch. 24, David casts Saul in the role of judge and himself as petitioner (vv. 18-25). He uses the court format to announce his own decision concerning his future course of action in light of Saul's continued and unrelenting pursuit, which will be to leave the territory of Israel, the landed property of Yahweh. He tries one last time to dissuade Saul from his chosen course by trying to make him realize that his continued pursuit has become an act of personal vengeance, not supported by Yahweh or his fellow men (v. 19). His petition to Saul that his blood not fall to the earth from before the face of Yahweh in foreign exile, which has become a pressing possibility because of the king's personal vendetta, is designed to remind the king that as Yahweh's anointed *nāgîd*, to be driven away from his heavenly Lord and the Lord's territory could result in a particularly calamitous situation for Israel.[1]

Referring to Saul's seeking 'a single flea' as a deliberate attempt to recall his previous plea to Saul in 24.15,[2] David further develops the image of the hunt that he also presented on that previous occasion (24.12), suggesting that Saul has undertaken a partridge hunt, trying to flush his prey out of the mountain hiding places into his nets. He is equating Saul's personal vengeance with the hunting down of a

1. Fokkelman (*Crossing Fates*, p. 545) contrasts David's use of material evidence to establish his innocence in 24.10-16 with his failure to do so here in vv. 18-20. However, the evidence has already been cited in the accusation against Abner and so is not necessary to establish his innocence again. Rosenberg (*King and Kin*, p. 138) observes that the theme of exile from Yahweh's inheritance is common in the Psalms.

2. The phrase is missing in the LXX and is considered to be a gloss in the MT by, for example, Wellhausen, *Text der Bücher Samuelis*, p. 138; Driver, *Notes*, p. 208; Ackroyd, *First Samuel*, p. 204; Hertzberg, *I & II Samuel*, p. 207; McCarter, *I Samuel*, p. 406; Klein, *1 Samuel*, p. 255. Fokkelman (*Crossing Fates*, p. 546) retains it. I retain it, presuming that it was deleted from the LXX because of its apparent inconsistency with the following partridge metaphor.

defenseless animal in an effort to drive home to him the error of his ways. The rejected king has forgotten the lesson he once knew in 11.12-13 and the lesson that David has just relearned from his encounter with Nabal: the king must look to Yahweh to avenge true enemies. The image of the partridge or the 'calling one' in the mountains plays off the depiction of David as the 'calling one' on the mountain and Abner's question, 'Who are you, O calling one?' in vv. 13-14.[1]

David's speech is effective, prompting Saul's confession of wrong before 'the people' and Abner. In 24.19-20, Saul's confession of his wrongdoing and his knowledge of David's destiny had been witnessed only by David and his men. Admitting he has sinned by having 'played the fool' (*hiskaltî*) and strayed (*'ešgeh*), he invites David to 'return' or 'turn' and states he will no longer act evilly (verb *rā'â*) because David has valued his life highly that day (v. 21). The sense of *šwb* is deliberately ambiguous; is David to return to the court with Saul or simply to turn from his intended course of exile outside the territory of Yahweh? Saul's confession and request that his confessor turn or return calls to mind his similar request to Samuel in 15.24-25 in the wake of his reconfirmed rejection by Yahweh,[2] which was honored by the prophet (15.30). The references to acting wickedly and to acting as a fool, on the other hand, provide two points of contact with Nabal in ch. 25; unlike Nabal, however, Saul has repented and avoided the instantaneous reprisal of Yahweh. This leaves the other two options of death by natural causes or death in battle as means of Saul's future demise.

David responds by returning Saul's spear (v. 22) and by summarizing the lesson he had learned from his encounter with Nabal: the need for a leader to rely on Yahweh, his lord, to deliver him from all pressing situations (*ṣārâ*) instead of resorting to self-help. While willing to restore to Saul his emblem of office, David indirectly answers Saul's request for his return negatively in his requirement that Saul send one of the attendants to fetch it.[3] His retention of the insignificant water jug carries symbolic repercussions. It expresses his ability to control Saul's life and death, should he so desire. As

1. So noted also by, for example, McCarter, *I Samuel*, p. 408; Fokkelman, *Crossing Fates*, p. 546; Klein, *1 Samuel*, p. 259

2. So noted by Gunn, *Fate of Saul*, p. 105; Fokkelman, *Crossing Fates*, p. 548.

3. So too, for example, Gunn, *Fate of Saul*, p. 105; Fokkelman, *Crossing Fates*, p. 549.

such, the jug highlights David's potential to use self-help in the future to secure from the rejected king the throne that is to be his, raising a question about his ability to rely on Yahweh as the king must learn to do.

David closes his statement to Saul with the hope that his actions have demonstrated the alignment of 'his eyes' with Yahweh's 'eyes' (v. 24). In light of the wordplay between 'eyes' and 'heart' in the preceding chapters, where the heart served as the seat of perception that linked one to God as opposed to the eyes, which tended to judge according to human standards, David's statement is somewhat ominous and misdirected. He needs to be aligning his heart with Yahweh's and learning to judge through it rather than through his eyes only. The audience is left to ponder over whether David has truly understood the lessons he was to have learned from his encounters with Saul and Nabal?

Saul closes their conversation by publicly blessing David, his 'son' or loyal servant, and predicting David's certain future action and success. His failure to reconfirm his earlier knowledge that David will certainly be king in the parallel scene in 24.20 is logical in light of the situation. Before, Saul was alone when he made the statement to David and his supporters. Now accompanied by his own troops, the king cannot lose the support of his men by publicly confessing his rejection by Yahweh and his knowledge that David has been divinely designated to be his successor. He can only allude to that knowledge through a deliberately vague or generalized statement. It is noteworthy that while Yahweh is certainly the implied agent of blessing, Saul does not specify that David's 'doings' will be 'with Yahweh', as for example, Jonathan's were thought to be in 14.45, so that his resulting ability to prevail will be the result of divine favor.

Saul's final statement allows room for David's prevailing through his own might rather than by relying on Yahweh, a tendency that the audience knows David is prone toward from the Nabal incident and possibly from his retention of Saul's water jug in the current situation. It is a tendency that might come back to haunt him if he does not learn to align his heart as well as his eyes with Yahweh's. Saul's parting words leave the audience reflecting upon David's character, self-understanding, and motivations, most of which have been deliberately left undescribed since his introduction in ch. 16. They cast a somewhat ominous tone over David's going *his* way, which may or may not be Yahweh's way, while Saul returns to his established place as king of Israel.

Chapter 22

1 SAMUEL 27

Picking up on the issue of David's ability to align his heart with Yahweh's, David 'says to his heart' that he believes he will be caught up (verb *sph*) one day by the 'hand' of Saul and there is 'nothing good' for him so that he must certainly escape to the land of the Philistines. He rationalizes that Saul will then lose hope of continuing to seek him within all the borders of Israel and he will thereby escape from the king's 'hand' (v. 1). Instead of listening to his heart, the seat of inspired perception, for direction, David is telling his heart what his predecided course of action is to be, rationalizing it according to human perceptions and logic. He is taking his possible course of action suggested to Saul in 26.19-20 as a means of impressing upon the king the error of his continued pursuit of the king-elect and turning it into reality, convincing himself that it is now the only option open to him. The term *tôb* may be intended to convey the overtones of treaty-loyalty that can be associated with it in addition to its more neutral sense: on a deeper level David may be stating that there is no point for him to continue to uphold his oath of loyalty to Saul (16.21) since the king has failed to act in good faith toward him.

Having just expressed his confidence that Yahweh will deal with the rejected king in his own time and way (26.10), David has lost sight of his own special relationship with Yahweh as the king-elect and has lost faith in Yahweh's continued protection and support. He is no longer relying upon Yahweh to guide him as his earthly vice-regent-in-training, but instead has decided on a course of action that represents a form of 'self-help'. Is he justified in using self-help to avoid a confrontation with Saul, or does the rule of avoiding self-help apply only to situations where one is aggressively confronting his enemy? Is Saul truly David's enemy? David's twice-stated concern in v. 1 is to escape from the power of Saul, expressed through the use of the motif *yād*, even though he has just demonstrated to Saul how he can 'overpower' the rejected king with little effort. Why this sudden attack of nerves and development of an inferiority complex?

In the narrative flow of events, David, together with his two wives and his 600 men with their families, 'cross over' to Achish, the king of Gath, and proceed to dwell with the Philistine ruler (vv. 2-3). Immediately, the audience is taken back to David's previous solo flight to Achish with the sword of Goliath in 21.11-16. Quickly realizing the danger he was in by listening to his heart, David had feigned madness to be thrown out of the town without reprisal. Now he has returned to the same town and ruler and has taken up residence in the Philistine urban center that lay closest to the border of Israel. He has 'crossed over', a term that carries with it overtones of betrayal or transgression as well as the movement across physical space. The audience is left to deduce from his ability to settle in Gath that he has been accepted by Achish this time. By contrastive analogy with 21.11-16, then, David's reputation as Saul's 'ally'-turned-traitor must have reached Philistine ears, making him welcome in the enemy camp.

Achish apparently has presumed that he and David share Saul as a common enemy. But David has explicitly rejected the suggestions by his men (24.4; 26.8) that Saul is his enemy. His constant reference to Saul as Yahweh's anointed and his self-characterization as Saul's servant tend to belie his viewing Saul as his enemy. Only his most recent statement in v. 1 suggests that he may have decided to abandon his loyalty to Saul, which would allow room for his characterization of Saul as his enemy.

In David's previous encounter with Achish, the Philistine courtiers had erroneously deduced that David had been 'king of the land' (21.11). Has Achish taken in David and his entourage in a gesture of political asylum, under the presumption that he is a king in exile, or has he taken him and his men in as mercenaries? Will David be able to deceive Achish again, as he had during his first visit, by eventually listening to his heart and following its divinely inspired guidance in contrast to Achish's dependence upon his eyes as a vehicle of humanly based perception?

No immediate answers are provided to the questions raised for the audience by the author's deliberate choice to withhold vital information. Instead, the ambiguity is sustained by the report that Saul has finally broken off his pursuit of the king-elect upon hearing of

David's 'flight' to non-Israelite Gath. The return of the verb *brḥ*, which was used in 19.12, 18; 20.1; 21.11; and 22.17 to characterize David's separation from Saul, implies that David's action is a final desperate attempt to elude the grasp of the rejected king, but does not elucidate any possible change of attitude in David toward Saul. If anything, it might reinforce the status quo in their relationship. The audience is simply informed that David's overt needs have been met by his physical removal from Saul's territory: he has freed himself from Saul's incessant obsession of trying to kill him and to foil the divine plan for Israel's new king. However, any ulterior motives in his move to Gath specifically remain unaddressed and become a highlighted issue.

David's motives continue to be the central focus of the story in vv. 5-7 as he requests as Achish's 'servant' (*'abdᵉkā*) a new place of residence in a town of the open land (*bᵉ'aḥat 'ārê haśśādeh*) instead of his current position in the city of the kingdom (*bᵉ'îr hammamlākâ*) with the king (v. 5). Does David's self-designation as Achish's servant indicate that he has sworn a new oath of loyalty to serve the Philistine king or is he simply using the standard courteous form of royal address to phrase his request? Are we to understand his reference to 'grace in Achish's eyes' to be polite speech or perhaps to be a deliberate and ominous echo of Saul's identical statement in 16.22? Will Achish's reliance on his eyes for perception cause him trouble? What has David done for the king or what will he agree to do to earn enough trust to merit an appointment outside the capital, away from the watchful eyes of the court?[1] Has he indeed betrayed his former country? David is given Ziklag as a personal fiefdom, which he holds for sixteen months (vv. 6-7).[2] The audience now is able to deduce that

1. In some ways, the situation anticipates David's house-arrest of Mephiboshet after reclaiming him from his political asylum with the king of Lidebir. It is reminiscent of the Assyrian practice of having deposed kings eat at the royal table. I find no textual support for the suggestion made first apparently by Hertzberg (*I & II Samuel*, p. 214), and adopted by Ackroyd (*First Samuel*, p. 206) and Klein (*1 Samuel*, p. 263), that the end of v. 5 hints that the move was posed as a means of relieving Achish from the necessary provisioning of David's large number of men at the capital. The writer seems to be deliberately vague here about David's motivations.

2. Hertzberg (*I & II Samuel*, p. 214) and McCarter (*I Samuel*, p. 414) believe that the 'days' and four months covers David's entire Philistine stay. However, the explicit contrast drawn by David between the royal city and a city of the 'field' in v. 5

David must have performed military service for Achish in exchange for the land grant.

The deduction is confirmed in vv. 8-11, with an ironic twist that resolves the issue of David's intentions. Yes, indeed, David made military raids, serving as Achish's hired mercenary. However, they were launched against inhabitants of the land from Telem[1] southward to Shur, even to Egypt—Israel's enemies, not against Israelite groups or territory (v. 9).[2] Included among David's targets were the Amalekites, Yahweh's sworn enemies whom Saul had failed to eradicate, an action that had resulted in Saul's rejection from the kingship (1 Sam. 15). The narrator has invited the audience to compare and contrast David's activities with Saul's Amalekite campaign (15.7) by repeating the boundary descriptions almost verbatim. A comparison indicates that David was picking up where Saul left off, eliminating Yahweh's sworn enemy within the region as well as other local groups and pushing his attack even further south, to the land of Egypt itself.

Verse 9 continues the deliberate comparison between David's raids and Saul's Amalekite campaign in ch. 15 by providing an echo of the list of Yahweh's intended victims in 15.3. Two changes are to be noted. First, in the present context no mention is made of toddlers or unweaned infants. Instead, clothing appears as an item joined to the otherwise duplicate list. Secondly, whereas Saul was instructed to destroy all human and all four forms of animal life, David kills only grown men and women, but takes the four forms of animals, together

suggests that the figure denotes only his time spent at Ziklag, 'in the field'.

1. I favor the widespread proposed emendation of MT *'lm* to *ṭlm*, presuming an early corruption of initial *ṭ* to ', which is supported by some twelve LXX mss.

2. It is popular to presume that the LXX text, which refers to *panta ton geseiri*, is a more ancient reading and that the references in the MT text to the similar sounding Geshurites and Girzites represent a conflation of doublets. So, for example, Wellhausen, *Text der Bücher Samuelis*, p. 139; Budde, *Bücher Samuel*, p. 173; Driver, *Notes*, p. 211; Hertzberg, *I & II Samuel*, p. 214; McCarter, *I Samuel*, p. 413; Klein, *1 Samuel*, p. 261. Klostermann (*Bücher Samuelis*, p. 117) proposes the emendation of *haggᵉšûrî wᵉhaggirzî* to *gidrôt hāhagrî* on the basis of Num. 32.16. However, as Fokkelman correctly points out (*Crossing Fates*, p. 563), David's reference in v. 10 to purported raids against three Negebite groups presumes the presence of three counterbalancing groups in v. 8. Thus, for literary reasons, both of the MT groups, the Geshurites and the Girzites, should be retained.

with clothing, as booty.[1] By implication, David spared the children alive during his raids, reasoning that they could not identify him. However, in taking clothing as booty, are we to assume that he left the children exposed to the elements alive but without the means to survive long on their own?

David's wars, while geographically a continuation of Saul's earlier campaign, are not being conducted directly as 'Yahweh's wars'. As P. Miscall points out, there are reminiscences here of the Deuteronomistic legislation for the treatment of disinherited cities captured during holy war in Deut. 20.10-18, but David is here securing his own position[2] and not devoting his booty to Yahweh, but to his own aggrandizement, with a token portion to Achish, his employer.[3] David's *mišpāṭ*, 'custom', is, for the time being, *pāšaṭ*, 'raiding'. With the intentional play on words[4] the narrator may be trying to draw a deliberate contrast to David's future destined *mišpāṭ* as enthroned king of Israel (8.11-18) to emphasize his present circumstances. Yet at the same time, the audience is aware that his overtly self-serving interests are indirectly benefitting Israel and serving Yahweh.

The narrator's foregrounding of the clothing as an item of the booty, accomplished through contrastive analogy to 15.3 and by its semantic association with the verb *pšṭ* which often is used to denote the stripping off of clothes, seems to be an intentional means of commenting on the stupidity of the Philistines, a trait already developed in 21.11-16. From Egyptian and Assyrian reliefs we know that different ethnic and national groups were distinguishable by their style of clothing. The ancient audience must also have been aware of this

1. Contrast the discussion of Gunn, *Fate of Saul*, p. 107, taken up by Klein, *1 Samuel*, p. 264.

2. Miscall, *1 Samuel*, pp. 164-65.

3. Miscall (*1 Samuel*, p. 165) sees the author deliberately introducing ambiguity over the fate of the booty. However, it is likely that the ancient audience's familiarity with booty-gathering practices would have made details unnecessary here. No one could appear empty-handed before their superior after a raid; how much legally was to go to the victorious participants and how much was illegally skimmed by David and his men before determining Achish's portion is another issue. Hertzberg (*I & II Samuel*, p. 215) has understood David's need to present booty to the king at Gath, but has misunderstood the nonhuman nature of the booty in his reference to Gath's slave-market as the booty's final destination.

4. The wordplay was previously noted by Fokkelman (*Crossing Fates*, p. 562) and Miscall (*1 Samuel*, p. 165).

fact. Therefore, Achish should easily have been able to discover the falsity of David's claim that he had made raids against 'Israelite' territories and groups simply by looking at the evidence supplied by the clothing that was part of the booty. However, Achish and his courtiers apparently were too stupid to work this out. With the evidence of David's nonloyalty placed literally before his eyes, Achish cannot evaluate it and concludes that David is fully trustworthy. Having certainly made himself stinking to his people, Israel, a false assessment of the actual situation in light of David's attacks against Israel's enemies, Achish foolishly surmises that David will become for him a perpetual servant (v. 12).[1]

Just as in 21.10-15 where the Philistine courtiers unknowingly proclaimed David's future status as king, so here, Achish unintentionally confirms David's unalterable identification with 'his people, Israel'. Achish has relied on weak human perception associated with the eyes and has been duped into believing that David can be separated from his people and made an oath-bound, fief-granted loyal mercenary. The audience, having already explored the dimensions of David's servitude to another human master, Saul, over against his higher master, Yahweh, is well aware of Achish's folly even to imagine that David could become his 'servant'. Only Yahweh can be David's master.[2]

1. Fokkelman (*Crossing Fates*, p. 560) draws a contrastive anticipatory link with 2 Sam. 15 where Ittai of Gath remains loyal to David through thick and thin.

2. Klein (*1 Samuel*, p. 265) notes the ironic contrast between the misunderstanding of the courtiers in 21.11-16, who refer to David as the king of the land, and Achish's currently misdirected belief that he would become a permanent servant or ally.

Chapter 23

1 SAMUEL 28

A new extended episode begins with v. 1, which will end in 31.13 with Saul's death and burial. However, the author has chosen not to give a straightforward, chronological account of the battle. Instead, he narrates its development in a nonsequential, nonlinear order to heighten audience suspense about David's possible role in Saul's death. Beginning with a focus on David's participation in a Philistine–Saulide battle as a Philistine mercenary, making him a potential killer of the Lord's rejected but still anointed king under circumstances out of his control, the writer jumps forward in time to the eve of the battle and Saul's consultation of the dead spirit of Samuel. Through Samuel, Saul learns of his certain death the following day. Suspense peaks as the audience realizes that David could unwittingly become the agent of death. The situation is then defused as the author goes back in time to the mustering stage and tells how David is dismissed from the Philistine ranks. He deliberately postpones his account of the final battle by describing instead David's actions at the very moment Saul is dying on the battlefield. Finally, in ch. 31 he relates in summary, anticlimactic form the actual battle at Mt Gilboa. Using this strategy, the author is able to underplay the actual battle and emphasize the interrelationship between the intertwined fates of his two central characters, Saul and David.[1]

Verse 1 introduces a new battle scenario, but provides a temporal link to the preceding scene in its use of the phrase *bayyāmîm hāhēm*, 'in those days', referring to David's service to Achish as a fief-granted

1. For similar and contrasting explanations of the literary structure of chs. 28–31, see, for example, Hertzberg, *I & II Samuel*, p. 217; McCarter, *I Samuel*, pp. 422-23; Klein, *1 Samuel*, p. 269; Gordon, *I & II Samuel*, p. 193.

mercenary.[1] The Philistines are gathering their forces to fight against Israel, and Achish tells David that he and his men will go *with him* into the Philistine camp, as David certainly knows. The grammatical construction of the sentence emphasizes David's knowledge through the use of the infinitive absolute + finite form of the same verbal root (*yādō'ᵃ tēda'*) and emphasizes 'with Achish' by pulling the pronoun *'ittî* forward before the verb *tēṣē'*. The duped Achish is stressing David's status as his loyal servant, which the audience knows is a figment of his imagination and an idea that could potentially lead to his demise by David's hand, given the right circumstances. The Philistines are Israel's most harassing enemy, and David's killing raids against less powerful enemies in the previous chapter demonstrated the king-elect's ability to act for the good of his nation, even in exile. Is he planning to destroy the Philistine enemy from within? What exactly does David 'know'; is he working out a plan devised by Yahweh or merely saving his own skin?

David's reply in v. 2 is deliberately multivalent. He reassures Achish that the king personally knows what his servant does, relying on Achish to continue to misinterpret the evidence of lying about David's raid victims and specious loyalty that is right before the king's eyes and to miss the true meaning of his reply. The audience recognizes the threat concealed in David's reply; he will continue to act as he has in the past, killing off Israel's enemies. In the forthcoming conflict where Israel will fight against the Philistines, the audience is to understand that David will work on behalf of Israel, wherever he and his men are positioned during the fight.

Nevertheless, at the same time, the audience should realize that David has now been put into a very dangerous situation. If he and his men go out into battle as Philistine mercenaries, he might be put into a position where he unwittingly kills Saul. In order to maintain appearances, they probably will have to kill a few Israelite soldiers while they are under the watchful eyes of the Philistine generals at the beginning of the battle. If Saul should disguise himself as a common

1. There is a tendency to make vv. 1-2 the end of the preceding Achish–Ziklag episode and to begin a new scene with v. 3. So, for example, Hertzberg, *I & II Samuel*, p. 211; McCarter, *I Samuel*, p. 412; Miscall, *1 Samuel*, p. 166; and Klein, *1 Samuel*, p. 261. However, I believe that vv. 1-2 introduce the larger unit comprising chs. 28–31, with v. 3 beginning a subsection within the unit.

soldier and not use his identifying royal weapons, David might inadvertently kill him. Or, should Saul maintain his royal weaponry, will David succumb to self-help and kill off the Lord's anointed in order to gain the throne, hoping that no one will know he did it and blaming the Philistines for his death? What does David really 'know' in his heart, the seat of divine perception?

True to form, Achish construes David's words as a pledge of loyalty and proceeds to appoint David as the 'guardian of his head' or personal bodyguard for the indefinite future (v. 2). The idiom *šōmēr hārō'š* indicates a fear of decapitation, which in turn suggests that such a custom was practiced by the Philistines themselves. This minor detail plays off David's earlier decapitation of the Philistine champion, Goliath, in 17.51.[1] Ironically, Achish places himself in mortal danger by allowing David to serve as his bodyguard because of his compounded stupidity in failing to see David's words and actions for what they really are.

In a parenthetical aside to provide background information for the coming scene, the narrator reminds the audience of Samuel's death and burial in his home in Ramah by all Israel in 25.1 (v. 3). He also informs us for the first time that Saul had ordered the removal of the ancestral spirits and ghosts from the land, in accordance with ritual law found in Lev. 19.31; 20.6; 27; and Deut. 18.11.[2] By implication, then, Samuel's spirit could not legally be consulted by any Israelite, and Saul was left to confront the Philistines without the benefit of a legitimate channel to Yahweh to learn of the heavenly regent's intentions and support for Israel in the present confrontation.

Returning to the battle scene being depicted as part of the narrative flow of events, the Philistines now advance and encamp in the vicinity of Shunem, on the northern side of the Esdraelon plain, while Saul assembles all Israel and camps at Gilboa, across the plain to the south

1. As noted previously by Miscall, *1 Samuel*, p. 166; Gordon, *I & II Samuel*, p. 193.

2. For *'wb* and *yd'ny* as types of spirits and not forms of human mediums, see J. Lust, 'On Wizards and Prophets', in *Studies in Prophecy* (ed. G.W. Anderson *et al.*; VTSup, 26; Leiden: Brill, 1974), pp. 133-42. Contrast the suggestions that connect *'ôb* with the Arabic verb 'to return' (W.F. Albright, *Archaeology and the Religion of Israel* [Baltimore: Johns Hopkins University Press, 1942], p. 203 n. 31) and with a Hittite word for pit (H. Hoffner, 'Second Millennium Antecedents to the Hebrew *'ôb*', *JBL* 86 [1967], pp. 385-401).

(v. 4).[1] It is not yet clear who the aggressors and defenders are in the battle. Both sides seem to advance to their positions simultaneously, and while the narrator has begun the episode by referring to the Philistine muster, the audience does not know whether that muster is in response to a first move by Saul or is a planned challenge to Saul. Saul's lack of prophetic guidance and ability to determine the divine will becomes crucial in either case, but particularly so if he has taken the initiative in the battle. How can he be certain that his actions will be backed by God?

Upon seeing the Philistine camp, Saul fears and his heart trembles, contrasting to his response to the Philistines at the Michmash pass in chs. 13–14. Before, the people had fled out of fear when faced with a Philistine horde like the sand on the seashore, but Saul had remained in control of the situation and resolute. Now, using the seat of human perception to size up the situation, the rejected king succumbs to fear, being unable to depend upon God's support as he had before. Whereas in the Michmash battle the people had trembled but followed their leader, Saul (13.7), here Saul himself trembles in fear, being unable to act as leader of the Israelite forces. His trembling also contrasts with the divine 'trembling' that was inflicted on the enemy in 14.15; with Yahweh's support, Israel need never tremble, even when outnumbered in battle (Deut. 20.1). Victory is brought about by Yahweh himself. Now Israel enters battle without Yahweh's known support, resulting in the rejected king's paralysis when faced with the grim reality of a strong enemy who, in his mind, cannot be defeated unless God intervenes on Israel's behalf. Saul's fear on this occasion parallels his fear

1. Gunn (*Fate of Saul*, p. 108) draws spatial parallels to the Philistine wars at the Michmash pass in chs. 13–14 and the Elah Valley in ch. 17. Since this would have been the common set-up when two ancient armies met in the open field for a confrontation, I am not sure how significant the parallels are. Herzog and Gichon (*Battles of the Bible*, pp. 72-73) suggest that the Philistines were the initiators of the war and planned to penetrate the hill country from the Esdraelon Plain at Ir Gannim (modern Jenin), enlisting the aid of Canaanite cities in the plain. Saul was then to have set up his forces on the south side of the plain to block Philistine access to the hill country. The report that the Saulide bodies were hung on the wall of Beth She'an, which would have been a victory display, if historically reliable, would indicate instead that Saul was the aggressor and that his target was Beth She'an, with the Philistines arriving as allies of the independent city-state.

at the Valley of Elah, where he also faced the Philistines uncertain of Yahweh's backing (17.11).

Seeking to determine Yahweh's will, Saul tries to inquire of Yahweh,[1] but is not answered in any of the conventional ways: by dreams, by Urim, or by prophets (v. 6). These three methods are listed as the legitimate forms of divine consultation elsewhere in Jer. 18.18 and Ezek. 7.26, and appear together in the Hittite plague prayer of Muršili II. Saul has reason to fear; he knows he has been abandoned by Yahweh and no longer has David to stand in his stead to ensure Israelite victory.

Determined to discover whether Yahweh will support Israel in the impending battle, Saul orders his servants to seek out a woman who is mistress of ancestral spirits so that he may go to her and may make divine inquiry (*drš*) through her (v. 8). His servants inform him that there is such a woman in En-dor (v. 8). The narrator has already informed the audience that Saul had ordered the removal of the ancestral spirits from the land, so his decision to attempt to determine the divine will by the agency of ancestral spirits highlights his own lack of integrity in the present situation. He is disobeying his own mandate, making himself liable to the death sentence for infraction of royal proclamation. At the same time, the audience should already suspect the identity of the spirit whom Saul wishes to contact from the pairing of the report of Samuel's death with the prohibition against spirits in v. 3. Since Samuel had formerly served as God's messenger to him, Saul hoped to be able to use his spirit once more to establish contact with Yahweh.

Perhaps risking capture behind enemy lines, Saul visits the medium at night, disguised and attended only by two men, and requests that she divine for him (v. 8). The traditional site of En-dor at Indur, northeast of Shunem, would mean that Saul would have had to have made his way undetected through the Philistine camp in order to have consulted the medium in En-dor, thereby risking his life even before the engagement of battle lines. His disguise seems, then, to have been designed to allow him to pass undetected through the Philistine ranks.[2]

1. Fokkelman (*Crossing Fates*, p. 598) points to the irony of the Hebrew phrase *wayyiš' al ˇsā' ûl*; Saul asks and it yields nothing.

2. So noted also by, for example, Ackroyd, *First Samuel*, p. 213; Fokkelman, *Crossing Fates*, p. 600; Klein, *1 Samuel*, p. 271; Gordon, *I & II Samuel*, p. 195.

As J. Fokkelman notes, Saul's removal of his royal attire and insignia has additional symbolic overtones; it marks his end as king.[1] Saul's request that the woman perform an act of *qsm* resounds with Samuel's pronouncement to Saul in 15.23 that rebellion is (as) the sin of divination, *qsm*.[2]

However, the medium's response to his request for her to call up a spirit that he shall name and to divine by the spirit (v. 8) indicates that at the same time, the disguise prevented the medium's recognition of her own king, who had outlawed the practice of her profession. The narrator seems to have deliberately delayed confirmation that Endor lay inside Israelite territory to allow for the possibility that the medium was plying her trade legitimately and that Saul was forced to go outside his own people to consult Yahweh. In v. 9, however, the woman confirms that she is indeed an Israelite citizen bound to Saul's decree and that her performance of his request could lead to her being put to death. Her reply to Saul echoes David's earlier statement to Achish in v. 2: *'attâ yāda'tā 'ēt 'ᵃšer-'āśâ*, substituting 'Saul' for David's 'your servant'. The result is a contrast between David's 'doing' and Saul's 'doing', involving the key term *'āśâ*, which is used elsewhere to express God's 'doing' on Israel's behalf by performing an act of deliverance.

Ironically, swearing by Yahweh, the very God who has abandoned him, Saul reassures the medium that no punishment will befall her in this matter, trying to alleviate her suspicion that the request is a trap (vv. 9-10).[3] Since Yahweh is presumably the reason why the dead-turned-lesser-divine beings are being removed from the land, his invocation in the oath perhaps would have been enough to quench the medium's suspicions about entrapment. Presumably, Yahweh would have been invoked in the original decree as the overseer of the execu-

1. Fokkelman, *Crossing Fates*, p. 600. Miscall (*1 Samuel*, p. 168) draws a connection with 10.6-9, where Saul receives an 'other' heart and becomes an 'other' man. This seems to be a distant echo at most. The emphasis in v. 8 seems to be on the removal of royal clothes, so that a closer echo would be with Jonathan's removal of his robe in 18.4. Polzin (*Samuel*, p. 270 n. 7) notes the implied wordplay between *béged*, 'clothing', and *bgd*, 'treachery'.

2. So noted by, for example, Miscall, *1 Samuel*, p. 168; Fokkelman, *Crossing Fates*, p. 602.

3. Fokkelman (*Crossing Fates*, p. 604) draws a link to the Michal episode in ch. 19 through the use of *nqs* via a woman.

tion of infractors. Here, then, the promise is being made that Yahweh will not act to punish the woman, whatever happens. Like any normal human being, however, the medium should have wondered what rank of authority allowed the man before her to make such an oath. Instead of questioning his motives further, she proceeds with the summoning of the spirit of Samuel.

The request for Samuel should perhaps have changed her wondering into suspicion about the true identity of the man before her, had she been aware of Samuel's relationship with Saul. The audience certainly knows which Samuel is intended because of v. 3. It is noteworthy that Saul provides no patronymic or identifying epithet for Samuel and that the woman merely parrots his request. Certainly there was more than one spirit who had been called Samuel in his lifetime! Perhaps we are to understand that the request need not have been more specific and that the spirit world, in watching events on earth, would identify the one seeking their assistance on earth and send the appropriate relative or close associate who bore the name requested. In this case, the medium might not have grown immediately suspicious at the call for a generic Samuel.

In any event, upon seeing the Samuel who materializes, the woman instantly understands that the man before her seeking her services is indeed Saul himself and crying out in a loud voice, she confronts him, asking why he has deceived her and identifying him as Saul (v. 12). It is in recognizing which Samuel is associated with the human individual that she is able to discern Saul's true identity. The close link between Samuel the prophet and Saul is once more highlighted.[1] The narrator's failure to report in detail the method the woman used to summon Samuel's spirit probably reflects a decision not to emphasize a practice that may well have been considered illegal in his own day.[2]

1. The MT text makes sense as it stands. There is no reason to follow the few Greek mss. that have substituted 'Saul' for 'Samuel' in an attempt to clarify the process of recognition, nor to follow the suggestion of Hertzberg to insert an allegedly dropped *šem* before Samuel (*I & II Samuel*, p. 219) for which there is no textual support. Nor does the woman's sudden recognition of Saul's identity seem to hinge on 'the prophetic power of Samuel', as suggested by W.A.M. Beuken ('I Samuel 28: The Prophet as "Hammer of Witches"', *JSOT* 6 [1978], p. 9).

2. Contrast the suggestion of Fokkelman, *Crossing Fates*, p. 605. The story is plausible as it reads, so there is no compelling reason to see the 'original' to have used Saul's imperious tone in v. 10 to alert the woman to Saul's identity and to

At the same time, it allows room for the audience to wonder whether Yahweh has not perhaps intervened and sent Samuel's spirit himself to permit Saul to learn of his appointed fate, as others have suggested.[1] The ambiguity leaves the door open for interpreting the event along more legally acceptable lines, although the whole point of the story seems to be to emphasize the depths of illegitimacy into which Saul has sunk through his despair. As R. Polzin notes, the woman's accusation of deceit by Saul echoes the king's earlier identical accusation against his daughter Michal in 19.17.[2]

Not wasting time on explanations, Saul tries to break off the medium's indignant cries with a curt 'fear not' as he focuses on confirming the identity of the spirit for himself (v. 13). His barked order not to fear now answers the question about the authority by which Saul can swear an oath exempting the medium from punishment. However, it does not answer her question as to why he had disguised himself to consult her, which remains hanging in the air. With a sense of urgency, Saul presses forward in breathless anticipation to learn if Samuel has responded to his call. The medium's first description of the spirit as a god rising up out of the earth (v. 13) is too nondescript to provide Saul with confirmation; he needs to be able to fasten upon a distinguishing aspect of the prophet's appearance to be certain. After all, did not all those who died become divinized ancestral spirits? Pressing for further details, Saul asks specifically about the spirit's outward appearance (*tō'ar*) and is told it is an old man[3] who is rising up and that he is wrapped in a cloak (v. 14). These two facts are enough for Saul to confirm that the spirit was indeed that of the desired Samuel, the prophet Samuel, and he then bows his face to the ground and does obeisance (v. 15). The *m*[e]*'îl*, while a common piece of clothing for those of rank, seems to have been especially

construe the intrusion of Samuel as secondary, as does McCarter (*I Samuel*, p. 423).

1. So, for example, Ackroyd, *First Samuel*, p. 214; Klein, *1 Samuel*, p. 271; Gordon, *I & II Samuel*, p. 195.

2. Polzin, *Samuel*, p. 270 n. 7.

3. Although the LXX's 'erect', presuming a Hebrew vorlage *zqp*, is the *lectio difficilior*, the term would play no role in establishing Samuel's identity. I therefore favor the adoption of the MT's *zqn*, 'old', as the original reading and suggest the LXX arose through the misreading of the final *nûn* as a *pēh*, *contra* McCarter (*I Samuel*, p. 419).

associated with the office of prophet (cf. 1 Sam. 2.19; 15.27; 2 Kgs 2.13-18).[1] This is the first occasion upon which Saul bows to another in an act signalling humility, submission and a plea for mercy; David has done it before Saul in 24.8 and Abigail before David in 25.23. The rejected king has finally learned the need for humility; yet he directs his act of obeisance and worship (*hištaḥ*ᵃ*wâ*) to a dead spirit instead of to his true master, Yahweh. Only once before, in 15.31, did Saul formally offer worship (*hištaḥ*ᵃ*wâ*)[2] and there it was properly directed to Yahweh, through Samuel's assistance.

The final exchange between dead prophet and king confirms for Saul what he already knows—that David will succeed him on the throne of Israel—and reveals to him his fate. Saul tells a bestirred Samuel that he is very distressed (*ṣār*) because the Philistines are on the verge of waging war against him while God has turned away from him and still has not answered, either through the hand of his prophets or through dreams. Under these circumstances, Saul explains, he has called Samuel and disturbed his rest,[3] to be taught (*l*ᵉ*hôdî'ēnî*)[4] what to do (v. 15). Saul's distress again recalls the situation on the eve of battle with the Philistines at the Michmash pass, where his men had been distressed (*ṣār*) (13.6) at the sight of the Philistine horde and had hid and deserted in desperation. Now, however, he is the one acting like a common soldier, using his eyes instead of his heart to judge the situation and failing as God's earthly vice-regent.

On the earlier occasion, Saul had failed to await prophetic instructions, resulting in his warning of possible rejection from the kingship (13.8-15). Now, having learned that hard lesson, he attempts to follow protocol and be instructed by the spirit of Yahweh's chosen spokesperson during the former part of his reign, having failed to be informed about the divine will through any new living prophet or by

1. Contrast Berlin (*Poetics of Biblical Narrative*, p. 35), who claims that the robe was not an identifying feature but was all the author cared to convey about what Samuel looked like and was apparently mimetic enough.

2. So noted also by Fokkelman, *Crossing Fates*, p. 608.

3. The connection of the root *rgz* with grave-robbing in Phoenician inscriptions (for example, McCarter, *I Samuel*, p. 421; Klein, *1 Samuel*, p. 272) is a subtle way for the narrator to emphasize the impropriety of Saul's use of necromancy to his contemporaneous audience.

4. Klein (*1 Samuel*, p. 272) notes the intentional pun involved in Saul's asking the dead spirit (*yd'ny*) to *hyd'*, 'enlighten' him.

dreams. No mention is made on this occasion of the failed attempt to establish contact with Yahweh through the Urim and Thummim, in contrast to v. 6. The omission is to be seen to be deliberate. Not only had Saul cut off Ahijah prematurely from determining God's will at Michmash (14.18-20), but he had also ordered the massacre of the priests of Yahweh at Nob (1 Sam. 22.17-20),[1] leaving himself liable on both occasions. Not wanting to incriminate himself, he apparently decided it was best not to mention this form of oracular consultation. Yet by its very omission, Saul reveals his guilt and leaves himself easy prey for Samuel, should he merely ask why Saul had not explored all avenues, including the Urim and Thummim.

Samuel spares Saul the embarrassment of self-entrapment and focuses instead on their past relationship as king and royal prophet. He points to the futility of attempting to contact Yahweh through any agency, even himself, when the Lord has himself 'turned' (*sār*) from Saul and is with his neighbor (v. 16).[2] The narrator's deliberate wordplay in vv. 15-16 on *sār*, 'turn away', and *ṣār*, 'distressed', emphasizes the cause and effect link between the two actions. Reminding Saul of his pronouncement at Gilgal in 15.28 after Saul's subsequent acts of disobedience against God (v. 18), Samuel drives home the point he made in the wake of the Amalekite incident: the everlasting of Israel will not lie or repent, for he is not a man that he should repent (15.26). Having confirmed Saul's assessment that Yahweh has turned from him, Saul must accept that there is nothing he can do to influence God's actions or decisions; the divine will is inscrutable by man.

In his parting words, Samuel nevertheless reveals to Saul Yahweh's plan for the battle to take place the next day. He has determined that Israel is to be defeated by the 'hand' of the Philistines (motif *yād*) and has ordained the death of the king and his sons (v. 19). As D. Gunn has correctly understood, the narrator has deliberately chosen to emphasize that the coming defeat will involve both the nation and king

1. This connection is seen as the basis for his lack of ability to use Urim by, for example, Hertzberg, *I & II Samuel*, p. 218; Fokkelman, *Crossing Fates*, p. 611; and Klein, *1 Samuel*, p. 271.

2. I favor seeing MT's *'rk* as a metathesis of *r'k*, as is common in scholarship. Fokkelman (*Crossing Fates*, p. 611) attempts to maintain *'rk* as a deliberate Aramaicism meaning 'your oppressor', serving as an intentional wordplay on the *r'k* that appears in v. 17c, quoting 15.28. But surely this is a contorted and unnecessary exercise.

in order to highlight the enactment of the divine punishment that was proclaimed in 12.25.[1] The futility of Saul's struggle against the divine plan is now highlighted; the king's attempt to have his son Jonathan or another son eventually ascend the throne after David's intervening kingship will not become a reality. Both the rejected king and his house, his dynasty, will die on the battlefield the next day.

Samuel's pregnant 'tomorrow' echoes the use of this term in the story of Saul's rise to kingship in ch. 9. Yahweh told Samuel that 'tomorrow' he would send him the man he was to appoint as *nāgîd* who was to save Israel from the 'hand' of the Philistines (9.16); here it is tomorrow that that same man will die at the hand of the Philistines and so illustrate his failure as king. David need not worry about his promise to Saul that he made in 24.21-22. There will be no need for a bloody purge to gain the throne since Yahweh has arranged for the elimination of the heirs as well as the king himself. The audience now knows which of the two remaining options that David posed for Saul's demise in 26.10 will occur. Saul will not die of old age, but in battle. He will be afforded an honorable death, dying while fighting Yahweh's war, but at the same time his death in battle against a foreign army will represent his divine punishment for breaking ongoing revelatory commands.

The exchange having ended, Saul instantly collapses, his full body-length sprawled on the ground, paralyzed by fear from Samuel's words and weak from hunger, having not eaten all day or night (v. 20). His position recalls the one he had assumed before Samuel at Naioth in Ramah in 19.24, after having prophesied naked under the influence of a divine spirit.[2] Once again, Saul is left paralyzed before God's mouthpiece, except here, it is the prophet's words that have

1. Gunn, *Fate of Saul*, pp. 108-109. For a proposed link with 18.10-11 and 8.20, see Polzin, *Samuel*, p. 220. The excision of vv.17-18 or vv. 17-19a as a secondary Deuteronomistic expansion (so, for example, Hertzberg, *I & II Samuel*, p. 217; Ackroyd, *First Samuel*, p. 215; Mauchline, *1 and 2 Samuel*, p. 183; McCarter, *I Samuel*, p. 423; Klein, *1 Samuel*, p. 270) is aptly characterized by Fokkelman (*Crossing Fates*, p. 616) as 'disastrous on at least four levels of the text and is a sign of literary illiteracy'.

2. So noted also by Fokkelman (*Crossing Fates*, pp. 618-19), who, in addition, sees it as a counterpart to the story of the call, where he *stands* a head taller than everyone else. As fallen king, he *lies* a head longer. Beuken ('Hammer of Witches', p. 6) contrasts his sprawl with his act of obeisance before Samuel in v. 14.

caused immobility, not those spoken by Saul. Saul's fear would seem to stem from the announcement of his and his sons' certain deaths the following day, since the other statements were merely confirmations of old knowledge. Saul's failure to have eaten all day and night raises the possibility that he may have been fasting before the forthcoming battle in an attempt to win God's favor and support, as he had done with the food ban that he had imposed on the troops in the battle at the Michmash pass in 14.24.[1] His reasons for not eating seem to have been deliberately shielded from the audience to raise the question of his intentions.

The medium, who had faded from the picture after having summoned up Samuel's ghost, re-enters in vv. 22-25 to take charge of the situation. Seeing Saul very disturbed (verb *bhl*), she urges Saul to let her feed him 'a morsel of bread'[2] so that he may have strength for his journey, politely characterizing herself as his *šiphâ*, female servant (vv. 21-22). It is not clear whether she and the two attendants witnessed the entire exchange between Saul and Samuel; the verb *bw'* need not be construed so literally that it must mean that she entered the room to find Saul. Even so, it is perhaps to be construed literally here, since the woman seems to assume that Saul's state derives from physical exhaustion only and that nourishment will suffice to restore his vigor, apparently not realizing that his collapse has been triggered primarily by emotional trauma. Or perhaps, as a skilled medium who is familiar with the emotional drain that results from such contacts with the spirit world, she has learned that the best way to bring people back to physical and emotional reality is to get some food into their system.[3] It is also plausible to think that the attendants and the woman

1. This is the conclusion of, for example, Gunn, *Fate of Saul*, p. 109. Fokkelman (*Crossing Fates*, p. 621) sees the refusal as the counterpart to ch. 14, where the army could not eat and so could not put a decisive end to war. McCarter (*I Samuel*, p. 421) suggests that the fasting was to purify himself for the seance. He seems to have taken up the prior position articulated by S. Reinach ('Le souper chez la sorcière', *RHR* 42 [1923], pp. 45-50).

2. As pointed out by Beuken ('Hammer of Witches', p. 12), the root *bhl* is used to describe reaction to unexpected events, including, specifically, a sudden confrontation with death.

3. According to Gordon (*I & II Samuel*, p. 196) the morsel of bread is a conventional expression of modesty, as in Gen. 18.5. According to Miscall (*1 Samuel*, p. 171) and Polzin (*Samuel*, p. 271 n. 10), the term 'morsel' evokes the

would have remained in another room granting the king privacy for his illicit exchange with Samuel. The attendants were there as body-guards for the journey, and the woman had performed her task of summoning Samuel's spirit and apparently was not needed further as an interpreter.

The woman's exchange with Saul has faint echoes of Abigail's petition to David in 25.24-31; in both instances the women are attempting to steer the king and king-elect toward a correct course of action. In the present instance, it may involve a simple attempt to fortify the king for the coming battle the next day, with no ulterior knowledge about his impending death. Whether the woman of En-dor is making sexual overtures toward the king as Abigail seems to have been doing to David is open to imagination.

After an initial refusal, Saul acquiesces to the second round of urging (read *pṣr* for MT *prṣ*) that has now involved the two attendants as well as the medium and bestirs himself to the bed (v. 23). Although his motives and thoughts are still hidden from the audience, as well as the knowledge or ignorance of the medium and the two attendants concerning Saul's certain death the next day, Saul has moved from his paralysis and returned to the realm of the living temporarily. He has decided to embrace life for the moment, return to his kingly duties, and accept his fate. The woman quickly prepares a meal befitting the king, killing her valued stall-fed calf and preparing fresh bread that has to remain unleavened because of the lack of time. She serves it to the king and his attendants. They eat and depart that same night (v. 24), strengthened physically at least for the impending battle. There is a sense of urgency in their need to return in order to participate in the battle at dawn. Fate seems to impel them home. While the audience and the king know that the meal will be Saul's last, it is not

judgment speech against the house of Eli in 2.30. Both scholars go on to develop parallels between the final battle at Gilboa and the battle at Ebenezer. Polzin goes so far as to suggest that David serves the same role as the Ark in his statement that David's stay among the Philistines was long enough to cause serious harm to the enemy, just like the Ark's stay was. However, David did not cause harm to the Philistines while serving under Achish; his raids against Negebite groups benefitted both the Philistines and Israel alike. This is a case where admittedly 'gross anatomical similarities' (Polzin, *Samuel*, p. 220) between the alleged beginning and end of a story have forced some questionable parallels and the overlooking of details.

clear whether the medium and the attendants also know this fact.[1] The poetic justice of Saul's final meal fit for a king is apparent. There is possible irony in the medium's unknowing preparation of Saul's final meal when she feared death herself as a result of her agreement to engage in a consultation of illicit ancestral spirits. Is the audience also to find poetic justice in Saul's imminent demise because of his breaking of his own mandate against the ancestral spirits?

1. Fokkelman (*Crossing Fates*, p. 619 n. 18) suggests that the wartime circumstances, the king's revealed identity, and his shattered state after the meeting with Samuel would have provided enough clues for any idiot to have deduced that Samuel gave the king bad news, i.e., a death announcement. Perhaps the narrator has deliberately failed to comment on the woman's knowledge of Saul's fate to indicate that it is irrelevant to the plot line; her actions are perhaps to be understood not to have been influenced by her possible knowledge that Saul is to die the following day.

Chapter 24

1 SAMUEL 29

Verse 1 returns the audience to the impending battle as it was introduced in 28.1, where the Philistines were mustering their forces for war against Israel and David was told by Achish that he was to fight with him. By framing the En-dor incident, which constitutes a fast-forwarding of the action, with the preparations for battle, the narrator has been able to inform his audience of Saul's certain death during the coming engagement. With ch. 29, he returns the audience to David's predicament of being obliged to fight against Saul and Israel, which now becomes an even greater potential danger in light of our privileged knowledge of Saul's imminent demise during the very same battle. Will David become the willing or unwilling agent of Saul's death after all?

The earlier ambiguity about the aggressor and defender in the impending war is now clarified: Saul has already positioned himself by the spring in the Jezreel plain and awaits the Philistine response to his challenge (v. 1). Although rejected by God, he has nevertheless taken the initiative in the present battle. In retrospect then, his concern about the outcome of the battle is more readily understood. Yahweh has chosen to defend Israel against hostile attacks in the past, but it is not clear that he will condone an aggressive move by Israel's rejected king.

The Philistines have accepted Saul's challenge and are mustering their forces at Aphek, a prominent town along the Via Maris in the northern part of the Sharon plain, at the northern end of Philistine territory.[1] The use of the name of Aphek in a military context should

1. There is no need to postulate the existence of an otherwise unknown Aphek in the Esdraelon Plain as the muster site, as was done by Smith (*Books of Samuel*, pp. 243-44). If one accepts the author's deliberate nonchronological ordering of chs. 28–31 for purposes of heightening suspense (*contra*, for example, Hertzberg,

immediately remind the audience of Yahweh's voluntary abandonment of Israel and their defeat at the hand of the Philistines in 1 Samuel 4,[1] reinforcing the negative overtones of the impending disaster to take place in the plain of Jezreel, where Israel is once again to fall victim to the Philistines.

The new scene takes place as part of the Philistine troop review prior to movement north to face Saul's forces. As part of a parenthetical aside introduced by disjunctive syntax in vv. 1b-2, the author contrasts Saul's stationary position (verb *ḥnh*) at the well in Jezreel with the Philistine active movement (verb *'br*) at Aphek. Although the information conveyed indicates that Saul was the initial agressor in the battle, the resulting picture tends to portray him as a sitting duck and defendant against the Philistine advance, reversing the role of agressor and defendant even before Saul's trip to the medium at En-dor.[2] He has issued a challenge but has lost heart even before the arrival of the enemy troops.

Upon seeing David and his men in the rear vanguard among Achish's forces, the Philistine commanders instantly question their presence (v. 3). They apparently are easily recognizable as 'hebrews' by their clothing,[3] a point that should lead the audience to remember Achish's inability to use the same criterion to catch David out in his lie about the targets of his raiding activities in ch. 27. An element of

I & II Samuel, p. 222), the alleged 'problem' of Aphek's location disappears. Nor is there any reason to relocate the entire battle scene to the Yarkon River area, near Aphek, as proposed by H. Bar Deroma ('Ye Mountains of Gilboa', *PEQ* 102 [1970], pp. 116-36). The lament in 2 Sam. 1 confirms the battle's location in the vicinity of the Jezreel Valley.

1. So noted also by Polzin, *Samuel*, p. 221.

2. Contrast Fokkelman (*Crossing Fates*, p. 570), who has contrasted the opening converted imperfect with the first participle in the circumstantial clause to conclude wrongly that the Philistines were the agressors. The correct situation has also been understood also Gordon (*I & II Samuel*, p. 197).

3. Clothing is the most obvious marker of identity in the context, rather than 'marked racial characteristics' as Hertzberg suggests (*I & II Samuel*, p. 222). His second suggestion that weaponry would have been a distinguishing feature is perhaps possible, but not necessarily conclusive. Common soldiers in all nations would have had fairly standardized weaponry, and by the period in question, the Aegean connections of the Philistines would have been 200 years in the past. It is likely that they would have shared weaponry design with their immediate neighbors, the Israelites.

suspense is now introduced as the audience is led to wonder whether the more astute Philistine generals will be able to discern David's true nature and loyalty and put him in jeopardy. While the explicit identities of David and his group do not appear to have been known by the commanders, their trustworthiness in the forthcoming battle against Saul and their fellow countrymen would be of central concern to the Philistine generals, especially in light of their experience at the Michmash pass, where the hebrews who had initially fought with the Philistines had defected back to the Israelite side during the course of the battle (1 Sam. 13-14).[1]

Achish immediately responds to the open question, taking responsibility for the hebrews and identifying their leader as David, the servant of Saul, who has been with him now for some time, stating that he has not found any problem with David from the day he defected (verb *npl*) until now (v. 3). While Achish may have intended his reply to be a boast about his ability to win over the loyalties of a renowned servant of Saul, his rhetorical question that identifies David as the servant of King Saul cannot help but reinforce the suspicions of the generals about David's true loyalties. In fact, Achish himself unwittingly identifies David as Saul's *continuing* servant in his failure to qualify David's servantship to Saul as a *past* status, i.e., 'Is this not David, the *former* servant of Saul?' By framing Achish's response as a rhetorical question, the narrator draws a link to the question that Achish's own servants had posed concerning David's trustworthiness when he had first appeared before Achish with Goliath's sword in 21.11.[2] Although misunderstanding the import of the song about David and Saul, concluding from it that David was king of the land, and, perhaps, that Saul was the servant of David rather than vice versa, they nevertheless had understood the close relationship between David, Saul and Israel. Now Achish has once again emphasized the ongoing close relationship between David, Saul and Israel, in spite of his intentions to do just the opposite and portray David as a defector who is now loyal to himself. The audience is aware of Achish's gross

1. The probable allusion of the Philistine generals to chs. 13–14 has been recognized by, for example, Ackroyd, *First Samuel*, p. 218; Mauchline, *1 and 2 Samuel*, p. 184; Fokkelman, *Crossing Fates*, p. 571; and Gordon, *I & II Samuel*, p. 197.

2. So noted previously by Fokkelman (*Crossing Fates*, p. 571).

misjudgment of David's postion and his gullibility from ch. 27.[1]

By having Achish characterize David as Saul's 'servant', the narrator is able to link him with Nabal, who likewise emphasized David's servantship to Saul (25.10-11). Whereas Nabal used David's former servanthood to Saul to highlight his later fugitive status and to deny him respect and supplies, Achish uses it to bolster his own self-image by deluding himself into believing that David is now his loyal servant and will remain so for the rest of his life. Both men become fellow fools in their failure to acknowledge David's true status as the servant of Yahweh, the anointed king-elect of Israel.

The enraged reaction of the Philistine commanders signals to the audience that they are not as guillible as their superior, Achish, reinforcing at the same time David's position of potential danger implied by their initial question in v. 3 (v. 4). They deal with the situation by demanding that Achish, one of the five supreme Philistine lords, order 'the man' who is his alleged underling to turn out so that he may return to the place to which he has been assigned by Achish. Whether their reference to David's assignment of a particular place by Achish is meant to allude to their further knowledge of his exploits as Achish's mercenary or whether they are merely presupposing that David would have been assigned land by Achish as a normal development had he and his men been in service for 'days and years' as Achish claimed is unclear. Either way, they are treating Achish with only some of the courteous deference due to the king of Gath. While they are allowing the king, as David's superior, to dismiss David, rather than defying him and highlighting his lack of good judgment by ordering David to fall out themselves, they nevertheless are overstepping their bounds as generals by *demanding* that Achish remove the hebrew contingent. Had they treated Achish with the proper respect due one of the *s^e^rānîm*, they would have reversed the order of their

1. W. Brueggeman ('Narrative Intentionality in 1 Samuel 29', *JSOT* 43 [1989], pp. 26-30) argues that Achish's threefold acquittal of David in vv. 3, 6, and 9 is the central interest of the narrative and that he serves to express the trust Israel has in David: 'a trust not based on facts, but on the strong habit David has of making his way through crises unscathed, even by blood-guilt' (p. 30). In light of Achish's portrayal in ch. 27 as a fool duped by David, together with the lack of respect his own countrymen show him and his own demonstrated weakness in this chapter, I find it highly unlikely that the Judahite author would have intended him to serve as a spokesperson for Israel's trust in David.

statement, beginning with the reasons for their suspicions and ending with a *request* that he dismiss them from service for the coming battle. Their demand reveals their lack of respect for Achish.

By carefully avoiding reference to David by name in their reply in vv. 4-5 until they quote the victory refrain crediting Saul with thousands and David with ten thousands of Philistine deaths, the generals are able to belittle his status in their own eyes and imply that he is a nobody of little import who is barely worthy of the present attention.[1] Yet their true concern about David's well-known status becomes more and more apparent as they continue their reply, betraying their familiarity with the man's reputation and the fact that he is indeed someone who needs to be reckoned with. The generals announce to Achish that David will not go with them into battle, explaining that they will not give him an opportunity to become their adversary, *śāṭān*, during battle. Continuing to develop their line of reasoning, they ask in what way 'this one' will or could make himself acceptable, *yitraṣṣeh*, to his lord and answer rhetorically, 'Is it not with the heads of these men?' (v. 4). They then finally reveal the source of their consternation and fear concerning David's loyalty to the Philistine cause, asking in a second rhetorical question if the David in question is not the well-known David about whom they sing in victory dances, 'Saul has slain his thousands and David his ten thousands' (v. 5).

The very same victory song that Achish's courtiers quoted in order to raise suspicions about David's intentions in defecting comes back to haunt him here in the mouths of the Philistine generals. The generals presume that David's loyalty to Saul is permanent and that the apparent break in relations is temporary at best. From experience at the Michmash pass, they know that hebrews can be turncoats during the heat of battle and cannot be trusted. In addition, they appear not to have forgotten David's exploit of beheading Goliath at the Elah Valley, an act that apparently launched him on his career with Saul, even if Achish has chosen to overlook this past exploit performed against his own citizens. The full irony of Achish's decision in 28.2 to appoint David to be the permanent 'keeper of his head' is driven home as the generals warn Achish that David may well be out to remove Philistine heads in the forthcoming battle[2] in an attempt to win back

1. So also Fokkelman, *Crossing Fates*, p. 574.

2. The play on 'head' imagery has been noted also by Klein (*1 Samuel*, p. 277)

the favor of his true lord, who by Achish's own admission is Saul, and regain his former position at the Israelite court. The Philistine generals would seem to have understood David's predicament all too well and do not want to give him an opportunity to display the source of his true loyalties on the battlefield. They have little tolerance for the foolish Achish, who cannot see through David's feigned loyalty.

Faced with being 'found out' again, as he had been in ch. 21, David is not afraid as he had been before. The changed circumstances account for his different reaction. In ch. 21, David had been seeking Philistine asylum and had had no defenders at the foreign court. Consequently, he had run the risk of being put to death as an enemy of the state before he could fully explain his position. In the present situation, he knew he had the protection of one of the five Philistine lords. Therefore, even though the generals were able to deduce the true situation, David did not run the risk of being executed on the spot as a probable traitor because of Achish's mislaid trust and influence.

Rather than challenge the generals' demand about David's dismissal and uphold his own decision to have David fight as a mercenary and, according to 28.3, as his personal bodyguard, Achish caves into the anger and orders of his subordinates. As David's superior, he summons him to dismiss him from the muster (vv. 6-7). Swearing in the name of David's god Yahweh, Achish proclaims that David has been upright (*yāšār*) and that 'in his eyes', the seat of human versus divine perception, he considers David's marching in and out with him in battle to be 'good' because he has not found any evil (*rā'*) in David during his entire sojourn with him. But, he goes on, 'in the eyes of' the Philistine lords, David is not considered to be 'good' (v. 6). His use of the phrase 'going out and coming in' to describe David's responsibilities in the coming battle seems intended to echo David's former performance of these identical duties in 18.13 as a commander in Saul's army.[1] He had carried out his job with such expertise for Saul, against the Philistines among other enemies, that he had earned the love of all Israel and Judah (18.16). The re-occurrence of the same phrase on the lips of Achish reminds the audience of the Philistine king's blindness and self-deceit concerning David's true loyalties and raise a question about how David would act, if forced to

and Fokkelman (*Crossing Fates*, p. 574).

1. So Fokkelman, *Crossing Fates*, p. 575.

'go in and come out' on behalf of the Philistines against Israel.

Achish's statement introduces the motifs 'eyes', with its implied opposite, 'heart', and the pair of opposites 'good' and 'evil'.[1] Like Saul before him, Achish has relied on human perception to judge David's actions and intentions and has come up short, straying to the side of misguided trust instead of straying to the side of misguided jealousy and rebellion against the divine plan, as Saul. Once again recalling the fool Nabal, who returned David 'evil' for 'good' (25.21), Achish has failed to acknowledge David's true status as the anointed king-elect of Israel, though for different reasons. It seems likely that the adjective 'good' is meant to have covenantal overtones in Achish's statement of his own position *vis-à-vis* David: in my opinion, your status as my mercenary or formally bound servant makes the participation of you and your men as members of the Philistine forces in the forthcoming battle legitimate and should not require further questioning by my cohorts. Nevertheless, the other four Philistine lords have declared that you are not 'good', i.e., trustworthy under the present circumstances.

The audience should note that Achish has told David that the decision about his dismissal has come from the highest body of authority, the Philistine lords themselves (*s^{e}rānîm*), when in fact it was the decision of the army generals. Apparently, he feels it is necessary to present the decision as an unalterable ultimatum from on high, so as not to be put in a position of having to lose face either before David for failing to appeal against the decision, or before the other lords, should anything go wrong during the battle and he be accused of introducing potential renegades among his forces.[2] His lie highlights his lack of integrity and leadership capabilities. He is unwilling to take command and tell the generals what to do, which is his right and duty as a lord. Do his words reveal a dawning, belated realization that David might not be as trustworthy as he had

1. Also noted by Miscall, *1 Samuel*, p. 174.

2. Miscall (*1 Samuel*, p. 174) develops the idea that Achish, like David, is a man 'prudent in speech'. He argues that Achish is to be seen 'not so much as gulled but as bought'; a man involved with David out of desire for personal gain who is on to David's schemes but feigns ignorance out of self-interest. I am not swayed by this reading, especially in light of the contempt his own Philistine generals express because of his lack of judgment. Miscall has also overlooked the ties drawn between Achish and the fool Nabal.

thought, or do they merely reveal his spinelessness?

With the echo of the commands of the Philistine generals in v. 4 still sounding in the audience's ears, Achish's variant commands in v. 7 highlight his desire to remain in the good graces of both David and his fellow Philistines simultaneously. He obeys the generals by ordering David to fall out of formation, thereby satisfying their insistence that David is not to participate as a Philistine recruit in the impending battle. However, he does not order David to return to Ziklag. Instead, he commands him to go peaceably and not to do anything that, in the 'eyes' of the Philistine lords, would be 'evil' (*rāʿ*). Apparently, he is afraid that by ordering David to be confined to quarters, he will alienate him. Finally taking some personal initiative instead of deferring to subordinates, he orders him to depart under peaceful terms,[1] accepting the decision in good faith in spite of its implications that David might not honor his oath of loyalty to him. Above all, Achish does not want David to create a scene.

In order to demonstrate his own trust in David's loyalty, Achish leaves him free to go wherever he chooses after his release from fighting obligations, indirectly stating that he trusts him implicitly by asking him not to do anything that the (other) Philistine lords would deem to be evil. By separating himself from the other lords in his previous statement in v. 6, he implies here that he disapproves of their decision, but must go along with it anyway. He strongly hints that he wants David to understand the bind he is in and that his judgment of David's 'good' and 'evil' in no way conforms to theirs. At the same time, he is appealing to David not to do anything that would get him into trouble with the other lords.

Realizing the position of compromise that Achish has put himself in, David decides to make the Philistine grovel even further in order to assert his own superiority in a psychological game of 'king of the mountain'. In the process, he catches Achish out in his own lie. Picking up on the phrasing of Achish's own statement of trust in David in v. 6, David, now characterizing himself as Achish's servant in a gesture of deference that is in fact a mockery of the Philistine fool, plays the injured party and demands to know what he has done

1. Fokkelman (*Crossing Fates*, p. 576) suggests that this statement is deliberately ironic, 'for the true David is only too glad to be spared a terrible dilemma in this way'.

wrong at any time during his service to Achish that has now prevented him from going to fight against 'the enemies of my lord, the king' (v. 8). The question 'What have I done?' resonates with the identically phrased protestations of innocence that David has made previously to Eliab in 17.29, Jonathan in 20.1, and Saul in 26.18.[1] In the present instance, however, the audience knows that David has duped his Philistine superior, who is the true enemy, while in the previous instances, his question expressed his innocence in situations where Saul had inappropriately classified David as his enemy. The closing desire to fight 'the enemies of my lord, the king' is meant to be ironic in light of David's demonstrated continuing loyalty to Saul in ch. 27.[2] It expresses the same sarcasm as David's reply in 28.2 to Achish's initial pronouncement that David and his men were to fight in the coming war.

In response, Achish reaffirms his misplaced trust in David, repeating his 'knowledge' that David is *ṭôb*, trustworthy.[3] He then reinforces his judgment by adding a metaphorical statement; 'in my eyes [the seat of his human misperception] you are like a divine messenger'—a totally reliable agent who will carry out the will of his liege majesty without hesitation. Of course, the irony of his characterizing David, the anointed *nāgîd* of Yahweh, as a 'divine messenger' is not lost on the audience.[4] Then comes the true confession, revealing his previous lie: only the Philistine *generals* have stated, 'he will not go up with us into battle'. In being forced to reiterate his position, Achish has not been careful enough to continue his original story line that claimed that the other lords had handed down the decision about David's exclusion from the Philistine forces and so has revealed the true

1. So noted also by Miscall, *1 Samuel*, p. 175. The echo with 26.18 is noted by Gordon (*I & II Samuel*, p. 198).

2. So noted also by, for example, Ackroyd, *First Samuel*, p. 219; McCarter, *I Samuel*, p. 427; and Klein, *1 Samuel*, p. 277.

3. Brueggeman ('Narrative Intentionality', p. 27) suggests that the use of *ṭôb* here echoes the earlier verdict Saul pronounced over David in 24.17; cf. 26.23.

4. Fokkelman (*Crossing Fates*, p. 576) sees *mal'ak 'ᵉlōhîm* to be the counterpart to *śāṭān bammilḥāmâ*. The subsequent appearance of *mal'ak 'ᵉlōhîm* in 2 Sam. 14.17 and 19.27-28 is pointed out by Ackroyd (*First Samuel*, p. 219) and McCarter (*I Samuel*, p. 426). The latter argues that the expression is probably intrusive here, citing its absence from LXXb and its judicial overtones in the later contexts, which do not fit in the present situation. The awkwardness of the phrasing as it stands, in addition to McCarter's points, make his suggestion attractive.

situation to his mercenary. He has indicated to David his cowardice or unwillingness to stand up to the generals by challenging their decision as one of the five supreme Philistine lords. He has cowered before the generals who are below him in rank, revealing his lack of self-esteem, leadership capabilities and integrity.

Apparently unaware of his slip, Achish completes his exchange by ordering David and his men to arise early and to go at the first morning light (v. 10). He begins by commanding that David arise early, but then, apparently to clarify any misunderstanding concerning the inclusion of all of David's party in the decision of the generals, hastens to add 'and the servants of your lord who have come with you—you (all) should arise early, and when light is with you (all), go'.[1] Achish's use of polite court speech temporarily places David on an equal (or perhaps even superior) footing by designating him 'lord' (*'ādôn*). In the continuing psychological game, it represents a triumph for David, who has brought the lord Achish 'to his knees' and wrung from him a confession of David's true lordship. In light of the play throughout the chapter on David's status as servant to Saul, to Achish, and to God as a divine messenger, it seems likely that Achish's statement is meant to be seen by the audience to be multivalent and, on another level of meaning, to be a slip in which he inadvertently confirms once again, as he did in v. 3, David's status as Saul's continuing servant.[2]

In light of the development of Achish's character in the earlier verses of the scene there is reason to suspect that the longer form of v. 10 found in the LXX is a later expansion rather than an original reading that has been lost through haplography, as is commonly asserted.[3] In spite of Achish's spinelessness in not standing up to the

1. The MT text, though awkward, makes sense in the context of a statement by a fool unable to think quickly as he tries to maintain face before David.

2. Its implicit reference to Saul is suggested also by Klein (*1 Samuel*, pp. 277-78), who stresses that all three uses of 'lord' in the chapter (vv. 4, 8, 10) probably allude to Saul and are intended to make clear that David's foreign sojourn was not treasonous.

3. The longer reading is adopted, for instance, by Driver, *Notes*, p. 221; Dhorme, *Livres de Samuel*, pp. 248-49; Hertzberg, *I & II Samuel*, p. 222; Ackroyd, *First Samuel*, p. 219; Mauchline, *1 and 2 Samuel*, p. 185; McCarter, *I Samuel*, p. 426; Klein, *1 Samuel*, p. 275. It is rejected as a secondary midrashic expansion by P.A.H. de Boer ('Research into the Text of I Samuel XVIII-XXXI',

insolence of the subordinate generals, he asserted his superiority over them by not ordering David to return to his appointed place, as the generals had commanded (vv. 4, 7). The Hebrew text maintains this decision intact by having Achish release David on his own recognizance at daybreak, which is consistent with his reiterated faith in David's trustworthiness in v. 9. It would seem that someone working with the LXX text felt Achish's words were too abrupt or perhaps too conversational in their presentation, seeming to be repetitive, and expanded his statement by building upon vv. 4 and 11 to command David and company to go 'to the place I have assigned you'. The subsequent command, 'As for these base remarks, take none to heart, for you have done well before me', has no explicit reference in the preceding episode, since David has not heard the speech of the generals in v. 5. It appears rather to be the attempt of a pious scribe who has not followed the logic of the scene too well to vindicate David before the insinuations of the Philistine generals.

The episode ends with David and his men obeying Achish's command and setting out in the morning to return to the land of the Philistines, while the Philistines go up to Jezreel.[1] In light of the implications that David's loyalties still lie with Israel, Achish's failure to order him back to Ziklag, as the Philistine generals commanded, and Achish's stress that David should not do anything that would make him seem evil in the eyes of the Philistine lords, the audience should wonder what actions David has in mind in his choice to return to Philistine territory. Is he going back 'in peace' or is he planning to launch his own countercampaign in the Philistine homeland while the troops are off fighting Saul up north? Does he plan to continue his policy enunciated in 27.11, but this time wiping out Philistine villages instead of Geshurite, Girzite and Amalekite ones while there were no watchful eyes to catch him at his game? Will he indeed reveal his true loyalty by helping the Israelite cause while the Philistines have left their home territory undermanned?

OTS 6 [1949], p. 87) and Stoebe (*Erste Buch Samuelis*, p. 499).

1. Miscall (*1 Samuel*, p. 176) asks if the emphasis on the early departure is meant to coincide with Saul's departure for En-Dor. Since no departure time was given in the previous chapter, the answer is probably no. Fokkelman (*Crossing Fates*, p. 578) contrasts David's passing through a long dark tunnel and coming out unscathed in the light at the end, as if a new beginning awaits him, with the very lonely darkness of Saul's last night.

Chapter 25

1 SAMUEL 30

The audience is not held in suspense for long about David's possible countercampaign after dismissal by the Philistine lords. He heads straight back home at a rushed pace, covering the sixty-odd miles in a little over two days (v. 1), without any side trips for retaliatory action. Meanwhile, however, the audience is informed that his own town has become the target of a retaliatory raid by the Amalekites, former Davidic victims from ch. 27, who have smitten and razed it (v. 1). The potential oppressor has ironically become a victim himself! The use of the verb *pšṭ* to characterize the Amalekites' activities in the Negeb and at Ziklag, as well as David's raids that were carried out against the Geshurites, Girzites and Amalekites in 27.8, 10, highlights the retaliatory nature of the strike.[1] The ironic situation raises the possibility that, in retrospect, the audience is to understand David's haste to return home to reflect his foreseeing of such a raid after he was required to serve as Achish's mercenary and leave his own home unprotected.

Yet, the Amalekites do not retaliate completely, for unlike David, they do not kill every living human to avoid the spread of rumors.[2] Instead, they take the women captive without killing anyone, leading them away and going on their way. The preservation of life is emphasized by the use of the phrase 'from the smallest to the biggest' to qualify the generic *'îš*, 'person'. Although they have not taken any lives, the Amalekites have rendered David and his men womanless. As others have noted, they undoubtedly planned to sell the women as

1. So, for example, previously, Mauchline, *1 and 2 Samuel*, p. 186; Fokkelman, *Crossing Fates*, p. 579; Gordon, *I & II Samuel*, p. 199.

2. So noted also by Gunn, *Fate of Saul*, p. 110; Klein, *1 Samuel*, p. 281; Miscall, *1 Samuel*, p. 178.

slaves,[1] realizing a profit for themselves while inflicting a painful reprisal upon David that would have the same effect as actual death. Different goals account for the different treatment of human life by David and the Amalekites, but both parties share the common motivations of self-service and self-aggrandizement.

Upon arriving home, David and his men find the town razed by fire and their wives, sons and daughters carried off (v. 3). Unlike the audience, they do not know who has retaliated against them, but they are able to establish that their families are still alive. Apparently, there are no visible body remains within the town or the fire rubble. In response, the entire group cries until they are utterly exhausted. The Hebrew phrasing seems to imply that David, as leader, initiated the crying and lamentation, which was the expected and customary response to such a disaster. In a parenthetical aside in v. 5, however, the audience is informed that David's two wives, Ahinoam the Jezreelite and Abigail the widow of Nabal, had been taken captive. Thus, the audience is to understand that his lament was not merely perfunctory, but personal as well.

As a result of bitterness of soul over the loss of their families, David's men seek to stone him, making the situation very 'pressing' (verb *ṣrr*) for their leader. The men's decision to put David to death by a legally prescribed means hints that they have perhaps held a mock trial and at least have deemed their leader guilty of a capital offense punishable by death. Their stance tends to reinforce the retroflective suggestion that David has perhaps foreseen, or should have been able to have foreseen, the retaliatory raid that was launched in his absence. Use of the phrase *wattēṣer lᵉdā́wīd* in v. 6 seems to resonate with the other occurrences of the root *ṣrr* in 13.6 and 28.15 in a similar impersonal construction.[2] Especially apposite is 28.15, since it involves Saul's experience of distress on the eve of his final battle of Gilboa, the battle from which David has just been dismissed to his own great relief. Through the use of the same phrase, the narrator draws a link between the king and the king-elect, both of

1. So Hertzberg, *I & II Samuel*, p. 227; Mauchline, *1 and 2 Samuel*, p. 186.

2. McCarter (*I Samuel*, p. 434) proposes more far-flung connections with Gen. 32.8; Judg. 2.15; 10.9; 2 Sam. 13.2, and Job 20.22. Miscall (*1 Samuel*, p. 179) asserts that this is only the second time that David is afraid or distressed, citing 21.3 as the first incident.

whom are experiencing the same loss of confidence in the face of an enemy attack. Yet, the link serves at the same time to contrast the two and to highlight the king's loss of divine favor to the king-elect. Whereas Saul is distressed not only because of the impending Philistine war but equally because of his lack of ability to consult God, who has turned away from him, David immediately is able to terminate his distress by turning to God for the strengthening self-confidence he needs (v. 6). The narrator probably also intends the audience to hear echoes of the uses of *ṣrr* in 25.29 and 26.24, where David's deliverance from 'distress' was intimately bound up with his reliance upon Yahweh.

David's ability to solve his crisis of self-confidence by 'strengthening himself in Yahweh his God' contrasts with his earlier crisis at Horesh in 23.15-18, where Saul's close pursuit had led him to fear.[1] At that time, Jonathan had taught him that he must 'strengthen his hand in God' (23.16) in order to conquer his personal fear or lack of self-confidence. Through the intervening chapters, David has learned that Yahweh is his special God upon whom he must rely, so that David's quick 'strengthening' by turning to Yahweh in particular in v. 6 demonstrates his mastery of the more generic advice that Jonathan imparted in 23.16. This time, David does not fear when his life is threatened by his own men, apparently because he has understood his close relationship to Yahweh, whose spirit he possesses as the anointed king-elect.

David consults Yahweh through Abiathar and the priestly ephod and learns that Yahweh will indeed help him overtake the raiders and rescue the missing families (vv. 7-8). Continuing the contrast between the divinely abandoned king of ch. 28 and the divinely supported king-elect, the narrator names Abiathar as the priest through whom David seeks to contact Yahweh, ostensibly in order to raise the specter of Saul's massacre of the priests of Nob in ch. 22, of which Abiathar was the lone survivor. As noted in 28.15 in Saul's exchange with Samuel, the king deliberately seems to omit reference to his attempt to

1. The connection between the two incidents is also noted by Hertzberg (*I & II Samuel*, p. 227) and Fokkelman (*Crossing Fates*, p. 582). Gordon (*I & II Samuel*, p. 199) contrasts it with Saul's ability to secure help or guidance in 28.15, while Mauchline (*1 and 2 Samuel*, p. 186) claims the last phrase of v. 6 bears the marks of hero-worship of David.

contact God through the priestly manipulated Urim and Thummim, even though they are mentioned in 28.6, apparently as an attempt to avoid dragging up memories of his massacre of the priests at Nob as well as his premature cutting off of Ahijah's priestly consultation at Michmash in 14.18-20. Armed with divine reassurance for his successful overtaking of the raiders and rescue of the missing families, which is emphasized through the use of the grammatical construction employing the infinitive absolute followed by a finite verbal form of the same root, David springs into action that will resolve the temporary distress caused by his distraught men.

Setting out with all 600 of his men in order to have the relief result from a united effort, David heads south (v. 9). His choice of direction is not reported to have been determined by oracular consultation. By implication, it is determined by the location of the groups against whom David had previously launched many raids, on the suspicion that one of them, the Geshurites, Girzites, or Amalekites, has tried to gain revenge. Upon reaching the brook, Besor, the narrator informs the audience, using a disjunctive grammatical construction, that 'the ones being left behind', *hannôtārîm*, stayed put (v. 9). The sense of the niphal participle is not immediately clear and appears to be deliberately ambiguous, forcing the audience to wonder about their identity.[1] Are they designated baggage-tenders, as known from 17.22 and 25.13, even if the baggage would be minimal at this point, or stragglers, exhausted from the long march that has been quickly resumed? The answer is given in the following verse. They are stragglers, numbering 200, or one third of the entire Davidic group, who were literally too 'corpse-like' (root *pgr*) to cross the river (v. 10). By implication then, the 400 who pursue the raiders with David are also extremely worn out and not particularly in the best condition for the rescue effort underway. The resulting image of a ragtag group of physically and emotionally exhausted men heightens the importance of the divine reassurance given in v. 8 that victory against the raiders will be forthcoming; there is no way that such a group would be able to prevail on their own.

The pursuing group stumbles upon an Egyptian who, after being revived with food, is able to lead them directly to the raiders without

1. *Contra*, for example, Ackroyd (*First Samuel*, p. 220) and Mauchline (*1 and 2 Samuel*, p. 186), who suggest its deletion as an addition because it adds nothing.

unnecessary effort or delay (vv. 12-16).[1] The man is instantly recognized by the group as an Egyptian (v. 12), once again reminding the audience of Achish's stupidity in trusting David when the clothing laid before his eyes after raids clearly revealed its owner's identity and David's lie (27.9-12). Like the Philistine generals (29.3), David's men can easily identify a man's origin by his clothing. Since the audience is told in the following verse that the man was unconscious when found, his clothing rather than his speech must have been the determining factor in identifying his background.

It takes two rounds of feeding to revive the man.[2] The initial bread and water is insufficient (v. 11). It is only after he receives an additional piece of fig cake and two clusters of raisins that his spirit returns to him. The audience is to note that David's men, while exhausted from the long march home from Aphek, the emotional trauma, and the subsequent march south, have food supplies with them. The audience is then informed that the Egyptian had not eaten or had water for three days and nights. This serves two functions. It explains his near-death condition from hunger and exposure, while at the same time, it raises an initial suspicion that the Egyptian may have had some sort of connection with the raid. His last meal was about the same time that David and his men were involved in the troop review at Aphek. The raid was some time during this same period. Is this only coincidence?

The suspicion grows stronger in v. 13 as David questions the man and learns that he is indeed an Egyptian, but a servant to an Amalekite man. The audience knows that the Amalekites raided Ziklag, while David apparently suspects them as one of the three groups who would have had reason to retaliate against him because of his earlier raids in ch. 27. The Egyptian's additional comment that he was left behind when he fell sick three days previously at first glance tends to allay the growing suspicions, suggesting mere coincidence, but upon reflection, intensifies them. After all, the slave's Amalekite owner could have

1. Echoes of Gen. 14.13-16 are suggested by Auzou (*Danse devant l'arche*, p. 209). Fokkelman (*Crossing Fates*, p. 584) sees echoes of Hagar from Genesis 16 and 21 in the Egyptian dying of hunger.

2. Fokkelman (*Crossing Fates*, p. 584) contrasts Saul's being fed in 28.20-25 with David, who gives food here. However, the slave needs two rounds of food unlike Saul, so the contrastive parallel is loose at best. Miscall (*1 Samuel*, p. 180) says the Egyptian 'intones' Saul's weakness from not eating.

been travelling on business. However, the repeated reference to 'three days' reinforces the memory of the three-day march from Aphek and David's absence from Ziklag, leaving it vulnerable. In addition, it seems somewhat strange that a man would abandon a servant along the way merely because he fell sick. One would expect him to take the servant back home and hope he would recuperate. Slaves would not have been so cheap that they would have been easily disposable.

The growing suspicions are finally confirmed in v. 14 as the Egyptian further clarifies the circumstances of his abandonment. He informs David that he had been part of an Amalekite raid against the Negeb of the Cherethites, the region belonging to Judah, and the Negeb of Caleb. At this point the audience knows that this is the same group that attacked Ziklag because of the information they were given in v. 1. David, on the other hand, while having cause to be strongly suspicious, cannot yet be certain that the same group attacked Ziklag, unless his town lay within the Negeb of the Cherethites. The raids appear to have been directed against both 'Philistines' and 'Israelites' alike, accepting the writer's understanding that Judah was part of Israel under Saul and that the Cherethites were closely associated with the Philistines. Thus, they were not overtly retaliatory, or they would have been limited to Philistine territory alone. Nevertheless, the last phrase in v. 14 provides absolute confirmation for David and the audience alike. The Egyptian ends by stating that they burned Ziklag with fire. Has he deliberately withheld this information until last because he knows who David is and the probable reaction it will provoke?

David's request that the Egyptian take him to the raiding band is surprisingly cool and collected (v. 15). However, the Egyptian's counterresponse reveals his fear and probable knowledge of David's reputation. He instantly demands that David swear by God not to kill him personally,[1] or to 'shut him up [verb, *sgr*] in the hand of' his (Amalekite) master. Only then will he agree to David's request. His use of the *Leitwort sgr* and the motif *yād* should remind the audience of the earlier uses of both terms to explore the relationship between rejected king and king-elect, Saul's stubborn attempt to thwart the

1. Miscall (*1 Samuel*, p. 180) sees the Egyptian to 'intone' Saul's earlier request for a Davidic oath not to kill him in 1 Sam. 24.22. Stoebe (*Erste Buch Samuelis*, p. 515) and Klein (*1 Samuel*, p. 283) suggest that the off-guard, feasting enemy recalls the situation in the Gideon story in Judg. 8.11.

actualization of the divine plan for his successor, and David's need to trust in Yahweh to resolve Saul's fate rather than taking control of the throne by his own hand. David's calmness in the face of learning that the Egyptian standing before him was party to the destruction of his town and capture of the families seems to relate to his divinely reassured confidence that he will be able to overtake the enemy and rescue the women and children. He understands instantly that the servant is his means of finding the whole raiding party, so that by killing him, an admitted member of the troop, he will lose his larger opportunity for revenge. The Egyptian understands the situation also and desires to ensure his survival beyond the imminent confrontation between David and the Amalekite band, realizing that he faces almost certain death at the hands of either party for participation in the raid or for betraying his master's party.

The Egyptian slave apparently knew the movements of his master well, even having been abandoned *en route*, for he is able to fulfill his end of the bargain and take David to the Amalekite camp (v. 16). Upon arrival, they find the enemy spread out over a wide area, eating, drinking and celebrating among, with, or on account of (*b*^{e}) all the great spoil they had removed from both the Philistines and the Judahites (v. 16). The scene is vaguely reminiscent of the Midianite multitude that Gideon encounters in the Jezreel valley in Judg. 7.6, but there are no deliberate repetitions of key phrases by the author to indicate that the two were intended to be related.[1] The use of the verb *ḥgg* to describe the Amalekites' activity may simply be intended to indicate that their revelry was set within the expected religious context of thanking their god for giving them victory.[2] In this case, the preposition *b*^{e} would be best rendered 'on account of'. On the other hand, if the verb is to be construed in its more regular sense to designate the celebration of an annually appointed pilgrim feast, it is possible that the audience is meant to understand that the Amalekites have made the raids just prior to a scheduled feast, perhaps as a means of having offerings from booty to use at the feast's celebration. In this case, the

1. Miscall (*1 Samuel*, p. 178) considers ch. 30 to read like a gloss on the destruction of the Midianites in Num. 31.

2. Thus the translation of 'behaving as at a *ḥag*', suggested by Driver (*Notes*, p. 223) and adopted, for example, by Mauchline (*1 and 2 Samuel*, p. 188) and McCarter (*I Samuel*, p. 435).

preposition b^e would best be assigned a sense, 'among' or 'with'. The acceptance of the normative meaning for *ḥgg* seems more likely to me because it provides a plausible reason in retrospect for the slave's ability to take David to the group, even though he had been abandoned three days earlier. He would have known where and when their scheduled annual pilgrim feast was to have taken place.

David springs into action in the narrative flow of events, smiting the enemy from twilight[1] until the evening of the next day,[2] almost a full 24 hours. The audience is not able to judge easily whether he delays his attack until twilight or whether he launches it then because that is when he has arrived on the scene. In either case, he has the advantage of rapidly approaching darkness (as well as the divine reassurance of success) to help his small force of 400 kill what would seem to be a larger Amalekite group. No factual figures have been provided for the size of the Amalekite group, and their coverage of a wide area does not necessarily mean that their numbers were large; according to custom, different clans might have preferred to tent separately. It may be that the narrator has deliberately refrained from providing the audience with figures to leave them to ponder how lopsided or even the odds may have been between the two sides.

The wide dispersal of the enemy group would have made a direct assault on the camp harder, and since David wanted to recover the women and children alive, his safest approach would not have been to

1. There seems to be no need to translate *hannešep* in its rare sense of 'dawn' instead of the normative 'twilight', as is done by, for example, Dhorme, *Livres de Samuel*, p. 252; Ackroyd, *First Samuel*, p. 221; Hertzberg, *I & II Samuel*, p. 225; Stoebe, *Erste Buch Samuelis*, p. 507; McCarter, *I Samuel*, p. 435; Klein, *1 Samuel*, p. 279; Fokkelman, *Crossing Fates*, p. 588. *Contra* especially Fokkelman, there would be no Amalekite advantage by engaging battle with darkness approaching; guerilla tactics are often launched at night to give the outnumbered side a tactical advantage.

2. I do not favor the emendation of *lmḥrtm* in v. 17 to *l^eha ḥ^arimām*, as suggested by Wellhausen (*Text der Bücher Samuelis*, p. 144) and followed by, for example, Budde (*Bücher Samuel*, p. 188) and Ackroyd (*First Samuel*, p. 223). Nor do the variant emendations *wyḥrmm*, proposed by Ehrlich (*Randglossen*, III, p. 267) or *b^ekol maḥ^anêhem*, proposed by Klostermann (*Bücher Samuelis*, p. 124) hold force. There is no textual support for the alteration of the consonants and there is no mention of a ban in the preceding verses of the narrative. Part of the deliberate contrast between David's battle against Amalek and Saul's battle in ch. 15 hinges on the different circumstances.

cause a great commotion in which the captives could have been killed in the mêlée and confusion. By using the cover of darkness, he could send guerilla teams against various clusters within the enemy ranks, kill them quietly, round up the women and children quickly, and herd them off to safety. If the Amalekites were to have been celebrating a pilgrimage feast, then David might have been able to send teams in to round up the women and children from their areas of confinement while the celebrants were gathered elsewhere for festivities and then move on to dealing with the revelers at their gathered places of revelry. By the arrival of daylight, the family members could have been safely retrieved and the enemy numbers reduced enough perhaps to make the odds more even, although again, the audience has no firm indication of how bad the odds might have been.

The narrator finally seems to confirm that David and his men were greatly outnumbered in the second half of v. 17 by mentioning that only 400 Amalekite men of *ná'ar* status had escaped from the slaughter by mounting camels and fleeing. All others had been put to death. The implication of the phrasing would seem at first reading to be that the 400 constituted a small fraction of the original Amalekite host. The ancient audience would have had more familiarity with the typical size of raiding parties and would probably have had a good idea whether the Amalekites would have required a number of parties to carry out their raids against both the Philistines and Judahites, or just a few select teams. The modern audience is less able to gauge this information. On further consideration, however, it seems possible that the comment is designed to indicate also, or instead, that there was nothing that David could have done about the group that managed to reach the camels and outrun his surprise attack.[1] In this case, the reported number of escapees may not have been intended to have had any bearing on the size of the larger group.

Since David would have no way of knowing how many of the enemy had escaped, the narrator appears to have relayed his privy figure of 400 to his audience for a particular purpose. The most noteworthy feature of the number is that it equals the size of David's entire force involved in the rescue operation. A number of impres-

1. This sense is favored by, for example, Ackroyd (*First Samuel*, p. 223) and Fokkelman (*Crossing Fates*, p. 589). Gordon (*I & II Samuel*, p. 200) sees the connection of the Amalekites with camels to be reminiscent of Judg. 6.3-6.

sions come to mind. One is that David and his band of physically and emotionally bedraggled men have been able to dispatch a veritable enemy horde, as God had predicted and reassured. Another is that they had killed off the Amalekites who were within their reach, in contrast to Saul in ch. 15, who had spared Agag and 'all that was good', perhaps including captives to be used as slaves. The resulting contrast highlights the actions of the rejected king who had failed to carry out a divinely ordered ban against Amalek and those of the king-elect, who has been left to carry on the battle against God's proclaimed enemy, whose ranks have swelled considerably since Saul's mission. Even without a specific divine directive to perform a ban against Amalek, David has killed off every Amalekite within reach of his group who was on foot, thereby indirectly demonstrating his suitability for coronation as Yahweh's earthly vice-regent. He is willing and able to undertake the elmination of Yahweh's enemies.

A third impression is that every one of David's tired men has been unable to prevent the escape of one of the enemy, so that the Amalekites will continue to be a thorn in Israel's side in the future. This somewhat negative aspect does not offset the overall suggestion of success associated with the first two impressions, however. The small band has been able to prevail over a larger enemy group in an unconventional 'battle', and the escape of the 400 camel-borne retainers has not interfered with the success of the mission, whose primary goal was not to eliminate Amalek from existence, as was the case of Saul's campaign, but to rescue alive family members in the Amalekites' possession.

The atypical nature of the rescue operation is emphasized by the use of the battle-report pattern in vv. 16-20. Instead of the conventional verbs of movement such as *yṣ'*, *hlk*, or *bw'* that report the positioning of the enemy lines, we have a niphal form of the verb *yrd*, placing David in a passive role (v. 16), and no report of the arrayal of the enemy troops for battle. The enemy is engaged in celebrational activities rather than activities of military preparation (v. 16). This variation from the norm prepares the audience for an atypical battle. The appearance of an unexpected verb of military activity, *nkh*, indicates that a battle took place, nonetheless (v. 17), and information on the length of the engagement (v. 17), as well as the outcome (vv. 17-19), follows the regular format. However, the concluding element varies from the expected report of the extent of the war and description of the defeat. Instead, we learn about David's success in 'bringing back all' and, in addition, of his capture of Amalekite herds (vv. 19-20). By indicating the success of the operation in terms of rescue rather than defeat, the author drives home to the audience the unusual nature of the encounter as a rescue operation instead of a standard battle. The catalogue of recovered goods mirrors the phrasing in vv. 3-6, emphasizing David's ability to have resolved the public and personal crises at hand. The people's initial loss of confidence in their leader is now replaced by restored confidence and gratitude, demonstrated by their ceding to him as personal spoil all the sheep and goat herds taken from the Amalekites (v. 20, MT). The cattle are reserved for distribution among the entire group.[1]

Harmony and unity have not been fully restored, however, since 200 of the group had been too tired to have been involved in the rescue. Confrontation occurs as the victorious group of people returns with David to the brook of Besor and meets the 200 who had remained behind (v. 21). Assuming his role as leader, David acts quickly to diffuse the inevitable hostilities and restore group unity. Drawing near to the people, the group returning with him from the Amalekite encounter, he asks them for peace (v. 21).[2] The implied situation requiring a peaceful resolution is the pending exchange with

1. I see no reason to adopt the LXXb reading, or a variant based on it. The MT's disjunctive syntax, which places *w*[e]*haṣṣō'n* before *nhgw*, seems intended to indicate that there was a deliberate separation of the sheep and goats from the larger herds as David's special portion. It seems likely that the verb *nhgw* should be repointed as a niphal, with *haṣṣō'n* to serve as its subject. Fokkelman (*Crossing Fates*, p. 589) points to the deliberate contrast between Saul, who does not take a single Amalekite beast for himself, and David, who takes all the livestock without ritual or cultic interest. My understanding is that he takes only the sheep and goats. Gordon (*I & II Samuel*, p. 200) cites Gen. 14.21 as a precedent for David's entitlement to all the spoil. By contrast, Hertzberg (*I & II Samuel*, p. 228) argues similarly to me that the author is trying to emphasize that the assignment of the booty to David was a mark of trust by his men after the surmounting of the crisis, rather than something due the leader by prearrangement.

2. I favor the retention of the MT text over adoption of the LXX reading, as do also, previously, Dhorme, *Livres de Samuel*, p. 254; Hertzberg, *I & II Samuel*, p. 229; Stoebe, *Erste Buch Samuelis*, p. 508; Gordon, *I & II Samuel*, p. 200; *contra*, for example, Wellhausen, *Text der Bücher Samuelis*, p. 145; Smith, *Books of Samuel*, p. 249; Driver, *Notes*, p. 224; Mauchline, *1 and 2 Samuel*, p. 188; McCarter, *I Samuel*, p. 433; and Klein, *1 Samuel*, p. 280.

the nonparticipants. David's request meets opposition; certain bad (*rāʿ*) and worthless (*b^eliyyáʿal*) men who had accompanied David in the rescue operation reject his proposal and respond by placing personal prejudices and greed above the group needs (v. 22). They proclaim that the failure of the 200 to have participated should deprive them of any portion of the Amalekite spoil gained during the rescue operation or of their recovered material goods; the men can merely have their wives and children back and are to leave David's ranks.

The return of the adjective *b^eliyyáʿal* recalls the dissension in ranks caused by a similar group that Saul experienced immediately upon his public designation in 10.27,[1] as well as Nabal's failure to agree to David's request (25.17, 25). In contrast to the two previous situations, however, the 'worthless' men here are not challenging the chosen leader's right to lead; they are challenging the definition of membership in the community on the basis of the failure of certain members to follow their leader into 'battle'. They are, in their own skewed way, defending the leader's honor and authority. Recognizing the disruptive potential of their challenge and the fact that it also attempts to usurp the leader's ability to define membership, David steps in as leader and exercises his authority by making a ruling. Acting as highest judge and authority of the group, he proclaims that the dissenters shall never do such a thing with what the Lord has given the group, using the durative, nonspecific formulation of the prohibition (*lōʾ* + imperfect) rather than the one for immediate, specific commands (*ʾal* + imperfect) (v. 23). Intending to impress upon all the need for maintaining group solidarity, he addresses the worthless men as 'my brothers', seeming to try to soften the blow of his forceful command by presenting himself as a *primus inter pares* to prevent instant alienation (v. 23). At the same time, he emphasizes to the men that their victory was not all self-earned, but determined by Yahweh, who had placed the raiding party 'in their hand', so that they have no reason to be so self-assertive or self-righteous (v. 23). His speech once again indicates his internalization of the need to rely upon Yahweh rather than self-help for vindication and victory.

1. So noted also by Klein (*1 Samuel*, p. 283). Polzin (*Samuel*, p. 223) claims that 'the king who hid himself among the baggage when called to rule (20.22) is replaced by one who stays by the baggage (30.24) as he waits for a chance to rule'. I find his comment inaccurate and off-target.

Seeking to diffuse the challenge posed by the worthless men once and for all, David quotes to them what appears to have been a well-known practice by his group concerning the division of spoil (v. 24).[1] By asking who would listen to their proposal, David strongly implies that the saying he goes on to quote was a standing, accepted policy among the group.[2] Those who remain with the group's supplies are to share the spoil captured by those who go into battle equally. The underlying recognition is that both jobs are necessary for the protection and well-being of the group. Those who go into battle face more immediate risk, but also gain more glory. Those who remain may also face surprise attack and so potential glory. Each has performed his assigned task and so is entitled to an equal share of the procured goods. By converting the status of the 200 who remained behind because of physical exhaustion to official 'baggage-keepers', a task that they probably legitimately performed even if they came to it through necessity rather than what was probably the more typical lot-casting procedure, David has been able to reintegrate the group and maintain its unity.[3] By having David convert the standing policy to an official statute and ordinance, the narrator depicts David as a

1. A number of scholars quote what they consider to be parallels to the ruling elsewhere in the Bible. Ackroyd (*First Samuel*, p. 224) cites Num. 31.27 and Josh. 22.8 as examples of the application of the same principle. Auzou (*Danse devant l'arche*, p. 209) also cites Josh. 22.8 but not Num. 31.27. Stoebe (*Erste Buch Samuelis*, p. 517) adds to Ackroyd's two examples Josh. 6.21 and Deut. 20.13-15, while Klein (*1 Samuel*, p. 283) adds only Deut. 20.14. I find none of the cited examples to be identical to the present one, where the booty is to be distributed equally among the *troops*, whether they went into battle or were 'assigned' baggage duty. Polzin (*Samuel*, p. 222) suggests that the reflection on the spoils of David in v. 20 as the portion of *all Israel* in v. 24 is ultimately exilic in nature, reflecting the related issues of culpability and fate. I believe he has extrapolated too far from the immediate context of the story, where I understand the spoils of David to have been separated from the spoils that are to be shared by *all members of his band*. I find no reason or justification to equate David's core group of 600 men with *all Israel* either; in the story, it is even clearly separated from the constituents of Judah!

2. Fokkelman (*Crossing Fates*, p. 590) sees David's rhetorical question in v. 24 to echo Saul's guilt in listening to the voice of the people in 15.24.

3. Similarly, Miscall (*1 Samuel*, p. 180), who sees the conversion of the 200 too tired to fight to baggage-watchers to demonstrate David's possession of *n^{e}bôn dābār* in keeping the band together.

legitimate law-maker, one of the tasks of a full-fledged king.[1] He seems to be hinting that David's final coronation is close at hand.

The episode ends with David returning to his home base of Ziklag and sending part of the Amalekite spoil to the elders of Judah, his 'friends' or 'fellow-citizens' (*rē'ēhû*) (vv. 26-31). In light of the immediately preceding dispute over who was entitled to share in the spoil, David's action seems to rock the boat slightly, since the elders of Judah had no legitimate claim to spoil whatsoever. The spoil sent to them is characterized by David as 'a blessing from the spoil of the enemies of Yahweh' (v. 26). The same term 'blessing' is used to describe the 'gift' or bribe sent to him by Abigail in 25.27 to head off his planned retaliation against her household. David's present 'blessings' also appear to be bribes, as indicated by the information delayed until the end of v. 31. The 'blessings' were sent to 'all the places where David and his men had roamed'. David has sent voluntary gifts from the Amalekite spoil to those in authority in the settlements within Judah with which he and his men had come into contact while escaping from Saul. More specifically, these were the settlements that, unlike Keilah and Ziph, had allowed him to go back and forth (*hithallēk*) freely, without reporting his movements to the king (cf. 23.13).

The report concerning the disposition of the booty in v. 20 now takes on new meaning. David is probably able to make these 'gifts' from his personal portion of the Amelekite spoils, the herds of sheep and goats (*ṣō'n*) that have been set aside for him from the captured herds of larger animals (*bāqār*). In this way, he need not dwell further on the already contested division of the spoils from the rescue operation. Everyone can have their fair shares and he can turn his to his personal and public advantage. Ironically, David is merely returning twice-stolen property to its original owners, since the booty he has taken from the Amalekites consists of the booty they had recently collected by raiding both Judahite and Philistine settlements. By offering it as a 'blessing', however, he is not claiming to be restoring the recovered property; he has converted the Judahites' former possessions to his own use and now is sending it back to them as a means of forging closer ties with his fellow countrymen, fellow citizens of

1. So noted also by Ackroyd (*First Samuel*, p. 224) and Klein (*1 Samuel*, p. 285).

Saul's state, who have shown him some respect at Saul's expense in the past.

David is asserting his kinship with the Judahites against the Amalekites and, more pointedly, against the Philistines, in whose employ he was supposed to have been. The settlements that receive his gestures of generosity all lie in the Negeb areas that David had told Achish in 27.10 he had been raiding.[1] David is using these people's former possessions as a bribe to convince them that he really is on their side, in spite of appearances. He has finally made an overt move to declare his true loyalties.

Having reasserted his leadership over his own small group of followers, David now appears to be attempting to expand his base of loyalty and power within the southern extremes of Saul's domain, to which he is imminent heir. If this is his intention, then David may not have mastered his lesson concerning the need not to resort to self-help to vindicate his position as thoroughly as he should have. By eroding Saul's base of power in the south, David is taking matters into his own hands and trying to 'steal' away Israelite loyalty from Saul prematurely, even granted the loyalty would have been shaky without David's interference. At the same time, he may have felt a need to provide himself with an alibi for his whereabouts during the battle in the Jezreel valley, to prove to the elders of Judah that he did not fight as a Philistine mercenary, but instead, was off fighting Yahweh's declared enemy, Amalek. In this way, he could assert at the same time that he was the true champion of Yahweh, in contrast to Saul.[2]

Alternatively, it is possible that the reports of David's law-making and booty distribution from 'the enemies of Yahweh' are intended to lead the audience to understand that Saul has already died on the battlefield near Jezreel. David's apparent 'usurpation' of royal prerogatives may be a deliberate clue that he is now, *de facto*, king. In light of the nonchronological sequencing of chs. 28–31, the two acts may be intended to serve as a signal that Saul's certain death predicted

1. So noted also by Fokkelman (*Crossing Fates*, p. 591).

2. So also Hertzberg, *I & II Samuel*, p. 229 and Gordon, *I & II Samuel*, p. 201.

in ch. 28 took place during David's rescue campaign,[1] so that David is now Yahweh's full vice-regent in every respect. All that is lacking is the people's acknowledgment of his full royal status at a formal coronation ceremony.

1. Fokkelman (*Crossing Fates*, p. 595) concludes that the two battles took place simultaneously. He goes through some contorted calculations to bolster his suggestion and then admits in the end that there is no irrefutable evidence in ch. 30 to support the hypothesis.

Chapter 26

1 SAMUEL 31

The issue of the simultaneousness of David's rescue operation and Saul's demise on the battlefield against the Philistines is resolved in the opening verse of ch. 31. The narrator opens with a participial construction stating that (meanwhile), the Philistines had been fighting against Israel. Grammatically, the phrase has the force of a circumstantial clause and represents an action that occurred simultaneously with the previous action, so that the Philistine–Israelite battle is thereby placed on a contemporaneous chronological plane with David's Amalekite operation in ch. 29. Thus, the narrator intends the audience to contrast David's life-preserving rescue of his families with death of Saul and his sons announced by Samuel at En-dor in ch. 28.[1]

Chapter 31 introduces the long-awaited final step in the regnal pattern, the death, burial and succession notices. The sixteen chapters between the summary of deeds in 14.47-48 and the death, burial and succession notices in ch. 31 have illustrated the fate of a disobedient king and the consequences for Israel: failed ability to lead the nation and secure for it divine blessings, resulting in internal divisions and the breakdown of bonding between people and king in certain sectors. Although two of the three items in the final step, the death and burial notices, will occur together, the succession notice will be delayed even further, into 2 Samuel (2.8-9 and 5.1-5), to highlight the unusual set of events that were depicted to have transpired.

With the groundwork for Israelite defeat already laid in ch. 28, the narrator is able to reinforce the inevitable, while at the same drawing a structural parallel between the two simultaneous 'battles' by using a

1. So understood also by, for example, Hertzberg, *I & II Samuel*, pp. 230-31; Klein, *1 Samuel*, p. 287; Fokkelman, *Crossing Fates*, p. 622; and Miscall, *1 Samuel*, p. 181.

variant form of the battle report, as he did in the preceding chapter. Although preliminary information concerning the parties to engage in battle and their respective camp positions has already been supplied in 28.1, 4 and 29.1, there are no details given here in the account of the battle itself about the arrayal of the troops on the battlefield for the actual confrontation. The same step was omitted in the account of David's attack against Amalek. The audience is merely told summarily that the parties 'had been fighting'. Instead of the expected verbs of smiting to report the progress of the Israelites in battle, which occur in David's engagement against the Amalekites,[1] the audience is informed that Israel's troops 'fled' (*wayyānusû*) and 'fell' (*wayyipp*^{e}*lû*) 'pierced' or 'dishonored' (*ḥ*^{a}*ālîm*) (v. 1). The root *ḥll* to seems to have been deliberately used to describe the Israelites' state because of both meanings associated with the term.

Israel is on the defensive and has become as it were a passive participant in the battle. The situation provides a contrastive echo to the hebrew conduct at the battle at the Michmash pass and the battle at the Elah Valley. In the first instance, because Saul was able to turn the situation around to Israel's advantage by putting the Philistines to flight, former deserters were able to rejoin the battle, regain a sense of honor, and fight for the larger glory of Saul and Yahweh (1 Sam. 13–14). In the second instance, the Israelites' flight before Goliath (17.24) was turned to a large-scale Philistine flight after David's killing of Goliath, in which the former deserters were able again to rejoin the battle with honor and conduct themselves appropriately.

It is the Philistines rather than the Israelites who do the expected smiting (verb *nkh*), killing off three of Saul's sons, Jonathan, Abinadab and Malchishua (v. 2), in addition to killing the Israelite troops at large.[2] They are characterized as having 'clung close' (verb *dbq*) to Saul and his sons throughout the battle at the beginning of v. 2, suggesting that the royal family was their primary target. Since

1. The contrast is noted also by Miscall (*1 Samuel*, p. 182).

2. It is noteworthy that Abinadab appears here without prior preparation in the narrative. He should have been named in 14.49 alongside the other family members who would appear subsequently in the Saulide narrative, following the standard biblical practice of character introduction. Either his name was erroneously dropped in 14.49 at a very early stage, or his inclusion in ch. 31 is a secondary textual expansion, based on his presence in the Saulide genealogies in 1 Chron. 8.29-40; 9.35-44.

the audience has already been informed that Saul and his sons have been ordained to die during this battle (28.19), the Philistines' dogged pursuit or 'shadowing' of the royal family takes on an air of divine predeterminism. The Philistines appear to become mere agents for the execution of Yahweh's will.[1] Contrastive echoes with the Michmash pass battle continue with the use of *dbq*, which was employed in 14.22 to describe the actions of the hebrews toward the Philistines after they rejoined the battle.

The narrator delays the summary of the outcome of the battle in order to focus on the precise circumstances of Saul's death in vv. 3-5. He has already indicated that the overall circumstances of Israel's defeat involved dishonor (root *ḥll* in v. 1) and has told of the smiting of the royal sons on the battlefield. Now he apparently wants to explore the issue of the honor or dishonor of Saul's final actions in light of the king's foreknowledge of his certain death. To announce that the battle 'grew heavy or burdensome' for Saul (v. 3), the narrator employs the root *kbd*, whose overtones of 'honor' certainly are deliberate. By using the multivalent term *kbd*, rather than, for instance, the root *ṣrr*, which has been employed on other occasions to describe the pressing circumstances of battle, the audience is introduced to what is personally at stake for Saul: individual honor when faced with imminent death, or dishonor, as for the soldiers who fled. By implication, Saul can gain honor only by facing the enemy instead of fleeing. Since he already knows he will die, he is left to make a choice concerning the circumstances of that death: whether standing his ground, as Yahweh's rejected earthly vice-regent, or in flight, like a coward.

The Philistines continue their dogged close pursuit, and Saul is found by 'shooters'[2] and is pierced greatly by them (v. 3). The appar-

1. A similar idea is expressed by Gunn (*Fate of Saul*, p. 157 n. 19).

2. *hammôrîm* and *'ᵃnāšîm baqqéšet* are often viewed to be ancient variant readings preserved by conflation: so, for example, Hertzberg, *I & II Samuel*, p. 230; Stoebe, *Erste Buch Samuelis*, p. 521; McCarter, *I Samuel*, p. 440; and Klein, *1 Samuel*, p. 286. Alternately, *'ᵃnāšîm baqqéšet* has been considered a secondary gloss on *hammôrîm* by, for example, Smith (*Books of Samuel*, p. 252) and Dhorme (*Livres de Samuel*, p. 258). Driver (*Notes*, p. 228), followed by Budde (*Bücher Samuel*, p. 190), rearranges the word order to read *'ᵃnāšîm hammôrîm baqqéšet*, while Klostermann (*Bücher Samuelis*, p. 127) proposes the emendation *hammôrîm 'ᵃbānîm baqqéšet*. I favor the second proposal, since the term

ent use of words with multivalent overtones continues, as evidenced by the term *hammôrîm* and the verb *wayyāḥel*. In its present form as a hiphil participle, *hammôrîm* could also convey the sense of 'teachers', carrying on the earlier implications that the Philistines are serving as divine agents to execute the divine will. As has already been discussed, two of the larger structuring patterns, the regnal pattern and the division of Saul's career into life under benevolent and malevolent guiding spirits, seem to share as a main objective the use of Saul's career to illustrate the fate of a disobedient king. In this context, the Philistines could be ironically portrayed to be Saul's executionary 'teachers'. The consonants of the participle also call to mind the homophonous roots *mrr* and *mrh*, adding at the same time overtones of rebellion and bitterness into the constellation of meaning raised by the term *hammôrîm*. Thus, the Philistine archers become 'rebel, bitter teachers' for the first king and the Israelite nation.

The verb *wyhl* similarly raises a constellation of meanings associated with the roots *ḥll*, *ḥlh* and *ḥwl*. On the most straightforward level of meaning associated with the root *ḥll*, which already has been used in v. 1 to describe the fate of the Israelite troops and which is most germane to the context of battle, Saul is 'pierced greatly' or inflicted with multiple wounds. The result also bears overtones of dishonor from the second meaning of the root *ḥll*. However, on another level of meaning associated with the root *ḥlh*, the archers[1] cause Saul to become very 'sick' (*ḥlh* I) or 'to entreat greatly the favor of' Yahweh, presumably (*ḥlh* II). Related to this semantic range is the implication that Saul 'writhed' in pain or anguish because of the archers,

hammôrîm, 'shooters' or 'throwers', could conceivably include spear and javelin throwers as well as archers.

1. I favor retention of MT's *mēhammôrîm* over LXX's 'in the belly', implying a Hebrew *vorlage* something like *mēhamnotnayim*. The grammatical construction and sense is straightforward as it stands. Fokkelman (*Crossing Fates*, p. 625) suggests that there is significance to be attached to the weapons mentioned in vv. 3-4. He notes that the bow, the weapon that brings Saul to the edge of death, is the weapon most closely associated with Jonathan in chs. 18 and 20, which is then transferred to David. By contrast, he asserts that the sword, which Saul uses to commit suicide, is his typical royal weapon. The latter statement is incorrect. Saul is primarily associated with the spear (19.9-10; 20.33; 22.6; 26.12, 22). The only references connecting Saul with a sword are 13.22 and 17.39. In the former instance, the spear is also mentioned and both weapons are connected with Jonathan as well as Saul. His attempt to find additional meaning in the weapons fails.

suggested by possible connections with the root *ḥwl*. The homophonous roots *ḥlh* and *ḥwl* are able to interject into the otherwise simple statement of fact concerning Saul's being wounded the issue of his state of mind and emotions as he faces death, amplifying the question begun in the first half of the verse concerning whether he will die honorably or dishonorably.

In v. 4 Saul orders his weapons-bearer to unsheath his sword and to run him through with it lest 'these uncircumcised' come and abuse him.[1] Already seeming to be mortally wounded and knowing that death is imminent, Saul's request to his weapons-bearer, who by definition is to be considered absolutely trustworthy and loyal, reflects his desire for a quick and merciful death and one that will cheat the noncovenantal Philistines out of a boast that they slew him themselves. His derogatory characterization of the Philistines as 'these uncircumcised' repeats Jonathan's words to his weapons-bearer in 14.6, reinforcing once again a contrastive link between the battle at the Michmash pass and the battle at Mt Gilboa. In 14.6, Jonathan, the potential king-elect, proposed a plan of action against the Philistines, nonmembers of the covenant community, that openly acknowledged the need of divine favor in order to triumph and destroy the enemy. Here, in v. 4, the rejected king of the covenant community, who knows his death has been divinely decreed, has accepted his fate, but seeks to eliminate nonmembers of the covenant community from interfering in an affair that he sees is between himself and Yahweh, the leaders of the covenant community. David used the same derogatory reference to the Philistines' lack of circumcision in 17.26 and 36 to highlight the need for nonmembers of the covenant community, enemies of Yahweh, to be destroyed.[2]

As in vv. 1-2, there is a contrast between the expected situation in which the Israelite leader takes the offensive against the enemy and the undesirable present situation where the enemy takes the offensive against the Israelite leader. Nevertheless, both situations have in common the presumption that the divine will is being fulfilled. On a

1. I accept the almost universal proposal to delete the MT phrase *ûd^{e}qāru̇nî* as intrusive, which is missing in the LXX. It contradicts the subsequent phrase, since the Philistines can only abuse Saul while he is still alive. It may have arisen through a copyist's error, being repeated from the first half of the verse.

2. The two uses of the phrase by David are noted by Stoebe (*Erste Buch Samuelis*, p. 526). All three uses are pointed out by Klein (*1 Samuel*, p. 288).

more immediate level, Saul wants to avoid humiliation and torture at the hands of the enemy before his final death. On another level, however, his request constitutes a final attempt to thwart the divine will, since it appears as though the Philistines were the intended agents of death and he wants to eliminate them from that role.[1]

The weapons-bearer does not consent to Saul's request because he was afraid (*kî yārēʾ*) (v. 4). His failure to lift his hand against the Lord's anointed, even at direct royal request, demonstrates his mastery of the lesson that David and his men grappled with, particularly in chs. 24–26.[2] At the same time, his refusal indirectly highlights Saul's continuing failure to grasp the same lesson. The king's consistent and persistent attempt to kill the anointed king-elect, set side by side with his deathbed order that his own loyal servant slay him, the Lord's anointed, demonstrates his failure to understand and honor the sacrosanctity of the bestowal of divine spirit through anointing. Since the weapons-bearer does not go on to explain to Saul the reason for his fear, Saul remains 'unenlightened' about the error of his perceptions concerning the meaning of anointing. The failure of Saul's weapons-bearer to follow his master's order contrasts with the willing service of Jonathan's weapons-bearer in 14.7, highlighting the inappropriateness of the royal death-order.[3]

1. This is the ultimate reading adopted by Gunn (*Fate of Saul*, p. 111), and Polzin (*Samuel*, p. 224). While clearly implied in this verse, I believe that Saul's suicide requires the audience to reject this understanding and see his act to be a personal surrender to his fate. Samuel announced only that Saul was to die the next day; he did not state the agency of death, and while the enemy would be the logical agent, it would not be the only possible agent.

2. That his fear stems from harming the Lord's anointed is concluded by, for example, Hertzberg, *I & II Samuel*, p. 232; Ackroyd, *First Samuel*, p. 227; Fokkelman, *Crossing Fates*, p. 625; and Gordon, *I & II Samuel*, p. 202. Klein (*1 Samuel*, p. 288) suggests as an alternative source for the fear the weapons-bearer's youth and the extreme circumstances. But we are not told the age of the weapons-bearer, so this is not a factor. Besides, given his responsibility for protecting the life of the king, it is extremely likely that the weapons-bearer would have been a seasoned veteran, not an inexperienced youth.

3. Miscall (*1 Samuel*, p. 182) emphasizes that at the last moment Saul is not supported by his current weapons-bearer or his former one, David (16.21-22). His observation is interesting. Perhaps the narrator intends the audience to speculate about what David would have done under these circumstances had he remained Saul's weapons-bearer.

The narrator seems to intend the audience to draw an additional contrastive connection between the actions of Saul's weapons-bearer and those of Abimelech's in Judg. 9.52-55.[1] Like Saul, Abimelech found himself mortally wounded and requested his weapons-bearer to draw his sword and run him through to save him from the dishonor of being killed by a woman (9.54). Both accounts share the vocabulary *nōśē' kēlîm, šlp, ḥéreb* and *dqr*, and the circumstance of the 'king' attempting to escape a dishonorable death by being slain by his loyal weapons-bearer. The contrast comes in the response of the two weapons-bearers: Abimelech's obeys his master's command, while Saul's does not. The difference in attitudes of the two servants seems to rest in the status of their respective masters. Saul is depicted to have been a legitimate king, *mélek*, crowned by all Israel and therefore sacrosanct, while Abimelech was king of Shechem (9.6), but only *śār* over Israel (9.22). Thus, he was not sacrosanct within Israel.

Saul resorts to the only remaining option to prevent his final death at the hand of the Philistines; he takes the sword himself and falls upon it, committing suicide (v. 4). Which sword Saul fell upon is not made immediately clear, apparently in order to introduce suspense. It is described simply as 'the sword', and the only sword previously mentioned in the account was the one belonging to the weapons-bearer. Has he fallen on the weapons-bearer's sword, so that those who find him will think that he was betrayed by his own most trustworthy servant, or has he fallen on his own sword that was in the care of the weaons-bearer, so that the enemy will clearly understand that he has taken his own life?

The sword's owner is revealed in the ensuing verse, quickly resolving the momentary suspense. Upon seeing that the king was dead, the loyal weapons-bearer fell on *his* sword also, and died with his master (v. 5). Since the audience was not told that the weapons-bearer removed the sword from Saul to fall on himself, there is a clear indication that two different swords were used. The weapons-bearer used his own sword to kill himself; by implication, the sword Saul used was

1. The connection between the two events has been noted, with different explanations as to the intended meaning, by, for example, Dhorme, *Livres de Samuel*, p. 258; Auzou, *Danse devant l'arche*, p. 215; Ackroyd, *First Samuel*, p. 228; Stoebe, *Erste Buch Samuelis*, p. 526; Klein, *1 Samuel*, p. 288; and Gordon, *I & II Samuel*, p. 202.

his own, which the weapons-bearer may have had charge of, in addition to the sword that he would have needed to protect the king. Otherwise, Saul may have been carrying his sword at this point in battle and simply drew it himself. The weapons-bearer's unhesitatingly quick suicide when faced with the death of his master, whose life he was sworn to protect at all costs, confirms the earlier impression that his fear in the previous verse was not a fear of dying for failure to carry out his duty, but rather a fear of harming the Lord's anointed. There is no mention of his having been wounded, like Saul, so it is conceivable that he might have been able to have fled and escaped alive. Instead, he chooses to do what he considered to be the honorable thing in light of his status as the king's weapons-bearer.

I am not convinced that modern readers will ever be able to know for certain how the writer intended his ancient audience to view Saul's act of suicide. While it is frequently asserted that suicide was not an accepted practice in ancient Israel, we have no actual legislation concerning it in the Bible, nor any clear instances that indicate it was viewed to be wrong or unacceptable under any circumstances. Reports of suicides occur in Judg. 16.30; 2 Sam. 17.23; and 1 Kgs 16.18, but the moral and legal ramifications of each are not certain. We simply do not know whether suicide was viewed negatively under all circumstances, viewed neutrally, or viewed positively under certain circumstances. In Saul's case, we must take into consideration the special circumstances of his royalty, the setting during war, and his foreknowledge that he was destined to die that day. It may well be that Saul's reported suicide was deliberately designed to question ancient Judahite standards for taking one's own life, just as it does for the modern reader, but we cannot know for sure. It is equally possible that the narrator's judgment concerning the honor or dishonor associated with Saul's suicide was explicitly determined by ancient Judahite *mores*. I tend to think that Saul's final act is to be viewed honorably, as a final surrender to Yahweh's will.

As the requisite summary of the outcome of the battle, the audience is informed that the Israelite forces died together on that day—king, royal princes, weapons-bearer, and troops in general. An immediate contrast is drawn between David's successful recovery of all his people from the Amalekites—'nothing was missing, whether great or small, sons or daughters, spoil or anything that had been taken' (30.19)—and the total loss of life under Saul's leadership. Although some scholars suggest that the phrase *'ᵃnāšāw*, 'his men', is intended to refer to some sort of royal bodyguard that would have been protecting the royal family,[1] this interpretation clearly ignores the summary nature of the verse, which includes all those who have been reported to have died in the previous battle account. 'Saul's men' are to be identified with the 'men of Israel' in v. 1 who were the first listed battle casualties.

There is no need to adopt the LXX reading over the MT and delete the phrase *gam kol-'ᵃnāšāw* as a secondary intrusion based on v. 1.[2] The completeness of the summary is clearly meant to highlight the utter Israelite devastation at the hands of Yahweh. Both king and nation have been punished for the disobedience of the first king, in accordance with the implied mutual responsibility for obedience and punishment that Samuel announced to the people in 1 Sam. 10.14-15, 25 and 12.25. Although in his speeches Samuel states only that the people's disobedience will result in the punishment of both nation and king jointly, his argument strongly implies that the same joint punishment will ensue from any disobedience on the part of the king as well. His speech is made in the context of addressing the nation alone, before the existence of a king, and in a context in which the nation was to declare their acknowledgment of the bonding of people and king in the ongoing Horeb covenant. Thus, there was no need to state specifically that royal disobedience would result in the same punishment of both parties: the king was a member of the people and was held to the same standards of obedience.[3]

Yet, Israel was not completely destroyed; men of Israel located across the valley and across the Jordan witnessed the Israelite defeat at Gilboa and abandoned their villages to the Philistines (v. 7). This additional news item in the summary of the extent of the battle changes the implications of the preceding verse. Now the audience learns that Saul entered the battle without the full support of Israel. Israelites living in the immediate vicinity, who would have been the most threatened by a Philistine victory, apparently did not join in the

1. So, for example, Driver, *Notes*, p. 229; Hertzberg, *I & II Samuel*, p. 232; Ackroyd, *First Samuel*, p. 228; Fokkelman, *Crossing Fates*, p. 623.

2. *Contra*, for example, Dhorme, *Livres de Samuel*, p. 258; McCarter, *I Samuel*, p. 440.

3. Polzin (*Samuel*, p. 223) also emphasizes that the fate of Israel and the king are depicted to be the same, quoting 12.25 only.

battle. While the audience might be allowed to speculate that they were specifically told to remain in their towns to serve as reserve rear forces in the event of a Philistine retreat, this impression tends to be countered by the reference to 'his men' in the previous verse. Saul died with 'his men', who constituted 'the men of Israel' (v. 1) who were loyal enough to fight with their king in the battle, responding to the troop muster of 'all Israel' in 28.4. By implication, then, the Israelite men in v. 7 had chosen to remain at home instead of supporting their king. Just as Saul's base of loyalty was said to have eroded in the south, so it apparently was also weakened in Galilee and northern Transjordan.[1] The underlying lesson is that a king who has been abandoned by his God cannot rule effectively and maintain the respect and support of his people.

As a result of Yahweh's punishment, Israel is once again occupied by the Philistines, returning to the position it had been in prior to Saul's reign. The net effect is that his kingship has not helped Israel eliminate foreign oppression. The nation had already been told in Josh. 2.1-3; 19–23 what it needs to do in order to end war and foreign oppression. It needs to remain faithful to its covenant with Yahweh. Then Yahweh will eliminate the foreign nations he has left surrounding them, to test them. The underlying presumption is that Israel does not need any form of military leader, either *šōpēṭ* or *mélek*, 'like all the other nations' to live in peace; it only needs to obey its God and his ongoing mediated commands.

Extending the summary of the battle outcome, the narrator details the fate of Saul's corpse in the remaining five verses of the chapter. The next day, the Philistines discover the bodies of Saul and his sons on Gilboa as they come to 'plunder' (verb *pšṭ*) the 'pierced' or 'defiled' Israelite corpses on the battlefield. Immediately noteworthy is the fact that it is only the next day that the Philistines confirm that Saul and his sons have died by 'discovering' their bodies among the carnage. This suggests in turn that, while injured by Philistine arrow fire, Saul may yet have been able to have been dragged to safety

1. The phrase 'and those across the Jordan' has been considered a secondary expansion by, for example, Dhorme (*Livres de Samuel*, p. 259). Its absence from 1 Chron. 10.7 should not serve as the primary basis for such a judgment however; the Chronicler has shaped his material to suit his own ideology. The presence of the phrase in all extant versions in 31.7 favors its retention, as does the role it plays in raising the status of the loyalty of Jabesh-Gilead in the ensuing verses of the episode.

during the course of the night by his uninjured weapons-bearer. His fear of being 'abused' by the Philistines, while certainly a real possibility, was not a foregone conclusion; the Philistines were not closing in on him and about to reach him as he made his request to his weapons-bearer. They were merely the enemy who would eventually find his resting spot, should he remain where he was on the battlefield. By implication then, neither the death of Saul nor of his sons was known to the Philistines until the aftermath of the battle; it did not mark the end of the battle, but was a bonus surprise in the aftermath.

The characterization of the Philistines' activity as 'plundering' (*pšṭ*) invites the audience to compare and contrast their activity with earlier references to plundering in the Saulide narrative. Significantly, *pšṭ* is not used to describe the raiding parties sent out from the Philistine camp during the battle at the Michmash pass in 13.7, nor the Israelites' despoiling activity after the battle in 14.36, as might have been expected in light of the many other echoes of that battle in this chapter. Occurrences of *pšṭ* in the Saulide narrative are restricted to the Philistines' actions in 23.17 that led Saul to break off his closing in on David at the Rock of Escape; David's activity against the Girzites, Amalekites and Girgashites in 27.8, 10; the retaliatory raid by the Amalekites in 30.1, 14; and Saul's action of stripping off his clothes before Samuel in 19.24.[1] A deliberate contrast seems to be set up between David's successful plundering raids against non-Israelite groups while in Achish's employ and Saul's defeat, which has led to the free advance of Philistine plunderers against Israel. Similarly, David's successful retrieval of all goods and people who had been plundered by the Amalekites is contrasted with Saul's defeat and death, which has left Israel the victim of enemy plunderers instead of victorious plunderers themselves. On a more symbolic level, Saul's stripping off of his own clothes before Samuel in 19.24 in retrospect foreshadows his fate and the fate of the 'dishonored, slain' (*hāḥᵃlālîm*) nation before Yahweh in ch. 31.

Saul's beheading in v. 9 calls to mind the reports of earlier beheadings or fears of loss of heads in the narrative. As widely acknowledged, Saul experiences at the hands of the enemy the fate of Goliath at the hand of David (17.51). There may be an intentional contrast being drawn between David's unsheathing of Goliath's own sword and

1. Miscall (*1 Samuel*, p. 181) notes its use in 23.24-28 and ch. 30.

using it to deal his final death blow before beheading him and Saul's use of his own sword to commit suicide, before being beheaded by the enemy. In the first case, David performs both actions, thereby gaining total victory over his opponent. In the latter case, Saul cheats the Philistines out of credit for his death, leaving them only the option of beheading his corpse. Saul's beheading also resonates with David's ironic appointment as 'keeper of Achish's head' in 28.2 and the rhetorical question posed to Achish by the Philistine generals in 29.4 that implied that the only way David could reconcile himself to his lord would be with the heads of the Philistine men there. In both instances, David is portrayed as the controller of the fate of enemy heads just as in ch. 17, in contrast to Saul, who loses his head to the Philistines.

The discovery of Saul's death, together with his subsequent beheading and the stripping off of his armor, is a newsworthy event in the Philistine world, leading to the gladdening of both idols and people with the good tidings (v. 9).[1] The defeated Israelite king's armor is said to have been deposited in the temple of Asthoreth (v. 10),[2] just as

1. Grammatically, MT's *byt* cannot stand. At the very least, a plural construct form *battê* is required in the context. Arguably, the phrase 'the temples of their idols' could stand as an accusative of place, but the resulting phrase yields an awkward parallelism. It is not clear why the glad tidings would be sent to temples and people, rather than gods and people. Presumably news sent to temples would reach both gods and people. The easiest solution is to follow LXX's presumed reading *'ēt* for *byt*, as is commonly done. Miscall (*1 Samuel*, p. 182) suggests there is a connection between the announcement of the death of father and sons on the same day here and the announcement concerning the fate of the Elides after the battle at Ebenezer in 4.17. The two situations are not identical, however, since Eli did not go to the battle with his sons and died afterwards, having heard of the death of his sons.

2. As widely acknowledged, the deity name should be construed as a singular, *'štrt*, in spite of the presence of the *mater lectionis wāw* before the final *tāw*. The text does not indicate that the temple of Ashtoreth was located at Beth She'an, *contra* McCarter (*I Samuel*, p. 443). Armor was quite portable and would have been deposited in a national sanctuary in the Philistine homeland, not in the hinterland which may or may not have become Philistine in the wake of the battle. Beth She'an's status and role in this war is only hinted at by the hanging of the bodies of the defeated royal family on its walls. Its ability to display the bodies as trophies suggests that it was the prime offensive of Saul's attack and that the Philistines were only called in as allied troops.

Goliath's sword was deposited in the temple at Nob, before Yahweh.[1] In each case, the winning nation was giving honor to their national god who had granted the victory. The narrator's attempt to belittle the Philistine deities is evidenced by his caricature of them as carved or fashioned artifacts, *'ᵃṣabbîm*, which by implication, lacked life force or real power. It is reinforced by the suggestion that the gods would not have known of their victory until being informed by their human agents.[2]

The nailing of the dead corpse so that it was suspended from the wall of the town of Beth She'an was meant as a graphic display of victory, as well as an object lesson to any future rebels or enemies.[3] There is no reason to emend the received text to yield the verb *hōqîᵃ'* instead of *tāqa'*, as was suggested long ago by P.A. de Lagarde.[4] The latter term bears overtones of ritual execution, which was not the case here. Saul's body has merely been fixed to the town wall for public display.

The valiant rescue effort on the part of the warriors (*kol-'îš ḥáyil*) of Jabesh-Gilead, who, upon learning what the Philistines had done to Saul, march all night to retrieve not only Saul's body, but the bodies of his sons as well, strongly implies that the public display of the corpses was considered a form of humiliation (vv. 11-12). Their 'rescue' of Saul's remains parallels Saul's earlier all-night march to take the Ammonites who were besieging Jabesh-Gilead by surprise during the morning watch and deliver the town from humiliation

1. This parallel has also been noted by, for example, Hertzberg (*I & II Samuel*, p. 232) and Ackroyd, (*First Samuel*, p. 228).

2. So also Gordon, *I & II Samuel*, p. 203.

3. Klein (*1 Samuel*, p. 289) and Gordon (*I & II Samuel*, p. 203) see the treatment of Saul's body to reflect a carrying out of the threat made by Goliath to David in 17.43-44 to expose his body to the birds and beasts. However, Goliath's words imply that he would leave David's body unburied on the ground, where the beasts could feed on it, while Saul's body was hung up for display and so was not accessible to beasts.

4. *Anmerkungen zur griechischen Übersetzung der Proverbien* (Leipzig: Brockhaus, 1863), p. iii. It has been adopted by, for example, Wellhausen (*Text der Bücher Samuelis*, p. 149), Budde (*Bücher Samuel*, p. 192), Smith (*Books of Samuel*, p. 253), and Dhorme (*Livres de Samuel*, p. 260), but has been rejected by most, for example, Klostermann (*Bücher Samuelis*, p. 128), Driver (*Notes*, p. 230), Ehrlich (*Randglossen*, III, p. 270), Mauchline (*1 and 2 Samuel*, p. 193), Stoebe (*Erste Buch Samuelis*, p. 522), and McCarter (*1 Samuel*, p. 442).

through bodily disfigurement (1 Sam. 11.2, 9-11).[1] Although not present at the battle of Gilboa, by implication they were not among the men of Israel who had remained beyond the Jordan and had not joined in the troop muster who were mentioned in v. 7. They lived far enough away from Gilboa not to have been able to have seen the battle, but had had to learn about it at second hand from messengers (v. 11).

Yet, in light of the report of Saul's muster of 'all Israel' in 29.4 and the characterization of the Jabesh-Gileadites as corporate members of Israel in 11.1-4, their failure to have participated in the actual battle at Gilboa strongly implies that they had not obeyed their monarch's summons to arms. Thus, they apparently also had lost trust in their king, like many others. It is only in the wake of the king's death that they feel an obligation to reverse the dishonorable treatment of the royal corpses, probably as a means of repaying the king for his earlier rescue of their town. Their efforts, while admirable after the fact, do not mitigate their betrayal of their king by failing to respond to his battle summons.

The Jabesh-Gileadites' intentions are implied to be honorable, so that their treatment of the recovered corpses for burial should presumably also reflect accepted and honorable practice for the disposing of royal remains. The bodies are said to have been burned (verb *śrp*) back at Jabesh-Gilead (v. 12) and the bones then buried under *the* tamarisk (*hā́'ēšel)* in Jabesh. Seven days of mourning were said to have been observed to honor the fallen royal family (v. 13). The interment of the bones under a tamarisk would not have been a cause of surprise to the ancient audience. It is perhaps to be understood that the tree in question was a sacred tree, especially in light of the report in Gen. 21.33 that Abraham planted a tamarisk in Beersheba, where he called on the name of Yahweh, El-Elyon. In 22.6 Saul's leadership is closely associated with his sitting 'under the tamarisk' on the height, so the choice of the same species of tree for the final resting place of his remains may be intentionally symbolic. The seven days of mourning also would have seemed appropriate and expected.

The burning of the royal bodies prior to the interment of the remaining bones seems more problematic, although again, the ancient

1. For a slightly different paralleling with 1 Sam. 11, see Fokkelman, *Crossing Fates*, p. 628.

audience would have known what was considered acceptable and unacceptable practice for a royal Judahite burial. To date, the available archaeological and textual evidence indicates that cremation was not an accepted Semitic custom among nonroyalty at least,[1] while, on the other hand, it was the preferred method of burial for Hittite royalty and an accepted form of honorable burial, alongside bodily interment, among the Greeks.[2] Since we have not been able to identify any royal Judahite tombs for certain, we cannot verify whether the cremation of kings was practiced in Israel, as in Hatti or Greece. The attempts to avoid the clear associations of the root *śrp* with burning the bodies in question by suggesting that the Jabesh-Gileadites 'burned spices' for the corpses (cf. Amos 6.10; Jer. 34.5; 2 Chron. 16.14; 21.19)[3] or that *śrp* can also signify 'smearing with resinous spices'[4] goes against the

1. *Contra* P. Bienkowski, 'Some Remarks on the Practice of Cremation in the Levant', *Levant* 14 (1982), pp. 80-89. He has failed to undertake a complete analysis of the context of the burials, the ceramic assemblages, and the range of accompanying grave goods. Had he done so, he would have realized that in the non-isolated instances, local wares are accompanied by imported goods that are particularly associated with crematory offerings in mainland Greece or that bear non-Semitic writings, indicating the presence of an intrusive group who had adopted local pottery traditions but were maintaining their inherited burial traditions. For the cremation cemeteries at Hama, see esp. P.J. Riis, *Hama, fouilles et recherches 1931-1938*, 2/3 (4 vols.; Nationalmuseets Skrifter; Copenhagen: Nordisk, 1958), p. 47 and A. Kempinski, 'Hittites in the Bible', *BARev* 5 (1959), p. 39. For the Amman airport structure and burials, see L. Herr, 'The Amman Airport and the Geopolitics of Ancient Transjordan', *BA* 46 (1983), pp. 223-29; V. Hankey, 'A Late Bronze Age Temple at Amman I: The Aegean Pottery', *Levant* 6 (1974), p. 139.

2. For Hittite royal burials, see K. Bittel, 'Vorläufiger Bericht über die Ausgrabungen in Boğazköy 1936', *MDOG* 75 (1937), pp. 68-70; *idem*, 'Hethitische Bestattungsbräuche', *MDOG* 78 (1940), pp. 12-28; H. Otten, 'Ein Totenrituel hethitischer Könige', *MDOG* 78 (1940), pp. 3-5; *idem*, *Hethitischen Totenrituale* (Berlin: Akademie Verlag, 1958). For cremation among the Greeks, see D. Kurtz and J. Boardman, *Greek Burial Customs* (Ithaca, NY; Cornell University Press, 1971), esp. p. 26.

3. The Targum follows this meaning. McCarter (*I Samuel*, p. 442) suggests that the phrase is a secondary, late expansion because of its absence from 1 Chron. 10. It is much more likely that the Chronicler omitted its mention because he viewed it to be a desecration that was too heinous, even for Saul.

4. This idea was initially proposed by G.R. Driver ('Hebrew Burial Custom', *ZAW* 66 [1954], pp. 314-15), but has no clear textual support. It has been adopted by, for example, L. Koehler, *Supplementum ad Lexicon in VT Libros* (Leiden: Brill,

clear grammatical implications of *wayyiśr^epû 'ōtām* in v. 12. It was the corpses themselves that were burned. Similarly, there is no need to emend the text to read *wayyisp^edû lāhem*, 'they bewailed them', as A. Klostermann suggests without any attested witness from manuscripts.[1] The text is straightforward and its meaning clear.[2]

The burning of the corpses would not have prevented the subsequent interment of bones, as is clear from descriptions of cremation practices among the Greeks and the Hittites. The *Odyssey*, Book 24, 11.60-80 presents an excellent description of the Greek cremation ritual, stating that it was the preferred form of burial for heroes and kings. The body was washed, oiled and shrouded with honey and unguent, and a mourning period preceded the burning. For Achilles' burial, animal sacrifices were added to the pyre. The pyre, once lit, was allowed to burn overnight to remove the flesh, and at dawn, the remaining bones were gathered from the ashes and stored in an amphora with wine and oil. The jar was then buried in a grave marked by a heap of stones. The burial of the Hittite king involved the burning of the body overnight, with the collection of the bones the next morning, just as the Greeks did. Women put out the fire with beer, wine and a liquid called *walḫi*. The remaining bones were gathered, rinsed in oil, put on a piece of cloth, covered over, and placed on a seat before a table spread with food. Everyone present then took a place at the funerary meal. Finally, the bones were placed in a 'Stone House' tomb, where they were laid out on a couch, with a lamp placed beside the bed. A comparative study of crematory practices suggests that such a treatment of Saul's body would have been considered a honorable form of burial, befitting a king, among surrounding non-Semitic nations.[3] Whether the same belief was held within Israel

1958), p. 175; Hertzberg, *I & II Samuel*, p. 231; Ackroyd, *First Samuel*, p. 229; Mauchline, *1 and 2 Samuel*, p. 193.

1. Klostermann, *Bücher Samuelis*, pp. 128-29.

2. Sternberg (*Poetics*, p. 498) suggests that the reported burning is due to the carrying forward of the intentional linking of Saul and Achan back in 15.19. In his opinion, the setting of the corpses on fire has been narrated in imitation of Achan's fate in Josh. 7.25 and the linkage of Saul with Achan in 15.19 was a deliberate move to foreshadow Saul's end.

3. The suggestion made by Hertzberg (*I & II Samuel*, p. 233) that the bodies of Saul and his sons were burned to remedy their disfigurement and the damage done by decomposition and carrion birds is unlikely if there was a general avoidance of the

remains to be determined. The implied honorable intentions of the Jabesh-Gileadites would tend to suggest that their cremation of the retrieved royal bodies was an honorable act. It is possible that the ancient narrator intended their actions to represent an ultimate irony; Saul was able to thwart Philistine mistreatment while still alive through suicide, only to be dishonored in death by them, as well as his own citizens. Such a message seems unlikely to me, however, in light of the larger implications of Jabesh's honorable intentions and its citizens' desire to reverse the dishonorable treatment of the corpses by the enemy.

destruction of the corpse in the Semitic world, which appears from burial practices known to date to have been the case. He is followed by Blenkinsopp ('1 and 2 Samuel', p. 318). Fokkelman's suggestion (*Crossing Fates*, p. 629) that the burning was a form of purification to counter the desecration the bodies had undergone has even less merit, since all corpses were considered unclean, no matter what their state. The burning would not have altered the association of death with polluting defilement.

Chapter 27

2 SAMUEL 1

The final element of the last step of the regnal pattern, the succession notice, remains to be presented and is the next logical topic the audience would anticipate. This chapter seems to be the conclusion to the narrative of Saul's career, with its presentation of David's lament over the fallen Saul and Jonathan. However, at the same time, this chapter begins a subsection ending in 2 Sam. 5.5, which narrates the process of succession. Since David was not a member of the Saulide house, the narrator needs to take extra space to explain how it was that he was able to actualize his coronation over Israel, as Yahweh's chosen successor to Saul. As the first step toward David's succession, the audience is informed in this closing chapter to Saul's career of how David came to possess the royal insignia of office, Saul's crown and armlet. Thus, the chapter forms a bridge to the continuing narrative.[1]

The opening verse switches the focus of attention from the dead and buried Saul back to the anointed and tested king-elect, as the audience would anticipate.[2] At the same time, taken together with v. 2, it reconfirms the simultaneousness of David's successful rescue operation against Amalek and Saul's unsuccessful demise during battle with the Philistines near Gilboa.[3] In this way the narrator is able subtly to

1. For a description of the structure of the chapter that focuses on the use of the ternary principle, chiasmus, and the construction of circles of meaning, see J. Fokkelman, 'A Lie Born of Truth, Too Weak to Contain It', *OTS* 23 (1984), pp. 40-44.

2. I think Gordon goes too far is arguing that v. 1 subordinates Saul's defeat to David's Amalekite victory 'as if to say that David's (relatively minor) success is more significant in the long run than is the major calamity that befell Saul and his army at Gilboa' (*I & II Samuel*, p. 208).

3. Also noted by, for example, Fokkelman, *Crossing Fates*, p. 631 and Gordon, *I & II Samuel*, p. 208.

reinforce in the audience's minds David's status as Yahweh's chosen king-elect who enjoys divine support and guidance in place of Saul. He is the divinely designated successor who needs now to claim what is rightfully his. How exactly will he do it?

On the third day after his purported return to Ziklag from Amalek, a man arrives from the battle, *mēʿīm* or *mēʿam šāʾûl*. The latter expression is ambiguous as to its intended meaning; is it 'from with Saul' or 'from the army of Saul'? The second option would seem to imply that the man was a Saulide partisan; the first could also be understood in this way, but is vague enough to allow for other possibilities, such as his being a Philistine partisan or sympathizer. The ambiguity seems designed to introduce an element of uncertainty and suspense into the narrative.

The man's clothes are torn and he has earth upon his head, both signs of mourning (v. 2). The audience is now placed in a situation of reverse dramatic irony, where David, being able to see the man's style of dress, would have been able to recognize the man's ethnic or national affiliation. The narrator has consistently used clothing as a marker of ethnic/national identification throughout the narrative. David would seem to know more than the audience at this point, and the man's ethnic/national affiliation therefore becomes a point of speculation, especially in light of the vague reference to his association with Saul in v. 1. Has David been able to surmise that the man is Israelite and that his state of mourning must mean that Saul is finally dead and he is *de facto* king of Israel at long last?

The man's first act is to fall to the ground before David and to do obeisance (v. 2). While such a gesture probably would have been normal court protocol, it takes on added significance in the present context, where the man is greeting David. Not only is he leader of Ziklag and so perhaps entitled to such courtesy, but he is also the widely acknowledged king-elect of Israel, Yahweh's chosen candidate to succeed Saul. For the audience, the man's actions should immediately take on overtones of obeisance before the new king, David.[1]

Whatever David has guessed from the man's physical appearance,

1. The possible dual levels of meaning to be attached to the bow is also noted by, for example, Hertzberg, *I & II Samuel*, p. 237; P. Ackroyd, *Second Samuel* (CambB, 10; Cambridge: Cambridge University Press), p. 20; and Fokkelman, *Crossing Fates*, p. 632.

he needs to establish the circumstances that have caused his arrival and his state of mourning, particularly if he suspects that the man has come from the Israelite–Philistine conflict on the Jezreel plain. Asking him where he has come from, the man responds that he has 'slipped away' or 'escaped from' (*nimlāṭṭî*) the camp of Israel (v. 3), emphasizing the camp of Israel by placing it as the first phrase of his reply. His response heightens the suspense introduced in the preceding verse. One would not expect a Saulide partisan to claim that he had 'escaped' from the Israelite camp; it now appears that the man may not have been part of the Saulide forces after all. David's ability to have guessed the outcome of the battle is thereby highlighted. If the man was a Philistine collaborator who had escaped from Israelite capture or detention, would his visible signs of mourning lead David to suspect that Saul had won the battle?

As would be expected, David anxiously presses for further details to learn from the eyewitness about the outcome of the battle (v. 4). His words are identical to those asked by Eli of the man who had arrived from the Israelite defeat at Ebenezer in 1 Sam. 4.16. In the latter account, the man was described to have had his clothes torn and earth upon his head, just like the man in the present instance (4.12). There may or may not be an intentional linking of the two instances of a man arriving from an Israelite–Philistine battle. It is noteworthy, however, that in the case of the battle at Ebenezer, the man responds to Eli's similarly phrased question by stating that he had *fled* (*nastî*) from the battle (4.16), in contrast to this man, who has said that he has *escaped* from the camp. If the narrator intends the audience to link the two scenes, then the identity of the man standing before David becomes further suspect by the use of the contrasting verbs of departure.[1]

The man informs David that the people had fled from the battle; in addition, he states that the majority of the people had fallen and were dead, and also that Saul and his son Jonathan were dead (v. 4). At this point, the audience cannot be certain whether the first two items in his report about the people refer to Israel or to the Philistines, since the

1. The literary similarity between vv. 2-5 and 1 Sam. 4.12-17 has been widely acknowledged, though in differing degrees of comparison and significance. See, for example, Auzou, *Danse devant l'arche*, p. 217; Ackroyd, *Second Samuel*, p. 20; P.K. McCarter, *II Samuel* (AB, 9; Garden City, NY; Doubleday, 1984), p. 56; Fokkelman, *Crossing Fates*, p. 634; and Gordon, *I & II Samuel*, p. 208.

speaker's allegiance has become suspect. Remembering that David is back at his home at Ziklag, where he serves as Achish's mercenary, the man may have come to inform him of the fate of his Philistine lord. If so, then the mention of extensive (Philistine) casualties would be compensated for by the death of the enemy leaders, Saul and Jonathan. In fact, the man may represent one of the heralds sent to deliver the glad tidings to the idols and the people of Philistia concerning Saul's death (1 Sam. 31.9).

However, two factors tend to reject this interpretation of the man's words. First, he has expressed signs of mourning, which would not be consistent with a mission of glad tidings, and secondly, the audience has already been informed by the narrator that the men of Israel fled before the Philistines and fell, 'pierced', on Mt Gilboa (1 Sam. 31.1). While it is possible that the Philistines also suffered heavy casualties and were forced to retreat at some point during the battle or had experienced defections like the Israelites, the audience would tend to construe the messenger's words to apply to the Israelite forces in light of the information they have been supplied by the narrator in the past. While it would be characteristic of a Philistine messenger to brag about the routing and death of most of the enemy forces, it would be somewhat unusual for him to designate the enemy simply as 'the people', *hā'ām*. His use of this term tends to imply that he has some form of relationship to the group being designated. Or has he carefully chosen his words to express David's relationship to the people he has just described, whom the audience knows from 1 Sam. 31.1 must be Israel? The man's national loyalties and motives for approaching David become the central focus of attention.

If the man is not an Israelite, but has made it a point to seek out David, a Philistine mercenary, to supply him with news of the Israelite casualties and the death of Saul and Jonathan, he must be aware of David's continuing interest in the fortunes of Israel, even though he is a Philistine mercenary. Once again, the audience is led to reflect on the meaning of his act of obeisance before David; was he merely showing respect, or was he demonstrating his allegiance to Israel's new king? Why was he mourning?

Having been informed of Saul's death, David seeks to confirm it for certain—a move that is understandable in light of all he has at stake. He therefore questions the eyewitness further to learn if his knowledge is hearsay or first-hand and to receive information that will unequivocally indicate that Saul is indeed dead. P. Ackroyd notes that the question asked, 'How do you know?', is a common device used in Hebrew narrative style to lead the respondent into committing himself to a statement that will bring judgment upon himself.[1] Thus, it is an entirely appropriate means for David to employ in order to get to the truth of the matter. While preparing the audience for the possibility that the witness may be capable of committing perjury, a suspicion that has already been raised by the preceding verses, the use of the stock device would reassure them that any such action will be able to be found out and the liar brought to justice in the end.

The audience is now informed that the man is a *ná'ar*, a term that must be intended to designate his professional status rather than his age, since he has already been described to be a man. Is this added piece of information intended to make the witness more credible because of his status as a professional fighting man, or to cast doubt upon his testimony, because he is merely a servant and not a trained warrior? The term's multiple levels of meaning make the significance of the piece of information ambiguous. However, both meanings provide links to the *nᵉ'ārîm* last mentioned in the narrative, those encountered by David in ch. 30 in connection with the Amalekite raid. On the one hand, the Egyptian who is found is described as a *ná'ar* to an Amalekite (30.13) and the group of 400 who escaped David's slaughter were described as *'îš ná'ar* (30.17). The former was a servant, the latter were apparently warriors.

The preferred meaning of *ná'ar* seems to be resolved by the man's subsequent response in v. 6, where his opening words assert forcefully that he just happened to be on Mt Gilboa. The use of the infinitive absolute + finite form of the same verb root (*niqrō' niqrêtî*) underlines the importance of this phrase, which asserts that the man in question was at Mt Gilboa strictly by chance as Saul lay dying during the course of the battle with the Philistines. His words strongly imply that he was neither a Philistine nor an Israelite partisan; instead, he was an outsider who happened to be passing through the vicinity where the battle raged and happened to stumble across Saul, perhaps as he was seeking a safe path around the battlefield.

The informant claims to have found Saul supporting himself upon or with his spear, the symbol of office most closely associated with

1. Ackroyd, *Second Samuel*, p. 20.

him, with the chariotry or cavalry (*hrkb*) and the lords of the horsemen 'clinging to' or shadowing him. Again, his words do not convey a clear-cut message as to Saul's situation, or the identity of the group shadowing him. The participle *niš'ān* may imply that Saul was using his spear as a crutch, suggesting in turn that he was wounded, or it may simply mean that he was 'trusting in' his spear as his main weapon of defense. In the latter case, he would not have been injured. The former option would be the one that would spring to the audience's mind first because of the report in ch. 31 that Saul had been wounded (31.3). The man's failure to identify the ethnic/national affiliation of *hārékeb ûba'ᵃlê happārāšîm* who were clinging to Saul leaves open the possibility that they were loyal Israelite troops surrounding him for protection against the Philistines, whether or not he was injured, as well as the possibility that they were Philistine troops closing in on him. The audience would be led to presume that they were the latter on the basis of the preceding episode in ch. 31, where they were explicitly told that the Philistines 'shadowed' Saul (31.2). However, in light of the uncertainty of the speaker's identity and trustworthiness, his failure to identify the affiliation of the riders and head horsemen in question clearly casts a suspicious shadow upon his report.

A. Berlin has noted the unusual use by the informant of two *hinnēh* clauses in rapid succession in his account of the battle circumstances in v. 6. She emphasizes that such a practice is very rare in narrative prose, but characteristic of dream reports, suggesting that the perceptive ancient reader should have picked up on this feature and suspected the reliability of the speaker.[1] It is noteworthy that the *hinnēh* clauses introduce the first two battle details that conflict with the narrator's authoritative account in ch. 31. There was no mention of the spear in the former account, and there was no clear indication that the enemy chariotry or head horsemen were 'shadowing' Saul; rather, the archers apparently unknowingly hit him from a distance (31.2-3, 8). As Berlin has suggested, the *hinnēh* clauses appear to be an intentional stylistic clue used by the narrator to cast suspicion over the informant's version of the events at Gilboa.

Continuing in v. 7, the informant claims that Saul looked behind

1. *Poetics of Biblical Narrative*, p. 81. Her suggestion is adopted by Gordon (*I & II Samuel*, p. 208).

himself, spotted the informant, and called to him, and that he in turn responded. This additional round of information tends to confirm the earlier statement that the man was not actively participating in the battle on either side, but was an outsider who happened to be in the vicinity of Mt Gilboa at a very inopportune time. Saul would not have expected a Philistine soldier to have approached him from the rear, only from the front, since his position on Mt Gilboa was said to have resulted from Israelite retreat. Unless the Philistines had set ambushes behind the Israelite lines in the mountains on the evening that Saul was away at En-dor, a Philistine assailant would have approached Saul from the plain below, in pursuit, and so in Saul's full view.

The informant's ethnic/national identity is finally revealed in v. 8 as he continues to narrate his account of Saul's death. In response to Saul's question about his identity, he identified himself as an Amalekite! Now many of the previous uncertainties and suspicions are answered, while new ones are raised. David would have been able to ascertain from the man's clothes that he was an Amalekite back in v. 2. In light of the Amalekites' independent raiding activity that was undertaken while Saul and the Philistines were both away (ch. 30), it is extremely unlikely that the man would have been a participant at Gilboa as an ally for either side. Thus, David would not have been able to have guessed the outcome of the battle based on the man's appearance when he turned up at Ziklag. David's pressing for firm details about Saul's and Jonathan's reported deaths would also make sense if the man was not involved in the battle, but a passing eyewitness.

The man's identity as an Amalekite *ná'ar* also takes on new significance. The possibility is raised that he was one of the 400 *'îš ná'ar* who had escaped from the 'camp of David' in 30.17 and had headed north to engage in further plundering activity, having known about the battle to be waged in the Jezreel Valley. Thus, his presence at Gilboa might not have been mere coincidence, but a deliberate destination for the purposes of looting of the slain.[1] At the same time, the man's Amalekite identity would have marked him as an untrustworthy, heinous character for the ancient Judahite audience, for

1. Contrast Fokkelman (*Crossing Fates*, p. 635), who concludes that the term *ná'ar* indicates the status of servant and that the man was a servant with the Israelite train since, as the son of a *gēr*, he would not have been liable for military service.

whom the adjective 'Amalekite' was synonymous with treachery and deceit. Bearing this in mind, the audience instantly should have doubted the reliability of the man's testimony, firming up their initial suspicions raised by the *hinnēh* clauses in v. 6. In retrospect, the ambiguity of all of his previous statements is again highlighted and becomes consistent with his slippery, underhanded character.

The Amalekite goes on to state that Saul requested that he (the Amalekite) kill him because *haššābāṣ* has taken hold of him because all of his life force was still in him (v. 9). The term *haššābāṣ* is a *hapax legomenon*, which is most unfortunate because of its key position in the Amalekite's story. While Saul's reported reasoning for wanting to die is no longer clear to the modern audience, but should have been to the ancient Judahite audience, the blatant contradiction between the Amalekite's claims about Saul's final request and the actual request as it was narrated in 31.4 jumps out at both audiences. Since the writer has carefully constructed 2 Samuel 1 to raise suspicions about the identity of the eyewitness and builds those suspicions to a climax that peaks as he reveals the man's Amalekite origins, the audience is certainly intended to conclude that the report in v. 9 is a fabricated lie and that 31.4 was the true situation. The testimony of an Amalekite can never be trusted. More importantly, the narrator's authoritative third-person account in 1 Samuel 31 must be given priority over a character's conflicting first-person account.[1]

The Amalekite's further claims to have obeyed Saul's command by slaying him and then to have taken his royal crown and armlet (v. 10) would come as no surprise to the ancient audience. Only an uncouth outsider would lay his hand upon the Lord's anointed and then have the nerve to strip him of his royal insignia in an act of common looting of the dead. His Amalekite character would have confirmed for the audience his ability to commit such sacrilegious, unthinkable acts that neither David not Saul's loyal weapons-bearer would do. The justification the man offered for performing the act, his certainty that the king would not have lived after he had fallen, would not have been accepted as a legitimate cause by the audience, since it was the king who was involved. Perhaps mercy killings were allowed under certain circumstances, but because of the king's sacrosanctity, they would

1. This rule of narrative construction has also been emphasized by Berlin (*Poetics of Biblical Narrative*, p. 80) and Fokkelman (*Crossing Fates*, p. 639).

never have been permitted within Judah against the national king. The Amalekite's explanation would have read as a feeble excuse to cover up his desire to gain fame and fortune for slaying a king and looting his corpse.

Yet why did the man deliver the crown and armlet to David, instead of taking them home as looted goods? Is it possible that he was capable of honorable intentions after all, even though he was an Amalekite? The audience knows from 31.3 that Saul had been badly wounded, so this part of the story is validated, and he did display the outward signs of mourning. Or, was he hoping to gain an even greater reward from David, having learned from rumor of David's former ties to Saul and Israel? It is noteworthy that there is no mention of the fate of Saul's sword or spear either in 1 Samuel 31 or here. The Amalekite's ability to have removed the two personal items from Saul's dead body strongly implies that he found the corpse on the day of Saul's death, prior to the Philistine looting parties that found him the next morning. Since the Philistines had only Saul's armor and body as a trophy, the audience is left to surmise that the Amalekite probably made off with Saul's weapons as well as the items of jewelry, but was keeping the former for himself as valuable booty.

Does the man's use of polite court speech, addressing David as 'lord', also reflect his desire to become part of David's band, now that his own people have recently been decimated by David? Knowing his treacherous nature as an Amalekite, should the audience suspect that he is trying to ingratiate himself with David, with an ulterior motive in mind of slaying him to avenge the death of his fellow Amalekites? His false claim to have killed Saul certainly suggests that he would have no hesitation in laying his hand on Saul's anointed successor.

Presented with Saul's personal items of jewelry, David is convinced that Israel's first king has indeed died. David's immediate response to the proof is to rend his own clothes as a sign of mourning. All his men followed his lead (v. 11).[1] As a community of exiles from Israel, they then observed an official period of mourning for the fallen king, royal heir-elect, royal house of Israel, and people of Yahweh, because

1. Fokkelman ('Lie Born of Truth', p. 44) notes that, unlike the messenger in v. 2, David and his men do not put earth on their heads. He suggests that this is a deliberate disjunction, separating David and his men from the false mourner who will end up with blood on his head in v. 16b.

they all had fallen by the sword. David, now king *de facto*, leads his own core group in mourning rites appropriate to those who had been defeated in battle. His decision to honor both people and king, while perhaps standard under the circumstances, nevertheless closely binds the fate of people and king together, reminding the audience that the people's request for kingship in 1 Samuel 8 had been granted as an additional burden they bore in addition to maintaining the Horeb covenant. David's mourning ceremony reinforces Samuel's warning that both groups will be punished by Yahweh for the wrongdoing of either (12.24-25).

Whether or not David believes the account of Saul's death that the Amalekite has reported to him remains unanswered. The audience must wonder whether he will be able to discern the lie or not, especially in light of his use of the leading question in v. 5 that should have been able to ensnare the man in his own lie. David is at the disadvantage of not having an alternative set of facts with which to compare the Amalekite's. His final question to the man in v. 13, while initially harmless, turns out to be designed to expose the man's motivations and intentions for seeking him out and to catch him out in his lie (vv. 14-16).[1] In response to a question about his origins, the informant states that he is the son of an Amalekite man with the official status of a resident alien, *gēr* (v. 14). He is thereby asserting that he has grown up under the protection of certain laws of the land, though not a native-born inhabitant, seeming to want to imply that he supports the Israelite cause and could be trusted by officials. He has not identified which nation his father received the status of *gēr* from,

1. Contrast the suggestion by G. Macholz ('Die Stellung des Königs in der israelitischen Gerichtsverfassung', *ZAW* 84 [1972], p. 164) and adopted by C. Mabee ('David's Judicial Exoneration', *ZAW* 92 [1980], p. 94) that the question begins the institution of criminal proceedings by establishing the 'soldier's'—now defendant's—identity and David's proper jurisdiction to adjudicate the case as military commander. Because of the Amalekite's foreign status, Macholz thinks that he would not have stood under the jurisdiction of the local juridical 'gate' authorities. I believe the unfolding of narrative events suggests that the Amalekite was not a soldier and that David's status as judge in the ensuing legal proceedings does not stem from his role as military commander, since the defendant was not one of his men, but rather from his status as leader of Ziklag, the town in which the Amalekite has confessed his crime. It is only after the Amalekite's claim to be a *gēr* in this verse that David has legal grounds to initiate criminal proceedings.

but his visible signs of mourning would suggest that it was Israel. His reply would seem to belie his identification with one of the 400 Amalekite *'îš ná'ar* who had escaped from David's recent retaliatory raid, but is his testimony trustworthy, or is he trying to gain David's confidence so he can kill him later?

Whatever the truth of his statement or his intentions, his reply provides David with legal grounds to execute the self-confessed royal killer. As someone enjoying the official status of *gēr* within Israel, the man would have been bound to uphold the sacrosanctity of the king along with native-born inhabitants.[1] His alleged mercy killing therefore becomes legal grounds for his own death. Since it is extremely unlikely that the Amalekite intended or foresaw such a development when he approached David with Saul's items and claimed personally to have finished off the king, the audience is left to suspect that the man did not receive the responses to his initial story that he had anticipated, and, fearing possible calamity, had tried to extricate himself from his predicament, only to worsen his situation with a further lie.

Unlike David during his first visit to Gath (21.10-15), the Amalekite was not clever enough to cover his tracks and get himself out of the dangerous situation he had entered in the hopes of personal gain. He did not have divine support as Yahweh's anointed. Instead, he is sentenced to death by Yahweh's anointed, one of whose primary jobs is to uphold justice. While his first act as *de facto* king may unknowingly have been to establish a new law in 30.23, his death sentence against the self-confessing Amalekite serves as his first cognizant act as *de facto* king.[2] Whether or not the new king has been able to discern the set of lies the Amalekite has spun, he has been able to bring about justice and execute the slayer of the former king. The

1. Although this is not stated in any extant law, it is self-evident and widely presumed: see, for example, Dhorme, *Livres de Samuel*, p. 267; Ackroyd, *Second Samuel*, p. 22; and Gordon, *I & II Samuel*, p. 209. Contrast the discussion of Fokkelman, *Crossing Fates*, p. 642.

2. For the legal proceeding implied in vv. 15-16, see Mabee ('Exoneration', pp. 90-98), who extends the procedure over vv. 13-16. Fokkelman adopts his proposal that a legal proceeding is depicted, but limits it to v. 16 and defines its elements and progression differently ('Lie Born of Truth', p. 50; cf. *Crossing Fates*, p. 643). He notes further that 'the killing of the exemplary Amalekite forms the counterpart and the rounding off of the slaughter of the whole band in ch. xxx' ('Lie Born of Truth', p. 43).

audience almost certainly would have felt that justice had been served, even though they knew for certain, unlike David, that the Amalekite's death was not a strict case of poetic justice.

The Amalekite's death does not completely remove the shadow his lie has cast on Saul's honorable suicide. Although the audience knows that Saul (probably) died honorably, it is not certain whether David and his men have been able, or will be able in the future, to learn the true course of events surrounding Saul's death. As D. Gunn notes,

> Saul really cannot win against these most hated of Israel's foes. He defeats them in battle but they provide the occasion for his undoing, nevertheless (chapter 15); he bravely takes his own life, but as far as the living (and that includes his rival David) are concerned, he ends with his life in hock to one of these hated people—is reduced to begging an Amalekite to kill him.[1]

With this in mind, the ensuing lament that will close the narrative of Saul's career serves to counter the negative lingering impression by having David himself eulogize Saul in a totally positive way, leaving the audience feeling that the shadow cast by the Amalekite over Saul's honorable death has been dispersed.

The narrative devoted to Saul's career closes with a lament over Saul and Jonathan (vv. 19-27) that David is said to have ordered to have been taught to the Judahites (vv. 17-18). The precise meaning of *qšt* is unclear.[2] It is said to have been written in the *Book of Jashar*, a written source quoted elsewhere in Josh. 10.13 and in the LXX text of 1 Kgs 8.53. The extant quotes from Joshua and 2 Samuel suggest that the 'book' was a collection of battle-related songs and laments. Both the statement that David intoned this lament (v. 17) and the fact that the final section of the lament is written in the first personal singular (v. 26) are intended to lead the audience to believe that he wrote the lament himself. As has often been noted, the poem does not bear the 'metric' markings expected of a traditional *qīnâ*. Since the piece is said to have been preserved in the *Book of Jashar*, its designation as a *qīnâ* can be attributed to the narrator's secondary use of the poem as David's final lament.

1. Gunn, *Fate of Saul*, p. 157 n. 21.
2. For the various options, see, for example, Dhorme, *Livres de Samuel*, p. 269; Driver, *Notes*, pp. 233-34; McCarter, *II Samuel*, p. 68; Fokkelman, *Crossing Fates*, p. 651.

In spite of the problems raised by the extant consonantal text, the main thoughts and overall structure of the poem are relatively clear. The present volume is not the proper context in which to undertake a full textual, grammatical, form-critical and historical analysis of this once independent piece of literature. For the purposes of the close literary reading almost completed, the eight verses of poetry need to be evaluated in terms of their current function as the conclusion to the larger narrative unit devoted to the career of Saul. How they connect with the preceding episodes, particularly the two accounts of Saul's and Jonathan's deaths, and what they reveal about Saul and Jonathan, the honorees, as well as David, the purported author, will be the primary focus of the ensuing discussion.

The division and translation of the opening half of v. 19 are problematic, but nevertheless can be seen to refer to the piercing (*ḥll*) of a person (or perhaps persons) of importance in Israel. The second half of the verse then reiterates the same theme of death (verb *npl*), but seems to expand it to include warriors (*gibbôrîm*) in general. Both groups (the royal family and the army) and both verbs were mentioned in the account of the final battle in 1 Samuel 31.

Verse 20 orders the hearers or readers not to tell (the news) in Gath or to proclaim glad tidings in the streets of Ashkelon, two of the five main cities of the Philistines. The verb *bśr* is used again, as in the first account of the defeat in 31.9. The reason for the silence is to prevent the daughters of the Philistines, the female portion of the population traditionally responsible for celebrating the victorious return of the home forces with songs and victory dances or for lamenting the defeat of the home forces with dirges and mourning rites, from performing their anticipated and obligatory celebrational functions. A parallel line refers to the Philistine women as 'daughters of the uncircumcised', repeating the derogatory characterization of Israel's traditional army as a noncovenantal group used elsewhere in the Saulide narrative in 1 Sam. 14.6; 17.26, 36; and 31.4.

In the following verse, the mountains in the Gilboa are cursed to become barren because they served as the final resting place of the castaway shield(s) of mighty warriors and Saul's unoiled shield (v. 21). The statement implies that the mountains were the site of the final defeat of the Israelite forces, including the location where Saul died. This information tallies with the situation as it was depicted in 1 Samuel 31. However, there was no reference in either ch. 31 or the

Amalekite's account of the battle earlier in this chapter to shields in connection with the battle. Sword, spear, armor, crown, armlet, chariotry or horsemen, and archers appear, but no shields. Perhaps shields are to be presumed to be a standard piece of defensive equipment used in war.

In v. 22, the poet moves on to praise the heroic efforts and exploits of the king and heir-elect during their careers. Jonathan, wielding the bow, is said never to have missed inflicting a wound on an enemy target, while Saul, wielding a sword, is said never to have missed an enemy's gut. Israel's leaders were heralded as having been diligent and skillful in their attacks against the enemy. By implication, they would have continued their customary aggressiveness during their last battle and so would have dispatched a number of Philistines before their own demise. While the poem stresses their dexterity and tenaciousness throughout their careers, ch. 31 focuses on the final battle of their careers and, more specifically, on the closing moments of Saul's life and the issue of whether he would die honorably or dishonorably. For this reason, Jonathan is overshadowed and his death noted quickly in passing, alongside those of his brothers (v. 2). No mention is made of his skillful use of the bow, although earlier in the Saulide narrative he was twice associated with this weapon (1 Sam. 18.4; 20.18, 36). By contrast, Saul's use of the sword is found in ch. 31, but with the ironic twist that he used it to dispatch himself in his own gut, not the enemy's.

As a final eulogizing characterization of father and son, the poet describes both men as beloved and delightful, asserting that they were not separated either while alive or in death. Both are said to have been swifter than griffon vultures and stronger than lions, two metaphors once again seemingly associated with their military prowess and accomplishments. The claim of close bonding and identification of the two royal figures, king and heir-elect, has been played upon and explored during the course of the narrative. While Jonathan begins as heir-elect and closely allied with his father (1 Sam. 13.2), his rejection by Yahweh at the battle at the Michmash pass (14.42) leads to his instant recognition of David's status as anointed king-elect (18.1-4), expressed through his symbolic bestowal of his clothes and weapons of office upon David as well as the covenant he made with him. His willing acceptance of Yahweh's decision contrasts with Saul's refusal to accept the divine plan and leads to eventual confrontations with his father over David (19.1-7; 20.1-42; 22.8) and what appears to be a clear split between the two (23.15-18).

Jonathan does not appear again in the narrative until his death is mentioned briefly in 31.2. In the meantime, Saul has confessed his knowledge that David will succeed him as king of Israel (24.20) directly to the anointed Bethlehemite, but still will not give up his attempt to thwart the divine plan that calls for David's succession to the throne in place of Jonathan. Jonathan's appearance in the battle of Gilboa alongside two of his brothers does not provide the audience with any firm indications as to whether the rift between father and son has been healed or remains open. Still, the fact that other brothers are mentioned for the first time in connection with their father in the context of national security may be intended to be a subtle clue, in retrospect, that the rift had remained unhealed and that Saul was grooming younger sons as possible heirs in place of the rejected Jonathan. The apparent bonding of Jonathan and Saul displayed by their joint participation in battle might have been illusory. In any event, David's purported assertion that the two were never separated constitutes a bald lie in the context of the larger Saulide narrative, suggesting in turn that his purportedly generous and ideal portrayal was motivated by factors other than reality.

In contrast to the daughters of Philistia, the daughters of Israel are commanded to provide the requisite mourning rites associated with defeat in battle for Saul. He is singled out for recognition because as king, he had provided his country with wealth and prosperity, allowing at least a certain segment of the population to afford to dress in scarlet-dyed cloth and to purchase clothing decorated with gold-sheathed ornamental appliques and brocades. The production of scarlet was an expensive and time-consuming task. It involved the collection by hand of eggs from females of the cochineal insect *Kermococcus vermilio Planch*. The eggs were deposited in small berry-like grains on branches of a certain type of oak tree, the *quercus coccifera*. After collection, the eggs were probably submerged in vinegar, dried, and then crushed to yield a dye soluble in water and alcohol.[1] Huge quantities would have been necessary to produce a deep

1. For the source of *šānî*, see, for example, H. Kurdian, 'Kirmiz', *JAOS* 61 (1941), pp. 105-107; J. Laudermilk, 'The Bug with the Crimson Past', *Natural History* 58 (1949), pp. 114-18; R.J. Forbes, *Studies in Ancient Technology*, IV

shade of scarlet. Verse 24 indirectly highlights Saul's success as a monarch, a characterization that was hinted at but was purposely abandoned after the summary of his deeds as king in 14.47-48.

In v. 25, the poet returns to the first verse, inverting its halves and expanding it slightly. He opens with the identical phrase that formed the second half of v. 1, 'how the warriors have fallen', but expands it with the circumstantial phrase, 'in the midst of battle' (v. 25). He then goes on to substitute the name of Jonathan, with the full divine element, *y^{e}hônātān*, for the opening consonantal text *hṣby yśr'l*, concluding with a repetition of the identical phrase that completed the first half of v. 1, *'al-bāmôteykā ḥālāl*, however *'al bāmôteykā* is to be translated. This play allows him to bring his main section of thought to closure, yet acts as a smooth transition to his further first-person testimony concerning Jonathan in particular.

In v. 26, the poet, who has been identified within the context as David, adds a personal note of lament to what has otherwise been a third-person eulogy. He returns to the two concepts of love (root *'hb*) and delight (root *n'm*) that he applied to both father and son in v. 23 and discusses how Jonathan's death in particular has affected him in these two spheres. Beginning with the statement that it is distressing for him on Jonathan's account, he characterizes Jonathan as his 'brother'. He then goes on to say that Jonathan delighted him very much, and that Jonathan's love for him was more extraordinary than female love. Links to the earlier narrative appear in the use of the impersonal construction with the verb *ṣrr*, which recalls the distress of the Israelites in 13.6, but more closely, Saul's distress in 28.15 and his own distress in 30.6.[1]

The exact sense in which Jonathan has 'pleased' or 'delighted' David greatly is not immediately clarified in the preceding narrative where that verb does not appear. Nevertheless, its close association with the root *'hb*, to love, could lead the audience to speculate that in its present context at least, it refers to Jonathan's decision to honor his covenant with David above his blood ties to his father. Certainly, the reference to Jonathan as his 'brother' and to Jonathan's 'love' for him is intended to be understood in connection with the covenant the two

(9 vols.; 2nd rev. edn; Leiden: Brill, 1964-1972), pp. 101-106.

1. Fokkelman (*Crossing Fates*, p. 678) overlooks the occurrence of the phrase in 1 Sam. 13.6 and so concludes that its use here completes a ternary series.

made in 18.1-4. That Jonathan's love was more extraordinary than the love of women perhaps can be seen in the larger associative context to be a sidelong reference to David's aborted marriage to Jonathan's sister Merab and his actual marriage to Jonathan's sister Michal. Michal is said to have loved David also (18.20), but did not seem to put her life on the line on his behalf as many times as her brother. In the narrative, Merab did not prove her love for him at all.

As a final closing to the entire poem, the poet repeats the refrain from v. 1b and v. 25a, 'how the mighty have fallen', and expands it with the phrase, 'and the weapons of war have vanished, been lost, or have perished'. The repetition creates an envelope structure for David's first-person lament over Jonathan, making it a kind of coda to the more public eulogy for Saul and Jonathan in vv. 19-25. The precise meaning to be attached to the verb *'ābad* depends upon whether its subjects, the weapons of war, are to be personified as they were in v. 22, or construed as regular objects, like the shields in v. 21. In the former case, the second phrase would represent a parallel member, with the weapons of war serving as a synonym to the mighty and the verb *'ābad*, 'perish', serving as a synonym to *nāp^{e}lû*, 'have perished'. A second possible level of meaning could be associated with this understanding of the verse. The 'weapons of war' could be used metonymically for their owners, expressing the view that in war men become mere instruments executing the will of their lords and gods, losing their human dimension.

In the latter case, the phrase 'and the weapons of war have been lost or vanished' would be a straightforward statement completing the thought begun in the first half of the verse through synthetic parallelism. On one level, the loss of weapons might be intended to refer to the enemies' practice of claiming the weapons of the conquered as victory booty, leaving the vanquished stripped of their former symbols of power. On a more basic level, however, the verse makes the statement that war merely results in the felling of human life and the loss of the weapons associated with destruction. While this may reflect an attitude of neutral acceptance of grim reality, it may also harbor undercurrents that express the painful futility of war from the perspective of the loser; no material gain has been realized. Instead, human life has been lost, along with the weapons that were designed to protect it.

CONCLUSIONS

How has Saul been characterized in the twenty-five chapters devoted to his career and what lessons was the ancient audience to have drawn from this portrayal? The following summary will go back through the story of Saul's career, focusing on personal character traits assigned to the king and lessons developed by the creator of the Saulide narrative. It will not be presumed that such features reflect historical reality. Rather, they are to be seen to represent the author's imagining of the first king of Israel from a retrospective glance of centuries. While the author has been guided in his portrayal by standard norms for kingly behavior and action, he also has been guided by larger theological concerns that have colored his final portrait significantly. In addition, it is not to be forgotten that in shaping his final portrait, the writer has used the three-part kingship installation pattern, the four-part regnal pattern, a pattern of 'Saul under Yahweh's good spirit' and then 'Saul under Yahweh's evil spirit', the contrastive word pairs 'good' and 'bad' and 'eyes and 'heart', the themes of covenant and power (*yād*), and a number of standard literary devices.

The biblical writer has introduced his readers to a man destined to greatness from birth who possessed the physical attributes of a natural hero (9.1-2). He has set forth Saul as Yahweh's own choice for the newly created office of king, an office with two divinely appointed tasks: 1) to deliver the Israelite people from Philistine oppression (9.15-16), and 2) to bind them to uphold and obey the terms of the ongoing covenant established at Horeb/Mt Sinai (9.17).

Saul is depicted to have undergone all three steps of the standard kingship installation. The first step of designation as king-elect has been presented as a two-step process. A private anointing as king-elect by Yahweh's agent Samuel (10.1) was followed by a public designation through the use of lots and the people's affirmation of Saul as Yahweh's chosen candidate (10.17-27). The middle step, a test of the candidate through his completion of a military deed, took place when Saul delivered Jabesh-Gilead from Ammonite oppression (11.1-11). His surprise attack at dawn confirmed his ability as a military strategist and provided a rationale for his selection by Yahweh to be first king, demonstrating his capability to carry out the first charge of kingship, the overthrow of Philistine oppression. After his official coronation as king (11.14-15), Saul was to set about fulfilling his first task of delivering Israel from the hand of the Philistines.

Once again, Saul's strategic abilities are highlighted as he formulates a daring plan to capture the Philistine garrisons on both sides of the Michmash pass so he can effectively take control of the pass himself. Dividing his forces, his plan was to have two divisions circle around behind the outpost at Michmash while a third moved in behind Gibeah. Then, attacking simultaneously, the enemy would be forced into the bottleneck of the pass where they could be finished off (13.2). The plan goes awry, however, when Jonathan, leader of the Gibeah contingent, launches his attack prematurely, forcing Saul to retreat from his position. Saul goes to Gilgal to formulate a new plan. While there, Saul equates his presence with an earlier ambiguous announcement (10.8) Samuel had made after anointing him. Samuel had added to the end of the three-part sign he announced as confirmation of Saul's divine choice as king-elect (10.2-7) a command that Saul was to wait seven days at Gilgal for the prophet to arrive, offer sacrifices, and instruct Saul in his plan of action.

With a Philistine retaliation imminent and Samuel's failure to arrive, at some point during the final seventh day Saul took action himself, only to have Samuel appear immediately and seemingly declare that his previous announcement in 10.8 was in fact a divine command that Saul had now broken (13.13-14). As a result, Saul's kingdom was not to be established and Yahweh would seek out 'a man after his own heart' to appoint as the new king-elect for Saul's disobedience to divine command. In retrospect from ch. 15, it becomes apparent that Samuel had not spoken on Yahweh's behalf in either 10.8 or 13.13-14; the narrator announces that Yahweh first repents for having made Saul king in 15.11. Therefore, the perfect verb form *biqqēš* and the ensuing *wāw*-consecutive verb form *wayṣawwēhû* in 13.14 probably should be interpreted as either 'perfects of confidence' or 'prophetic perfects' spoken to emphasize the surety of the fulfillment of the announced predictions. In either case, they probably are meant to be understood as future predictions. The list of Saul's military victories in 14.47-48 also serves to raise suspicion about the divine source of Samuel's pronounced rejection in 13.13-14 since the king cannot fight successfully without the support of the nation's god.

Saul runs into trouble in fulfilling his second royal task of restraining the people. In the wake of the successful rout of the Philistines at the Michmash pass, he builds his first official altar to Yahweh, a standard royal duty, but only after he is told that the people are sinning against Yahweh by eating 'with the blood' (14.33-35). He has failed to hold the people to observance of proper ritual law. A subsequent failure to restrain the people takes place shortly thereafter as they ransom Jonathan from Saul's declared death sentence after mistakenly believing that he had Yahweh's divine support throughout the preceding battle (14.45). While Yahweh initially used Jonathan as an agent to launch the second phase of the battle for the Michmash pass (14.6-13), he subsequently condemned him through the priestly oracle of Urim and Thummim (14.41-42). Saul should not have allowed the ransoming to take place.

A third failure to restrain the people occurs during the battle against Amalek and costs Saul his kingship. He 'listens to the voice of the people' (15.24) and believes that they have pure motives for sparing the best animals and all that was good in spite of the specific divine command to destroy Amalek utterly and all that they had (15.15). In conversation with Samuel, he comes to realize that he wrongly presumed that they shared his desire to act in good conscience by sparing some of the booty for later dedication to Yahweh at Gilgal. In fact, he realizes too late that they deliberately followed the letter of the divine command instead of its spirit, saving alive animals not explicitly listed in the original command, for selfish reasons. It is his repeated failure at the second divinely appointed task for the king that costs him his kingship according to the writer (15.11, 26, 34). A king must be more than a great military strategist; he must be able to hold the people to observance of the divinely sanctioned law and ongoing divine command. More specifically, a good king will not judge by human perception ('eyes') and outward appearances; he will align his heart, the seat of divine perception, with Yahweh's, relying on inner strength and divine inspiration for judgment.

As divinely rejected king, Saul is depicted to be extremely concerned with maintaining a semblance of ongoing divine support and legitimation; after all, he is still king *de facto*. His demonstrated weakness toward the opinion and support of the people becomes a primary and consuming concern (15.30 and *passim*). After a coded exchange with his courtiers (16.16-18), we learn that Saul sent out spies to learn the identity of Yahweh's newly anointed king-elect, the 'man after his own heart': he knew David's name even without it being pronounced by his courtier (16.19). Here we see Saul testing the knowledge and ongoing loyalty of members of his court in the wake of his privately announced rejection; Saul has become afraid that as a lame-duck king, he will be killed to make room for the new candidate.

We also see a calculating Saul, who binds David to him personally in a formal pact as his royal weapons-bearer (16.21), thereby hoping to keep David under constant surveillance while at the same time ensuring the inability of the king-elect to kill the lame-duck king without suffering death himself as punishment for laying a hand on the sacrosanct person of the king. The ability to formulate plans and carry them through, which earlier had been a positive trait allowing Saul to be a great military strategist, now becomes a negative trait with the loss of Yahweh's good guiding spirit. It will continue to come into play throughout the remaining narrative. Saul's plan apparently is thwarted when Jesse fails to acquiesce to the king's command to have David remain permanently at court (16.22); David is needed at home to tend the family flock in place of his three elder brothers who become part of Saul's forces (17.13-15).

Saul confirms to David his knowledge of the youth's identity as the divinely appointed king-elect in their private discussion concerning Goliath (17.31-40). In response to David's assurance that Yahweh would deliver him from Goliath, Saul says, 'Go, and Yahweh (himself) will be with you'. He then dresses David in his royal armor and gives him his sword, but David rejects these items because he is not yet entitled to them: he is only the king-elect and has not yet been 'tested' (17.39). After the battle, Saul tests Abner's understanding of the significance of the victory for the king-elect by asking him if he knows who David's father is. He once more is trying to ascertain whether an official in his court knows of David's anointing and now his successful testing and whether he will continue to support the existing king or not. Saul wants to know if Abner has detected that Yahweh is David's adoptive father.

Saul seeks to solve his problem of loss of divine support by appointing David over the men of war, knowing he has Yahweh's support and can lead Israel to continued victory (18.5). His strategy to maintain a semblance of continued divine favor backfires somewhat, however, as David's success wins him the support and respect of all the people, including the court (18.5). Realizing David's growing popular support, Saul worries that he will be made king by force (18.6-8), fulfilling his earlier fears, and becomes suspicious of David (18.9).

After he attempts to kill David himself under the influence of an evil spirit (18.10-11), Saul removes him from his personal reach and appoints him to the position of commander of a thousand, apparently to remove the Lord's new anointed, who was now a sacrosanct individual, from mishap at his own hand (18.12-13). After David's continued success and sworn loyalty from both Israel and Judah, however, Saul embarks on an active campaign to eliminate the perceived threat David poses to his own life by having the king-elect killed by others. He begins with the Philistines (18.17, 21, 25), but moves subsequently to members of his own court as he becomes more desperate (19.1). Saul's resolve to kill David intensifies as David's military success continues and his charisma grows, strengthening his position among the people. David's success feeds Saul's apparent fears of assassination to the point where he comes to consider David his enemy, someone out to kill him (19.17). David, for his part, senses the danger Saul poses and flees (19.18).

Saul's fear of David gaining the kingdom involves not only his personal fear of assassination, but also his fervent hope that his own son Jonathan might yet be able to succeed him on the throne (20.30-31). While he has acknowledged that David is indeed Yahweh's chosen successor, he also seems to have decided that if David dies, as heir-elect, Jonathan would have a secure path to the succession. He either has not understood or has not accepted the clear implications of Jonathan's rejection by Yahweh as a suitable king-elect that the guilty verdict back in 14.41-42 revealed. On the other hand, he may be counting on the loyalty of the people to install the heir-elect as the natural successor, in spite of Yahweh's lack of support for him. They clearly have not understood the meaning of the guilty verdict Yahweh rendered in 14.41-42 since they ransomed him from death.

Saul's active, calculated attempt to thwart the divine plan to place David on the throne as his successor instead of Jonathan is further highlighted by Jonathan's own acceptance of his rejection as king-elect by Yahweh in favor of David and his own attempts to forestall a possible bloody *coup d'état* in that would forcibly remove Saul from office. After witnessing David's defeat of Goliath, Jonathan seems to understand David's new status and instantly moves to enter into a formal personal pact with him, bestowing upon him the symbols of the office of king-elect (18.1-4). He subsequently intercedes on David's behalf with his father, reminding Saul that he has no just cause for killing the slayer of Goliath, Yahweh's now-tested king-elect (19.2-7). Eventually, the audience learns that the basis for the covenant was not altruism on Jonathan's part. He uses it as a means of pressuring David into concessions guaranteeing David's loyalty to 'his house' and his own personal safety as Saul's attempts to kill David become more frequent and David's safety diminishes (20.14-17, 42). Later, he uses the covenant to extract an amended pact in which Jonathan would be David's right-hand man after David became king (23.17-18). Having already extracted the former promise not to wipe out the royal Saulide line through Jonathan at least, Jonathan now 'ups the ante' by effectively inserting David as a single interloper on the Saulide throne. He is willing to forego ruling himself to allow his descendants to reclaim the throne on David's death. Is he trying to thwart the divine plan in his own way?

Saul's growing fear over the strength of David's support base among the people and their knowledge of his own rejection by Yahweh in favor of David leads him to accuse his own son and courtiers of conspiracy with David (22.7-8). As a result, the king turns to outsiders to supply him with the information, feeling his own people are no longer trustworthy. With this action he reverses in his mind his true enemies and true supporters. His reliance on the deliberately skewed testimony of Doeg leads to the massacre of his own priesthood as co-conspirators with 'the enemy', David (22.9-19). He relies on the testimony of the non-Israelite Ziphites to lead him to David (23.19-24) and still is unable to catch him, only to have David turn around and feed the Ziphites deliberate misinformation to lure the king to him for a subsequent confrontation (26.1-5).

A chance encounter with David in a cave near Ibexes' Rocks fails to divert Saul from his determined calculations to kill David, thereby thwarting God's plan for the succession. He will not take the strong hint David drops that no one can kill Yahweh's anointed with impunity, even though he has already personally confessed to David his knowledge that David is indeed Yahweh's anointed (17.37-38) and Jonathan has told David of Saul's knowledge as well (23.17). Indeed, here he openly confesses to David in unequivocal terms that he knows David will be king and that the kingdom of Israel will be established in his hand (24.20). He uses the confession to pressure David into swearing not to kill either him personally or his descendants, arriving at an arrangement similar to the one Jonathan extracted through their covenant in 20.14-17, 42.

Yet, Saul's weeping in response to David's mock trial scene reveals his inability to accept David's words at face value and his reinforced conviction that Yahweh intends to use David as the agent of his premature assassination. Saul seems to have a faint glimmer of hope, as he invokes Yahweh's just reward for David as payment for David's failure to kill him, that Yahweh will punish the king-elect, perhaps even reject him, for his failure to carry out a falsely perceived divine command for David to take the throne by killing Saul. His failure to invite David back to the court, however, tends to override this misplaced hope; he still considers David an enemy out to kill him. While David refutes his men's assertion that Saul is his enemy (24.4-7), Saul has completely lost perspective on this issue.

In a second more public confrontation with David where the same lesson concerning the sacrosanctity of Yahweh's anointed is emphasized by David, the other living anointed one, Saul is not willing to repeat his earlier confession to David in 24.20 about the certainty of his successful kingship. Under the public spotlight with his troops hearing his exchange with David, he can only allude in general terms to his more specific private announcement. At the same time, since David has once again failed to kill him even though Yahweh gave him into the king-elect's hand, on the basis of his previous misapplied logic, David should be in even more trouble for disobeying Yahweh a second time. Perhaps then, his weaker statement is also intended to reflect his growing hope that David had sabotaged his position of favor with Yahweh and may not be granted the kingship after all.

Saul's decision to launch an offensive attack in the valley of Jezreel (29.1) in spite of his lack of divine support might signal his conviction that David has been neutralized by his own disobedience and by his flight beyond the borders of Yahweh's territory. Nevertheless, on the eve of the battle Saul experiences extreme anguish and lack of confidence and, in attempting to communicate with Yahweh, is not answered through any of the standard channels of communication (28.6). Sentencing himself to death by breaking his own decree forbidding the consultation of a medium, Saul summons Samuel's spirit to learn what he should do concerning the battle (28.11). His former strategic abilities have now been paralyzed in the wake of his loss of divine support and his inability to align his heart with Yahweh's. Once again, proper perception is emphasized as the key to a good king. Samuel, Yahweh's former spokesperson whose role was to 'tell the king what he should do' (10.8), provides no guidance, but reveals Saul's impending fate to die in battle the next day alongside his sons (28.19). Saul now learns that his hopes are misplaced and that Yahweh considers him an enemy to be destroyed.

Samuel's revelation of Saul's fate gives the king a final opportunity to try to thwart the divine plan. He can choose not to be present at the battle and so not to die in the conflict at the hand of the Philistines. He can also choose to spare his sons in the same way. While he does not thwart the plan concerning the fate of his sons (31.2), he alters the plan for his own death by committing suicide instead of dying by the agency of the Philistines (31.4). When he is wounded by blindly launched long-distance volleys of arrows and has the opportunity to be dragged to safety by his weapons-bearer, he seems at first to surrender to his fate by asking his weapons-bearer to finish him off (31.3-4). However, the audience learns that his dead body was only discovered the following day when the Philistines were stripping the slain (31.8) so that they had had no knowledge that he had died. This in turn indicates that Saul's argument aimed at persuading his weapons-bearer to kill him was deliberately specious. Failing to grasp the death sentence he was passing on his weapons-bearer by his request, he finally commits suicide, thereby surrendering to his fate while at the same time defying Yahweh by dying in a way other than was intended. Realizing the hopelessness of his situation now that he was Yahweh's declared enemy, he nevertheless defied Yahweh in his very act of dying.

Saul ends his career fighting the enemy from whose oppression he was charged as king to deliver Israel. His tendency to use human perception instead of inward, divinely inspired perception by aligning his heart with Yahweh's led him to fail at his task of restraining the people to obey the divine will. This in turn affected his ability to function as a military leader and to complete his first task of delivering Israel from the Philistines. At his death, Saul's failure became apparent and his long-standing fears were realized: the Philistines were able to occupy former Israelite cities (31.7), continuing their oppression, and groups within Israel had lost confidence in Saul as king and had abandoned their loyalty to him, failing to support him in his final campaign. Israelites in the immediate vicinity of the battle had not rallied to Saul's support (31.7), nor had the Jabesh-Gileadites, who had personally benefitted from Saul's earliest military exploit (31.11; 11.1-11).

To summarize the writer's depiction of Saul's career, we see a man who was chosen in good faith by Yahweh as an able ruler and endowed with the proper heart to succeed (10.9), but one who ultimately failed because, in his exercise of free will, he eventually failed to rely on inward, divinely inspired perception and trusted instead in his own human perception. The writer is emphasizing the need for the king to align his perception with that of his heavenly regent, Yahweh, to be a successful ruler. Such alignment is the source of all wisdom and good judgment, without which natural character traits will become skewed and used for nonproductive purposes. The king is expected to forego human allegiance and not to be swayed by popular opinion or demand; since humanity relies on imperfect, limited human perception to judge, a collective decision can still be wrong and should not be trusted or acted upon. As earthly vice-regent for Yahweh, the king must transcend his human weaknesses and limitations by surrendering himself to become an agent of the divine will so that the nation can be constrained to obey the divine will. If the king accomplishes this necessary task, the nation will prosper; if not, both king and nation will be swept away.

BIBLIOGRAPHY

Books

Ackroyd, P., *The First Book of Samuel* (CamB, 9; Cambridge: Cambridge University Press, 1971).

—*The Second Book of Samuel* (CamB, 10; Cambridge: Cambridge University Press, 1973).

Ahlström, G.W., *Royal Administration and National Religion in Ancient Palestine* (SHANE, 1; Leiden: Brill, 1982).

Albright, W., *Archaeology and the Religion of Israel* (Baltimore: Johns Hopkins University Press, 1942).

—*The Biblical Period* (Pittsburgh: Pittsburgh University Press, 1950).

Alt, A., *Kleine Schriften zur Geschichte des Volkes Israel* (3 vols.; Munich: Beck, 1953-1959).

Alter, R., *The Art of Biblical Narrative* (New York: Basic Books, 1981).

Auzou, G., *La danse devant l'arche* (Connaissance de la Bible, 6; Paris: Editions de l'Orante, 1968).

Avigad, N., *Hebrew Bullae from the Time of Jeremiah* (Jerusalem: Israel Exploration Society, 1986).

Berlin, A., *Poetics and Interpretation of Biblical Narrative* (Bible and Literature Series, 9; Sheffield: Almond Press, 1983).

Birch, B., *The Rise of the Israelite Monarchy: The Growth and Development of 1 Samuel 7-15* (SBLDS, 27; Missoula, MT: Scholars Press, 1976).

Boecker, H.J., *Die Beurteilung der Anfänge des Königtums in den deuteronomistischen Abschnitten des ersten Samuelisbuches* (WMANT, 31; Neukirchen–Vluyn: Neukirchener Verlag, 1969).

Budde, K., *Die Bücher Samuel* (KHC, 8; Tübingen: Mohr, 1902).

Campbell, A., *The Ark Narrative. A Form-Critical and Traditio-Historical Study* (Missoula, MT: Scholars Press, 1975).

Carlson, R.A. *David, the chosen King* (trans. E.J. Sharpe and S. Rudman; Stockholm: Almqvist & Wiksell, 1964).

Cross, F.M., Jr, *Canaanite Myth and Hebrew Epic* (Cambridge, MA: Harvard University Press, 1973).

Crüsemann, F., *Die Widerstand gegen das Königtum* (WMANT, 49; Neukirchen–Vluyn: Neukirchener Verlag, 1978).

Culley, R., *Studies in the Structure of Hebrew Narrative* (Missoula, MT: Scholars Press, 1976).

Damrosch, D., *The Narrative Covenant* (San Francisco: Harper & Row, 1987).

Day, J., *God's Conflict with the Dragon and the Sea* (Cambridge: Cambridge University Press, 1985).

Dhorme, P., *Les Livres de Samuel* (Ebib: Paris: Lecoffre, 1910).

Driver, S.R., *Notes on the Hebrew Text of the Books of Samuel* (2nd rev. edn; Oxford: Clarendon Press, 1913).

Eaton, J.H., *Kingship and the Psalms* (SBT, Second Series, 32; London: SCM Press, 1976).

Ehrlich, A., *Randglossen zur Hebräischen Bibel* (7 vols.; Leipzig: Hinrichs, 1908-1914).

Eslinger, L., *Kingship of God in Crisis. A Close Reading of 1 Samuel 1-12* (Bible and Literature Series, 10; Sheffield: Almond Press, 1985).

Farber, W., W. Kümmel and W.H.Ph. Römer, *Rituale und Beschwörungen*, I (Texte aus der Umwelt des Alten Testaments, II/2; Gütersloh: Mohn, 1987).

Fokkelman, J.P., *Narrative Art and Poetry in the Books of Samuel*. II. *The Crossing Fates* (Assen: Van Gorcum, 1986).

Forbes, R.J., *Studies in Ancient Technology* (9 vols.; 2nd rev. edn; Leiden: Brill, 1964-1972).

Foresti, F., *The Rejection of Saul in the Perspective of the Deuteronomistic School* (Studia Theologica-Teresianum, 5; Rome: Edizioni del Teresianum, 1984).

Friedman, R.E., *The Exile and Biblical Narrative* (HSM, 22; Chico, CA: Scholars Press, 1981).

Gevirtz, S., *Patterns in the Early Poetry of Israel* (Studies in Ancient Oriental Civilization, 32; Chicago: University of Chicago, 1963).

Good, R., *Irony in the Old Testament* (London: SPCK, 1965).

Gordon, R.P., *I & II Samuel: A Commentary* (Library of Biblical Interpretation; Grand Rapids, MI: Zondervan, 1986).

Graetz, H., *Geschichte der Jüden von de altesten Zeiten bis auf die Gegenwart* (11 vols.; Leipzig: Leiner, 1874-1911).

Gray, J., *I and II Kings* (OTL; Philadelphia: Westminster Press, 1963).

Gunkel, H., *Schöpfung und Chaos in Urzeit und Endzeit* (Göttingen: Vandenhoeck & Ruprecht, 1895).

Gunn, D., *The Fate of King Saul* (JSOTSup, 14; Sheffield: JSOT Press, 1980).

Halpern, B., *The Constitution of the Monarchy in Ancient Israel* (HSM, 2; Chico, CA: Scholars Press, 1981).

Hertzberg, H.W., *I & II Samuel* (trans. J.S. Bowman; OTL; Philadelphia: Westminster Press, 1969).

Herzog, C. and M. Gichon, *Battles of the Bible* (New York: Random House, 1978).

Hestrin, R. and M. Dayagi-Mendels, *Inscribed Seals, First Temple Period. Hebrew, Ammonite, Moabite, Phoenician, and Aramaic. From the Collections of the Israel Museum and the Israel Department of Antiquities and Museums* (Jerusalem: Israel Museum, 1979).

Jamieson-Drake, D., *Scribes and Schools in Monarchic Judah: A Socio-Archeological Approach* (SWBAS, 9; Sheffield: Almond Press, 1991).

Jobling, D., *The Sense of Biblical Narrative*, I (JSOTSup, 7; Sheffield: JSOT Press, 1978).

—*The Sense of Biblical Narrative*, II (JSOTSup, 39; Sheffield: JSOT Press, 1986).

Johnson, A.R., *Sacral Kingship in Ancient Israel* (2nd edn; Cardiff: University of Wales, 1967).

Klein, R., *1 Samuel* (Word Biblical Commentary, 10; Waco, TX: Word Books, 1980).

Klostermann, A., *Die Bücher Samuelis und der Könige* (Kurzgefasster Kommentar zu den heiligen Schriften Alten und Neuen Testamentes, III; Nördlingen: Beck, 1887).

Koehler, L. and W. Baumgartner (eds.), *Supplementum ad Lexicon in Veteris Testamenti Libros* (Leiden: Brill, 1958).

Kurtz, D. and J. Boardman, *Greek Burial Custom* (Ithaca, NY: Cornell University Press, 1971).

Kutsch, E., *Salbung als Rechtsakt im Alten Testament und im Alten Orient* (BZAW, 87; Berlin: Töpelmann, 1963).

Lagarde, P. de, *Anmerkungen zur griechischen Übersetzung der Proverbien* (Leipzig: Brockhaus, 1863).

Lemaire, A., *Les écoles et la formation de la Bible dans l'ancien Israël* (OBO, 39; Fribourg: Editions Universitaires, 1981).

Lipiński, E., *La royauté de Yahwé dans la poésie et le culte de l'ancien Israël* (Verhandelingen van de Koninglijke vlaamse Academie voor Wetenschappen, Letteren en schone Kunsten van België-Klasse der Letteren, XXVII/55; Brussels: Paleis der Academiën, 1965).

Long, V.P., *The Reign and Rejection of King Saul. A Case for Literary and Theological Coherence* (SBLDS, 118; Atlanta: Scholars Press, 1989).

McCarter, P.K., Jr, *I Samuel* (AB, 8; Garden City, NY: Doubleday, 1980).

—*II Samuel* (AB, 9; Garden City, NY: Doubleday, 1984).

McKane, W., *I & II Samuel: The Way to the Throne* (Torch Biblical Commentary; London: SCM Press, 1963).

Mauchline, J., *1 and 2 Samuel* (NCB, 6; London: Oliphants, 1971).

Mayes, A.D.H., *The Story of Israel between Settlement and Exile: A Redactional Study of the Deuteronomistic History* (London: SCM Press, 1983).

Mettinger, T., *King and Messiah* (ConBOT, 8; Lund: Gleerup, 1975).

Miscall, P., *The Workings of Old Testament Narrative* (Semeia Studies; Chico, CA: Scholars Press, 1983).

—*1 Samuel. A Literary Reading* (Bloomington, IN: Indiana University Press, 1986).

Mowinckel, S., *Psalmenstudien* (6 vols.; Kristiana: Dybwad, 1921-1924).

Nelson, R.D., *The Double Redaction of the Deuteronomistic History* (JSOTSup, 18; Sheffield: JSOT Press, 1981).

Noth, M., *The Deuteronomistic History* (trans. J. Doull *et al.*; JSOTSup, 15; Sheffield: JSOT Press, 1981).

Otten, H., *Hethitische Totenrituale* (Berlin: Akademie Verlag, 1958).

Pardee, D., *et al.*, *Handbook of Ancient Hebrew Letters* (SBLSBS, 15; Chico, CA: Scholars Press, 1982).

Plöger, J., *Literarkritische, formgeschichtliche und stilkritische Untersuchungen zum Deuteronium* (BBB, 26; Bonn: Paul Hanstein, 1967).

Polzin, R., *Moses and the Deuteronomist* (New York: Seabury Press, 1980).

—*Samuel and the Deuteronomist* (St Louis: Harper & Row, 1989).

Provan, I.W., *Hezekiah and the Books of Kings* (BZAW, 172; New York: de Gruyter, 1988).

Richter, W., *Traditionsgeschichtliche Untersuchungen zum Richterbuch* (BBB, 18; Bonn: Paul Hanstein, 1963).

Riis, P.J., *Hama, fouilles et recherches 1931-1938* (4 vols.; Nationalmuseets Skrifter; Copenhagen: Nordisk, 1948-1988).

Rosenberg, J., *King and Kin* (Indiana Studies in Biblical Literature; Bloomington, IN: Indiana University Press, 1986).
Sasson, J., *The Military Establishments at Mari* (Studia Pohl, 3; Rome: Pontifical Biblical Institute, 1969).
Schmidt, L., *Menschlicher Erfolg und Yahwes Initiative: Studien zu Tradition, Interpretation und Historie in Überlieferungen von Gideon, Saul, und David* (WMANT, 38; Neukirchen–Vluyn: Neukirchener Verlag, 1970).
Seters, J. van, *In Search of History* (New Haven: Yale University Press, 1983).
Smith, H.P., *A Critical and Exegetical Commentary on the Books of Samuel* (ICC, 9; New York: Charles Scribner's Sons, 1899).
Sternberg, M., *The Poetics of Biblical Narrative* (Indiana Studies in Biblical Literature; Bloomington, IN: Indiana University Press, 1985).
Stoebe, H.J., *Das erste Buch Samuelis* (KAT 8/1; Gütersloh: Mohn, 1973).
Tur-Sinai, H.N., *The Book of Job: A New Commentary* (rev. edn; Jerusalem: Kiryath Sepher, 1967).
Vannoy, R., *Covenant Renewal at Gilgal* (Cherry Hill, NJ: Mack, 1978).
Vaux, R. de, *Ancient Israel. Religious Institutions* (New York: McGraw–Hill, 1965).
Veijola, T., *Das Königtum in der Beurteilung der deuteronomistischen Historiographie. Eine redaktionsgeschichtliche Untersuchungen* (Suomalainen Tiedeakatemian Toimituksia Annales Academiae Scientiarum Fennicae Series B, 198; Helsinki: Suomalainen Tiedakatemia, 1977).
Volz, P., *Das Neujahrsfest Jahwes (Laubhüttenfest)* (Tübingen: Mohr, 1912).
Wakeman, M., *God's Battle with the Monster* (Leiden: Brill, 1973).
Weiser, A., *Samuel: seine geschichtliche Aufgabe und religiose Bedeutung. Traditionsgeschichtliche Untersuchungen zu 1. Samuel 7-17* (FRLANT, 81; Göttingen: Vandenhoeck & Ruprecht, 1962).
Wellhausen, J., *Der Text der Bücher Samuelis* (Göttingen: Vandenhoeck & Ruprecht, 1871).
Wénin, A., *Samuel et l'instauration de la monarchie* (1 S 1-12) (European University Study Series, 23.342; New York: Peter Lang, 1988).
Westermann, C., *Grundformen prophetischer Rede* (BEvT, 31; München: Kaiser Verlag, 1960).
Yadin, Y., *The Art of Warfare in Biblical Lands* (trans. M. Pearlman; New York: McGraw–Hill, 1963).
Yonick, S., *The Rejection of Saul as King of Israel* (Jerusalem: Franciscan Printing, 1970).

Articles

Ap-Thomas, D.R., 'Saul's Uncle', *VT* 11 (1961), pp. 241-45.
Bar-Deroma, H., 'Ye Mountains of Gilboa', *PEQ* 102 (1970), pp. 116-36.
Barrick, W.B., 'On the "Removal of the High Places" in 1-2 Kings', *Bib* 55 (1974), pp. 257-59.
Barton, G.A., 'Tiamat', *JAOS* 15 (1893), pp. 1-27.
Beuken, W.A.M., 'I Samuel 28: The Prophet as "Hammer of Witches"', *JSOT* 6 (1978), pp. 3-17.
Beyerlin, W., 'Die königscharisma bei Saul', *ZAW* 73 (1961), pp. 186-201.

Bienkowski, P., 'Some Remarks on the Practice of Cremation in the Levant', *Levant* 14 (1982), pp. 80-89.

Bietak, M., 'Vorläufiger Bericht über die erste und zweite Kampagne der österreichischen Ausgrabungen auf Tell ed Dab'a im Ostdelta Ägyptens (1966, 1967)', *MDAIK* 23 (1968), pp. 79-114.

Bin-Nun, S.R., 'Formulas from Royal Records of Israel and Judah', *VT* 18 (1968), pp. 414-32.

Birch, B., 'The Development of the Tradition on the Anointing of Saul in 1 Sam 9:1-10.16', *JBL* 90 (1971), pp. 55-68.

Birnbaum, S., 'The Lachish Ostraca', *PEQ* 71 (1939), pp. 20-28, 91-110.

Bittel, K., 'Vorläufiger Bericht über die Ausgrabungen in Boğazköy 1936', *MDOG* 75 (1937), pp. 68-70.

—'Hethitische Bestattungsbräuche', *MDOG* 78 (1940), pp. 12-28.

Blenkinsopp, J., 'Jonathan's Sacrilege. 1 Sm 14, 1-46: A Study in Literary History', *CBQ* 26 (1964), pp. 423-49.

—'1 and 2 Samuel', in *A New Catholic Commentary on Holy Scripture* (ed. R.C. Fuller; London: Nelson, 1969), pp. 305-27.

Boer, P.A.H. de, 'Research into the Text of 1 Samuel XVIII-XXI', *OTS* 6 (1949), pp. 1-100.

—'Vive le roi', *VT* 5 (1955), pp. 225-31.

Brauner, R.A., '"To Grasp the Hem", and 1 Sam 15:27', *JANESCU* 6 (1974), pp. 35-38.

Brueggemann, W., 'Narrative Intentionality in 1 Samuel 29', *JSOT* 43 (1989), pp. 21-35.

Buber, M., 'Die Erzählung von Sauls Königswahl', *VT* 6 (1956), pp. 113-73.

Cheyne, T.K., 'Critical Gleanings from Samuel', *ExpTim* 10 (1899), pp. 520-22.

Conrad, D., 'Samuel und die Mari- "Propheten". Bemerkungen zu 1 Sam 15:27', *ZDMG* Sup 1 (1969), pp. 273-80.

Crenshaw, J., 'Education in Ancient Israel', *JBL* 104 (1985), pp. 601-15.

Cross, F.M., 'The Ammonite Oppression of the Tribes of Gad and Reuben: Missing Verses from 1 Sam. 11 Found in 4Q Sam[a]', in *History, Historiography and Interpretation: Studies in Biblical and Cuneiform Literature* (ed. H. Tadmor and M. Weinfeld; Jerusalem: Magnes Press, 1983), pp. 148-58.

Deem, A., 'And the Stone Sank into his Forehead. A Note on 1 Samuel xvii 49', *VT* 28 (1978), pp. 349-51.

Driver, G.R., 'Some Hebrew Words', *JTS* 29 (1927–28), pp. 390-96.

—'Hebrew Burial Custom', *ZAW* 66 (1954), pp. 314-15.

Edelman, D., 'Saul's Rescue of Jabesh–Gilead (1 Sam. 11.1-11): Sorting Story from History', *ZAW* 96 (1984), pp. 195-209.

—'Saul's Journey through Mt Ephraim and Samuel's Ramah (1 Sam. 9:4-5; 10:2-5)', *ZDPV* 104 (1988), pp. 44-58.

—'The Asherite Genealogy in 1 Chronicles 7:3-40', *Biblical Research* 33 (1988), pp. 13-23.

—'The Manassite Genealogy in 1 Chronicles 7:14-19: Form and Source', *CBQ* 53 (1991), pp. 179-201.

Emerton, J.A., 'Sheol and the Sons of Belial', *VT* 37 (1987), pp. 214-17.

Eppstein, V., 'Was Saul also Among the Prophets?', *ZAW* 81 (1969), pp. 287-304.

Eves, T., 'One Ammonite Invasion or Two? 1 Sam. 10:27-11:2 in the Light of 4QSam[a]', *WTJ* 44 (1982), pp. 308-26.

Fokkelman, J.P., 'A Lie Born of Truth, Too Weak to Contain It', *OTS* 23 (1984), pp. 39-55.

Fox, M., '*Ṭôb* as Covenant Terminology', *BASOR* 209 (1973), pp. 41-42.

Freedman, D.N., Review of *Patterns in the Early Poetry of Ancient Israel*, by S. Gevirtz, *JBL* 83 (1964), pp. 201-203.

Golka, F., 'Die israelitischen Weisheitsschule oder "des Kaisers neue Kleider"', *VT* 33 (1983), pp. 257-70.

Gooding, D., 'An Approach to the Literary and Textual Problems in the David-Goliath Story: 1 Sam. 16-18', in *The Story of David and Goliath* (ed. D. Barthélemy *et al.*; OBO, 73; Göttingen: Vandenhoeck & Ruprecht, 1986), pp. 145-54.

Gordon, R., 'David's Rise and Saul's Demise: Narrative Analogy in 1 Samuel 24-26', *TB* 31 (1980), pp. 37-64.

—'Saul's Meningitis According to Targum 1 Samuel XIX 24', *VT* 37 (1987), pp. 39-49.

Gros-Louis, K., 'The Difficulty of Ruling Well: King David of Israel', *Semeia* 8 (1977), pp. 15-33.

Gunn, D., 'Narrative Patterns and Oral Tradition in Judges and Samuel', *VT* 24 (1974), pp. 286-317.

Hankey, V., 'A Late Bronze Age Temple at Amman I: The Aegean Pottery', *Levant* 6 (1974), pp. 131-59.

Harris, S.L., '1 Samuel viii 7-8', *VT* 31 (1981), pp. 79-80.

Herr, L., 'The Amman Airport and the Geopolitics of Ancient Transjordan', *BA* 46 (1983), pp. 223-29.

Hoffner, H.A., 'Second Millenium Antecedents to the Hebrew 'ôb', *JBL* 86 (1967), pp. 385-401.

Honeyman, A.M., Review of *Lexicon in Veteris Testamenti Libros*, ed. L. Koehler, *VT* 5 (1955), pp. 214-23.

Humphreys, W.L., 'The Tragedy of King Saul: A Study in the Structure of 1 Samuel 9-31', *JSOT* 6 (1978), pp. 18-27.

Jason, H., 'The Story of David and Goliath: A Folk Epic?', *Bib* 60 (1979), pp. 36-70.

Jobling, D., 'Saul's Fall and Jonathan's Rise: Tradition and Redaction in 1 Sam 14:1-46', *JBL* 95 (1976), pp. 367-76.

Kempinski, A., 'Hittites in the Bible', *BARev* 5 (1979), pp. 21-45.

Kessler, M., 'Narrative Technique in 1 Sm 16, 1-13', *CBQ* 32 (1970), pp. 543-54.

Krenkel, M., 'Einige Emendation zu den Büchern Samuels', *ZAW* 2 (1882), pp. 309-10.

Kurdian, H., 'Kirmiz', *JAOS* 61 (1941), pp. 105-107.

Kutsch, E., 'Die Wurzel עצר im Hebräischen', *VT* 2 (1952), pp. 57-59.

Lang, B., 'Schule und Unterricht im alten Israel', in *La sagesse de l'Ancien Testament* (ed. M. Gilbert; BETL, 51; Gembloux: Duculot, 1979), pp. 186-201.

Lasine, S., 'Guest and Host in Judges 19: Lot's Hospitality in an Inverted World', *JSOT* 29 (1984), pp. 37-59.

—'Fiction, Falsehood and Reality in Hebrew Scripture', *Hebrew Studies* 25 (1984), pp. 24-40.

Laudermilk, J., 'The Bug with the Crimson Past', *Natural History* 58 (1949), pp. 114-18.

Lemaire, A., 'Vers l'histoire de la rédaction des livres de Rois', *ZAW* 98 (1986), pp. 221-36.

Levenson, J., '1 Samuel 25 as Literature and History', *CBQ* 40 (1978), pp. 11-28.

Lindblom, J., 'Saul inter Prophetas', *ASTI* 9 (1974), pp. 30-41.

Lipiński, E., 'Nāgîd, der Kronprinz', *VT* 24 (1974), pp. 497-99.
Lust, J., 'On Wizards and Prophets', in *Studies in Prophecy* (ed. G.W. Anderson *et al.*; VTSup, 26; Leiden: Brill, 1974), pp. 133-42.
McCarthy, D., 'Compact and Kingship: Stimuli for Hebrew Covenant Thinking', in *Studies in the Period of David and Solomon and Other Essays* (ed. T. Ishida; Winona Lake, IN: Eisenbrauns, 1982), pp. 75-92.
MacDonald, J., 'The Status and Role of the Na'ar in Israelite Society', *JNES* 35 (1976), pp. 147-70.
McKane, W., 'The Gibbôr Ḥayil in the Israelite Community', *Glasgow University Oriental Society Transactions* 17 (1957–58), pp. 28-37.
Mabee, C., 'David's Judicial Exoneration', *ZAW* 92 (1980), pp. 89-107.
Macholz, G., 'Die Stellung des Königs in der israelitischen Gerichtsverfassung', *ZAW* 84 (1972), pp. 157-81.
Miller, J.M., 'Saul's Rise to Power: Some Observations Concerning 1 Sam 9:1-10:16; 10:26-11:15 and 13:2-14:46', *CBQ* 36 (1974), pp. 157-74.
—'The Moabite Stone as a Memorial Stela', *PEQ* 107 (1975), pp. 9-18.
Moran, W., 'The Ancient Near Eastern Background of the Love of God in Deuteronomy', *CBQ* 25 (1963), pp. 77-84.
—'A Note on Some Treaty Terminology of the Sefire Treaties', *JNES* 22 (1963), pp. 173-76.
Morgenstern, J., 'David and Jonathan', *JBL* 78 (1959), pp. 322-25.
Otten, H., 'Ein Totenrituel hethitischer Könige', *MDOG* 78 (1940), pp. 3-5.
Phillips, A., 'The Ecstatic's Father', in *Words and Meanings* (ed. P.R. Ackroyd and B. Lindars; Cambridge: Cambridge University Press, 1968), pp. 183-94.
Ploeg, J. van der, 'Le sens de *gibbôr ḥaîl*', *RB* 50 (1941), pp. 120-25.
—'Les chefs du peuple d'Israël et leurs titres', *RB* 57 (1950), pp. 40-61.
Polzin, R., 'The Monarchy Begins: 1 Samuel 8-10', in *SBL Seminar Papers 1987* (ed. K.H. Richards; Chico, CA: Scholars Press, 1987), pp. 120-43.
Preston, T.R., 'The Heroism of King Saul: Patterns of Meaning in the Narrative of Early Kingship', *JSOT* 24 (1982), pp. 27-46.
Rabinowitz, P., 'Truth in Fiction: A Reexamination of Audiences', *Critical Inquiry* 4 (1977), pp. 121-41.
Reinach, S., 'Le souper chez la sorcière', *RHR* 88 (1923), pp. 45-50.
Robertson, E., 'Samuel and Saul', *BSRL* 28 (1944), pp. 175-206.
Rofé, A., 'The Acts of Nahash according to 4QSam[a]', *IEJ* 32 (1982), pp. 129-33.
Rose, A., 'The "Principles" of Divine Election. Wisdom in 1 Samuel, 16', in *Rhetorical Criticism* (ed. J.J. Jackson and M. Kessler; Pittsburgh Theological Monograph Series, 1; Pittsburgh: Pickwick Press, 1974), pp. 43-67.
Rouillard, H. and J. Tropper, '*trpm*, rituels de guérison et culte des ancêtres d'après 1 Samuel xix 11-17 et les textes parallèles d'Assur et de Nuzi', *VT* 37 (1987), pp. 340-61.
Sasson, J., 'Reflections on an Unusual Practice Reported in ARM X: 4', *Orientalia* 43 (1974), pp. 404-10.
—'A Genealogical "Convention" in Biblical Chronology?', *ZAW* 90 (1978), pp. 171-85.
Schelhaas, J., 'De instelling van het koningschap en de troonbestijging van Israëls eerste koning', *Geformeerd Theologisch Tijdschrift* 44 (1944), pp. 241-73.

Seebass, H., 'Traditionsgeschichte von 1 Sam. 8, 10:17ff., und 12', *ZAW* 77 (1965), pp. 286-96.

Seters, J. van, 'Oral Patterns or Literary Conventions in Biblical Narrative', *Semeia* 5 (1976), pp. 139-54.

Shaviv, S., '*nābî'* and *nāgîd* in 1 Samuel ix 1-x 16', *VT* 34 (1984), pp. 108-12.

Stamm, J.J., 'Der Name des Königs David', *VTSup* 7 (1960), pp. 165-83.

Sternberg, M., 'The Bible's Art of Persuasion: Ideology, Rhetoric and Poetics in Samuel's Fall', *HUCA* 54 (1983), pp. 45-82.

Sturdy, J., 'The Original Meaning of "Is Saul also Among the Prophets?" (1 Samuel 10:11, 12; 19:24)', *VT* 20 (1970), pp. 206-13.

Thomas, D.W., '*belliyya'al* in the Old Testament', in *Biblical and Patristic Studies in Memory of Pierce Casey* (ed. J. Neville Birdsall and R.W. Thomsen; New York: Herder, 1963), pp. 11-19.

Thompson, J.A., 'The Significance of the Verb "Love" in the David–Jonathan Narratives in 1 Samuel', *VT* 24 (1974), pp. 334-38.

Vaux, R. de, 'Le roi d'Israël, vassal de Yahvé', in *Mélanges Eugène Tisserant*, I (Studie Testi, 231; Vatican: Biblioteca Apostolica Vaticana, 1964), pp. 129-33.

—'Single Combat in the Old Testament', in *The Bible and the Ancient Near East* (ed. G.E. Wright; Garden City, NY: Doubleday, 1961), pp. 122-35.

Wallis, G., 'Eine Parallele zu Richter 19, 29ff und 1 Sam. 11, 5ff aus dem Briefarchiv von Mari', *ZAW* 64 (1952), pp. 57-61.

Weinfeld, M., 'Covenant Terminology in the East and its Influence on the West', *JAOS* 93 (1973), pp. 190-99.

—'The Emergence of the Deuteronomic Movement: The Historical Antecedents', in *Das Deuteronium: Enstehung, Gestalt, und Botschaft* (ed. N. Lohfink; BETL, 68; Leuven: Leuven University Press, 1985), pp. 76-89.

Weippert, H., 'Das "deuteronomistischen" Beurteilungen der Könige von Israel und Juda und das Problem der Redaktion der Königsbücher', *Bib* 53 (1972), pp. 310-39.

Westenholtz, J., 'The Heroes of Akkad', *JAOS* 103 (1983), pp. 327-36.

Wiesmann, H., 'Die Einführung des Königtums in Israel (1 Sam 8-12)', *ZKT* 34 (1910), pp. 118-53.

Willis, J., 'The Function of Comprehensive Anticipatory Redactional Joints in 1 Samuel 16-18', *ZAW* 85 (1973), pp. 294-314.

Yonick, S., 'The Rejection of Saul: A Study of Sources', *AJBA* 1 (1971), pp. 29-50.

Indexes

Index of References

Hebrew Scriptures

INDEX OF HEBREW WORDS

INDEX OF AUTHORS

JOURNAL FOR THE STUDY OF THE OLD TESTAMENT

Supplement Series

35 SAGA, LEGEND, TALE, NOVELLA, FABLE:
NARRATIVE FORMS IN OLD TESTAMENT LITERATURE
Edited by G.W. Coats
36 THE SONG OF FOURTEEN SONGS
M.D. Goulder
37 UNDERSTANDING THE WORD:
ESSAYS IN HONOR OF BERNHARD W. ANDERSON
Edited by J.T. Butler, E.W. Conrad & B.C. Ollenburger
38 SLEEP, DIVINE AND HUMAN, IN THE OLD TESTAMENT
T.H. McAlpine
39 THE SENSE OF BIBLICAL NARRATIVE. II:
STRUCTURAL ANALYSES IN THE HEBREW BIBLE
D. Jobling
40 DIRECTIONS IN BIBLICAL HEBREW POETRY
Edited by E.R. Follis
41 ZION, THE CITY OF THE GREAT KING:
A THEOLOGICAL SYMBOL OF THE JERUSALEM CULT
B.C. Ollenburger
42 A WORD IN SEASON: ESSAYS IN HONOUR OF WILLIAM MCKANE
Edited by J.D. Martin & P.R. Davies
43 THE CULT OF MOLEK: A REASSESSMENT
G.C. Heider
44 THE IDENTITY OF THE INDIVIDUAL IN THE PSALMS
S.J.L. Croft
45 THE CONFESSIONS OF JEREMIAH IN CONTEXT:
SCENES OF PROPHETIC DRAMA
A.R. Diamond
46 THE BOOK OF JUDGES: AN INTEGRATED READING
B.G. Webb
47 THE GREEK TEXT OF JEREMIAH:
A REVISED HYPOTHESIS
S. Soderlund
48 TEXT AND CONTEXT:
OLD TESTAMENT AND SEMITIC STUDIES FOR F.C. FENSHAM
Edited by W. Claassen
49 THEOPHORIC PERSONAL NAMES IN ANCIENT HEBREW
J.D. Fowler
50 THE CHRONICLER'S HISTORY
M. Noth
51 DIVINE INITIATIVE AND HUMAN RESPONSE IN EZEKIEL
P. Joyce

52 THE CONFLICT OF FAITH AND EXPERIENCE IN THE PSALMS:
A FORM-CRITICAL AND THEOLOGICAL STUDY
C.C. Broyles

53 THE MAKING OF THE PENTATEUCH:
A METHODOLOGICAL STUDY
R.N. Whybray

54 FROM REPENTANCE TO REDEMPTION:
JEREMIAH'S THOUGHT IN TRANSITION
J. Unterman

55 THE ORIGIN TRADITION OF ANCIENT ISRAEL:
THE LITERARY FORMATION OF GENESIS AND EXODUS 1–23
T.L. Thompson

56 THE PURIFICATION OFFERING IN THE PRIESTLY LITERATURE:
ITS MEANING AND FUNCTION
N. Kiuchi

57 MOSES: HEROIC MAN, MAN OF GOD
G.W. Coats

58 THE LISTENING HEART: ESSAYS IN WISDOM AND THE PSALMS
IN HONOR OF ROLAND E. MURPHY, O. CARM.
Edited by K.G. Hoglund

59 CREATIVE BIBLICAL EXEGESIS:
CHRISTIAN AND JEWISH HERMENEUTICS THROUGH THE CENTURIES
B. Uffenheimer & H.G. Reventlow

60 HER PRICE IS BEYOND RUBIES:
THE JEWISH WOMAN IN GRAECO-ROMAN PALESTINE
L.J. Archer

61 FROM CHAOS TO RESTORATION:
AN INTEGRATIVE READING OF ISAIAH 24–27
D.G. Johnson

62 THE OLD TESTAMENT AND FOLKLORE STUDY
P.G. Kirkpatrick

63 SHILOH: A BIBLICAL CITY IN TRADITION AND HISTORY
D.G. Schley

64 TO SEE AND NOT PERCEIVE:
ISAIAH 6.9-10 IN EARLY JEWISH AND CHRISTIAN INTERPRETATION
C.A. Evans

65 THERE IS HOPE FOR A TREE:
THE TREE AS METAPHOR IN ISAIAH
K. Nielsen

66 SECRETS OF THE TIMES:
MYTH AND HISTORY IN BIBLICAL CHRONOLOGY
J. Hughes

67 ASCRIBE TO THE LORD:
BIBLICAL AND OTHER ESSAYS IN MEMORY OF PETER C. CRAIGIE
Edited by L. Eslinger & G. Taylor

68 THE TRIUMPH OF IRONY IN THE BOOK OF JUDGES
L.R. Klein

69 ZEPHANIAH, A PROPHETIC DRAMA
P.R. HOUSE

70 NARRATIVE ART IN THE BIBLE
S. Bar-Efrat

71 QOHELET AND HIS CONTRADICTIONS
M.V. Fox

73 DAVID'S SOCIAL DRAMA:
A HOLOGRAM OF THE EARLY IRON AGE
J.W. Flanagan

74 THE STRUCTURAL ANALYSIS OF BIBLICAL AND CANAANITE POETRY
Edited by W. van der Meer & J.C. de Moor

75 DAVID IN LOVE AND WAR:
THE PURSUIT OF POWER IN 2 SAMUEL 10–12
R.C. Bailey

76 GOD IS KING:
UNDERSTANDING AN ISRAELITE METAPHOR
M. Brettler

77 EDOM AND THE EDOMITES
J.R. Bartlett

78 SWALLOWING THE SCROLL:
TEXTUALITY AND THE DYNAMICS OF DISCOURSE IN EZEKIEL'S PROPHECY
E.F. Davies

79 GIBEAH: THE SEARCH FOR A BIBLICAL CITY
P.M. Arnold

80 THE NATHAN NARRATIVES
G.H. Jones

81 ANTI-COVENANT:
COUNTER-READING WOMEN'S LIVES IN THE HEBREW BIBLE
Edited by M. Bal

82 RHETORIC AND BIBLICAL INTERPRETATION
D. Patrick & A. Scult

83 THE EARTH AND THE WATERS IN GENESIS 1 AND 2
D.T. Tsumura

84 INTO THE HANDS OF THE LIVING GOD
L. Eslinger

85 FROM CARMEL TO HOREB: ELIJAH IN CRISIS
A.J. Hauser & R. Gregory

86 THE SYNTAX OF THE VERB IN CLASSICAL HEBREW PROSE
A. Niccacci

87 THE BIBLE IN THREE DIMENSIONS
Edited by D.J.A. Clines, S.E. Fowl & S.E. Porter

88 THE PERSUASIVE APPEAL OF THE CHRONICLER:
A RHETORICAL ANALYSIS
R.K. Duke
89 THE PROBLEM OF THE PROCESS OF TRANSMISSION
IN THE PENTATEUCH
R. Rendtorff
90 BIBLICAL HEBREW IN TRANSITION:
THE LANGUAGE OF THE BOOK OF EZEKIEL
M.F. Rooker
91 THE IDEOLOGY OF RITUAL:
SPACE, TIME, AND STATUS IN THE PRIESTLY THEOLOGY
F.H. Gorman
92 ON HUMOUR AND THE COMIC IN THE HEBREW BIBLE
Edited by Y.T. Radday & A. Brenner
93 JOSHUA 24 AS POETIC NARRATIVE
W.T. Koopmans
94 WHAT DOES EVE DO TO HELP? AND OTHER READERLY QUESTIONS
TO THE OLD TESTAMENT
D.J.A. Clines
95 GOD SAVES: LESSONS FROM THE ELISHA STORIES
R.D. Moore
96 ANNOUNCEMENTS OF PLOT IN GENESIS
L.A. Turner
97 THE UNITY OF THE TWELVE
P.R. House
98 ANCIENT CONQUEST ACCOUNTS: A STUDY IN ANCIENT NEAR
EASTERN AND BIBLICAL HISTORY WRITING
K. Lawson Younger, Jr
99 WEALTH AND POVERTY IN THE BOOK OF PROVERBS
R.N. Whybray
100 A TRIBUTE TO GEZA VERMES. ESSAYS ON JEWISH AND CHRISTIAN
LITERATURE AND HISTORY
Edited by P.R. Davies & R.T. White
101 THE CHRONICLER IN HIS AGE
P.R. Ackroyd
102 THE PRAYERS OF DAVID (PSALMS 51–72)
M.D. Goulder
103 THE SOCIOLOGY OF POTTERY IN ANCIENT PALESTINE:
THE CERAMIC INDUSTRY AND THE DIFFUSION OF CERAMIC STYLE
IN THE BRONZE AND IRON AGES
Bryant G. Wood
104 PSALM-STRUCTURES:
A STUDY OF PSALMS WITH REFRAINS
Paul R. Raabe

105 ESTABLISHING JUSTICE
Pietro Bovati
106 GRADATED HOLINESS
Philip Jenson
107 THE ALIEN IN THE PENTATEUCH
Christiana van Houten
108 THE FORGING OF ISRAEL:
IRON TECHNOLOGY, SYMBOLISM AND TRADITION IN
ANCIENT SOCIETY
Paula McNutt
109 SCRIBES AND SCHOOLS IN MONARCHIC JUDAH
David Jamieson-Drake
110 THE CANAANITES AND THEIR LAND:
THE TRADITION OF THE CANAANITES
Niels Peter Lemche
112 WISDOM IN REVOLT:
METAPHORICAL THEOLOGY IN THE BOOK OF JOB
Leo G. Perdue
113 PROPERTY AND THE FAMILY IN BIBLICAL LAW
Raymond Westbrook
114 A TRADITIONAL QUEST:
ESSAYS IN HONOUR OF LOUIS JACOBS
Edited by Dan Cohn-Sherbok
115 I HAVE BUILT YOU AN EXALTED HOUSE:
TEMPLE BUILDING IN THE BIBLE IN THE LIGHT OF MESOPOTAMIAN
AND NORTH-WEST SEMITIC WRITINGS
Victor Hurowitz
116 NARRATIVE AND NOVELLA IN SAMUEL:
STUDIES BY HUGO GRESSMANN AND OTHER SCHOLARS 1906-1923
Edited by David M. Gunn
117 SECOND TEMPLE STUDIES
Edited by P.R. Davies
118 SEEING AND HEARING GOD IN THE PSALMS:
PROPHETIC LITURGY FROM THE SECOND TEMPLE IN JERUSALEM
R.J. Tournay
119 TELLING QUEEN MICHAL'S STORY:
AN EXPERIMENT IN COMPARATIVE INTERPRETATION
Edited by David J.A. Clines & Tamara C. Eskenazi
120 THE REFORMING KINGS:
CULT AND SOCIETY IN FIRST TEMPLE JUDAH
Richard H. Lowery
121 KING SAUL IN THE HISTORIOGRAPHY OF JUDAH
Diana Vikander Edelman